WITHDRAWN

I hope you will find something of interest in this over-generous life-story of the
undersigned.

D1300429

WILLIAM F. MAAG LIBRARY
YOUNGSTOWN STATE UNIVERSITY

William Chapin Deming
Of Wyoming

William Chapin Deming

WILLIAM CHAPIN DEMING
OF WYOMING

Pioneer Publisher, and
State and Federal Official

A BIOGRAPHY

by

AGNES WRIGHT SPRING

former State Librarian and State Historian of Wyoming

WITHDRAWN FROM
WILLIAM F. MAAG LIBRARY
YOUNGSTOWN STATE UNIVERSITY

Privately printed in a limited edition by
THE ARTHUR H. CLARK COMPANY
Glendale, California, U.S.A.
1944

WILLIAM F. MAAG LIBRARY
YOUNGSTOWN STATE UNIVERSITY

Copyright, 1944 by
WILLIAM CHAPIN DEMING

All rights reserved including
the right to reproduce this
volume or parts thereof
in any form.

PN
4874
.D4S65
1944

WITHDRAWN

The story of a newspaper man who, according to Kent Cooper of the Associated Press, "not only pioneered in his own field but found happiness in contributing constructively to the public good."

WILLIAM F. MAAG LIBRARY
YOUNGSTOWN STATE UNIVERSITY

Contents

APPENDIX

Illustrations

Foreword

A biography is necessarily personal. When a reasonably modest man reads his own life story, he knows that he has not deserved all of the tributes that have come his way. Because he may be mentioned frequently in various movements and enterprises, it does not follow that others did not play an even greater part.

This is the thought that recurs to me in reading Mrs. Spring's narrative of my life. I am indebted to her for her untiring work in gathering the material from my files, scrap books, documents, etc., kept over a period of forty years and in supplementing it with interviews and correspondence.

I make no pretense to being a major or even minor prophet; only an average citizen, deeply interested in Wyoming, who did a little preaching in the desert during the decades of residence in the West. The texts were not religious but social, economic or political – the latter sometimes, I fear, too partisan. Age and retrospect temper even the most ardent crusader.

It is my hope that this volume may serve not only to record the story of the Deming family but to preserve some of the early atmosphere of Wyoming during a vital and picturesque era.

WILLIAM C. DEMING

Preface

Newspaper publishers have played a very important part in the development of the West.

It is a distinct privilege to present this story of William Chapin Deming, whose public service has been so outstanding.

Through a combination of publishing the leading newspaper in his state, his vision, his enthusiasm, and his exceptional business ability, Mr. Deming has materially helped in promoting good roads movements, including the Lincoln highway; in developing arid farming, tree planting, and irrigation projects; in encouraging transcontinental airways; in furthering city and state public works; in conserving natural resources; and in advancing things educational and cultural. His interest in the agricultural and industrial development of the West was enhanced by his work on the St. Louis World's Fair commission, celebrating the Louisiana Purchase, and on the Portland Exposition commission, commemorating the Lewis and Clark expedition.

Although a lawyer by profession, Mr. Deming early began his newspaper career in Kentucky, followed it to Ohio, and then, at the turn of the century faced westward to cast his lot in the Rocky mountain region.

Starting in Cheyenne, Wyoming, with a small, neglected news sheet that was manned by a discouraged personnel, he gradually built the Wyoming *Tribune* into the leading newspaper of the state and made it one of the best known newspapers of the West.

Coincident with his newspaper work, Mr. Deming inaugurated various business ventures, including the organization of a prosperous realty operating company.

Through his personal achievements and successes and his interest in public welfare, he has won high national recognition. He has attended important White House conferences, and has served under five presidents of the United States upon official commissions.

As a young Ohio newspaper editor, Deming was among the first to nail to the masthead the name of Governor William McKinley as the most likely candidate for the national presidency. Later, with James R. Garfield, son of President James A. Garfield, he campaigned in behalf of McKinley.

As a member of the Wyoming legislature he initiated important laws.

He was appointed Receiver of Public Moneys in the United States Land Office at Cheyenne by President Theodore Roosevelt and re-appointed by President William H. Taft. His commission extended a few months into the Woodrow Wilson administration. His duties were administrative and judicial.

Mr. Deming always worked willingly to advance his friends politically, but seldom asked for anything for himself. In 1923, he was signally honored in being appointed to the U.S. Civil Service commission in Washington, D.C., by President Warren G. Harding. He was re-appointed by President Calvin Coolidge and by President Herbert Hoover.

Almost immediately upon assuming his duties in Washington, he was elected president of the commission and was responsible for accelerating many improvements in the merit system.

Aside from his newspaper work, Mr. Deming has

William Chapin Deming and his Ancestors

William Chapin Deming, lawyer, newspaperman, lecturer, businessman, and public official, is descended from a New England family, industrious, law-abiding, public spirited, and useful through many generations.

The name Deming, according to some authorities, found its source in the name of d'Hammond, an ancient and well-known family of Blois and Cherbourg, in France. The name reached Surrey and Buckinghamshire in England during the Norman conquest, gradually taking its present form by Anglo-saxon usage and the English of a later date.

The original American Deming was John Deming, called "The Settler," who came to Wethersfield, Connecticut, in 1635, only fifteen years after the landing at Plymouth Rock. So far as known, all American Demings were descended from "The Settler." A number of Demings were conspicuous in the early days of American colonization, particularly in New England. The most outstanding of them was John Deming, who was chosen deputy to represent Wethersfield in 1645, at the general court, and was a member of the jury of the particular court for many sessions. In 1657, he was appointed to give advice as to the policy of the government in dealing with the Indians. His name is found in the famous charter granted by King Charles "to the original founders and to those who should later become associated with them in the lands of Connecticut." Trumbull, the historian, said, "John Deming was one of the fathers of Connecticut."

A later John Deming, born january 28, 1760, the great-grandfather of William C. Deming, was doubtless a descendant of John, "The Settler," and though young, served in various commands in the Continental forces during the Revolutionary war in 1776-77 and 1779. He was an early settler of Saratoga county, New York, and the father of David W. Deming, who was the father of Osmer S. Deming.

David W. Deming, on march 20, 1833, married Almira Sage, whose people were of Scotch-irish descent. Almira Deming was an educated woman. Her maiden sister, who was known to the family as "Aunt Eliza," was gifted in many ways. She lived alone in a modest home in Pennsylvania, and, according to William C. Deming, she "made the best tea and baked the best cookies I ever ate." Both grandparents, Almira and David, were deeply religious.

The records show that large families were the rule among the Demings and most of them lived to a mature age. They were a substantial class of people, who migrated westward from New England into New York, then to Pennsylvania, Ohio, and Indiana. They participated in public affairs, encouraged schools and supported the churches. Occasionally a family moved South after the Civil war. There were doctors, lawyers, and literary men among them, also artists, farmers, and merchants. In 1868, Henry C. Deming, a former member of congress, wrote a popular *Life of General Ulysses S. Grant.* Grant was elected President that year. Judson K. Deming, a banker of Dubuque, Iowa, prepared a complete *Genealogy of the Deming Family in America* about twenty-five years ago. Edwin Willard

MR. AND MRS. DAVID W. DEMING
father and mother of Judge O. S. Deming

JUDGE OSMER SAGE DEMING
OF KENTUCKY

LEONA C. DEMING
as a young woman

father and mother of William C., David S., and Thomas H. Deming,
and Adah D. Morrison

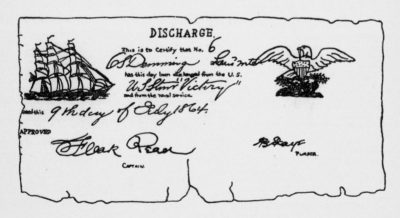

OSMER S. DEMING IN CIVIL WAR
metal identification tag in 1863 and discharge july 1864

Deming, born in Ohio, became a famous artist, specializing in western scenes and Indian life. He maintained homes in Colorado Springs and New York City.

Osmer S. Deming, the son of David W. and Almira Sage Deming, was born in Otsego county, New York, december 22, 1837. He went through the public schools in New York and later attended an academy at Waterford, Pennsylvania, where he received a classical education and graduated with honors. For two years he remained as a member of the faculty of the academy and taught Latin, Greek, and Philosophy.

When his health began to fail, he was sent south by his cousin, William Deming, of Erie, Pennsylvania, with a party of men taking a large raft of commercial lumber to towns and cities on the Ohio river. The young man landed at Ripley, Ohio, where, without much delay, he was engaged to teach school and subsequently served as a member of the Ohio State Militia.

He later enlisted for service with the United States Navy in the Civil war and was assigned to the gunboat "Victory," which was plying the Ohio and Cumberland rivers. He frequently recalled the defiant attitude of John Morgan, the Confederate raider, when Morgan was captured by the Union forces. He contributed timely articles to the press concerning the activities of General Nathan B. Forrest, Confederate cavalry leader who kept the border states on edge.

At the close of the war, Osmer S. Deming, impressed by the climate in northern Kentucky, became a resident of that state and was instrumental in the organization of a new county, made up from sections of other counties and given the name of Robertson, after a well-known jurist of the Blue Grass state. Mt. Olivet was designated as the county seat.

It was here that O. S. Deming met and married Leona C. Rigg, daughter of the Reverend Thomas G. Rigg, who had come to Mt. Olivet from Carlisle in Nicholas county, Kentucky, some years before. O. S. Deming had diligently studied law in Kentucky and was admitted to practice in that state. He held various offices, including that of prosecuting attorney and judge of the court. The Republicans of northeastern Kentucky, in 1895, were determined to support him for governor. A statement in the press read:

Judge Deming is one of the best known Republicans in the State, having been prominently brought before the people in 1879, when he made the race for Lieutenant Governor, with Hon. Walter Evans. . . In that campaign he stumped the State, speaking in most every county. He was also a Hayes Elector for the tenth district, and in 1876 he was made the Republican nominee for Congress only a week before the election and made a fine race in this district, which was overwhelmingly Democratic, being defeated by only a small majority. . . Judge Deming is a sterling republican, a man of wide experience and broad, liberal views. One of the foremost lawyers in the state, and one of the best stumpers in the party.

Judge Deming had the honor of being the first republican to preside over a republican electoral college in Kentucky. This followed the victory of William McKinley in 1896, when Kentucky went republican.

He was an excellent lawyer and his standing at the Kentucky bar was always high. He was a student, a lecturer, and an eloquent speaker. For many years he was in demand as a speaker in all parts of Kentucky, particularly for Memorial Day exercises in the large cities. In recognition of the fact that he was the first prominent citizen to advocate a union observance of Memorial Day by both the North and the South, he was chosen by the National G.A.R. to speak at the great union meeting of the Blue and the Gray at the St. Louis

WILLIAM C. DEMING
as a baby

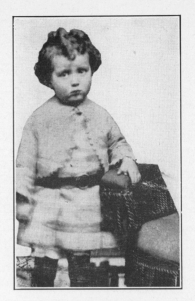

DAVID S. DEMING
at an early age

ADAH DEMING
at an early age

THOMAS H. DEMING
at an early age

Exposition in 1904. He was a member of the Christian church and of the Masonic lodge.

Judge Deming invested to a considerable extent in farm lands and houses, but was not very successful in his real estate ventures. "He could make money," said his son, William, "but could not keep it. One reason for this may have been that he had a big family and also helped many of his relatives."

To Judge and Mrs. Deming were born three sons: William Chapin, David S., and Thomas H., and a daughter, Adah, who became Mrs. William H. Morrison of Lexington, Kentucky, now of Wheatland, Wyoming.

Mrs. Katherine Evans Ross was orphaned at an early age, and was reared by her uncle and aunt, Judge and Mrs. O. S. Deming, parents of William C. Deming, David S. Deming, Thomas H. Deming and Adah Deming Morrison. She grew up as a member of the family and was much devoted to them as long as she lived.

All have attained success and a high place in their respective communities. Perhaps there is much in heredity. William C. Deming once remarked, "I never have known or heard of a Deming who had been charged with an offense or crime against his fellowman."

On the maternal side, the history of the family is equally worthy. Leona Rigg, daughter of Reverend Thomas G. and Julia Rigg, was born in Carlisle, Kentucky. Her mother, Julia, was a member of the Ruddell family. Other children were Mary, Julia, Sarah, and Thomas.

According to record, James Ruddell, a lineal ancestor, served in the Revolutionary war in the years

1777-79, under Captain Isaac Ruddell and Col. John Bowman in the Virginia campaigns. He enlisted in Shenandoah county, Virginia, and lived to be seventy-five years old, being a resident of Boone county, Kentucky, at the time of his death.

Rev. Thomas G. Rigg, the maternal grandfather of William C. Deming, was a remote descendant of General Anthony Wayne, of Revolutionary war fame. The Reverend Rigg was a kind, tall, angular, dignified man.

"I recall that in cold weather he sometimes wore a dark shawl over his shoulders, a custom that then prevailed among a few old-fashioned men," said his grandson. "Some men wore capes."

During his younger days, Rigg had a number of charges or rural congregations. Upon one occasion, according to tradition, while taking a short cut across a big pasture, with his Bible under his arm, he was pursued by a very ferocious bull. Rigg squared away and at the psychological moment threw the book, hit the animal between the eyes, knocked the bull to his knees, and then made his escape. This story, doubtless apocryphal, says William C. Deming, served to illustrate the power of God.

The Rigg family moved to Virginia in the early days from Pennsylvania. It is something of a coincidence that the father of William C. Deming had migrated to Kentucky from Pennsylvania. William C. frequently said he was a product of both the North and the South in temperament and tastes.

Leona Rigg Deming, mother of William C. Deming, a public school graduate, like many other women of her day, did not attend college, since institutions of higher learning for women were rare, especially in the South. The Civil war also interfered.

WILLIAM H. MORRISON
as a bridegroom

ADAH DEMING MORRISON
as a bride

It may be of interest here to refer to a war incident during the school days of Leona Rigg. A confederate soldier, whose wife and children lived near the home of the Reverend Thomas Rigg and family, had been captured by the Union forces and was in a federal prison. He became very seriously ill. All efforts of his family and friends to have him exchanged were without success.

Feeling deep sympathy for the family, Leona Rigg, a mere school girl, decided she would write to President Abraham Lincoln.

The story in Mrs. Deming's own language, as she prepared it years later at the request of the Warren (Ohio) *Tribune,* follows:

"L. E. Burden of Paris, Kentucky, was a confederate soldier. He was taken prisoner and incarcerated in Camp Morton, Indiana. Owing to the vicissitudes of the cruel war, his home and business house were burned. The helpless wife and baby daughter sought refuge with her mother at Carlisle, Kentucky.

"Near by lived my father, the Reverend T. G. Rigg. I was a school girl and often stopped to see the lovely little girl and her disconsolate mother. Short letters were permitted during the war to pass between prisoners and their families. Mr. Burden wrote to his wife to spare no effort to have him exchanged, as the hardships of war and long months of imprisonment had broken down his health and he could not live through the winter in his present quarters.

"I listened to this tale of woe as told by Mrs. Burden, and of how impossible it would be to pay a lawyer to go to Washington City in behalf of her husband's release.

" 'Why not write to President Lincoln yourself,' I

suggested,' and ask him to have your husband exchanged?' 'I could never do that,' replied Mrs. Burden, 'and I don't think it would do any good, anyway.'

" 'I think it would,' I said, 'and I am going to write to him myself.'

"The letter was written. In it I told of the sorrowing wife and the baby girl who had never looked upon her father's face; of the broken-down confederate soldier confined in Camp Morton, Indiana, who, unless exchanged and returned to his home to be nursed back to health, would die. To Lincoln I wrote –

" 'I am but a school girl, but I have faith in the kind heart of President Lincoln and believe that he will do this act of mercy. For references I will give my father, Rev. T. G. Rigg, and United States Senator Garrett Davis, who have, each in his way, done much to keep Kentucky in the Union.'

"I addressed the letter, carried it to the postmaster, well knowing the gauntlet of curiosity it would pass through otherwise. Notwithstanding this caution, I became the target of many jokes as to when I expected to hear from 'Father Abraham,' etc.

"My faith never wavered and in due time an answer came from President Lincoln. He replied:

" 'The school girl's friend shall be exchanged and given transportation to his home. I trust that he will be restored to health and live many years with his family.

" 'I need no references; am only too glad to do this 'act of mercy' as I hope to live to do many more. Very respectfully,
'ABRAHAM LINCOLN.' "

"It is needless to say that there was great joy in the confederate family when the father returned home."

Through reading and study, which she kept up all her life, Leona Rigg Deming became a very highly

LEONA RIGG DEMING
Mother of William C. Deming

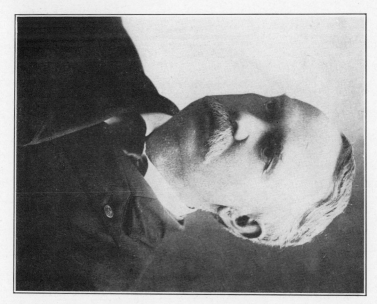

JUDGE OSMER S. DEMING
Father of William C. Deming

educated and cultured woman, rearing a family of four children of her own and a young niece, Kate Evans, an orphan, who was taken into the family at an early age.

Mrs. Deming was more inclined to be reserved than was her husband, who was exceedingly democratic in all of his tastes and activities. She was dignified and conservative in her methods and gave her children careful, systematic training in all things.

She organized a reading circle for the young people of Mt. Olivet, Kentucky, which met regularly at the Deming home once a week for the study and discussion of the books in her well-selected library of standard prose and poetry. In those days, libraries were scarce in most towns and communities. Mrs. Deming's favorite writings were the poems of Tennyson and the novels of Scott and Dickens. Mrs. Deming was a member of the Methodist church and all of her children attended services there with her.

Judge and Mrs. Deming made their home in Mt. Olivet until about 1907, when they moved to Warren, Ohio, to be with their son, Thomas, who was recovering from a serious illness and wished to have his parents with him. They purchased a home there and occupied it until their deaths in 1917 and 1918.

In recognition of the consistent interest and support that Judge O. S. Deming gave throughout his life to the cause of education, the new consolidated county high school, on the site of the former home of the Deming family in Mt. Olivet, was named the Deming High School. The dedication was held June 29, 1931. The third generation of the Deming family is among the students. In athletics, as well as scholarship, the Deming High School ranks well in northern Kentucky.

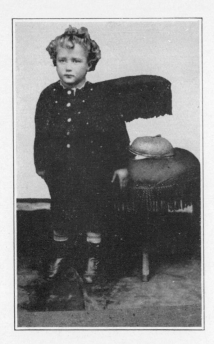

at an early age

as a Junior in Allegheny College

in his early teens

WILLIAM C. DEMING

Boyhood and Young Manhood

William Chapin Deming, eldest child of Judge O. S. and Leona Deming, was born december 6, 1869, at Mt. Olivet, Kentucky, near which occurred some of the most dramatic events of Revolutionary war times. A few miles away was the site of the Battle of Blue Licks. Here on august 19, 1782, was fought the last battle of the Revolution between 182 Kentuckians, commanded by Colonel John Todd and Lieutenant-colonel Daniel Boone, on one side, and about two hundred forty Indians and Canadians on the other, under Captain William Caldwell. It is now a state park with an interesting and attractive museum. Some interesting mementos of the Deming family have a place among the exhibits.

Less than twenty miles from Mt. Olivet is the Ohio river, on which Osmer S. Deming, father of William C., served as a gunner's mate in the Civil war. While in the naval service he was stricken with fever and was seriously ill. D. B. Chapin, a young lawyer, and a friend of his, cared for him and on september 19, 1863, wrote a letter to his father, David Deming. Among other things, Mr. Chapin, after some reassuring statements said, "When I wrote you first, I feared your son, O. S. Deming, would never be better, but I think now he is entirely out of danger. You need have no uneasiness, as everything is being done for his comfort here. I am happy to be of service to your son at this time."

In recognition of his friend's personal care and attention at that critical time, Osmer S. Deming named his first born William Chapin Deming.

Although in the little home town it was difficult to tell where the boundaries of the village left off and the country began, the boy had the advantage of coming in touch with more phases of life than if he had lived in a city. However, the Deming family were frequent travelers and sometimes spent the summer months with their relatives in Pennsylvania. Will Deming recalls many trips and thrills on the steamboats "Bonanza" and "Wildwood," down the Ohio river, before the Chesapeake and Ohio railroad was extended from Cumberland, Maryland, and Huntington, West Virginia, to Cincinnati.

"My most interesting recollection of a train trip," he says, "was when my father took me and my brother, David, to the World's Fair and Great International Cotton Exposition at Atlanta, Georgia in 1881. I was not quite eleven years old and my brother was two years younger.

"En route father related many incidents of General William T. Sherman's campaign in the South and the various bloody battles that occurred before Atlanta fell into the hands of the Union army. While General Grant was my father's favorite military hero, he gave great credit to General Sherman who persisted, after many heavy losses, in forcing himself through the enemy's country and closing his campaign with his famous march from Atlanta to the sea.

"The trip south took us through sections in which General Joseph E. Johnston had staged so many gallant fights against the invading forces. Our attention was called to Dalton, Ringgold, Resaca, Decatur, and Kenesaw mountain where thousands lost their lives.

"Like other broadminded men, who had fought on either side, my father bore no ill will and spoke then and frequently afterward of the great generals upon the staff of both Sherman and Johnston, the latter being succeeded by General Hood before Atlanta fell."

William Deming's early schooling was in the short-term public schools and select or pay schools, which followed immediately after the close of the public schools.

According to Dr. J. E. Wells, of Cynthiana, Kentucky, a friend of the family, "For a Kentuckian to become a great man or an outstandingly successful one, he must claim to have been born in a log cabin and in his boyhood days to have hunted coons and sold their skins to help provide for a large family of brothers and sisters. Will Deming is the exception. He was not born in a log cabin and as a child was not of the Tom Sawyer type. I remember him always clean, handsome, and courteous. I think he owes his success to heredity and environment or development. . . We bear within ourselves countless fragments of our ancestors' bodies. Our qualities and defects proceed from theirs. Strength and courage are hereditary. Besides his heredity, W. C. Deming had good development. . ."

He may not have been of the Tom Sawyer type, but William C. very early displayed one of his most outstanding characteristics – the ability to face problems squarely and with courage.

A friend relates that once as a small boy, when engaged in a scuffle with his companions, some older fellows persisted in knocking off Will's hat. Promptly he gave notice that the next individual who interfered with his headgear, either accidentally or otherwise, would "suffer a moss-agate face." His antagonizers respected his statement and there was no further annoyance.

During his boyhood, he participated in only one real fist fight. His antagonist was both taller and larger, and was a sort of school bully. It was a give-and-take combat and Will Deming's friends recall that he landed the last blow. The big boy was much humiliated thereby.

Will, however, found when he returned home that he had a big black eye and had to do some quick thinking to prevent his mother from learning he had engaged in a fight. Only frequenters of the saloons and some colored folk on saturday nights were supposed to participate in brawls. While there still were shooting scrapes in Kentucky, the old-fashioned duel between aggrieved gentlemen was outlawed.

In sports, Will Deming was a good wrestler, a baseball enthusiast, and successful in playing marbles "for keeps." Later in life, he played a fair game of golf.

One of his early associates says: "Will Deming was a clean-cut, manly boy, and always made the best personal appearance in the manner of dress and bearing of any of the boys of his age. He was very far advanced in his studies and a leader in school."

He seemed to "leap from boyhood to manhood entirely escaping the follies of youth." He was so sincere and natural, and loved people so well, that his extraordinary abilities never caused others to be jealous of him. He was always a favorite among both the boys and girls who grew up with him in Robertson county, Kentucky.

There were no night clubs or cocktail rooms for young folks in those days, but parties and picnics galore in the fine oak woods or at some near-by estate. Skip-to-my-lu, Charades, and the Virginia Reel were popu-

Delta Tau Delta Fraternity House, Allegheny College, Meadville, Pa.

William C. Deming third from right

lar. Buggy riding by moonlight or on sunday afternoon was common among the boys and girls.

William C. Deming's recollections as a boy hover around the activities of attorneys and courts. His father was an excellent lawyer and he says of him: "It seemed to me in those days that he won nearly all of his cases. Perhaps he did not mention those he lost. Those were the days when lawyers wore long Prince Albert coats and either silk hats or large black felt hats of some sort. An event in our town life was the regular term of the circuit court. The lawyers came from the neighboring county-seat towns." This early stimulated Will's interest in the profession of law. During his vacations he did copying work in his father's law office and picked up much legal phraseology.

Long before he graduated from college he could frame an ordinary complaint, a contract, deed, assignment or plain note as a result of frequent practice and opportunity to read or transcribe such documents.

GOES TO ALLEGHENY COLLEGE. Because his father's people resided in western Pennsylvania, William C. was, in 1886, sent to Allegheny college at Meadville, Pennsylvania. There, after four years, he received the degree of B.A. Later, in 1893, he received the degree of M.A., and in 1924, the honorary degree of LL.D., from the same institution.

Among the important activities of college life at that time were dramatics and debating. In both of these he excelled.

A file of the *Campus of Allegheny College* states:

The inter-society of Ossoli and Allegheny, held last friday evening, was an event long to be remembered by those present. The societies were entertained by a play (farce) in three acts presented by the following members of the societies: Misses O'Neal and Sherman, Messrs.

Proper, Bodley, McNair, Barrett, and Deming. The rendition of "The Sleeping Car" met with great favor, and the players are to be highly complimented upon the manner in which they acted their parts.

At different times during his college career, he was business manager and editor of the college journal, and was active in the Delta Tau Delta fraternity.

Upon graduation, he was president of his class and also represented Allegheny Literary society in the annual commencement inter-society debate at the Opera house with a representative of the Philomathean society.

"The annual contest," said the *Meadville Tribune-Republican*, "is the most important literary event of the whole year, and the friends of the college always look to the result of the contest as the real deciding point of superiority of one society over the other. In the debate, on the question that the government should own and control the telegraph systems of the United States, the negative was presented by Mr. W. C. Deming, who led his opponent from the first both in argument and delivery. He very successfully combatted the points of the affirmative and fairly earned his victory."

Young Deming was very happy over his success because his father was in the audience.

About the time Will entered Allegheny, his father began the erection of an imposing new home on the crest of a hill, the highest point in Mt. Olivet. Judge Deming then owned a number of farms and from one of them he brought enough limestone to build an elaborate stone wall in front of his new home and extensive grounds.

Shadrach Williams, quaint artisan, lived on one of Judge Deming's farms – the one from which the building material was obtained. Shadrach, like Judge Deming, had been in the Civil war and enjoyed swap-

ALPHA CHAPTER DELTA TAU DELTA FRATERNITY, ALLEGHENY COLLEGE, MEADVILLE, PA.
William C. Deming standing rear row right with hands on shoulder of student in second row

ping stories with the Judge. Shad's favorite tale was an exploit of bearing a wounded officer off the field in the battle of Franklin, Tennessee.

Upon one occasion when Will came home from college, he brought a fellow student from the East, and Judge Deming introduced the young man to Shad as being a son of the same man Shad had so bravely rescued from death. Shad's version of the rescue was much enjoyed by the Deming family and the guest.

Shad was a better stonemason than farmer. A neighbor recalled that upon one occasion when the temperature was around 100° Shad was plowing corn. Both he and his plow animal were being attacked vigorously by flies. The neighbor, who was near by, heard Shad talking to himself and finally made out that he was repeating at frequent intervals, "Git up, damn ye, I'd ruther do nuthin' than to plow ye." Many people feel that way about any kind of work.

The Old Kentucky Home, Mt. Olivet, Kentucky, now site of Deming High School.

Left to right, Katharine Evans - Father - Dave - Tom - Mother - Will - Adah

Getting Started In Life

Will Deming recalls that he did not do very much during the first summer after graduation except visit around and receive congratulations upon being a college graduate. His youngest brother, Tom, who was quite a humorist, was accustomed to remark that about the only thing that Will learned at college was to carry a cane, wear a silk hat, and tie a four-in-hand, instead of the bow tie more or less common among the young men of the period.

TRIES SELLING BOOKS. A classmate from the North, who had been his guest, suggested that they see a little of the world before they settled down. This sounded all right, but opportunties were few. His friend had known a young chap in college who had made a lot of money selling books and suggested that they both get in touch with the publishers of the *International Encyclopedia*. Correspondence with the New York house painted a very rosy picture and invited them to come to New York for training.

It was a fine experience and young Deming got a real thrill seeing the city between lectures on book selling. After about ten days' training, each man was assigned to a territory. The friend went somewhere in New Jersey and Deming was sent to Pennsylvania. To make a long story short, Deming said, "It was the toughest job I ever tackled." In the first place, a set of *International Encyclopedia* sold for more than one hundred dollars and it was not so easy in those days to find subscribers for that amount. He did, however, dispose of a few sets, but his commissions scarcely paid his expenses.

"I think," he said, "it was in Plainfield, New Jersey, where I later decided that, though I might be more or less literary, I couldn't sell books, and forwarded my resignation to the head office.

"For some reason, the manager of that department, a Mr. Fowler, declined to accept my resignation and asked me to continue, with my expenses guaranteed, so I resumed, but without much enthusiasm. After another sale or two and many disappointments, I sent the office a letter thanking them for their consideration and returning such paraphernalia, including brief cases and the like, as had been supplied for the work. My recollection is that a condition precedent to becoming a representative of Dodd, Mead and company was the purchase of a set of the *Encyclopedia,* which I still have and have found very useful.

EXCERPTS from his diary relative to the book-selling experience follow:

Mt. Olivet, Kentucky, Thursday, September 4, 1890. I shall leave in the morning for New York, in pursuance of an agreement with Dodd, Mead and company of that city, to enter their employ in selling the *International Cyclopedia.* I feel very hopeful of success.

Friday, September 5. Family all breakfasted at 5:30. Bus ride to Maysville. Will remain here until saturday night with Will Heiser, a college friend. Boys all seem to envy me because I am going to New York.

Saturday, September 6, 9:30 P.M. Some friends came to the train with me – The FFV, Fast Flying Virginian. Good-byes and Good Luck, etc., etc. The train is dashing away into the night. For the first time, I begin to think earnestly about my destiny. A strange foreboding

WILLIAM C. DEMING
as a freshman of Allegheny College

THOMAS H. DEMING
in Allegheny College

or question rather takes possession of me for an instant.
But it is soon dismissed, and I fall asleep – to reawaken.

Sunday, September 7. In the heart of old Virginia,
beautiful scenery and cities engage my attention all day.

Sunday evening, 9:30 P.M. Jersey City is reached.
"All Out." Follow the crowd on to the ferry-boat.
My first view of New York at night – impressive sight
– somewhat bewildering. Being unfamiliar with the
street car lines in New York, took a hack to the Grand
Central hotel. Cab hire, one dollar and fifty cents.
Lesson number one.[1]

September 8. Reported at Dodd, Mead and company.
A Mr. H. from Victor, New York, a nice country
gentleman, was there also.

September 9, 1890. We took our first training lesson
selling *International Cyclopedia.*

September 10. Early this morning, before reporting
for study, Mr. H and I walked up Broadway to the
Fifth Avenue hotel. Mr. H came very near going
through a large mirror in the rear end of the office
lobby. I caught him just in time.

September 11. The training is very complete and
interesting. I begin to feel as if the *International Cyclopedia* is the best in the world, and that I could sell
it to anyone. The enthusiasm, transmitted by the training crew, I guess, is infectious.

September 12, 13, 14, 15 and 16. We have had a lot
to memorize, but the company thinks we have gotten
along very well. Meantime, have attended some theatrical performances and have seen something of the
city. Mr. H is somewhat doubtful of the outcome of
our efforts. I try to encourage him.

September 17. Leave tomorrow evening for my first
"territory," Lock Haven, Pa., a coal mining town.

---

[1] McAdoo had not then built the tunnel under the Hudson river. A.W.S.

September 18, 8:15 P.M. Crossed ferry to Jersey City and boarded train for Lock Haven.

September 19. Called upon an Episcopal minister, whose name had been given me as a prospect. He was very courteous and directed me to a good family boarding house, a small hotel. Lock Haven is a little town nestling down under the Allegheny mountains on the Susquehanna river. Called upon another prospect and talked as I never talked before. He is to advise me tuesday evening.

Saturday, September 20. Went to the Normal School building to call on Professor ————, another "prospect," stated my business and proceeded to open my brief case. His hand went up as he told me he did not care to invest. My third failure and my spirits began to waiver.

Had the name of a Mr. C, a wealthy gentleman. He set an afternoon when I should call and see his daughter who might be interested. I fully expected to make a sale. Found a bright little school girl who looked attentively for a few minutes at my "work," but assured me that her old *Appleton Encyclopedia* was good enough for her. Notwithstanding my argument in behalf of the *International Cyclopedia* she stood firm. For the first time I began to feel discouraged.

September 22. A good sunday dinner and night's rest renewed my hope and I began my round of calls. Stopped at a young lawyer's office. He looked at my grip or brief case suspiciously. I politely asked him if he was at leisure. "That depends upon what you want," he replied. I stated my business and he stated that he was not interested.

Called next upon an alderman, admitted he did need an encyclopedia but began to tell me about his golden wedding which he had just celebrated; showed me how well he could write, notwithstanding his seventy-five years, read me a piece of poetry he had written in honor of his wife, which was little better than doggerel. That's all I got out of the visit.

Observing a sign, Practical Surveyor, dropped in, now somewhat curious to see what his attitude and reaction would be. To my surprise he was both pleasant and polite. Seemed interested, although he has an *Appleton,* will consider exchanging for *International.* We were permitted to make sales on that basis.

September 23. The Mr. M who had promised to call on me at eight o'clock in the evening limped into my room. I held him spellbound by my eloquence and enthusiasm and got his order. Tonight I feel easier for the first time since reaching Lock Haven.

September 25. Called upon the Democrat Publishing company, found the editor, a fine, old man. He liked the *Cyclopedia* and I made a deal taking half in advertising. Things seem to be looking up.

September 26. Someone referred me to a clothing merchant as a man with a family who might be interested. Stated my business, whereupon he exclaimed, disclosing his nationality, "Great Scot, mein frendt, cyclopeda! Vy I got a whole show vindow full of those things and give one away with ebery suit of clothes."

September 27. Called on Dr. T. He was just working himself up to the point of saying, yes, likes the seventy-five dollar binding and would pay cash. My hopes rebound like a rubber ball. Continued to talk and push order blank and pen toward him.

At this instant there was a rush to the door and I hear a woman's voice fairly shrieking, "No, no, Harry, you should not. You know how enormous our expenses will be this year and you shall not buy any more books."

Apparently she had been listening to the conversation from an adjoining room.

Discretion being the better part of valor, I withdrew. Politely agreeing with her that she knew best, meantime, hoping the Doctor's judgment would prevail.

Sunday, September 28, 1890. Managed to write a cheerful letter home, although I have not yet actually made my expenses.

September 29. Called on some of the middle class or working people who mostly appreciated the cyclopedia but were unable to buy as they had lost heavily in the recent flood.

September 30. Returned to the professional class, called on one or two lawyers. Did not have time to look at the book.

Wednesday, October 1. Am becoming accustomed and in a measure, hardened, to unpleasant receptions and failures. Common politeness seems to be rare when a book salesman approaches.

Thursday, October 2. Have decided that I am eminently unfitted for the work. Have not the first element of a good canvasser of any kind. So, have decided to return to New York, resign, and turn in my supplies. What I shall do after that I cannot tell. There may be difficulties but I am willing to face them alone. Cannot help thinking as I eat my last good supper in Lock Haven, that I may not fare so well in New York. Take night train, counted my money after I bought my ticket. I left home with ninety dollars, out of which I paid railroad fare to New York, living expenses while there and in Lock Haven, and now have just nineteen dollars left out of original funds and commissions on sales and exchanges.

Friday morning, October 3, 10 A.M. Crossing Jersey City ferry only about two weeks from the date I crossed going in the opposite direction. It all seemed a bit queer.

This time I take a street car. Report at Dodd, Mead and company, state my decision to quit, manager somewhat surprised and prevailed upon me to delay final decision until monday.

Saturday, October 4. Walked down Wall street. Do not feel because I cannot sell books that I could not succeed in a more congenial line. Must be some place where I would fit in. Would like opportunity for steady work.

Sunday morning, October 5. Attended services at the old Trinity church. Sunday afternoon strolled up Fifth avenue, saw New York life at its best, enjoyed the elegance and wealth displayed even if my few dollars were dwindling away. Experienced no feeling of envy as it seemed better that some, at least, should enjoy success rather than all should be held down.

Monday, October 6. Must give my answer to Dodd, Mead and company today. I see no reason for resuming work although I am unable to find anything to do elsewhere. I have made up my mind that I will not go home and will not tell the folks of my present plight. It is a difficult situation.

Told the assistant manager of my decision. He informed me that the manager, Mr. Fowler, who from the first had shown so much consideration for me, wished to see me before I left.

The result is I am to start all over again on the morrow with my expenses paid by the firm. After listening to Mr. Fowler for a few minutes I was made to feel that I could succeed in the line of work for which I was positive a short time before I had no qualifications.

October 8, 1890. On recommendation of the company, I came to Plainfield, New Jersey, called upon the Reverend Charles B. Mitchell, pastor of the First Methodist church,[2] whom I had met once before in Meadville, Pennsylvania, when he visited my fraternity, Delta Tau Delta. He is a charming character and seemed interested in helping me.

Paid for a week's board and now have one dollar and a half left. The week in New York had about exhausted my cash, however, will send in my expense account saturday and that will help some.

October 9. Called at the office of Mr. J. H. V———, an attorney. He was a pleasant gentleman. Likes the *International* much better than his *Brittanica*. Am to see him again later in the week. Also saw a Mr. S. He liked *International Cyclopedia* but has a *Brittanica*. Met a Mr. H, an attorney. He has a *Brittanica* but will think about exchanging. Have done a lot of talking in making comparisons and hope to get one order out of the three. Perhaps Mr. Fowler was right. Somebody was able to sell *Brittanicas*.

October 10, 1890. I became acquainted today with a young dentist, Doctor R, who is at the same hotel. Made a number of calls but the parties were not in. This business tries one's patience if nothing else. Also it is hard on one's endurance as I have walked several miles today.

October 12. Went to the Methodist church this morning and heard the Reverend Mitchell preach. He is very talented.

October 13. No encouragement today. Beginning to feel that the prospects for success are hopeless. One thing I have observed is that politeness and courtesy are not so common as one would surmise. I have almost

2 Later a bishop in the Methodist church. A.W.S.

learned to recognize a boorish man even before I have addressed him.

Doctor R and I have become quite congenial. It is a relief to have a new friend.

October 15. Made a return call on a Mr. V. He would give me no satisfaction, although I had reasons for believing he was actually interested. In a way that was a straw that broke the camel's back. Mr. Fowler had too much confidence in my ability to stage a comeback. Returned to my room, tired, discouraged but found surcease in sleep. "Now, blessings light on him that first invented this same sleep! It covers a man all over, thoughts and all, like a cloak." I used to pride myself on being able to parse or analyze that sentence in school.

Tonight I received a long letter from my mother. I have not told her about my present plight and apparent failure.

Each day Doctor R and I have become better friends. He, too, is away from his home in Philadelphia and is just starting in his profession in Plainfield. He is subject to attacks of blues and in buoying him up I forget my own situation.

Doctor R found today his bank account was overdrawn by a very small amount. His allowance from home not having arrived, I loaned him the amount necessary which leaves me with only one dollar, but he does not know it.

October 16. Called at the office of Mr. R. Changed my tactics, did not take my brief case. It seemed like a Jonah or handicap. Was ushered into his private office; he dropped his work, even acted as if he wanted to shake my hand. Anticipating the transformation that might take place when I stated my business, decided to prolong the preliminary interview. His suspense and with all his profusion of smiles were enjoyable as he doubtless assumed I was a prospective client.

After the somewhat ridiculous prelude I asked him how he was supplied with encyclopedias. Words fail me. The disappointment and vexed tone and manner in which he exclaimed, Oh! easily interpreted as "Is that all?" was amusing which he followed up by snatching his pen and saying, "I have more books than I want and more too." I suppose he was justified because of his disappointment. Called on one man today who continued to read a newspaper all the time I was talking to him.

Wrote letter to firm. Think Company will no doubt realize I am unfitted for further work of this kind. After supper, Doctor R came to my room. He was exceedingly depressed, told me the cause of his present state of mind, a love affair, and I did my best to cheer him. Life seems full of inconsistencies. Here is Doctor R with a fine office, only a few miles from his home city, receiving cash allowances from his parents and yet worrying over "The girl I left behind me."

October 17, 1890. A long, tiresome day. I called upon the Reverend Mitchell and related my experiences of the last few weeks. He asked me to call again and I will see him tuesday evening.

October 18. Received letter from Dodd, Mead and company in New York. Seemed to understand my position and accepted resignation.

I am fully aware of my unpleasant and uncertain position at this time.

At noon my friend, Doctor R, the young dentist, informed me he had to leave for Philadelphia at five o'clock in the evening and that he would hire a rig and we could drive around during the afternoon. It was a swell turnout. I could not help contemplating that in a few days I might not have enough money to pay for a passage over the Brooklyn bridge. Whole situation seems ridiculous. Doctor R is depressed today, as usual, of late, and I try to cheer him up. We both felt badly when we said good-bye at five-thirty. He seemed much disappointed because I would not be here when he returned to Plainfield a month or two later.

Sunday, October 19. After breakfast read New York paper and went to hear the Reverend Mitchell preach.

At one o'clock the Reverend Mitchell called to inform me he had made an engagement for me with Dr. H. K. Carroll, a director of the United States Census, relative to my securing something to do in the branch office of the United States Census department in Plainfield. I am to see Doctor Carroll monday.

October 20, 9 P.M. Called upon Doctor Carroll, found him a pleasant gentleman who gave me considerable encouragement.

Tuesday, October 21. Called at Census office, presented letter of application which must be forwarded to Washington, D.C. I was told. Hope to hear within a week. There is usually so much delay and uncertainty about government appointments that I still feel some doubt.

Strangely enough, received a nice letter from Dodd, Mead and company suggesting that I resume work if I chose enclosing check for ten dollars due me for expenses.

This came in very handy as I had but sixty cents left, paid five dollars for board. Cannot understand Company's reluctance to accept my resignation.

Wednesday, October 22. Went to New York this

morning and finally surrendered my grip and papers to Dodd, Mead and company. I hated to do so as the firm had been so considerate but I could not continue conscientiously drawing expenses when I was not doing the job justice. I am sure I have few, if any, of the requisites of a salesman of that character.

While walking down Broadway this afternoon, I was accosted by a nice looking, neatly dressed young man. He asked me if I knew where he could find something to do; his manner interested me and I felt he was sincere. He gave me his name, saying his home was in New Orleans. He had been in New York since friday, did not know a soul, and had pawned everything he had but the clothes he wore. Said he had had nothing to eat all day. I questioned him closely and was satisfied his story was true. He looked pale and weak and he could hardly help crying when he talked. Since friday said he had wandered around in search of work. If he was a fraud he was a good actor.

Although I had only about three dollars left, I gave him a quarter and he warmly shook my hand as he thanked me and said good-bye.

At eight o'clock in the evening I attended a big ratification meeting of the county democracy at Cooper institute. The crowd was enormous. Mayor Grace presided. Francis M. Scott, candidate for mayor, spoke. I returned to Plainfield at one-thirty o'clock in the morning.

Thursday, October 23, 1890. A rainy, disagreeable day. Nothing to do but wait for news from Washington.

This evening I attended a small reception at the home of the Reverend Mitchell. First time I have been in ladies' society for two months, enjoyed the evening very much.

Friday, October 24. Spent greater portion of the day with Doctor R who had returned and was surprised to find me still in Plainfield.

October 25. Still waiting to hear from Uncle Sam.

Sunday, October 26. Attended church this morning, read sunday paper, wrote letters, retired early. Feel a bit discouraged, but must keep up appearances.

Monday, October 27. Had first letter from my father since he became aware that I have severed relations with Dodd, Mead and company. Seemed to think I had made a mistake in doing so.

My finances again reduced to about sixty cents, and a week's board will be due on friday.

This evening I went around to the Electric Light station to talk with Will McClurg of Meadville, Pennsylvania, who is employed there. We smoked and talked of college days at Allegheny.

Tuesday, October 28. Still anxiously awaiting word from Doctor Carroll's office. The uncertainty is becoming very depressing.

Wednesday, October 29. For the first time, notwithstanding our friendship, I made a confidant of Doctor R.

No one could have been more kind and sympathetic. Asked me to room with him if I wished to. Thanked him sincerely, but declined.

Decided to call on Doctor Carroll. As I half-way expected was told that the powers in Washington would not appoint me to a position in the Census Bureau because I am from Kentucky and not from New Jersey.

Doctor Carroll said Washington headquarters stated they would not have hesitated if I were a resident of New Jersey.

This all seemed a bit disgusting to me. I presume

the reason is that New Jersey is a doubtful state and politics is considered in filling these places.[3]

Have not the slightest idea what I shall do now but will not give up. Had a letter from my mother and as I feared she had seen the letter I had written my father and of course is worrying about me.

Friday I shall owe for a week's board and room, suppose I will have to pawn my gold watch. Seems queer as I never pawned anything in my life. Hate to part with it even temporarily, as it was given to me by my father while I was in college.

Doctor R is now trying to brace me up, while a short time ago I was the comforter.

Thursday, October 30, 1890. Called again on the Reverend Mitchell to tell him the result of my application in the Census Department. He was very sorry, but true to his own fine character, said everything would be all right yet.

He promised to make an engagement for me to see Mr. P. Minturn Smith, president of the Union Iron Works and Easton Electric company, New York City. Mr. Smith lives in Plainfield and commutes to his office. He is a member of the Reverend Mitchell's church.

Will have to wait until saturday night to see him.

Friday, October 31. Am counting the hours until saturday evening. Spent morning at the Public library. Must raise some money by tomorrow. Do not feel very hopeful about position in New York as I know nothing about the business.

Meantime, I am delaying the study of law at home which I am supposed to begin sometime. Never realized before how necessary it is to have some ready

---

[3] Thirty-three years later Mr. Deming became president of the entire United States Classified Civil Service with headquarters in Washington D.C. A.W.S.

money available. At supper Doctor R and I were both pretty blue. He proposed several schemes to pass the evening as it is Halloween and we ought to be celebrating.

Ironically enough, I asked him to go with me to a pawnshop as I was going to hang up my watch there but he protested saying we will get the money some way tomorrow. However, I pawned the watch.

My mother wrote suggesting that I come home, but much as I would like to see the family, I cannot think of giving up yet.

Saturday, November 1. One more day upon the "anxious seat." Spent afternoon in the Public library. Hour has arrived for my call upon Mr. Smith. The Reverend Mitchell and his wife accompanied me, met Mr. Smith's interesting family, all talked generally for awhile when Mr. Smith and I proceeded to his library and talked business. He catechised me pretty closely but pleasantly. He is a shrewd businessman. The result is that I am to report to his office on 45 Broadway monday morning for trial.

He seems to prefer that I continue to live in Plainfield. Perhaps because it is less expensive or more likely because he doubted I would be very useful in his organization.

Sunday, November 2. This afternoon Doctor R and I took a drive.

Monday, November 3. Went to New York and began work in Mr. Smith's office. Routine duties. Returned to Plainfield and heartily enjoyed my dinner.

Tuesday, November 4. Today we have a holiday as it is Election day in New York.

Wednesday, November 5. Went to New York, worked all day, and am beginning to feel something at home in a New York business office.

The latest news shows that the Democrats swept everything in tuesday's election.

George Wallace Delamater, republican of Meadville, defeated for governor in Pennsylvania and William McKinley meets a similar fate for re-election to congress in Ohio. The next congress will be overwhelmingly democratic. Reaction from high tariff days and depression, no doubt.[4]

Thursday, November 6, 1890. Everything quiet after election.

Friday, November 7. Was late in arriving at office this morning because of delay in crossing the ferry. Too much fog. The worst in years. Am very tired tonight.

Saturday, November 8. Arose at 7 A.M. and caught 8 o'clock train for Jersey City and New York.

Although I am a college graduate, this afternoon I received my first regular week's wages or salary, ten dollars. True, it was very small but I felt I had actually earned it and what is more, am learning something about the value of money.

Because of the ferry delays from fog and the expense of commuting to and from Plainfield, I have engaged board and room with Mr. Tremaine of the Easton Electric company at his home in Brooklyn and feel quite fortunate in getting into a nice family. After paying my bills in Plainfield, tomorrow will have about twenty-five cents left, but happily I have a return ticket to New York.

But even with this small balance, I don't feel discouraged now as I have a job, such as it is. This will be my last night in Plainfield and a month spent at this family hotel.

Sunday, November 9. After breakfast and reading

---

[4] A few years later, William McKinley, after serving as governor of Ohio, returned to Washington as president of the United States. A.W.S.

papers, packed my grip, preparatory to leaving for New York and Brooklyn. Came down to dinner at 1 P.M. and told Doctor R good-bye, settled for my board, and had twenty-three cents left. It has taken close figuring.

Left Plainfield at 2:30 p.m. and reached New York an hour later. This time I did not even take a street car for every nickel counts. Carried two heavy valises from the ferry dock at Liberty street to the Brooklyn bridge, a long distance. Had to rest nearly every block. By the time I reached the bridge, it was almost impossible for me to carry them because my hands and arms were so weak or numb. Paid three cents to ride over the Brooklyn bridge and five cents street car fare to Carlton avenue where Mr. Tremaine lives.

It's a nice old style brownstone front house in a pleasant but old fashioned neighborhood. Was kindly received by Mrs. T. At tea met some very nice people who take their meals there. A Reverend Mr. H and wife are among the boarders. As Mrs. T is quite religious I guess my morals will be properly cared for, as this seems to be a hot-bed of Methodism. Attended church, put five cents in the plate, which leaves me with a net balance of thirteen cents. Don't know where my bridge fare and luncheon will come from this week.

Monday, November 10. Was at the office at 8:30 A.M., worked hard all day, paid out three cents for bridge fare, leaving balance of ten cents. Made my lunch or dinner on a piece of pie costing five cents, bought it from an old woman on the corner of William and Wall streets. Leaned up against a lamp post and ate it with gusto.

After I left the office this afternoon, I realized I must have a little money this week before receiving pay check. So I have pawned my last pawnable article, my college fraternity pin.

Got only ninety-five cents on it, but that may see me through until saturday. At earnest request of the Reverend and Mrs. H and Mrs. Tremaine, I attended a young people's meeting this evening.

Tuesday, wednesday, and following days were spent in same routine at office. Considering my obscure position am somewhat puzzled at courtesy and consideration shown me by all employees and members of the firm. Maybe because I am a Kentucky Gentleman, or a recent college graduate, but more likely because they think I am a protegé of President Smith.

Sunday, November 16, 1890. Beautiful fall day. Mr. T and I strolled through a nearby park, attended church again in the evening.

Monday, November 17. We have quite an acquisition at our boarding place. A Mr. and Mrs. C—— of the Brooklyn navy yard and their daughter who is a bright, young girl. We became good friends.

This afternoon Edwin L. Mattern, whom I knew well in Allegheny college, and now a reporter on the *Brooklyn Eagle,* called. He has arranged to board here and will room with me. We have taken a beautiful, large room and the winter promises to be very pleasant, even if my finances do remain at a low ebb.

Tuesday, November 18, 1890. This is a delightful day. The big United States warship, the "Maine." [5] was launched from the Brooklyn navy yards today.

December 3. I substituted for Mattern on one of his double assignments. Very interesting. He works too hard. Doesn't get enough sleep.

There was another big failure in Wall street.

---

[5] Early in 1898 the "Maine" was blown up in Havana harbor resulting in the war with Spain. A.W.S.

February 1, 1891. An occasional five or ten dollar bill received from my mother has enabled me to remain solvent and redeem my watch from Plainfield pawn-broker.

At this point Mr. Deming's diary closed. He remained in New York with the same company until march when he returned home, having received a check from his father for the necessary travel expenses.

True to his instinct for seeing the country, Mr. Deming made a stop-over in Washington and other interesting points en route home, not knowing when he would get away again.

Mr. Deming says he learned many things of value during his winter in New York and returned home in good health and "rarin' to go" in the study of law.

"Here I was, age twenty-one, a college graduate, with a Bachelor of Arts degree and a record in literary societies and other organizations, yet I was not a typist or a stenographer or a bookkeeper. In fact, I was not much of anything of value to a business organization, and knew it. However, the president and his associates were very considerate and cordial and tried to find something suitable to my talents.

"The company was erecting, at 29 Broadway, one of the then early steel structures, called the Columbia building, nine stories high, surmounted by a very high peaked roof and containing a series of dormer windows." [Illustrated in King's *Handbook of New York,* published about 1904.]

"Indicating the rapid growth of that district, the Columbia building was replaced in one generation by a thirty-two story office building. I am indebted to F. J. Adams of McKim, Mead and White for information about changes on lower Broadway."

"My duties were chiefly outside of the office, covering considerable territory, and giving me an opportunity to learn something about the city and its environs."

"I acted as timekeeper, distributed the pay roll, contacted supply houses in New York, Brooklyn, and Jersey City which were slow in delivering material, and looked after many similar things. The telephone was not so generally used as it is today."

Ed. L. Mattern later became a successful Pittsburgh lawyer, and oddly enough, Deming became a successful newspaper writer and publisher.

It is possible Mr. Deming's later interest in real estate and construction was inspired by that early superficial experience during which time he became acquainted with architects, contractors and craftsmen.

Referring further to that winter spent in New York, Mr. Deming says: "My diary shows that I had great difficulty in living on my weekly wage. My luncheon rarely cost more than ten cents, consisting of a glass of milk and a sandwich, for instance, and it goes without saying that I enjoyed the big family dinner in the old-fashioned Brooklyn home in the evening.

"With the exception of an occasional Shakespearean play or a lecture or a concert at the Cooper institute, I indulged in no extravagances.

"When spring arrived, I decided it was time for me to settle down if I ever expected to become a lawyer.

"About the first of march I purchased an unlimited ticket for home, desiring to make as many stops as possible for fear I might never see that part of the country again. My first was Washington, which I toured thoroughly, including the rooms in the White House that were open to the public. I made stops at Richmond, Virginia, White Sulphur Springs, and other historic points en route, arriving home ready for the next act or duty, whatever it might be."

Apparently not yet ready for serious work, or as he expresses it, "still possessed of the wanderlust," Mr. Deming deferred his law study and went to Chautauqua Lake, New York, as correspondent for at least a half dozen metropolitan newspapers. Among them were the *Pittsburgh Dispatch,* the *Philadelphia Inquirer,* and the *Chicago Herald.*

In connection with his work there, he relates the following, which he entitles, "How I didn't get Fired:"

"Frederick Palmer, later the well-known war correspondent, and I had attended college together. He started out to be a newspaper man, while I hoped to be a lawyer. We decided to spend the summer together, he to arrange with at least three dailies and I to secure at least three.

"When I reached Chautauqua, however, in june, 1891, I found a letter from Palmer containing his list of newspapers but saying that he would be unable to come because of other employment. It therefore happened that I had a string of New York, Pittsburgh, Cleveland, Cincinnati, Louisville, and Chicago newspapers, for which I was doing space writing, being paid only for what was published. Out of the entire number, however, I had an income for two or three months which seemed princely; particularly in those good old days when hotels and boarding houses and railroads were willing to take care of newspaper men without money and without price. This is not literally true, but almost so.

"The big hotels at Lakewood, which catered to society people from the East and South were particularly courteous and my greatest trouble was in dividing up

my 'patronage' in such a way as not to offend any one
of them. When I checked out, I always found that
my bill was marked "Paid."

"My headquarters were at the 'Assembly Grounds,'
or Chautauqua proper, which had justified the vision
of Bishop John H. Vincent and the Methodist church
so many years before, as a great foregathering each year
of people of all ages for self-education and the development of religious culture.

"One evening in mid-summer, when I thought my
day's work was about over, I received a telegram directing me to proceed at once to Lakewood, at the other
end of the lake, and meet a special train bringing in
the injured from the most disastrous wreck the Erie
railroad had ever had. The wreck occurred in northeastern Ohio near Ravenna, and many very prominent
Cincinnati people were among the injured. The telegram was signed Marshall Halstead, managing editor,
Commercial Gazette.

"Marshall Halstead was a son of the famous Murat
Halstead, who was a contemporary of Greeley, Reid,
Bennett, Dana, and other editorial lights of that period.

"I was delayed somewhat in reaching Lakewood by
reason of slow transportation, and it was nine o'clock
before I got into action. Meantime, the relief train had
arrived and the injured were placed in hotels and private cottages. Under very difficult circumstances, I interviewed doctors, nurses, and passengers in various
stages of dress and undress.

"The only commercial telegraph wire out of Lakewood was operated from one of the hotels, and when
I reached the telegraph office at eleven o'clock, the
operator was closing up for the night. I stated my case
and he agreed to get my report over the wire.

"Up to this time, I had merely the data and had not written the story, but there was another problem yet to be solved. Unknown to the *Commercial Gazette,* I was also correspondent for the *Cincinnati Enquirer,* which, as a matter of fact, was my best paper from the standpoint of space used.

"A great variety of questions, involving newspaper ethics, ran hastily through my mind. The upshot of the matter was that I sat down inside the telegraph office, wrote my report, and directed the operator to send it to both the *Commercial Gazette* and the *Cincinnati Enquirer.* Before I had written the last page, the first was no doubt in type.

"It was of such local importance and contained so many details as to names and injuries that the *Commercial Gazette* made it the big story the following morning on the first page.

"No one but a newspaper man can properly appreciate the feeling of anger of Marshall Halstead, managing editor of the *Gazette,* when he saw the same story, word for word, on the first page of the *Cincinnati Enquirer.*

"Having done my duty, as I saw it, I retired and got a reasonably good night's sleep. After breakfast I awaited with both interest and curiosity the reaction of my supposed duplicity. I did not have long to wait. My name was paged as I sat at the luncheon table, and when I opened the telegram, it read: 'You duplicated to the *Cincinnati Enquirer* story I ordered concerning Erie wreck. This is unpardonable. Your services are no longer needed at Chautauqua Lake.'

"I placed the message in my pocket and finished my meal, after which I did two things. I first wired Mr. Halstead briefly and enigmatically suggesting that he wait for a letter before passing final judgment. The second was to prepare a good follow-up story and duplicate that to both papers, believing full well that neither would dare omit it, not wishing to be outdone on matters of such important local concern.

"As I anticipated, both papers published the second story. My letter explained all the circumstances attending the situation and emphasized the fact I was not on a salary basis, but a space writer. There was no opportunity to rewrite the story and this justified what otherwise might seem to be an inexcusable offense.

"Whether it was because my argument carried weight or whether the *Cincinnati Gazette* found no other correspondent, Mr. Halstead continued to take my stories, exclusive, at my suggestion, until the end of the season. He later gave me one of the most important newspaper assignments of my early life and paid me well for the work. It was of an investigative nature, and had to do with rates for natural gas, electric light, and coal prices in northern Kentucky."

At Chautauqua, Deming interviewed a man named Jones of Binghamton, a successful manufacturer of scales, running from grocery store balances to heavy platform mechanism. One of his advertising slogans was: "Jones, He Pays the Freight." Because of his success and his unique advertising, Jones received consideration as a candidate for governor of New York.

Mr. Deming called upon Jones in his large private suite in the old Athenaeum hotel. Despite the fact that Jones was an advertiser and ambitious, he balked at being interviewed. In fact, he was not very gracious. Recognizing the futility of endeavoring further to obtain an interview with Jones as to his possible candidacy for governor, Mr. Deming picked up his hat and started to leave the room.

"I presume I may state that you still pay the freight?" the young reporter asked. This seemed to strike Jones just right and he gave the interview.

When in college at Meadville, Pennsylvania, Will Deming had done a little rowing on French creek, so he decided to try his hand as an oarsman on Chautauqua Lake. Once when enjoying the water with an attractive young woman, a sudden summer storm rocked the boat, and he remembered the old revival song "Pull for the shore, sailor, pull for the shore." His fair companion, he is sure, never knew how near she came to being upset.

"One of my pleasant recollections of this summer spent at Chautauqua," he says, "hovers around a young football coach who was much in the public eye at that time. Upon one occasion when the newspaper men and others were drafting talent for an impromptu evening's entertainment, it was my pleasure to introduce Alonzo A. Stagg, a Yale man, and I was much impressed with his modesty and his easy stage presence. Occasionally throughout the years I have met him and he has continued to hold the admiration and respect of all true sportsmen, both in this country and in Great Britain. Today he is retired, of course, but his opinion is frequently sought on matters affecting football and baseball."*

At the end of the Chautauqua season, Deming returned to his home in Kentucky, where he resumed the study of law in the office of his father, Judge O. S. Deming, and was later admitted to the bar.

About 1892-93, as a side line, he joined Professor R. H. Keyes and J. W. Riley in establishing the first advanced school in the community. This was called the Mt. Olivet Male and Female Academy and was conducted in rooms on the second floor of the court house.

*Since the above was written Mr. Stagg has resumed coaching in California.

It was said to have been "one of the best private schools
ever taught in the county." Deming taught English,
Rhetoric, Political Economy, and German.

Having taken a prominent part in college debating,
William Deming started a literary and debating society
in Mt. Olivet and helped establish a "traveling" library.
Parliamentary rules were studied and practiced in executive session. The public was admitted to the literary
discussions. Deming was also the moving spirit in starting an annual banquet for the home-town boys, especially those who had removed to other communities.

The literary society and the banquets were said to
have had a visible effect on the morale of the young
men and to have improved the standing and character
of many.

Helm Woodward, one of these home-town boys, now
a prominent lawyer in Covington, Kentucky, says:

"Will Deming was my ideal, and no doubt the ideal
of many other young men and boys in the neighborhood. His praise was more valuable to me than that of
any other person I knew. At the time he was teaching,
I studied English under him, and I remember on one
occasion I read a paper at some public gathering on
the subject, 'Is the World Going Forward?' Later in
the meeting, Will took occasion to praise my paper
publicly, and I was so happy that I felt sure that some
day I would be a writer. Although this happened many
years ago, I still remember the pleasure I felt at the
time."

While waiting for a law practice to develop, young
Deming turned his attention also to acting as local correspondent for his old friend, the *Cincinnati Commercial Gazette*. This gave him some standing in the newspaper profession. In fact, Lem Atwood, a native of

Kentucky, then the editor of the *Cincinnati Post,* a Scripps paper, offered him a job which he declined because he was more interested then in the law, and also doubted the wisdom of taking a salaried job and becoming one cog in a big machine. His judgment was vindicated later in life, as he usually got in at the top. Meantime, he had demonstrated that he could carry on a number of activities concurrently.

There were two weekly papers in Mt. Olivet at that time. The editor of the *Democratic Weekly* was a typical young southern gentleman of the old school about the same age as William Deming. He, too, was a lawyer. Notwithstanding the fact that Deming was a strong republican, the two were good friends. One day he came into Deming's office and after some hesitation and considerable circumlocution said that he was going to get married and that Susie insisted on at least two weeks honeymoon trip.

"I don't know," he said, "how I am going to keep this paper going unless you do it for me."

"All right," answered Deming, "if you are willing to trust a republican at the editorial helm of the official democratic organ of this county for two weeks, let Susie have her way."

Thus it happened that his first practical experience in conducting a newspaper was to help a friend get married. When the bridegroom returned, he was made the butt of many good-natured jibes by his friends, because he had come back so soon. They said that for two weeks, at least, they had had a readable newspaper.

The lure of the printed word continued to intrude itself in the life of the young lawyer. The leading weekly of the community was owned and edited by a very interesting man named John W. Zoller. Zoller had learned the printing trade in the old days before type was generally designated according to the point system, and he published his weekly upon a Washington hand press. He called it the *Tribune-Democrat.* It was a consolidation of two papers and was independent in politics. The old printer could take his composing stick and "set" a column editorial in nonpareil, brevier, or small pica type without writing a word on paper.

Mr. Zoller was in rather poor health and he had the habit of not publishing his paper promptly if he did not feel like it. Eventually, however, he would complete his volume and maintain his record of never having missed an issue. His subscribers were indulgent and stayed with him.

One day Deming said, "Mr. Zoller, I understand, of course, how you can satisfy your neighbors and friends, and even the local advertisers, by these intermittent issues, but how do you satisfy the foreign advertisers – the fellows in New York and Chicago who give you the contracts for Carter's Little Liver Pills, Peruna, Paine's Celery Compound, and Dr. Caldwell's Cough Syrup?"

Zoller looked at his visitor with a rather pained and quizzical expression and said, "Why, Will, all these people know me," and let it go at that.

Mr. Deming often has stated that the few simple principles and the knowledge of newspaper psychology gained from old John W. Zoller and his weekly in Kentucky have been no small factor in whatever success he has had as a publisher, both in Ohio and in Wyoming.

One day Zoller intimated that he would like to have Will operate his paper for a time. After giving the

THOMAS H. DEMING
when editor of the Mount Olivet (Ky.) Tribune

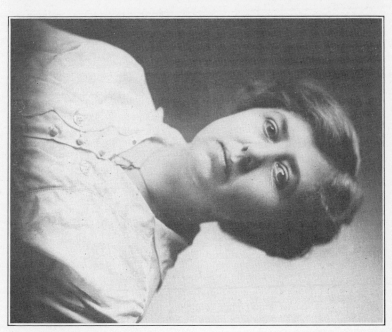

ADAH DEMING MORRISON
Wheatland, Wyoming

matter some consideration, Will told him that if he would make an absolute lease for three years, placing the paper entirely under his control, editorially and otherwise, during which time Zoller would have no more to say concerning its management or policy than the rankest outsider, Deming would take it over. Zoller agreed to the proposition, and William Deming became, on the side, the full-fledged editor-manager of a weekly paper.

Although he had never learned the printer's trade, Will was fortunate in having a younger brother, Thomas, who had been an apprentice in Zoller's office and was then an employee. Tom had not only learned to set type for ordinary straight matter, but could do the average bit of job work that came to a small office, such as sales, stud horse bills, cards of candidates, etc. Being rather vigorous for his age, he could also make up the forms and handle the Washington press. With Tom, and one other good printer, Coleman B. Rigg, a cousin, Will Deming managed the business and began to sense the real influence of a newspaper.

He profited by having watched Zoller's paper for several years. He readily saw the value that Zoller placed upon a personal news item, the number of names of people he brought into each weekly issue, and the careful attention he paid to birth notices, marriages, and obituaries. When the farmers came to town they all called on the editor.

It should be understood that, notwithstanding his procrastination, Zoller had the popular paper and from time to time absorbed aspiring rivals.

In following many of Zoller's principles, enlarged by his own views, Deming made excellent progress with the *Tribune Democrat* in Mt. Olivet.

As junior member of the law firm of Deming, Holmes and Deming, his individual court cases were not important. His first was a defense of a well-known citizen charged with disturbing religious worship while intoxicated. Deming convinced the jury that his client always quoted scripture when drinking and that his interruption of the minister was merely interest in the sermon. Acquittal followed. He said later, "I never quite liked the technical side of court practice. I always preferred a game in which all cards could be laid upon the table. In after years I found that Thomas Jefferson made the same criticism of the law, particularly as to the controversial side of the practice."

Turning Point in his Life

During the Christmas holidays of 1893, Fred Russell, son of Hon. J. W. Russell, general manager of the Aetna Machine and Foundry company of Warren, Ohio, stopped en route to Florida for a short vacation to visit Will Deming. The two had been classmates at Allegheny college and both had served on the staff of the Allegheny college *Campus,* the former as business manager and the latter in an editorial capacity.

Young Russell discussed a pending proposition for buying the *Warren Daily Tribune* and asked Will if he would be interested in going into it. His reply was in the negative, as he had expected to follow in his father's footsteps by devoting all of his attention to the practice of law, and there had been too many interruptions already.

After the departure of his friend, he dismissed the Ohio proposition from his mind. Early in march 1894, however, he received a telegram from Russell saying that a company was in process of formation to buy the *Warren Tribune* and requesting that he come to Warren and give the benefit of his advice and experience.

Flattered at being considered an expert in newspaper matters, young Deming accepted the invitation promptly. "Moreover," he says, "I guess I was ready for another trip."

Upon his arrival at Warren, Ohio, he was at once impressed with the beauty of the town and the substantial character of its business houses, homes, and the surrounding farming country. Although the plant of the *Tribune* was but little more modern than that of the paper he was running in Kentucky, and despite the fact that the depression of the early nineties was still acute, with the steel mills idle and men out of work filling the parks, he felt that there was an opportunity in Warren. Once the capital of the "Western Reserve of Connecticut," it antedated Cleveland and many of the early land records were housed in Warren.

When, after ten days, he was asked to become one of the company which was organized for ten thousand dollars to buy the daily, he accepted. He was chosen editor at seventy dollars a month. Likewise, eight hundred forty dollars a year was the salary of Fred Russell, the business manager. Those were the days when men built good homes and reared families on one hundred to one hundred twenty-five dollars a month.

With considerable assurance, William Deming subscribed his pro-rata of stock and agreed to return as soon as he could settle his affairs in Kentucky. He asked for only thirty days for that purpose.

This decision, made on the spot, without further consultation with his father, mother, or brother, or Zoller, was typical of Will Deming's ability to recognize a real opportunity, notwithstanding the depression, to visualize the future, and to reach sound conclusions without delay. Perhaps he relied on a unique perversion of the Scripture, common among the colored folks in Kentucky – "The Lord will divide."

This was Deming's first business venture requiring any particular outlay of capital or use of his credit. His experience with the school and the Mt. Olivet *Tribune-Democrat* and time spent in his father's law office, however, had taught him the rudiments of business and given him confidence. His two younger brothers, David and Tom, were perhaps a bit more frugal than he or, at least had fewer opportunities for spending or fewer demands upon their funds. At any rate, the brothers seemed to have made small loans to one another from time to time. One source of youthful income was to "set" tobacco on nearby farms. When the season for planting came, the farmers gathered up town boys and paid them a dollar a day for ten or twelve hours work. Will was always in demand.

He recalls also working for sixty cents a day in a brick kiln "off bearing" brick – mighty hard and hot work in summer for a boy in his early teens.

The following copy of a receipt from David S. Deming is interesting only in that it involved such a small settlement in view of the larger operations in which W. C. Deming was to engage in later years. The receipt, prepared by W. C. Deming, shows in its language that he could make proper use of legal terms at that time, and that he was leaving home for Ohio with a clean slate.

Office of TRIBUNE DEMOCRAT, DEMING & RIGG, *editors*

Mt. Olivet, Ky. march 26, 1894

I have this day received of W. C. Deming $1.50 for balance in full of all past transactions and obligations express or implied between W. C. Deming and myself.   D. S. DEMING

Tom Deming succeeded him as editor and manager of the *Robertson County Tribune Democrat,* but he did not have as much patience with Zoller as William had, and evidently could not handle him quite so well when the old editor came into the office and gave advice. A year or so later when Tom's patience was exhausted, he reached down in his pocket, pulled out the office keys, tossed them over to Zoller, walked out, and never went back. He entered Allegheny college and later joined his brother in Warren, Ohio. Coleman B. Rigg, the printer cousin, followed Tom and both became stockholders in the Ohio paper. The five hundred dollars which Will Deming urged his cousin to invest sold for ten thousand dollars twenty-five years afterward. Tom Deming saved his money, became a stockholder, editor, and well-to-do citizen.

William C. Deming was deeply moved at the thought of leaving Mt. Olivet. "Perhaps the most trying situation in which a man ever finds himself," he wrote, "is when, with swelling heart and ill-repressed emotion, he stands bidding farewell to those people and those things which by nature are nearest and dearest to him. The opportunity in Ohio was one I could not well afford to ignore. However strong my predilections are for home, friends, and the scenes of my boyhood, the day of separation had to come, sooner or later, no doubt. Little given to profuse and extravagant display of my feelings on any subject, I have cherished your friendship more than any of you have reason to suppose. I love my native state, and I love my native people. As the years roll by, a beautiful mind picture of home and boyhood in Kentucky will oft appear before me and cause me the same heartache I feel today. . ."

And thus William C. Deming at twenty-four severed his home ties and took up his work in a new state – Ohio, never to return to Kentucky except as a visitor.

He wrote also about Kentucky and its people. "Yet I am willing to leave all this and cast my lot with strangers, amid strange scenes, feeling that upon no one state or section has benign Providence bestowed all its temporal blessings. . . Come easy; go easy – such is life in old Kentucky. No strikes; few aliens; no unemployed

(don't smile) at least not in the northern acceptation of
the term; no Coxey army marching on to Washington
to demand better roads, for Kentucky has a network of
turnpikes à la Macadam. The iron horse snorts at rare
intervals and in rare places. The smoke of the mill and
furnace is almost a stranger, although Kentucky's mountains are filled with the choicest coal, and iron ore. 'Mid
the black smoke of roaring furnaces; 'mid the mad rush
of northern enterprise, I have long desired to find myself, even though an insignificant factor – to go, to be,
to work where life is not lived because it is easy, but
where labor, enjoined by the great Master Mechanic,
bringeth its own reward."

To go, to be, to work where life is not lived because
it is easy – has been the pattern which William C. Deming has followed. He has always been industrious, setting a pace in his writing work for his associates, attempting new and difficult tasks, pioneering in new
fields where trail-breaking was necessary.

The Warren, Ohio, Tribune. The young men of the
newly organized *Warren Tribune* threw themselves
into the enterprise with great enthusiasm. At that time
there were fewer than one thousand subscribers and the
paper circulated for six cents a week.

Having been accustomed to covering a good deal of
ground, William Deming did not restrict himself to
writing editorial articles but made a full hand on the
news staff. Opportunities to meet people both in the
city and county came thick and fast, even invitations to
make commencement speeches and to speak on various
occasions.

Every month Deming saved something out of his
salary to apply upon his stock ownership. He has said
many times since, "Whatever financial success I have

had comes from the fact that I learned early to save, and not wait until my income was larger before beginning the habit. I began at once and found I could live within my income and have something left."

Some time during the first year of the new ownership of the *Warren Tribune,* Mrs. Zell P. Hart, a young widow, came to the editor's office with a voluntary contribution concerning the wedding of a friend, a member of a prominent family. Up to that time the owners had specialized in general news, free want ads, obituaries, and county correspondence to make the paper popular.

Will Deming had learned by experience on Zoller's weekly in Kentucky that names counted and that an obituary should be complete in every detail, as it saved the family the trouble of writing long letters. Furthermore, the relatives bought the paper that contained the best death notice. Marriages were in the same category.

The *Tribune* had not, however, installed a regular society column. Mr. Deming was so much impressed with the work done by Zell Hart, then and in subsequent contributions, that she was engaged as society editor at a modest salary.

Being a native, and with a large acquaintance and relationship, she did not confine herself to society news but was soon turning in stories that the regular reporters had overlooked, thereby making herself still more valuable to the paper. Incidentally, Mr. Deming recalls that the standing society head was embellished with a cut from the Lydia Pinkham advertising service. As the lady selected appeared handsome as well as wholesome, the picture served well for the time being.

Meantime, the campaign for subscriptions was bringing results and the spirited news columns were attracting attention. In fact, the paper was growing so rapidly that at times it was difficult to get to press on time or issue promptly because the old-fashioned Campbell press was operated by water motor. If there happened to be a fire in town at press time, the paper was delayed until the blaze was extinguished.

It was, indeed, an event when the *Tribune* company replaced the water motor with a Webster gasoline engine and later installed a Duplex eight-page cylinder press.

During the early years of editorship in Warren, Ohio, Deming worked day and night to get the *Tribune* established against the old and formidable rival. To increase his income and enlarge his experience, he syndicated certain classes of special news and feature stories. His system was very simple. He made half a dozen or more copies and sent them to widely scattered sunday papers with the hope that some of them would be accepted and printed. He had fair success.

In telling of this syndicate work, he says: "One day I prepared what I thought was an unusually interesting and timely historical article, growing out of a nationally famous murder trial of the period. I was so fearful that someone else would have the same idea about an article that I wrote my story hastily, the chief concern being to market it before some competitor beat me to it. It bore the caption, 'Tragedies of Kentucky governors and their sons.'

"Charles A. Dana was still the active editor of the *New York Sun,* although he was an old man and had turned over all the publishing details to younger associates. For some reason I selected the *New York Sun* as the metropolitan newspaper to honor with my contribution. Perhaps I thought of my article as a classic and in keeping with the Dana standard of style.

"You can imagine my surprise when I found that the story had fallen under the personal scrutiny and judgment of the great editor himself. On a piece of print paper, newspaper copy size, written with a blue pencil, and in Dana's familiar hand, and certainly in his most characteristic style, appeared the following:

Your manuscript is herewith returned. The subject is most interesting, but the treatment is meager and disappointing. It is not a satisfactory work of art — C. A. DANA

"Strange as it may seem, I was not a bit displeased. In the first place, at least a half dozen papers published the story for its current news value and paid me well for it, indicating that my judgment as to the timeliness of the story was correct. At the same time I had received from Charles A. Dana a typical expression of his personality and critical judgment, an original signature, and a bit of helpful advice through the language of his rejection, which stood me in good stead for many years to come. In other words, 'Make haste slowly' and 'Nothing is lost by taking time'."

Much interest was aroused by the *Tribune,* not only through its lively news columns but also through various "contests," inaugurated by the staff.

The *Tribune* made itself the medium through which three hundred and fifty needy children received Christmas remembrances for many years. To the *Tribune* staff it meant weeks and weeks of work, coupled with anxiety and expense. One year, presents were solicited ranging from dolls to dresses and five-dollar bills. The following year was the "Children-for-the-children" year and not so much soliciting was done from the local merchants.

As the result of hard work, relentless effort, and a

The subject is most interesting, but the treatment is meagre & the absence of important details makes the article very disappointing. It is not a satisfactory work of art.

C. A. Dana

May 10 '95

FACSIMILE OF LETTER FROM CHARLES A. DANA TO W. C. DEMING

desire to please and satisfy readers, *The Daily Tribune* in due time rapidly increased its business in every department, established itself firmly as a popular newspaper, and accomplished in a few years what it had taken decades for others to attain.

About this time, Fred E. Russell, business manager, decided to sell his interest in order to assist and succeed his father in the manufacturing business. William C. Deming, Zell P. Hart, Thomas H. Deming, George Braden, and Coleman B. Rigg bought Russell's stock in the Tribune company. Mr. Braden had been a worthy member of the news staff for a long time and later became prominent in county and state politics.

With the retirement of Fred E. Russell as business manager, William Deming's duties were considerably enlarged, as he was not only editor and manager, but supplemented the advertising staff in soliciting space and also took a hand in collecting some of the bad accounts.

If the old organization was enthusiastic, then there is no word to describe the vim with which the new members entered into their work and their greater opportunity. Mrs. Hart demonstrated not only much literary ability but also keen business judgment, a rather rare combination. She even kept the books for a while. Her responsibilities were enlarged as time went on. Tom Deming, reporter, was a good mixer and made many friends with all classes. Young Rigg, the cousin, did likewise.

Correspondents were obtained in all the townships and the name of nearly everyone got into the *Tribune* sooner or later. If they were not subscribers, the newspaper sent marked copies to them with the result that the subscriptions grew like the proverbial green bay tree.

If county subscribers could not pay cash, the *Tribune* sometimes took maple syrup. If the office became over-stocked with cans of syrup, the extras were used as door-stops until a member of the firm needed another supply.

As the business grew, more floor space was needed, but the company did not wish to move from the Opera house block. It was directly across the street from the public park and Court house and in the same block on the east with the county jail. The fire department, in the City hall, was less than two blocks west on the banks of the Mahoning river and in the same building were all the municipal offices. Thus, it did not require much leg work to obtain official news promptly.

Fortunately, the Opera House company owned a vacant strip of land adjoining the Opera block on the east. Mr. Deming induced the company to erect a one-story addition to the imposing three-story Opera house building, much to the surprise of some of the old timers. They were not slow in declaring it looked like an ex-crescence and spoiled the symmetry of Warren's hand-some theatre which, from time to time, was visited by the leading opera companies, Shakespearean actors, and star comedians of the day, despite the fact that the city had less than ten thousand people. Deming found he could "sit in" with business men and get results.

The *Warren Tribune* was among the first newspapers in Ohio to nail Governor William McKinley's name to the masthead as a deserving candidate for president of the United States. William C. Deming took much interest in the McKinley campaign, traveling in north-eastern Ohio with James R. Garfield, son of President James A. Garfield. Both spoke against free silver and for sound money, and the return to a protective tariff through the election of McKinley. Years afterward

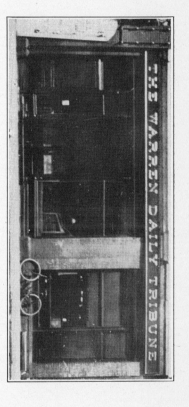

TRIBUNE OFFICE, WARREN, OHIO

Above – In Opera House about 1900; below – Present building

they were to meet again, both in the West and in Washington. James Garfield became Secretary of the Interior, and William C. Deming, Receiver of Public Moneys in the United States land office at Cheyenne under President Theodore Roosevelt.

Deming's work in the McKinley campaign was not confined to Ohio, but was carried also into Kentucky. Upon a visit to Mt. Olivet, he wrote, "I came down to this state of blue grass and horses of every color to visit and to rest, but I find that the Chicago platform has preceded me and there is no rest." His father in the 1896 campaign was a McKinley elector and presided over the Electoral College when the vote was cast.

Speaking of Kentucky – when one of the rival Ohio newspapermen referred to William C. Deming as "Colonel," he disclaimed the honor, saying that there were only four ways of obtaining the title of colonel in Kentucky, and that he could claim none of them: fight a duel, owning race horses, running for office, or making a fortune. In his youth he owned saddle horses and rode well, but recalls going to sleep one night when returning late from a party in the country and falling off, doing some slight damage to his anatomy.

While living in Warren, Ohio, William Deming was elected president of the Warren Y.M.C.A. He was a member of Old Erie lodge, no. 3, F. AND A.M., and the Knights of Pythias. In his third year of residence in Warren, he was made president of the Joshua R. Giddings club, the leading republican organization of the district, and acted as toastmaster at the annual banquet.

Throughout his career, Deming made it a point to get acquainted with prominent public men. In 1897 he interviewed James R. Greene, of Ellsworth, Ohio, then ninety-nine years old. Greene as a boy had witnessed the Battle of Waterloo and had seen Napoleon. Years later, Mr. Deming put the interview into printed form in order to preserve it for his friends and for others interested in historical data. Young Greene's brother was in the British army under Wellington, and Jim had followed the troops to Belgium in some capacity.

Data for another extremely interesting historical document was obtained during the Ohio residence. "How a Letter of a Country Lawyer became International Law," is the title of a manuscript which Mr. Deming wrote regarding the war against Spain in 1898. He knew intimately the men concerned and says:

William McKinley was born at Niles, Ohio, only five miles from the county seat town of Warren, Trumbull county. When he was ready to be admitted to the bar, Frank E. Hutchins, a contemporary of James A. Garfield, later president, and of General J. D. Cox, later governor, was upon the committee which examined William McKinley. Among McKinley's neighbors was Judge William R. Day, an able lawyer, whom McKinley subsequently made assistant secretary of state. Judge Day was elevated to the supreme court bench. It was my good fortune to have known these men. I knew one of them, Mr. Hutchins, intimately. In the fall and winter of 1897-98, the entire country was wrought up over the revolution in Cuba and the brutal methods pursued by Spain to perpetuate her power in the western hemisphere. There was a growing and a very insistent demand and public sentiment for action on the part of the United States.

. . . In February 1898, Frank E. Hutchins, a lawyer of Warren, Ohio, who had reached the age of three score and ten, was in Washington visiting his daughter. He made a personal call upon his friend the President and, incidentally, discussed the Cuban situation and the destruction of the United States battleship 'Maine' in the Havana harbor. President McKinley referred him to Secretary of State Day, who requested Judge Hutchins to put his views in writing.

The letter prepared by Mr. Hutchins was so pointed that Mr. Day referred it to President McKinley who used most of it as the basis for his message to congress. In fact, there was little or no change in thought or diction.

JUDGE OSMER SAGE DEMING OF KENTUCKY
father of William C., David S., and Thomas H. Deming, and Adah D. Morrison

Thereafter, upon the grounds prepared by Frank E. Hutchins, a plain country lawyer, and adopted by President McKinley, congress immediately declared war against Spain with all the momentous results not even yet foreseen.

The position of congress in that crisis has never been questioned in this country or abroad. William R. Day, now Justice of the supreme court of the United States, has since done Mr. Hutchins the honor to say that this letter contained the clearest and best statement he had ever seen of the sufficient reason for American intervention in Cuban affairs. It was to the credit of President McKinley that he had the good judgment and quick grasp of legal principles and wise discretion to incorporate Mr. Hutchins' argument as the vital portion of his message.

Mr. Hutchins always insisted that his part of this chapter of the Spanish-American War should not be magnified beyond its deserts.

Perhaps Mr. Deming's best human interest story was based upon the strange disappearance of William Packard, grandfather of William D. and James W. Packard, inventors of the Packard incandescent lamps, transformers, and the Packard automobile. He had been harassed by Indians while en route to California during the gold rush in 1849, and given up as lost by his family. Likewise his letters home never got through. It was not until the four sons were grown that, through a chain of circumstances, in 1874 they located their father in California living alone at the foot of the Greenhorn mountains. He did not recognize any of them for some time and then only the youngest son, Warren, who was to become a rich lumber merchant in Warren, Ohio, and father of the Packards of automobile fame. The old gentleman had become prosperous in California and was a local judge, but did not live to return to Ohio and join his family. W. C. Deming's first automobile ride was with James W. Packard in his earliest successful horseless carriage, manufactured in Warren before the plant was moved to Detroit.

"I have known only one man who talked less than Calvin Coolidge and that was James W. Packard, inventor of the Packard automobile," says Mr. Deming. "Upon one occasion when visiting in Warren, Ohio, I remarked to him, 'A favorite horseless carriage in Cheyenne is the Great Smith.' He replied, 'What is great about it?' I said, 'Not being an expert, I don't know unless it is the red paint.' 'Great Smith,' a somewhat unusual name, had been adopted; the prevailing color was bright red."

William C. Deming's interest in political matters continued and in 1898 he received a letter of commendation from the republican national committee for his excellent work in the Hanna senatorial contest. The letter was signed by O. P. Austin and said in part: "No factor of that memorable struggle was so potent as the work of faithful editors and newspapers who pictured the intense public sentiment throughout Ohio in favor of the recognition of party pledges and integrity, and nobody appreciates this work more highly than do Senator Mark Hanna, Major Charles Dick, and others familiar with the facts. . ."

From his editorial days, Mr. Deming believed in equal rights for all law-abiding citizens. When the Ohio senate passed the bill giving women the right to vote at school elections and to hold school offices, Mr. Deming wrote: "The passage . . of the bill . . marks a distinct advance for the Buckeye state and is in line of universal progress. . . If there is no constitutional bar to the granting of school suffrage to women, what reason can there be for refusing to grant it?"

Very early did his fair-mindedness become apparent in his editorial columns. For example: "The *Tribune* has the warmest and deepest sympathy and fellow-feeling for every honorable, hard-working, and law-abiding man, but it has no sympathy for any man, be he prince or pauper, who wantonly and willfully disregards law and order. The capitalist has rights that the laborer, for his own self-preservation, must respect; the laborer has rights, which for his own happiness and prosperity the capitalist must respect. Without ready and available wealth there would be very few railroads, iron mills, woolen factories, colleges, and hospitals built. Capital and labor are interdependent."

From the beginning of his newspaper days, he favored expressions of opinions from the readers of his publication and offered to give space to articles on controversial subjects.

After seven years in Ohio, William C. Deming found that the damp, heavy, foggy climate of the Lake Erie district in winter, with the rainy seasons and smoke from the steel mills in the Mahoning valley, did not agree with him. He experienced some nose and throat trouble.

An opportunity came to him – almost as suddenly as the one in Warren – to reside in a dry climate and to take charge of the *Wyoming Tribune* in Cheyenne, Wyoming. By coincidence it was in march, also, when he made his first visit of investigation. He never had been west of Chicago, which he first visited during the Columbian Exposition in 1893 and later when he went to Chicago to buy some modern equipment for the *Warren (Ohio) Tribune*.

The Move to the West

Among the old-time families in Warren, Ohio, was the Fuller family. One daughter, Harriet, had married Charles W. Burdick, a young lawyer of Toledo, who early in territorial days came to Wyoming. Later, Mrs. Burdick's brother, Robert P. Fuller, came west and settled in Cheyenne, where he became deputy secretary of state under Mr. Burdick who had been elected secretary of state.

Upon a visit to the home-folks in Ohio, Mr. Fuller told William C. Deming that the Cheyenne *Tribune,* then owned by ex-Senator Joseph M. Carey, a cattle-grower of Wyoming, was without a manager and possibly could be purchased at a reasonable price. He said there was need for an up-to-date paper in Cheyenne.

An inquiry to Judge Carey brought the following letter:

Cheyenne, Wyoming, March 8, 1901

WM. C. DEMING, ESQ., Warren, Ohio.

DEAR SIR: I have your letter of march 5th. The morning *Tribune* of this city is virtually without an editor.

A number of persons have applied for the management of the paper but none of them have been just the man that we want. We will sell the entire plant but we prefer to retain an interest in it. It is worth about $12,000.00, has two linotype machines (as good as new), a Campbell power press, a gas engine and the other paraphernalia that goes with a newspaper office.

The paper has never been pushed very much. It has a circulation of about 1,200. I think it would now be easy to run the circulation in this State up to 3,000 but I confess that I am not as well acquainted with this matter as I should be. There is a place in this State for one

good daily paper. It should be a strictly Republican paper, with
sufficient independence to criticize that which is wrong in its own
party.

Assuming that you are the right kind of man, I would be glad to
make an arrangement with you either for whole or part of the paper,
provided that you wish to go into it to make it a success. Very truly
yours,

JOSEPH M. CAREY

Desiring to take a vacation, William Deming decided
upon the trip west.

His introduction to the "wide open spaces" was enlivened by a raging blizzard en route, which held the
train forty-eight hours at Ogallala, Nebraska. In writing to Ohio about the storm, he said: "Hardy trainmen
fought their way three miles back to Ogallala, where
in time an engine was secured, which in addition to our
own took us back to this melodious town – once the
end of the Texas cattle trail. In an hour a big train
from Omaha caught up with us and a grand rush was
made for its dining car. . . As the trains from the east
arrive here today, the engines are detached and sent
ahead to help shove the big Union Pacific snowplow
that is endeavoring, while I am writing, to clear the
way for us. But I am enjoying it. We are comfortable
within, while the 'Northwester' sighs and moans and
piles up the snow around us. The passengers are all
good natured and if we are not delayed too long, I shall
not regret the experience. Our dining car had been
detached during the night."

When he arrived in Cheyenne, he found the city
digging itself out of the snow. To his surprise, in a few
days, all was clear and the snow had vanished.

The description of this first trip to Cheyenne, which
he wrote for the *Warren Tribune,* was a forerunner
of the series of travelogues which he maintained for

his papers as long as he was actively engaged in the publishing business.

Arriving in Cheyenne, he opened negotiations with Judge Carey. He was immediately impressed by the number of interesting people in Cheyenne, many of whom had come from the East or South and some from European countries. The citizenship was highly cosmopolitan.

Although he encountered some heavy spring snows, he liked the climate – the dry, invigorating air, the blue skies, and the warm sunshine, even at that very early season.

He was surprised to find that no paper published in Wyoming had anything more than a local circulation. He saw at once the opportunity for a paper of state-wide influence.

Too, there were phases of the republican political situation in Wyoming which interested him deeply. First, he learned there was a rather bitter feud between the friends of former Senator Joseph M. Carey and the senior United States senator, Francis E. Warren, both men of outstanding ability and success in the new state of Wyoming. Mr. Deming thought it possible eventually to bring these factions together.

Not wishing to commit himself too definitely to a prolonged stay in the West, he entered into a temporary arrangement as editor and manager, with an option to buy the paper, if mutually satisfactory.

Returning to Warren, Ohio, after having made a decision as promptly as when he left Mt. Olivet, Kentucky, seven years before, he closed his personal affairs there. He did, however, retain his large interest in the *Warren Tribune,* leaving the paper in the hands of his associates.

By agreement, he continued as long-range editor and manager of the *Warren, Ohio, Tribune* for the time being and contributed a letter on general topics at regular intervals. In fact, he may have felt, and his Ohio associates possibly believed, he would return to Warren in a year or two.

In time, his growing duties in Wyoming as a publisher made it advisable for him to retire from active work on the *Warren Tribune,* although he did not relinquish his position as president until later. He was succeeded as editor by his brother, Thomas H. Deming, whose experience and ability as a writer and his personal popularity fitted him for the larger responsibilities. Zell P. Hart became business manager, a position for which she had become fully equipped.

New factories came to Warren, old ones were enlarged, steel mills pushed up the river from Youngstown and the city grew substantially. During the World War and with the establishment of the large Republic steel plant, Warren experienced a boom and the population of the city in time exceeded forty thousand people. The World War II has greatly increased these figures.

William Deming had continued his semi-annual visits to Warren and was quick to see the opportunity and future offered by well located real estate. Upon his recommendation, his associates joined him in the purchase of business property which became very valuable.

With the increased business, a practical circulation man was required and C. E. Gilliam came to the *Tribune* from the Scripps-Howard league. His excellent work brought him rapid promotion and he became business manager and a stockholder in the company.

THOMAS H. DEMING
Editor, Tribune Chronicle, Warren, Ohio

KATHERINE EVANS ROSS
reared by her uncle and aunt, Judge and
Mrs. O. S. Deming

Frank Ritezell, editor, son of the pioneer, the Honorable William A. Ritezell, being in poor health, in 1925 offered the Tribune company the opportunity to purchase the *Chronicle,* said to be the first newspaper published in what is known as the Western Reserve of Connecticut, now northern Ohio. It had been in the Ritezell family since the Civil War. When the *Warren Tribune* was purchased in 1894, the *Chronicle* was the home paper of the city and county. Many of the old-timers thought the new *Tribune* organization would go the way of its predecessors – down the road to failure. But the young, like fools, sometimes rush in where angels fear to tread. The *Tribune* had succeeded beyond all expectations.

W. C. Deming was called to Warren to assist in the negotiations and was instrumental in reducing the price the Ritezells had asked.

It was a proud day for the *Tribune* owners when they took over the name and franchises of the *Chronicle,* long since distanced in circulation and advertising by its younger rival.

In the meantime, the Tribune company had erected a modern building on Franklin street, planned largely by the manager, and the plant and office are said to be the most complete of any in the same class in the entire country.

A telegram on july 21, 1921, from the president and manager of the *Tribune,* stated that she was printing the first copy of the *Warren (Ohio) Daily Tribune* in the new model building and plant just completed and asked when Mr. Deming would honor her with a call. (The daily circulation (1943) is more than twenty-five thousand copies.)

Having retained an interest in the *Tribune Chronicle*

through the years, William C. Deming took as much satisfaction in its growth and prosperity as if he himself had been in command throughout its history. He is now vice-president of the company and keeps in touch with the present management.

There was no magic about the growth and development of the *Warren Tribune-Chronicle*. Its success resulted from the industry, faith, and loyalty of its owners and employees. It is the popular paper in Trumbull county. The county is twenty-five miles square and fast auto trucks deliver the evening *Tribune* to carriers in the remotest districts within forty minutes from the time the paper rolls from the press. The daily output is nearing thirty thousand copies, with from twenty-four to thirty-six pages each.

The *Cheyenne Tribune,* established in 1884, had had a checkered career and many ownerships. William C. Deming brought a new, active, intelligent, and aggressive force into the newspaper and business life of Wyoming. His type of journalism enabled the *Tribune* to become the state's largest and best newspaper.

From the beginning of his editorship, he was an earnest advocate of those things most important to the state of Wyoming. He did not seek controversy, yet did not evade any issue squarely presented by a contemporary.

The *Tribune* was then a morning newspaper, but the new editor thought the evening field was the better one and that in the small cities the morning papers were destined to decrease in numbers and influence. He realized that the evening paper reaches the homes of the people at a time when the working man and the business man have the most leisure in which to read and digest the day's happenings. After careful consideration, mature preparation, and well-ordered anticipation of obstacles to be overcome, without notice to anyone, he changed the *Wyoming Tribune* from a morning to an evening paper.

The fact that his competitor, the *Leader,* was already in that field was not taken into consideration except in contemplating how and under what circumstances the evening newspaper would yield to the new intruder. He estimated that the *Leader* would give up the fight and take the morning field within six months.

As a matter of fact, Colonel E. A. Slack, an able and impulsive man, did not wait one month to withdraw from the evening field and made the mistake of increasing the price of his paper.

The two papers were circulated at that time for fifty cents a month each. Mr. Deming said that he expected to lose a few hundred subscribers temporarily by reason of the shift, but in time would get most of them back.

Colonel Slack, in entering the morning field, put on the full Associated Press service and used that as a reason for raising the monthly price to seventy-five cents. The result was that the people would not pay the increased price, even for increased service, and the *Tribune,* instead of losing subscribers, showed a net gain within the first month after the change in publication was made.

Says Mr. Deming: "When I arrived in Wyoming in 1901, there were a number of veteran editors, notably E. A. Slack of the *Cheyenne Leader,* A. J. Mokler of the *Casper Tribune,* William E. Chaplin of the *Laramie Republican,* Will Reid of the *Rawlins Journal,* A. H. Duhig of Thermopolis, George W. Perry of Rawlins, Colonel Peake of Cody, Joe Magill of Basin, J. K. Calkins of Lusk, John W. Cook of Lander, Frank

Crumley of Rock Springs, H. J. Wendt of Green River, George Ewer of Evanston, Hayden M. White of Buffalo, M. C. Barrow of the *Douglas Budget,* and J. T. Booth of Evanston.

"Tragedy overtook one well known Wyoming newspaper man but not while he was a publisher.

"Ira O. Middaugh settled in Wheatland about 1890 and became publisher of the *World,* a weekly newspaper, which he edited very ably for fourteen years.

"In 1904 he sold the World and with his interesting family moved to Cody, Wyoming and started a bank. After about four months Cody was visited by bandits who shot and killed Mr. Middaugh.

"Mrs. Middaugh is now Mrs. J. V. Parker of Ontario, Calif., and the three lovely daughters of Ira Middaugh are still living.

"Colonel Slack, as he was called, was a strong character in many ways. He had served with distinction in the 19th Illinois Infantry from may 1, 1861, until june 1864. He then entered Chicago university. During the time he was in school, there was fear of an uprising among the many confederate prisoners of war at Camp Douglas. Young Slack received orders from the general in command to organize a company of cadets for the purpose of police patrol.

"In '68 Slack located at South Pass, Wyoming, a center of gold excitement, and established a newspaper there. In '71 he married Sarah F. Neeley, a sister of Mrs. John M. Palmer, wife of the Governor of Illinois. His mother, Esther Slack Morris, was the first woman actively to champion woman's suffrage in the new territory.

"In due time, Slack established the *Laramie Independent* in partnership with Thomas J. Webster. Some time in 1875, he and his partner, Judge C. W. Bramel, purchased Webster's interest. They changed the name to the *Laramie Daily Sun*.

"Colonel Slack was a powerful man physically, energetic to the nth degree, but with little or no control of his temper. This, together with the fact that he had not only been a crusader but was also quite partisan, resulted in a good many enemies, such as an active newspaper man usually finds camping upon his trail.

"Mr. Slack was appointed Receiver of Public Moneys in the United States Land office in Cheyenne in 1898 and served until 1907 when he was succeeded by me. In the meantime, however, about 1901 or 1902, Governor De Forest Richards had appointed a provisional commission for the Louisiana Purchase Exposition at St. Louis and named his friend, Colonel E. A. Slack, chairman of the board.

"Colonel Slack's eldest daughter, Harriet, an accomplished young woman, was married to Wallace C. Bond, prominent newspaper man and active in republican politics for many years. His second daughter, Dora, a brilliant young woman, was married to William Dubois, whose sons and daughters are well known in Cheyenne. Mrs. Dubois lost her life in an automobile accident in 1938, a tragedy that saddened the community. Mrs. Bond passed away in 1940."

Upon Mr. Deming's arrival in Cheyenne in march 1901, to take up his residence, he found a young high school boy, John Charles Thompson, acting as reporter, telegraph editor, and general utility man on the *Tribune*. The paper was then published in the basement of the old Opera house building on Capitol avenue.

In december 1902, the building burned while Mr. Deming was east on a business trip. While circumstances indicated the fire originated near the stage of the Opera house, the real cause was never established. The message from Judge Carey read: "Fire in Opera house last night destroyed building and *Tribune*. Nothing left but the name." Deming went to Chicago at once and purchased new equipment.

When the fire destroyed the plant, young Thompson was equal to the occasion. Despite the fact that the manager of the *Leader* refused assistance to the *Tribune,* Thompson issued the *Tribune* from the Bristol job printing office and did not miss an issue. A tabloid paper was published until enough new machinery, type and equipment had been assembled to enable the *Tribune* to resume publication from its own plant. Its facilities were enlarged from time to time and the paper came back bigger and stronger than before the fire.

One of Mr. Deming's earliest moves was to promote a canvass of the entire state for subscribers, believing that many of the livestock men, lawyers, doctors, bankers, and business men, generally, would like to have a paper from the capital of the state, if it was a clearing house of Wyoming news. Most certainly, he reasoned, the widely separated office holders and politicians would be interested.

He had known James H. Walton in Warren, Ohio, when Walton was principal of a school. The latter had done some effective circulation work on the *Warren Tribune* during summer vacations. In the strenuous days following the Cheyenne fire, when it was necessary to strengthen all along the line, Mr. Deming sent for Mr. Walton, who came to Wyoming at once and toured the entire state on horseback, by stagecoach, by train, and possibly sometimes on foot.

Mr. Walton made his first trip to Wyoming in the

summer of 1901, and spent about three months soliciting subscribers for the *Tribune* throughout the state.

Together, Deming and Walton organized a new company that in 1904 bought the *Tribune* outright from Senator Carey. Even so, it was still believed by many in both Cheyenne and Warren that Deming would return to Ohio, but fate and destiny held him bound to the West.

When asked if Cheyenne was a bit wild and woolly at the turn of the century, when he arrived in Wyoming, Mr. Deming said: "There were lots of sheep hereabouts, so I guess it was a bit woolly. Senator Francis E. Warren even then had attained the distinction of being the most extensive flockmaster in the Rocky Mountain region. His big shipments of fleeces were something of an event in local circles. Cattlemen all liked Warren for many reasons, including the fact that he was for a high protective tariff, but they did not all like sheep.

"There was some cattle stealing by small settlers, as evidenced by the fact that Tom Horn, a tall Texan, former Pinkerton sleuth, and a professional range detective, was said to be in the employ of the big cattle ranchmen. Horn made the mistake of killing Willie Nickell instead of Willie's father, Kels P. Nickell, who had defied the unwritten law of the district by bringing in sheep. At least, that was the reason Nickell gave for his own unpopularity with his neighbors. The killing occurred july 19, 1901, a rock being placed under the boy's head, an incident or clue that attracted attention at the time. Horn was presumably a cowboy on a ranch in Albany county.

"After a lapse of several months, during which suspicion was directed at Horn, Joe LeFors, a Deputy

United States marshal, on a pretext of obtaining a new position for Horn in Montana, arranged a conference in Cheyenne. Horn, who was then out of work, was drunk when he arrived. Later in the day Horn, assuming he was talking confidentially to a friend, told the entire story of the killing. He said Willie Nickell had recognized him, Horn, and began running home, so he let go with his 'thirty-thirty,' remarking incidentally it was the best shot he ever made and the dirtiest deed he ever did.

"Charles J. Ohnhaus, a court stenographer, who was concealed, but within easy hearing, took down the entire conversation including Horn's explanation of the stone under the boy's head, which Horn said was his mark for the benefit of his employers.

"Horn was arrested in february 1902 and was tried the following october. Despite alleged influence in his behalf and brilliant attorneys for the defense, he was convicted and hanged in the old Laramie county jail. W. R. Stoll was prosecuting attorney.

"I recall seeing him celebrating at Thanksgiving time 1901 in Cheyenne. He was pretty well loaded with liquor and amused himself by roping bell boys and guests in the old Inter-ocean hotel lobby where I was taking my meals at that time.

"About two years later, on november 20, 1903, the last rope with which Horn came in contact was placed around his neck by under-sheriff Dick Proctor. Sheriff Ed J. Smalley was in general charge of the proceedings. Horn, a six-footer, was impressive in appearance and strode forward to the gallows calmly. While he was being supported on the trap by T. Joe Cahill and the sheriff, Horn remarked, 'Joe, I hear you have a new baby at home. Congratulations.' Horn had known

Cahill for a long time, and Joe was present largely because he was county clerk and called in to assist in the final preparations. There was a rather weird and somewhat mournful song by Charlie Irwin and Frank Irwin, friends of Horn. When asked what he preferred Horn replied, 'Make it the old railroader's song, 'Keep your hand upon the throttle and your eye upon the rail.' The Reverend George W. Rafter attended Horn in the closing hours of his life. The trap was sprung and in a few seconds Tom Horn had passed over the range.

"A chapter in Gene Fowler's *Timberline* contains an extended and intimate history of Horn's life and a full report of the entire case.

"The *Wyoming Tribune* had made all preparations for an extra edition and awaited only a word from the death chamber. Griffin Cochran, a young reporter on the staff, immediately after the drop fell, telephoned me at the *Tribune* office and the edition was upon the street in a very few minutes. There were other prominent witnesses to the execution.

"Yet despite that fact, occasionally one hears the statement that Tom Horn was never hanged.

"William F. Cody, popularly known as Buffalo Bill, had established a residence in Wyoming. He still owned a valuable ranch home at North Platte, Nebraska, where Mrs. Cody spent most of her time, I recall. Cody had not only become interested in the budding new municipality in the Big Horn country which had been named for him, but was promoting an irrigation enterprise and, according to rumor, also had become an admirer of an attractive young actress. He frequently stopped over in Cheyenne to exchange news and views with his old friends, R. S. Van Tassell, Harry P. Hynds and John H. Fullerton of the Inter-ocean hotel. I have seen him leaning on the bar, but never saw him intoxicated. As a boy, I had attended his wild west show and had been thrilled when he dashed around the arena shooting glass balls as they were tossed into the air.

"Cody, like most men of his type, was inclined to exaggeration, particularly as to the number of buffalo he had slain and Indian scalps he had taken. Likewise, he had some sense of humor. I recall one occasion in Cheyenne, when he was feeling in good spirits, hearing him compare himself to Barnum.

"Buffalo Bill said: 'As a matter of fact, I am a better showman than Barnum. Since he became rich and attained more or less world prominence, especially after he met Queen Victoria, Barnum has been too seclusive. He depends upon Jumbo, his big elephant, and the Siamese twins to draw crowds. I give 'em plenty of noise and action, hordes of Indians, stage holdups and train robberies. I always lead the parade and find that it pays.'

"Cody lost much of his popularity in Wyoming when he sued his splendid wife for divorce. I do not recall the grounds for the action, but the public did not consider them serious and sentiment was against Buffalo Bill. While the *Tribune* did not risk contempt of court by taking sides, we gave Mrs. Cody's defense liberal space. The case was shifted about from one Wyoming county seat to another and the divorce was finally denied by the district court.

"Mr. and Mrs. Cody were the parents of fine, attractive daughters who married well.

"In those days, Cheyenne was a bit primitive so far as modern improvements are concerned. From the standpoint of law and order, there never was a time

The Old Cheyenne Club House (1884)
later Chamber of Commerce

when I did not feel perfectly safe, notwithstanding the fact the *Tribune* was doing quite a good deal of crusading that was not popular with all classes. One's opponents were usually good sports and played the game above board.

"The streets of Cheyenne were of the native soil and had not yet been systematically surfaced with gravel, which preceded the later stage of oil and concrete. It will be understood that there was plenty of dust in the winter and spring when the wind blew.

"Socially, I think there was even more formality than today. That is probably true throughout the country. I refer especially to dinners and dances at the old Cheyenne club, Keefe hall, and the Post hall at Fort Warren.

"Life as a whole, however, was free and easy. There were many saloons and open gambling, because gambling was licensed as well as liquor selling. On the whole, I doubt whether there were any more infractions of the law relatively than there are today, because many so-called recreations now were not acceptable in good society, at least, at that time.

"Cheyenne's churches were reasonably well supported and the ministers, while mostly young were men of ability. The exception in matter of age was the Reverend George W. Rafter, D.D., then the active minister of St. Mark's Episcopal church, and, years later, rector emeritus. Doctor Rafter was a man more than six feet tall, wore a gray beard, well-trimmed, which not only added to his dignity but gave him some resemblance to an apostle. Dr. Rafter was probably the most popular and lovable character in Cheyenne. He lived for years at the Cheyenne club and his presence there never interfered with the festivities. I recall an interesting period when about a dozen unattached men had a table at the Inter-ocean dining room, over which Dr. Rafter presided, being himself a life-long bachelor.

"Dr. Rafter could not be with us always, but Divine Providence has a way of compensating for deep sorrows and great losses. Otherwise, in time the world would become an aching void. About 1912, Bishop Patrick A. McGovern, of Omaha, arrived in Cheyenne to become the Catholic Bishop. Likeable and loveable, popular with catholic and protestant, for a generation Bishop McGovern's gentle personality and abounding kindness have brought good cheer to multitudes. He has well earned his high place in this community and the beautiful home erected for him by the church, at the intersection of Carey avenue and Pershing boulevard.

"Speaking of the old Cheyenne club, then located on the present site of the Chamber of Commerce and the Harris Furniture company's store, the dining room was most attractive. It was finished with hardwood paneling, at least five or six feet high, while the fireplace and mantel were both attractive and unique.

"There were private dining rooms, and, before state-wide prohibition all necessary bar and sideboard facilities. On the wall of the lounge hung a large replica of Paul Potter's bull, done in oil and quite impressive. It contained two or three distinct bullet holes, and thereby hangs a tale, told and retold probably thousands of times.

"Among the young and strenuous ranchmen of the early days was John Coble, who, upon one occasion, desiring to try his six-shooter, used a number of discharges upon the historic picture. Coble later married a most estimable young woman and settled down upon his holdings in Albany county.

"Percy Hoyt, a member of an old and distinguished and prosperous family in New York, for some reason or other settled in Cheyenne. He never had or needed, so far as I know, any active business or visible means of support. The rumor was that he had difficulty in spending his income. During the time covered by my recollections, he lived in his one-story home on east Eighteenth street, which could be identified by the two porcelain dogs standing in front of the house. He donated the home to his yard man, Charley Anderson. Hoyt kept a number of fine saddle horses, but mostly rode a beautiful dappled gray animal. An elaborate stable was connected with the house.

"While it is still popular in the East to speak of Cheyenne as being out in the wide open spaces, with all that that implies, and special emphasis upon the wild and woolly, forty years ago there were a surprisingly large number of highly educated and aristocratic men and women in Cheyenne.

"A young lawyer, Willis Van Devanter, associated with his brother-in-law, Judge John W. Lacey, was coming into national prominence and had been appointed assistant attorney-general of the United States. He later became judge of the United States circuit court and an associate justice of the United States supreme court. Justice Van Devanter and Mrs. Van Devanter were a remarkably charming couple. Mrs. Van Devanter died a few years ago and Justice Van Devanter in february 1941 in his eighty-first year.

"On east Seventeenth street was a number of fine homes, mostly planned by the architect George D. Rainsford, who came out from New York, and subsequently engaged actively in the horse breeding business in Wyoming. Elsewhere in this book mention is made of Rainsford's profanity, in which he indulged upon the slightest provocation.

"I spent a good many pleasant hours at the home of Mr. and Mrs. William Sturgis, later known as the Charles Carey house, which was sold to Walter Flora.

"East of the Sturgis home was the commodious place of R. S. Van Tassell and across the street on the north, the Lane house, then owned by the Union Pacific and occupied by its local ranking official. I little dreamed in 1901 when I occupied a room in the home of Mr. and Mrs. Valentine Baker on Seventeenth street, that I would now own and occupy the historic Lane house, sometimes called the Peters home, with its comfortable rooms and beautiful grounds.

"The Tom Sturgis home, northwest corner of Seventeenth and Pebrican avenue, an immense brick structure with stables, is in the same neighborhood and is now an apartment house owned by the Warren Mercantile company.

"The most popular bars and gambling places operated under the law at that time were owned by Harry P. Hynds and Thomas A. Heaney. Both were remarkable characters. I recall the lay-out of the Hynds Capitol saloon, because those were the days of free lunches. I never could quite understand how any business could afford to give a customer access to the most delicious ham, roast beef or cheese sandwiches, with white or rye bread, pickles, olives, and all the fixings, even if he bought only one five cent glass of beer, but that was the custom and it lasted for years.

"Harry Hynds was very public spirited and the same may be said of Tom Heaney. Both were willing to donate at any time for a worthy public purpose, as I well recall, having served upon numerous committees for soliciting funds. Hynds always dressed well and paid more attention to the sartorial side of his make-up than Heaney did. Mr. Heaney's diversion, outside of his business, was literature and particularly poetry. Being an Irishman, he was especially partial to Tom Moore. One of his favorite quotations was:

> 'The harp that once through Tara's halls
>   The soul of music shed,
> Now hangs as mute on Tara's walls
>   As if that soul were fled.
> So sleeps the pride of former days,
>   So glory's thrill is o'er;
> And hearts that once beat high for praise
>   Now feel that pulse no more.'

"He was also fond of Robert Burns, Scotch poet.

"Watching the sweep of the dry movement from Kansas westward, both Hynds and Heaney realized that Wyoming, sooner or later, would adopt state-wide prohibition. I don't think either felt badly about it, and each was looking toward anchoring himself in another line.

"When Senator Warren and associates built the Plains hotel about 1910, Harry Hynds secured a long-time lease, furnished the building in a most attractive and modern style, and conducted a hotel and dining room which attracted attention from coast to coast. There were few better known hotel men of that period and certainly none abler from the standpoint of giving his guests value received. Having no false pride, Mr. Hynds placed in the lobby a photograph, made early in his life, showing himself wearing a leather apron and shoeing a horse. At the time of my arrival in Cheyenne, he both rode and drove good horses. On the side, Harry Hynds took advantage of the oil and gas boom in Wyoming, and left a fortune to his widow, Mrs. Nellie Hynds, who still resides in the beautiful home on Eighteenth street where she entertains her many friends.

"While living, Mr. Hynds built a handsome twenty-five thousand dollar stone lodge in the Pole mountain region for the Boy Scouts of Cheyenne. It is also used for general recreation purposes.

"Mr. Heaney, sensing the development of the moving picture business, became the owner and proprietor of the Atlas theatre on Sixteenth street, and built a commodious stucco home which was called Heaney Castle on east nineteenth street, overlooking Lake Minnehaha.

"When he was not busy at his theater he was devoting a good deal of time to city improvements and talking books and quoting poetry with congenial friends. He was among the first promoters of the Alta Vista addition, now a popular residential district, in East Cheyenne."

Mr. Deming's friends were by no means confined to republicans. Among the democratic citizens were Mr. and Mrs. John Charles Thompson, who had come to Wyoming in the 1880's and were rearing a most interesting family of boys and girls. General Thompson, as he was known, having been surveyor-general of Wyoming, was a brilliant orator and Mrs. Thompson a most delightful, cultivated woman. She was the daughter of the Civil war governor of Kentucky, the Honorable Beriah Magoffin, and a great granddaughter of Isaac Shelby, the first governor of Kentucky — certainly a lineage of which anyone might be proud.

Mr. and Mrs. Gibson Clark presided over a household of boys. The Clarks were leaders socially and politically. Gibson Clark was a confederate war veteran and arrived in Wyoming as early as 1866, according to records. He became an able lawyer, a justice of the supreme court and influential citizen. One son, John D. Clark, is an outstanding Wyoming attorney and economist; another, Frank, is collector of internal revenue for Wyoming.

Other democratic families who were equally prominent and public-spirited were Mr. and Mrs. John L. Murray and Mr. and Mrs. E. S. Johnston, whose hospitable homes were always the center of activity. Doctor and Mrs. J. H. Conway were among the younger social set, the doctor, then having an office in the old Opera House building, was a frequent caller at the *Tribune* office. Mr. and Mrs. L. H. Bresnahen and family resided at the corner of Warren and Seventeenth streets and that spacious home is still occupied by the Misses Bresnahen.

In making his decision to come to Wyoming as editor and manager of the *Wyoming Tribune,* William C. Deming had seen unlimited possibilities for the industrial and commercial development of the state because of its vast undeveloped resources.

From the beginning of his residence in the West, he displayed loyal devotion to public interests. To quote one of his early editorials: "Wyoming needs working mines, flowing oil wells and new railroads a thousand times more than it needs any one man for governor or the perpetuation of any one political organization." It was such bold statements as this that challenged attention and established the *Tribune* as a popular paper with the masses.

Deming arrived in Wyoming at a most opportune time. In the preceding decade, the state's population had increased almost forty-eight per cent, but even then with its 92,531 people, it had plenty of elbow-room – less than one person to the square mile. Approximately half of the total population was in the southeastern quarter of the state.

Wyoming had just refused to endorse free silver and had cast its electoral vote for McKinley and Roosevelt. Prosperity was returning to the United States after the serious depression of the 1890's. There was an unprecedented expansion of governmental activity which materially affected Wyoming, including the conservation of natural resources, especially the setting aside of forest areas and the development of great reclamation projects.

Irrigation canals were being constructed under the reclamation act; the Grand Encampment mining district was booming; a merger had been perfected between the Southern Pacific and the Union Pacific lines; surveys for new railways were being run; and agricultural colonization was progressing rapidly.

Wyoming's total valuation of assessed property increased approximately fifty per cent in the years 1898-1904.

Deming frequently visited the Wheatland colony with Judge Joseph M. Carey. This colony had been sponsored by the Wyoming Development company, the oldest irrigation enterprise financed by private capital under the Carey act. Realizing the splendid possibilities of this area, Deming purchased an eighty acre farm which he sold three years later at an excellent profit. Through the years he has retained his interest in that section and today owns valuable business property in Wheatland, which now has 2500 people.

The first important state meeting in Wyoming, in

which Mr. Deming actively participated, was the original Wyoming industrial convention held at Laramie, december 11 and 12, 1901.

It was called to consider Wyoming's various interests, agricultural and industrial, and to find ways and means of extending the same.

The program included the following subjects among others:

Fine Cattle Breeding in Wyoming, by the Honorable B. B. Brooks.

Mineral Resources of the State, by H. C. Beeler, state geologist.

Wheatland System and its Results, by Judge J. M. Carey.

Present Conditions in Wyoming, by Clarence B. Richardson.

Petroleum in Wyoming, by W. C. Knight.

Higher Education in Wyoming, by Elmer E. Smiley, president of the University of Wyoming.

Finances of Wyoming, by Harry B. Henderson, state examiner.

Coal Mines and Mining, by the Honorable P. J. Quealy.

Irrigation and Reservoirs, by Fred Bond, state engineer.

Wyoming Forests, by the Honorable W. H. Holliday.

Sugar Beets in Wyoming, by E. E. Slosson, chemist, Wyoming agricultural experiment station.

Resources of Big Horn county, by Colonel W. F. Cody (Buffalo Bill).

Wyoming – Our Commonwealth, by the Honorable Fenimore Chatterton, secretary of state.

The full proceedings of the convention were assembled and published by the secretary, Colonel C. G. Coutant.

It is worthy of note that the address delivered by the Honorable B. B. Brooks upon cattle breeding was such a fine effort from the standpoint of contents, excellent English and fascinating delivery, that it was common talk he would be the logical successor of Governor DeForest Richards. For many years Mr. Brooks' speech at Laramie was referred to as "the address that made him governor." It was called a classic upon cattle.

The executive committee of the first Wyoming industrial convention consisted of Governor DeForest Richards, chairman; William E. Chaplin, vice-chairman; C. G. Coutant, secretary; William H. Reid; Professor F. H. Roberts, of the University of Wyoming; M. C. Barrow; W. C. Deming; W. H. Holliday; J. L. Baird; and Professor W. C. Knight, state geologist.

Mr. Deming's constructive ability was early recognized in a political way, and he was elected to the Wyoming house of representatives which convened in january 1903, less than two years from the time of his migration westward. Along with the majority in the Laramie county delegation, he voted for the "mine tax" bill, despite much political pressure against the act.

In the first republican convention held after his arrival in Wyoming, he was astonished to find that there was more Cheyenne interest in the nomination of a candidate for state treasurer than there was for a governor. Inquiry brought forth the reason that the treasurer had complete control of the deposits in any bank or banks of all of the state funds, and was not accountable for any interest. In other words, there was no law requiring banks to pay interest upon the state funds. Thus, the selection of a state treasurer was largely a contest between the two leading Cheyenne national banks – The First National and the Stock Growers National. George E. Abbott was the candidate of the former and William R. Schnitger, of the later.

Deming found that at least one state, Wisconsin, had a state depository law. He opened correspondence with Governor Robert M. LaFollette, the father of the present senator. Upon his election to the Wyoming legislature, Deming introduced a bill for a state depository law, which was approved by the house, but was put to sleep in the senate.

The *Tribune* carried the fight over the state deposits to the people of the state generally, and in the republican convention held in 1906, Mr. Deming offered a plank pledging the party to this legislation. The succeeding legislature, largely through the insistent editorials in the *Tribune,* and the good work of Senator Fred Blume of Sheridan, who introduced the bill, passed a depository law, which has saved the tax payers thousands and thousands of dollars. In fact, for years it brought to the state and the several political subdivisions – counties and school districts – enough money to meet the major portion of the salaries of all officers. Present low interest rates have reduced the amount.

Believing that a newspaper should be something more than a mere purveyor of news, or counting house for dividends, the *Wyoming Tribune* was more or less of a crusader. It took the lead as a spokesman of the republican party, in helping place upon the statute books many excellent laws. Among them have been a provision for payments or compensation for injured workmen, an independent state judiciary and a mine tax law affecting products shipped from the state – also the primary election law, for which Deming has received both the credit and the blame. Local and state improvements were given a prominent place.

By act of the seventh legislature of the state of Wyoming in 1903, provision was made for the appointment by the governor of a commission of seven members to secure a collection of the resources and products of Wyoming and to display properly and care for the same at the Louisiana Purchase Exposition at St. Louis in 1904, celebrating the one hundredth anniversary of the acquisition of the Louisiana territory from the government of France. William C. Deming fathered the bill.

Governor De Forest Richards appointed the following commission: president, Robert H. Homer; vice-president, Bryant B. Brooks; secretary, William C. Deming; commissioner-in-chief, Clarence B. Richardson; and Willis George Emerson, George E. Pexton, and Charles A. Badgette. Later, upon the resignation of Mr. Homer, Bryant B. Brooks became president and J. L. Baird was appointed to the commission. W. H. Holliday became a member of the commission upon the death of Mr. Badgette.

The commission offered a list of premiums for a variety of farm products, fruit, wool, minerals, etc., exhibited at the convention of the State Industrial association held in Sheridan in october 1903. The winning exhibits were turned over to the commission. An educational exhibit, a forestry exhibit, and exhibits of minerals, oils and scenic photographs by J. E. Stimson were also assembled.

Although all of the members of the commission gave much time and thought to the exhibit, the bulk of the actual work devolved upon Clarence B. Richardson and William C. Deming. H. E. Crain, of Cheyenne, was made superintendent of exhibits at the Fair. The three spent many months in St. Louis.

Wyoming exhibitors received one hundred twenty-five awards, a larger number than any other state or country received in the two departments of mines and agriculture. The grand prizes awarded Wyoming grown grains were the result of actual tests by weight for the excellent quality and size of the grain. The agricultural display comprised more than one thousand four hundred classified exhibits; there were one hundred fifty-six varieties of minerals – three thousand classified exhibits, a larger number than was shown by any other state. Gold medals were also won by two of the Wyoming wool exhibits and by the forestry products.

The total cost of collecting, caring for and installing the exhibits was about twenty thousand dollars, or five thousand dollars less than the amount appropriated by the state for that purpose.

In obtaining and preparing the exhibits, the commission had in view the idea of making them of a permanent character. After the World's Fair closed, the forestry, onyx and iron products, as well as the oil exhibit, show-cases, cabinets, and pictures valued at three thousand dollars were returned to Wyoming and were used for years as exhibits.

In connection with the work of assembling the minerals and oil exhibits, Mr. Deming became well acquainted with Doctor Wilbur C. Knight, an authority on Wyoming geology, and in later years as president of the board of trustees of the University of Wyoming, he was closely affiliated in a number of ways with his son, Doctor Samuel Howell Knight, who now occupies a position similar to that of his distinguished father as head of the department of geology of the University.

When Mr. Arthur H. Marble, president of the Stock Growers bank of Cheyenne, presented a fossil fish specimen to Mr. Deming, from the Green river formation of southwestern Wyoming, Mr. Deming learned through Doctor S. H. Knight that it was one of the most unusual ones ever found.

Although there is a somewhat general impression that the Wyoming fossil fish resulted from being buried in the lava of erupting volcanoes, this does not hold true relative to those found in the Green river formation.

According to Doctor Knight's "Notes on the Occurrence of Fossil Fish in the Green river formation of Southwestern Wyoming":

The fossil fish occur in shales which were deposited in a large fresh-water lake which existed in southwestern Wyoming during the deposition of the Green river formation.

It is estimated that this lake (called Lake Gosiute by Clarence King in 1878) came into being approximately fifty million years ago (Eocene time) and lasted from five million to eight million years.

The lake during its maximum expansion covered an area of more than ten thousand square miles. Its drainage basin is believed to have reached from the Laramie mountains, Wyoming, to the Wasatch mountains, Utah, and from the Uinta mountains to the Wind river mountains.

The level of the lake is estimated to have been approximately one thousand feet above sea level. Fossil plants preserved in the Green river formation indicate that the climate which prevailed in the lake basin was similar to the present climate of the Gulf coast states.

The enclosing mountains, notably the Wind river, Uinta and Wasatch ranges in all probability stood somewhat higher above the lake level than they now stand above the floor of the Green river basin.

An alluvial floodplain of varying width separated the mountain front from the lake.

Flood from the surrounding mountains carried large amounts of rock debris onto the alluvial floodplains and into the lake.

A possible explanation of the fossil fish occurrence at Fossil, Wyoming, is as follows: During a period of unusually heavy precipitation in the watershed of the lake, flooded rivers discharged an exceptional amount of silt into the lake, which suffocated and rapidly entombed large numbers of fish. The excellent state of preservation of the fish is explained by rapid burial, which prohibited them from being devoured by scavengers.

The interest aroused in the natural resources by the

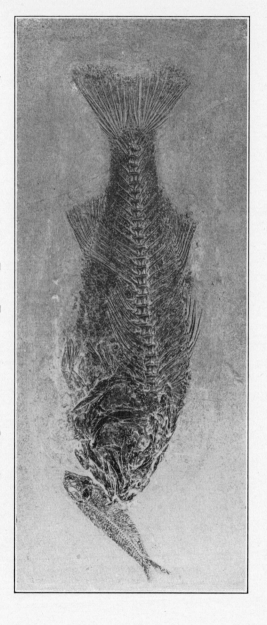

A MOST UNUSUAL SPECIMEN OF FOSSIL FISH FOUND IN THE GREEN RIVER BEDS
It appears that the large fish was in the act of grabbing the small fish when the cataclysm occured. Reduced from about eighteen inches long

work with the World's Fair commission has been continued by Mr. Deming down through the years.

As a result of the excellent work done by the St. Louis World's Fair commission, the publicity given the state and the businesslike manner in which the appropriation was administered, Governor B. B. Brooks appointed Clarence B. Richardson as president of the Wyoming commission at the Portland Exposition in 1905, and William C. Deming, secretary. Their work at Portland was equally efficient, economical, and successful. The friendship begun in 1904 between Mr. Richardson and Mr. Deming was never broken. Deming has often said, "Clarence Richardson is a natural organizer and has a remarkably keen business mind. Mr. Richardson laid great stress upon the bottled samples of oil refined in Doctor Salathe's plant in Casper and said some day the Salt creek field would be developed and that oil would be the state's biggest industry. Dr. Frederick Salathe had come to Wyoming in 1897 as chemist for the Pennsylvania Oil and Gas company to test the Salt creek product. He was associated with C. H. King in constructing the Casper electric light plant.

No other single industry has contributed so much financially and otherwise to the development of Wyoming and the enrichment of its citizens as the oil business.

Without any disparagement of many others who have shown foresight and energy in connection therewith, it is only fair to state that Clarence B. Richardson, of Cheyenne, was proclaiming the extent of Wyoming's underlying wealth in oil and predicting its value and use even before the automobile had supplied a general market.

Mr. Richardson was born in Pittsburgh, Pennsylvania, september 7, 1867, the son of Warren and Mary Anna (Kabis) Richardson, who migrated to Wyoming in territorial days. He was educated in the public schools, and later took special courses, which developed his business instinct. Clarence Richardson learned the printer's trade and became news-editor of the old *Cheyenne Daily Sun* in 1886 and continued in that capacity until 1891, being very closely associated with the editor, Colonel Edward A. Slack, for many years.

Realizing even then the importance of Wyoming as a mining and mineral state, he began the collection of data and general information along many lines, particularly as to the undeveloped oil territory. He went to New York in 1893 and for two years was an active member of the New York Consolidated Stock Exchange. Encouraged by his experience and contacts in the East he proceeded to London in 1895 and, although a very young man at the time, he interested a group of English capitalists in the oil fields of Wyoming.

Enthused by the reports of the gold findings at Klondike, Alaska, Mr. Richardson visited that country in 1898 and gained much valuable experience in mining. Returning to Wyoming he was associated with his brothers, Warren Richardson and Emil Richardson in the management of the Richardson financial interests and maintaining assessment work upon their oil claims in the Salt Creek Wyoming fields.

Meantime, Governor De Forest Richards appointed Mr. Richardson Commissioner-in-Chief of the Louisiana Purchase commission at St. Louis in 1904 and he held the same position at the Lewis and Clark exposition in Portland, Oregon, 1905.

With an eye always for big business Mr. Richardson

CLARENCE B. RICHARDSON
pioneer in development of oil industry in Wyoming

went to Mexico in 1906 where he was manager of the Chihuahua Lumber and Manufacturing company, but this enterprise was more or less nullified by the Pancho Villa revolution.

In 1915 the demand for crude oil products had become so widespread that Mr. Richardson, in association with former Governor B. B. Brooks and others, organized the Consolidated Royalty Oil company which he has managed since 1917. The company erected a modern office building in Casper and has paid much more than a million dollars in dividends.

Mr. Richardson has been identified with a number of other oil companies and is an active member of the Casper Chamber of Commerce. He is a Mason, Elk, Knight of Pythias, and Son of the American Revolution.

Mr. Richardson married Anna May Stanley of Cheyenne, september 26, 1900.

According to an eminent banker of the state: "In every community we find one or a few men to whom the term builders can be properly applied; men who are willing to devote time, resources, and talent to the up-building of their community; men who are always ready and willing to serve on boards and committees for civic improvements. Mr. Deming always has been and still is one of this type, and at the same time has not been a seeker of publicity or public glory."

Realizing that there were in Cheyenne an unusually large number of active and resourceful young men whose combined efforts and opinions could be made a real force, Deming saw the opportunity for a splendid public forum. Others, notably the young attorneys Matson and Kennedy, and also Clyde M. Watts, had been thinking along the same line and concurred heartily.

The idea of such a club was suggested by the organization of similar character which Deming had fostered at Mt. Olivet, Kentucky, just after his graduation from college, and from reading of a Young Men's Lyceum organized by Benjamin Franklin, which became a strong influence in Philadelphia, and helpful to its members.

With R. N. Matson, T. Blake Kennedy, W. E. Chaplin, Paul Bailey, Wm. B. Ross, Clyde M. Watts, J. Q. Mathews, and others, Deming assisted in the organization of the Young Men's Literary club in 1902,* and became its first president. Twenty years later, in 1922, he again served in that capacity. He is still an honorary member.

This organization has meant much to Cheyenne and to Wyoming. One of the secrets of its success has been its limited membership of thirty. The waiting list is always large.

In addressing the club, thirty years after its organization Mr. Deming observed "that in all the essentials which have gone to make the organization a success there have been few changes."

Through the years, tolerance of conflicting opinions and good fellowship always obtained in the club, notwithstanding occasional seemingly bitter debates.

Democrats and republicans, protestants and catholics, capitalists and representatives of labor organizations, and sons or grandsons of union and confederate Civil war veterans, Spanish-american war veterans, World war veterans have gathered weekly to exchange views informally and to listen to a well-prepared paper. Subjects have included current events of worldwide scope and local matters of importance to Cheyenne.

*For current and early membership *see* APPENDIX.

William C. Deming was chairman of the committee that brought the first chautauqua to Cheyenne and likewise chairman of the committee that raised a bonus of nearly ten thousand dollars toward building the new opera house on Capitol avenue.

The Young Men's Literary club fathered the movement for a new theater, urged homesteading and agriculture in Laramie county, and worked for a modern highway across Wyoming, thus serving in the dual capacity of an agency for culture as well as an aid to the Chamber of Commerce in local development.

The Cheyenne *Tribune* of june 24, 1903, reported a large meeting at the Court House of subscribers to the new opera house. A building committee was selected.

The old Carey Opera house on Capitol avenue had burned in the previous december, and there was a growing demand for a new structure. W. C. Deming called the meeting to order and Louis Kirk was made chairman, with Paul Bailey, secretary.

The Young Men's Literary club had appointed the following committee to solicit subscriptions for a bonus; W. C. Deming, Paul Bailey, Louis Kirk, R. N. Matson, C. W. Riner, and C. B. Richardson.

R. N. Matson was the first one to subscribe and in characteristic fashion paid his pledge on the spot in cash. The committee reported pledges to the amount of eight thousand dollars.

The meeting resulted in a building committee as follows: T. A. Cosgriff, R. S. Van Tassell, Joseph M. Carey, Francis E. Warren, Henry Altman, C. W. Riner, R. N. Matson and P. S. Hoyt. Timothy F. Burke was selected as trustee.

The result was that a strong company was incorporated by Senator Warren and others which resulted in building the new opera house called the Capitol Avenue theater, now the Paramount theater.

Coming from a section of the country where trees and flowers thrive and grow with but little encouragement, the new *Tribune* editor was quick to see the opportunities and needs for beautification in Cheyenne, and allied himself actively with J. F. Jenkins, Thomas Heaney, Fred Hofmann, George E. Brimmer and others in behalf of tree planting, improved streets and extension of the city parks and boulevards. "The best work along this line in Cheyenne," he says, "was done by Mayor Cal Holliday, Mayor Archie Allison, and Commissioners Art Trout and Ed Warren, subsequently elected mayor."

It is probably difficult for the present generation to realize that the beautiful and well shaded Randall boulevard is only about thirty-six years old.

During the administrations of President Theodore Roosevelt and President William H. Taft, United States Senator Warren obtained large appropriations for buildings and improvements generally at Fort D. A. Russell. At that time there was no direct road or street from Cheyenne to the gateway of the reservation. It was necessary to go around many blocks and follow numerous right angle turns. Senator Warren promised the War department that Cheyenne and Laramie counties would open a direct highway from the Capitol to Fort D. A. Russell.

For some reason the matter dragged, possibly because of the necessity of condemnation proceedings affecting privately owned real estate. In keeping with his vigilance and alertness in such matters, Senator Warren wrote William C. Deming among others, to see what could be done to expedite the negotiations.

According to Verner H. Franson, county clerk, the records show that on april 1, 1906, a committee composed of the Honorable D. W. Gill, mayor; the Honorable Frank E. Johnston, councilman of the city of Cheyenne, and the Honorable W. C. Deming, representing the Young Men's Literary club, appeared before the Laramie county board of commissioners in the interest of a boulevard from Fort D. A. Russell lane to the Capitol.

Daniel McUlvan was appointed viewer. On june 8, 1906, he reported favorably upon the establishment of said road. Notice was given and a date set for receiving objections. D. W. Gill, A. D. Kelley, and J. W. Griffin were appointed appraisers for property in Hellman's Addition, Holdrege Addition and Kenwood Place. Property owners having been indemnified, on august 9, 1907, the board decided to name the new county road extending from Fort D. A. Russell lane to the head of O'Neil street, Cheyenne, Wyoming, Randall boulevard in honor of Major-general George M. Randall, retired.

The members of the board of commissioners in april 1906 who cooperated were: James B. Boyer, chairman; Samuel Corson and Harry Farthing, commissioners. In may Mr. Boyer resigned and I. W. Gray of Wheatland, then in Laramie county, was appointed to fill the unexpired term. Harry Farthing succeeded to the chairmanship. In january 1907, however, a new board was organized with Samuel Corson, chairman; I. W. Gray and James W. Gilmore, commissioners, and the road was completed.

William Dubois, Wyoming's best known architect, who married Miss Dora Slack and reared a fine family, was among the first to erect a fine residence along Randall boulevard.

The triangular small parks on both sides add much to its beauty.

The new *Tribune* editor in the early 1900's experienced some resentment every time a funeral notice included the following: "The interment will be at the City Cemetery."

It sounded too much like a pauper's field, so he instructed all reporters to drop the name City Cemetery and call it Lakeview Cemetery, because it overlooked Lake Minnehaha – and Lakeview Cemetery it is today.

J. K. Stoddard, city clerk, finds a plat marked "City cemetery, Cheyenne, Wyoming, 1884. W. G. Provines, city engineer."

The next reference is a plat marked "Lakeview Cemetery and Additions, august 25, 1926. Approved and accepted by the City council, october 25, 1926." P. R. Revis was city engineer.

However, the first ordinance recognizing the name Lakeview Cemetery apparently was not adopted until april 4, 1932 when J. F. Weybrecht was mayor. A plat bearing this name was later placed on file.

Hence, it appears that the original official name was "City Cemetery" and that news items in the *Wyoming Tribune* over a long period of years resulted in giving that well-kept cemetery its present name, Lakeview.

Having served on the two Exposition commissions, Mr. Deming and Mr. Richardson became intensely interested in Wyoming's agricultural possibilities. They saw that the trend of farming and settlement in Nebraska indicated that the movement would reach Wyoming. Many ranchmen were accepting the opportunity to dispose of their holdings to large companies from Iowa and other states, who were bringing in settlers.

GRAIN STACKS ON DRY-FARM NEAR CHEYENNE

SIXTEEN-FOOT TROUGH, 7″ DEEP, IN VIRGIN PRAIRIE NEAR CHEYENNE

As early as the 1890's there was a Scandinavian settlement in and around Albin, north of Pine Bluffs, Wyoming, but for one reason or another it was generally assumed that the immediate section which had been settled was the only part of Laramie county suitable for arid agriculture.

Most of the lands to the west and south, as well as north, were occupied by large cattle and sheep ranches. The second and third generations were less interested in ranching and the pioneers, having attained a competency, naturally gravitated to the towns.

The lands on either side of the Union Pacific railroad were in the "checker board system," caused by the land grants by the Federal government to the Union Pacific railroad when it was constructed. Each alternate section for twenty miles north and south was sold or leased cheaply by the railroad to the ranchmen and they were able to use the adjoining public or government lands without charge. In some cases they even fenced them, different areas being divided among different ranchmen.

Under the Cleveland administration and later that of Theodore Roosevelt, the ranchmen were compelled to take down their fences. This presented a real problem, because the cattlemen and sheepmen found difficulty in controlling their herds and they frequently became trespassers upon government land.

A number of stockmen, who merely had followed custom on the range, were hailed into the United States district court. Among them was Addison A. Spaugh. Mr. Deming interviewed him at the old Cheyenne club. When asked where he lived, Spaugh replied, "Manville."

"Where is Manville?"

"On my ranch," Spaugh replied half-humorously. This was almost literally true, as his fences surrounded the town. Uncle Sam fined him fifty dollars and a day in jail, which was likely spent as the house guest of the sheriff.

Spaugh never seemed worried by the experience and probably considered it "just one of those things."

Others who spent twenty-four hours either constructively or otherwise with the sheriff, or were fined, were as follows: George D. Rainsford, who probably did some tall swearing when called upon to pay a five hundred dollar fine; Henry J. Weare, Julius Bock, Robert P. Allan, John J. Underwood, Joseph C. Underwood, Willard Carpenter, Alexander Nimmo, David Nimmo, George A. Montgomery, Alexander D. Adamson, William McDonald, John L. Jordan, and Albert J. Bothwell.

These men were all highly respected citizens and members of the republican or democratic parties. They had felt for a long time that their fences would have to come down and some of them lightly referred to the "gathering" in Cheyenne as "The Roosevelt Roundup." Theodore Roosevelt had been a ranchman in North Dakota.

The *Wyoming Tribune* began to discuss "dry farming" or "dry land farming" in Wyoming, a term then used to distinguish such agriculture from irrigated farming. The contention was that these lands, which were fertile enough to produce rich native grasses that cured upon the sod like hay in the barn, would produce grain crops, at least forage crops. There were certain vegetables and some grains which would thrive in this altitude with fourteen or fifteen inches of precipitation. Albin farmers had long succeeded in growing potatoes for market.

Clarence T. Johnston, state engineer of Wyoming at that time, although a practical irrigationist, had some faith in arid farming as a science, and urged Mr. Deming to write a paper for the Young Men's Literary club on "Is Dry Farming around Cheyenne practicable?"

As a result of the interest which the paper aroused, a committee was appointed consisting of the late A. D. Kelley, H. B. Henderson sr., C. B. Richardson, C. T. Johnston, and William C. Deming. Funds were solicited which ultimately resulted in bringing to Wyoming Dr. V. T. Cooke, an expert dry farmer from Oregon. That movement, inaugurated by the young men of Cheyenne, later resulted in a state department of Agriculture, with Doctor Cooke as its head.

In the meantime, H. B. Henderson sr., A. D. Kelley, C. B. Richardson, and William C. Deming purchased four hundred eighty acres of land south of the present site of the veterans' new hospital, which was used as an experiment farm. John H. Gordon, a pioneer, was hired as a practical farmer. The year that Doctor Cooke arrived, there was excessive moisture, and he made such an excellent showing on the land that the state later established the Archer Experimental Farm, a few miles east, now one of the show places in Laramie county, with A. L. Nelson as superintendent. Thousands of farmers came into Wyoming, but of course not all remained. Enough stayed, however, to build up substantial communities such as Pine Bluffs, Hillsdale, Carpenter, Burns, and Egbert. Irrigation from wells is now supplementing dry farming around Pine Bluffs, while electricity from the Seminoe power dam is being supplied farm houses for both power and illumination all over the county.

In the most rosy days of early dry farming, when real estate agents in Cheyenne were displaying sheaves of home-grown grain and baskets of potatoes in their windows, no one dreamed of planting corn. It was naturally assumed that the altitude was too high and the season too short to mature a corn crop. Later corn became one of the staple dry farming crops of Wyoming, especially for forage.

The precipitation records showed that some years there was as little as nine inches (too little), occasionally sixteen or seventeen inches, while the average was only about fourteen inches. Fourteen inches of precipitation spread out over twelve months on a sandy soil is not very much encouragement for a farmer from Iowa accustomed to thirty-five or forty inches, absorbed and held by the black loam, but many Iowans remained and are among Wyoming's best citizens today.

The Cheyenne Board of Trade, in 1906, issued a little pamphlet entitled, "Some Suggestions relative to Dry Land Farming."

According to the publication, "The first thing to learn about dry land farming is that it requires thorough work and careful preparation of soil. The land should be plowed as early in the spring as the weather and conditions will permit. Preserve moisture with a dirt mulch and alternate crops and rest land by re-sodding. Plow and harrow top soil to prevent crust and evaporation of moisture."

In addition to sound, scientific advice, the committee and Doctor Cooke furnished persons desiring to engage in dry farming, seed grain (at cost price, delivered), purchased from localities where dry land farming had been successfully conducted.

Among those who took a leading part in the movement and helped to build dry farming communities in Laramie county were: J. Ross Carpenter, Alexander Hastie, Stephen H. Sibley, A. J. Moeckly, Ernest Hieber, V. W. Smith, D. J. James, T. W. Bastion, of Burns, E. W. Burrows, George A. Baker, Tracy Bomhoff of Egbert, Ed Jacobson, Rex Nichols, Judson Hardy of Carpenter, J. C. Towns, C. A. Keslar, W. F. Whitehead of Hillsdale, L. Larson, John Lusk, Frank Linn of Albin, Ralph H. McFarland, Joe Siemsen, William Barkell, C. E. Kaser of Pine Bluffs.

The state commission on dry farming experiments near Cheyenne, Wyoming, comprised the following: H. C. Beeler, state geologist, president; R. P. Fuller, state land commissioner; C. T. Johnston, state engineer, secretary; Doctor V. T. Cooke, director. Interest in dry land farming increased at a rapid rate. Professor B. C. Buffum, former head of the department of agriculture in the University of Wyoming, published a four hundred page book in 1909 called *Arid Agriculture*.

Indicating that the movement was not a mere flash in the pan, A. L. Nelson, long-time superintendent of the experiment farm at Archer, near Cheyenne, states there are one thousand farms and small ranch units in Laramie county and scores of rural district and centralized schools. Truly tall oaks from small acorns grow!

In an early editorial, Mr. Deming wrote: "Of all the achievements permitted to mankind, to my mind the greatest is to find a desert and make it vibrate and pulsate with new vegetation and all the fine things that go with farm life. Brigham Young and his Mormon followers had this vision and made the Deseret valley a bee hive, indeed. I want to see Wyoming in 1950 when it shall have been written in deeds of men, that

the stone and soil which were so long rejected have
become the backbone of the nation."

One of Mr. Deming's earliest friendships in Wyoming and one which has been steadfast through the
years is that of William E. Chaplin, editor of the
Laramie Republican, and register of the United States
land office at Cheyenne for seventeen and a half years,
later secretary of state of Wyoming. Mr. Chaplin, now
in his eighties, is retired and living in Van Nuys,
California.

Mr. Deming once remarked, "In borrowed parlance,
he is the noblest Roman of them all."

William E. Chaplin laughingly tells how he
"scooped" Mr. Deming with the news of his arrival
in Wyoming. It seems that Mr. Nissen, a Laramie resident, who was coming west on the same train with Mr.
Deming, queried his fellow passenger about his destination and business. Upon arriving in Laramie, he
reported the incident at once to Mr. Chaplin who announced in the *Laramie Republican* that Mr. Deming
had arrived in Cheyenne to edit the *Tribune,* before
the *Tribune* had time to announce the news itself.

In the early 1900's before Mr. Chaplin's family
moved from Laramie, the two men roomed at the same
house in Cheyenne. While the *Tribune* was still owned
by Judge J. M. Carey, they had a few good-natured
tilts in their editorial columns. Mr. Chaplin was one
of the main standard bearers for the republican organization headed by Senator Francis E. Warren. Judge
Carey was more or less independent in state politics.

"For about twenty-five years the rivalry between
the Honorable Joseph M. Carey and the Honorable
Francis E. Warren," says Mr. Deming, "created more
or less factional strife among Wyoming republicans.

It was popularly referred to as the Carey-Warren feud.

"I think the term a bit too strong, as many members of the party were friendly to both and declined to be drawn into a conflict which was more often emphasized by subordinates than by the principals.

"It is difficult to assign any one reason for the feeling that grew up between Warren and Carey. They were unusually big men, physically, mentally, financially and politically. In fact, it would have been remarkable had two such natural leaders, with contrasting though equally strong personalities, continued to live peaceably side by side in a small community.

"Carey had been United States district-attorney, judge of the territorial supreme court, mayor of Cheyenne, a delegate in congress, and had fathered the statehood bill.

"Warren had been mayor, state senator, territorial treasurer and territorial governor. Carey had entered the cattle business on a large scale while Warren's sheep and wool interests were very large. Both were builders and owned and operated commercial structures in Cheyenne.

"It is believed by some of their friends that in an early mayoralty campaign there arose a difference in opinion that engendered feeling. However, the main contention came later over a more important matter.

"When statehood had been acquired in 1890, Senator Warren was elected the first governor, september 11 of that year. When the Wyoming legislature met a few weeks after the election, they proceeded to choose two United States senators. The men honored were Francis E. Warren and Joseph M. Carey. Warren immediately resigned his four year term as governor, and secretary of state Amos W. Barber became acting governor.

"Carey and Warren drew lots for the short and long terms, one being for two years and the other for four, because it was an interim election for senator. Warren drew the two year term and Carey the four year term.

"When the legislature assembled early in 1893, Wyoming as well as the entire country was in the midst of political turmoil under Grover Cleveland's administration, and the question of sound money or the gold standard was becoming a paramount issue even before William J. Bryan made his 'Cross of Gold' speech in the democratic national convention in 1896. The democrats had elected Doctor John E. Osborne of Rawlins to the position of governor in 1892. One result was that there was no election for senator by the legislature in 1893, a deadlock having resulted. On march 9, after adjournment, Governor Osborne appointed A. C. Beckwith, of Evanston, United States senator. Several senate committee hearings were held and it was recommended that Mr. Beckwith's credentials be accepted. However, on july 11, 1893, he sent his resignation to Governor Osborne. Beckwith was allowed two thousand dollars expense money by the senate.

"I am indebted to Attorney Charles E. Lane for the above facts concerning Mr. Beckwith.

"When Carey came up for reelection by the legislature in 1895, he was defeated, and representative in congress, the Honorable Clarence D. Clark, of Evanston, an able lawyer, was awarded the honor.

"The state was growing in population, and then as now there was some prejudice against Cheyenne. Other sections wished a senator and it was realized by many leaders that Cheyenne could not always retain two. The question was – which should it be, Warren or Carey?

"Warren survived the situation and served continu-

Joseph M. Carey
Governor, United States Senator, and Cattleman
of Wyoming

Francis E. Warren
Governor, United States Senator, and Sheepman
of Wyoming

ously in the United States senate until his death in november, 1929.

"It is commonly believed that Carey's defeat for the senate and Warren's return to that body constituted the real origin of the feeling between Senators Carey and Warren which so divided the republican party that Judge Carey, failing to receive consideration by the republicans for governor in 1910, accepted a nomination at the hands of the democrats and was elected over the Honorable William E. Mullen, the republican candidate.

"Judge Carey was long inclined to attribute his failure to return to the senate to the fact that he was known as a sound money man at a time when there was much free silver sentiment in Wyoming.

"The breach in the republican party was not healed until Governor Carey's son, Robert D. Carey, was nominated and elected governor by the republicans in 1918. Senator Warren approved the nomination and worked for Robert D. Carey.

"As a friend of these two big men, Francis E. Warren and Joseph M. Carey, and as a friend of their families, I take pleasure in recording here that notwithstanding the feeling which certainly did exist between them, they were "to the manner born" when it came to the external niceties that obtain between gentlemen, who in the course of events may be frequently thrown together.

"Cheyenne, being on the cross roads, then as now, was visited from time to time by national characters including presidents. Warren and Carey kept open house and both were hospitable hosts. Upon such occasions frequently I have seen them together and no one would have suspected that in their hearts there was some bitterness which required years to overcome."

While editing the *Tribune* for Judge Carey for two or three years, Deming conformed to his policies, but managed to retain the respect of the regular organization, especially the friendship of Senator Warren. Warren's aides sometimes became very critical but the "Old Man" could take it, some one has said.

Deming's knowledge of politics and psychology made the situation easier because both factions read his paper, thus placing him in a strong position when he should buy the *Tribune* from Judge Carey. Thus he could and did support Warren always for senator and Robert D. Carey wholeheartedly for governor in 1918. The fact that Deming was defeated for United States senator in 1930 in the primary did not deter him from giving full support to Robert Carey who was elected. In time the Warren-Carey family differences were healed, to the relief of their many mutual friends.

In 1907, President Theodore Roosevelt appointed William C. Deming as receiver of public moneys in the United States land office at Cheyenne, where he worked side by side with Register Chaplin who had been named by President McKinley.

Three years previous to this time, the 60,000,000 acres of land in Wyoming had been classified as to ownership and control as follows: state lands, 4,000,000; assessed land, 7,500,000; 43,000,000 acres either filed upon or still open for settlement; and 8,000,000 acres in forest reserve. Hundreds upon thousands of acres of this open land were filed for settlement during Mr. Chaplin's and Deming's term of service in the land office.

According to Mr. Chaplin, "In the dispatch of the public business, Mr. Deming was always courteous, obliging and efficient. Much of the vast area of land lying in Goshen, Platte and Laramie counties was settled during our administration."

JOHN C. FLEMING
Information Librarian, the Mountain States Telephone
and Telegraph Co., Denver

WILLIAM E. CHAPLIN
last surviving member of Wyoming constitutional
convention, pioneer editor of the Laramie
Republican, and former Secretary of State

Fred J. McDermott, a pioneer of Wyoming, says: "I recall an early practice of the United States land offices in Wyoming. The rich and powerful livestock interests that had lost the stream valleys to the settlers through squatting and homesteading of these lands, were determined to hold the many springs and water-holes, which was necessary, yes, vital, to their control of the public domain – the so-called range – and through such control they could harass, and drive out the small settler. The powerful interests would invest in right to lands, commonly known as 'scrip' and leave such rights or such scrip in the hands of a prominent local attorney.

"Then when an application for entry on any lands which contained water was made in these land offices, the attorney was frequently notified and a delay followed for a few hours or days as the case required, while the attorney entered the lands under these scrip rights, leaving the bona fide, would-be entryman, completely out through prior filing. This practice was unfair and Chaplin and Deming put a stop to it at the Cheyenne office, which of course stopped it elsewhere in the state.

"Not only were frauds perpetrated by the larger 'interests,' but also by many of the 'homesteaders' who perjured themselves. Thus our alert editor-administrators put the service on a fair and honest basis."

This is the statement of Mr. McDermott, who is a very out-spoken citizen and small ranch owner, who from time to time contributed vigorous articles to the press.

In making decisions upon the various land cases, Mr. Chaplin and Mr. Deming alternated. After writing their opinions, they would confer with each other for

March 18, 1935.

Mr. William C. Deming,
Wyoming State Leader,
Cheyenne, Wyoming.

Dear Mr. Deming:

I greatly appreciate your thought in sending me the article recently published in the Wyoming State Leader. It brings to mind many interesting associations.

With best regards.

Sincerely yours,

[signature: James R. Garfield]

LETTER FROM JAMES R. GARFIELD, SON OF PRESIDENT GARFIELD with whom William C. Deming had many contacts a final decision. Their records show that they never had a decision reversed by the secretary of the Interior when an appeal was taken. Deming says: "Wm. E. Chaplin was, in my judgment, the best authority in the West on the public land laws and their administration."

Mr. Deming's knowledge of law was of exceptional worth to him in the land office work. On may 6, 1910 he was admitted to practice in the courts of Wyoming, upon his certificate issued in Kentucky many years before. This courtesy was granted by the supreme court of the state of Wyoming, but he never engaged in active practice. He remains a member of the Wyoming Bar association and has occasionally addressed the Colorado and Nebraska associations as well as the Wyoming body. "The Making of a Nation" has been his favorite theme.

During the Chaplin-Deming administration, a visit was paid to the Cheyenne land office by James R. Garfield, secretary of the Interior, whom Deming had known in Ohio, in the 1890's.

"How much do you personally know about your district?" he asked Mr. Chaplin.

Mr. Chaplin explained that the area included some thirteen million acres and that his knowledge of it had been gained from various hunting and fishing expeditions, and casual visits to the counties and towns.

When Mr. Garfield said that he thought Mr. Chaplin and Mr. Deming should have more intimate knowledge of their territory, Mr. Chaplin asked the following question: "Mr. Secretary, in case we are to decide important matters, which would you prefer we rely on: 'law and evidence' or personal knowledge?" The secretary immediately decided in favor of law and evidence.

In keeping with the times, the land office was investigated by a special commission sent out from Washington. The members of this commission were Gifford Pinchot and William A. Richards, assistant commissioner of the general land office. During the investigation, Mr. Chaplin suggested that a thorough inspection of lands should be made by the government before patents were filed. He said that the existing manner in which the examinations were made was farcical, and cited the case of Old Sailor Jack who had been granted a patent upon the testimony of witnesses. Later a protest was entered and it was proven that Sailor Jack had never lived a minute on the place in Albany county. The entry was cancelled. Chaplin explained that rich mineral oil lands could be secured by homestead or direct entry through false witnesses.

"What would be your remedy?" Mr. Pinchot asked.

"We would have the federal government represented by field men," was the prompt answer.

The outcome of the meeting was the creation of a field division for the land office with at least one field man for each office in the state. Some of these special agents later became leading citizens of Wyoming, notably Adelbert Baker, Harry B. Durham, E. O. Fuller, and former United States senator Harry H. Schwartz of Casper.

While in the land office, Mr. Deming made a large acquaintance among the settlers and was much in demand as a public speaker at community gatherings.

During the Wilson administration, a special representative of the department of the Interior, a Mr. Tallman, made a complete examination of the Cheyenne land office. After he was through, he said: "I had in mind to make some alterations and changes to coincide with the manner in which the San Francisco office is run, but I am not going to. Your methods are entirely satisfactory."

Mr. Deming resigned july 1, 1913, before the expiration of his term as receiver, in order that he might give more personal attention to his rapidly growing publishing and real estate affairs.

A letter dated january 1914, from the auditor of the Treasury department at Washington, reported that William C. Deming's account as receiver of public moneys for the period ended june 30, 1913, had been settled and balanced to the cent. His accounts were always in order.

Strenuous Years of Editorial and Political Work

William C. Deming early displayed marked business ability. He had the characteristics which make for financial success: honesty, industry, tolerance and thrift. He visualized opportunities, conserved his income and profits from his newspaper and diverted them to other lines of investment.

He inherited a taste for real estate from his father and realized that although his father had more real ability as a lawyer, he himself might make a better business man.

Mr. Deming said: "My first actual experience or personal interest in handling real estate was in college. I was a member of the committee that leased and helped furnish the first Alpha chapter, Delta Tau Delta house at Allegheny college, and managed the business details during my junior and senior years."

In addition to the *Tribune,* he published the *Wyoming Stockman-Farmer,* a monthly livestock and agricultural journal, which he planned and founded in 1908.

While his attention and efforts had been concentrated largely upon the development of his newspapers, with an occasional investment in other companies, Mr. Deming took an interest in real estate, particularly business property. He watched the trend of growth in Cheyenne, observing that the original commercial districts were Sixteenth street on the south and old Eddy street, now Pioneer avenue, on the west, with a consistent movement northward and eastward as the decades passed.

When he arrived in Cheyenne, Ferguson street, now Carey avenue, was probably the principal shopping street, with a block on Seventeenth street eastward suggesting the trend. By 1910 and 1911 there was some activity on Capitol avenue and indications that Eighteenth street might in time develop. Thus he could understand the foresight of Senator Warren and T. A. Cosgriff in selecting Central avenue as a location for new investments, including the Plains hotel.

He noted also that there was a Carey building, a Warren building, an Idelman building, a Bresnahen block, as well as a number of others, which had been erected many years before. He felt that the time had come to branch out somewhat in his business activities and probably construct a block to be known as the Deming building.

In pursuance of this ambition, he acquired the southwest corner of Central avenue and Seventeenth street, north of the Plains hotel, then under construction. Senator Warren encouraged him in this enterprise.

While Mr. Deming did not have all the necessary funds for completing and paying for the building, that was no deterrent, because he had learned from his newspaper experience the advantages of an incorporated company in which stock might be sold. Furthermore it was comparatively easy to place a mortgage, with the right to make payments upon the principal at frequent intervals.

Although his credit and standing by this time were so well established that it would not have been difficult

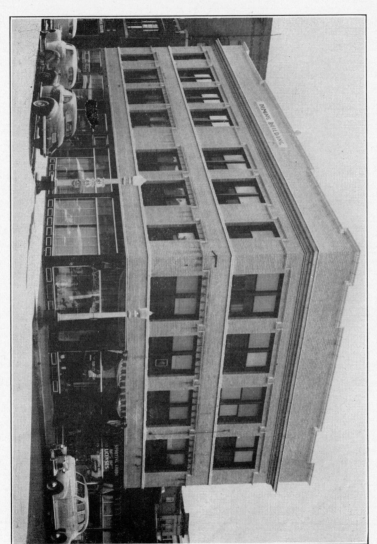

DEMING BUILDING, CHEYENNE, WYOMING

erected 1911

to sell stock to his friends or others, he decided to restrict his business associates in the realty company to those who had been affiliated with him in the publishing business. He had learned, furthermore, in business financing as well as in many other phases of life, that four, five, or six individuals may be able to do what one person would not be able immediately to achieve. In other words, by pooling his own capital and credit with that of his associates, it was possible to raise the necessary funds with which to begin business. Thus, in 1911, the first building to be erected by the new company was known as the Deming building. It was the first exclusive business block on Central avenue. The stock holders were W. C. Deming, T. H. Deming, D. S. Deming, Zell Hart Deming, and James H. Walton. In answer to the question why he did not sell stock to the public in any of his enterprises, he said, "I never desired to commercialize or over-expand my credit. If my investments were sound it was sufficient that I and my immediate associates should receive the profit. If they were doubtful, I did not wish to involve outsiders."

The Deming Realty company was not a real estate agency in the usual acceptation of the term but a company created to construct, own, and operate business property.

Mr. Deming's three thousand dollars a year salary as receiver of public moneys in the United States land office, added to his income from the *Warren Tribune* and the *Cheyenne Tribune,* enabled him to discharge his personal obligations promptly as they came due.

Although Deming was never handy with tools like his father, he probably compensated for it in that he could conceive and plan or remodel buildings even if he could not make the detailed sketches and specifications.

By 1912, the *Wyoming Tribune* had outgrown its rented quarters on Capitol avenue and his company purchased from John Thomas, the old Keefe amusement hall (north of the Post Office), which he converted into a newspaper office. The walls were raised and fourteen attractive small living apartments were provided in the second and third stories. The financing of this building was accomplished along the same line as that of the Deming building.

In due time, the Deming Realty company purchased other property, vacant or improved, and today, in addition to the above named Deming building, owns the New Tribune building on Seventeenth street, occupied by the *Tribune-Eagle,* the Little Shop building east of the *Tribune* office, the Texas filling stations on the corner of Nineteenth street and Pioneer avenue, and on Twentieth and Central avenue, the old Tribune building containing the fourteen living apartments on Federal street, and the former Thomas building adjoining on Carey avenue, containing the Star restaurant and twelve apartments on the second and third floors. Later renamed the Belmont block.

Personally, Mr. Deming owned The Gables on Eighteenth street, that historic old home which was demolished in 1940. It is now the site of the Cheyenne Light, Fuel and Power company's headquarters.

In addition to the Deming Realty company, Mr. Deming has been interested in two home-building companies in Cheyenne.

As the Union Pacific railroad expanded its shops in Cheyenne, more houses were needed.

Mr. Deming was chosen as a member of the board of directors of the Cheyenne Home Builders' association to which William Dubois, A. D. Kelley, Fred

TRIBUNE BUILDING, CHEYENNE, WYOMING
erected 1929 – property of Deming Realty Company

Hofmann, A. H. Marble, Charles W. Hirsig, and R. N. LaFontaine belonged. The association had an authorized capital stock of two hundred fifty thousand dollars.

The company erected many houses in northwest Cheyenne and the Cheyenne Apartment house. The latter is now owned by the Hofmann estate. The company was a success financially.

The same is true of a later company which erected homes for employees at the airport. It was called the Home Builders company with a capital of fifty thousand dollars. The incorporators were: A. E. Roedel, John D. Clark, Fred Warren, Charles Hirsig, Archie Allison, W. C. Deming, William Dubois, R. J. Hofmann, George Klett, Harry Freed, and Ed Bartley. All the houses were sold and the company liquidated.

Mr. Deming's success as a business man comes of his natural caution, his ability to see and grasp opportunity, his recognized integrity, and his correct appraisal of men in the selection of his business associates. Notable examples of this trait are indicated by his partnership and association for many years with James H. Walton, of Cheyenne, and his retention and promotion from subordinate positions on the *Tribune* to editor and manager, respectively, of John Charles Thompson jr., and John C. Fleming.

During the World war, Mr. Walton resigned to become cashier of the Stock Growers National bank, and later, head of the Walton Motor company.

"When I first knew James H. Walton," Mr. Deming said, "he was principal of a school in Warren, Ohio. During the early weeks of a certain summer, the *Warren Tribune* was preparing to cover a sensational murder case very fully and in preparation therefor sent solicitors for subscriptions throughout the county. There were at least five men upon the list of salesmen, including the principal of another school.

"The result was that they began to drop out after a day or two and the only one who completed his job and got results was Mr. Walton. That was his introduction to the newspaper business and the reason I invited him to come to Cheyenne and canvass the state in 1903 for the *Wyoming Tribune.*"

Later, Fred H. Ware and William H. Owens became associated with Mr. Deming, chiefly in the Deming Realty company management. They were efficient, dependable, and loyal, enabling Mr. Deming to spend many months each year in California or Florida.

During Mr. Deming's boyhood in Kentucky, there was a very general movement in the northern section of the state to improve the country roads, many of which were almost impassable in wet weather. Crushed limestone, called "metal," laid upon a bed of flat rocks, dirt and gravel was generally used and was known as the macadamized system. Sometimes bonds were issued by counties or districts for the purpose and at other times private companies improved the roads and established toll gates upon them. Deming's father, Judge Deming, was a leader in the movement for hard surfaced highways in his section.

W. C. Deming had been through something of the same experience in Trumbull county, Ohio, when experiments were being made with brick roads.

Therefore, he came naturally by his interest in improved highways, and was among the first to advocate gravel roads and modern surfacing in Wyoming.

With navigable waters in Wyoming lacking, roads always have been of the utmost importance because of

BELMONT BLOCK, CHEYENNE
property of the Deming Realty Company
The rear portion of this building was occupied by the Wyoming Tribune, 1913 to 1929

the vast distances between settlements and the necessity for hauling supplies hundreds of miles from the railway or nearest supply center.

From the earliest territorial days, the road matters were placed in the hands of the county commissioners, who constructed as many roads as local funds permitted.

In 1891 the legislature requested the federal government to establish a wagon road from Fort Washakie to Yellowstone park. It was claimed that the establishment of such a government highway would allay the constant fears and dangers of Indian outbreaks and would aid western immigration. It was also asserted that the proposed line of road passed through the haunts of the notorious horse thieves, and general range bandits of the Wind River mountains, who had so long, as an organized band, been a source of annoyance, danger, and loss to the stock growers of Wyoming, Idaho, Utah, and Montana, as well as to the Indians on the reservation. And that the road in question would have as one of its results the breaking up of this mischievous robber band.

Nothing of consequence resulted from the legislative memorial and the Wyoming roads continued to remain the problem of the separate counties.

Although bills were before congress in 1904 proposing an appropriation of more than twenty million dollars for distribution among the various states for help in road building, it was not until 1909 that the matter received official attention in Wyoming. In that year, Governor B. B. Brooks said in his legislative message that "it would seem that some intelligent system could be outlined providing for better and more permanent road construction."

During the 1909 session, the legislature set aside the

proceeds of the inheritance tax law of 1903 as a special fund to be expended by the county commissioners "for the sole purpose of permanent improvement of the county roads." The income from this source, however, was comparatively small.

With the general development and the increasing settlement in the state, bringing demands for centralized high schools, rural mail service, and the like, interest in good roads was aroused.

The advent of the automobile emphasized the necessity for new roads in Wyoming – wider and straighter ones. A prime mover in awakening interest in good roads was Ez Emery, a civil engineer, who in 1910 attempted to pilot a French automobile across the west end of Wyoming in what was called a New York-to-Paris automobile race. He found that a "gas machine" was far different from the trusty buckboard with which he had been accustomed to negotiate Wyoming roads. Emery, however, was convinced that the automobile had come to stay, so he purchased a Lambert friction-drive machine, and began a campaign for good roads. It took him three days and innumerable hardships to drive from Rawlins to Rock Springs, about one hundred ten miles, where he was met with flags flying. He told the interested greeters how automobiles were going to fly across the country in scores within a few years.

In 1911, Governor Joseph M. Carey emphasized the importance of good roads in his message to the legislature saying, "No one can now contradict the fact that the automobile is to become an every-day feature on our public highways, both for pleasure and for business. If Wyoming could adopt some measure, without its becoming burdensome to the people, whereby great highways, well constructed, could be built across the

JOHN CHARLES THOMPSON   JAMES H. WALTON

Both associated for many years with William C. Deming on the Wyoming Tribune
Thompson now editor of the Wyoming Tribune

state from north to south and from east to west, touching the county seats and principal towns, it would tend to be one of the greatest factors in the rapid development of the state."

Accordingly, the legislature appropriated ten thousand dollars for road improvement, outlined seven state roads and created the state commission on prison labor, which was authorized to use the labor of convicts in the construction, repair, and maintenance of certain public highways. This may be said to be the first designation of a state highway system although the jurisdiction over the roads still remained with the boards of county commissioners.

At this time, a Cheyenne contingent inaugurated a movement for an automobile transcontinental highway – quite some time before Carl Fisher and Henry B. Joy fathered the Lincoln highway. What is said to be the first automobile log made in Wyoming covered the road from Pine Bluffs to Cheyenne. Emery drove the car and W. C. Deming made the notes for the log. Cheyenne officials and the Laramie county commissioners named the route "The Transcontinental Highway."

Soon afterwards, Emery and a man named Strawman drove an automobile from Cheyenne to Evanston, following the only trail then open and seeking bridges, as they were unable to ford most of the streams with the car. It took ten days to reach Evanston, with a total distance covered of five hundred twenty-five miles from state line to state line. The route included bridges at McGill, Fort Steele, Oakley (near Kemmerer), and then turned southward by the way of Cumberland Flats to Evanston.

The map of this route was lithographed, reduced,

and printed in the daily *Tribune*. Hundreds of copies, both large and small, were mailed throughout the country from the Tribune office, boosting the new automobile highway.

This created much interest and enthusiasm, and on november 1, 1911, more than two hundred Cheyenne business men organized the Laramie County Good Roads association and each paid a membership fee of two dollars. With this money, enthusiasm was aroused in the other counties in southern Wyoming along the proposed Transcontinental highway and "good roads days" were held with splendid success by volunteer workmen. Payson W. Spaulding, of Evanston, joined heartily and became an outstanding factor in western Wyoming. He was later an official of the "Lincoln Highway" which followed. Mr. Spaulding continues his interest in the Lincoln highway and presided at the dedication of the monument to Henry B. Joy at the continental divide near Creston in 1939.

The most constructive early work was done by Warren Richardson and his colleagues on the board of Laramie county commissioners. They did the first real work on the Lincoln highway and also laid out and improved the Yellowstone highway, north, almost as straight as the crow flies. Mr. Richardson was one of the few road builders who refused to follow cow paths and old trails. He condemned private and public lands, thereby eliminating many curves and saving mileage. Richardson says that in Laramie county hundreds were interested and many gave substantial encouragement to highway improvement.

The good roads idea spread throughout the state and on march 11, 1912, a meeting was held at Douglas attended by representatives from every section.

Volunteers in one day painted black, yellow, and white rings on fence posts across southern Wyoming – thus making it possible to follow the proposed automobile route. These colors were replaced later by the red, white and blue of the Lincoln highway.

Wyoming's present system of oiled highways amazes all who use it.

In the summer of 1912, Wyoming representatives who attended a national good roads meeting in Cincinnati distributed two thousand pamphlets giving the facts about crossing the state of Wyoming by auto and were instrumental in starting an ocean-to-ocean highway.

Ez Emery became known as "Ez, the Good Roads Moses" (a term which he credited to Mr. Deming) while Gus Holm's, Jacob Schwoob, B. B. Brooks, and L. L. Newton were doing yeoman service for the cause in northern and central Wyoming.

The Lincoln Highway association was organized in 1912 and those most active in the work in Wyoming the first few years included: Laramie county: Warren Richardson, Herbert V. Lacey, Harry Hynds, Frank L. Dildine, and W. C. Deming; Albany county: Elmer Lovejoy, John Ernest, Otto Gramm; Carbon county: Homer A. France, J. M. Rumsey, Dr. Raymond Barber, W. W. Daley, F. A. Hadsell, J. R. Doty, and L. E. Armstrong; Sweetwater county: John Hay, W. B. Dunton, Dr. E. S. Lauzer, T. S. Taliaferro jr.; Uinta county: Maurice Groshon, W. A. Carter, W. F. Normandy, George Pexton, Dr. J. L. Wicks, H. L. Williams, Shirley Kastor, George Spencer, Dr. C. H. Solier, George Snyder and P. W. Spaulding.

In 1913 the legislature increased the designated highways in the state to twelve and passed the first automobile law providing for the registration, identification, and regulation of automobiles on the state's public highways.

The next legislature (1915) provided for the construction and improvement of public roads and highways in whole or in part by the state, "either direct or by extending aid to counties."

Naturally, the first extensive road activities were across southern Wyoming along the route of the heaviest travel. Later the road improvement extended northward through Casper to Basin and Cody. Then came the organization of the Park-to-Park Highway association.

By the act of july 11, 1916, congress provided federal aid in the construction of roads. Immediately following the passage of the act, Secretary of the Interior Lane called a meeting at the Canyon hotel in Yellowstone park for the purpose of discussing a park-to-park highway, that would link all national parks in the nine different states with a permanent automobile road. Mr. Deming, a delegate from Cheyenne, presided as chairman of the committee which outlined the plan for the permanent National Park-to-Park Highway association, and was elected vice-president of the organization. Other officers elected were: Gus Holm's, president, and L. L. Newton, secretary-treasurer. Assistant-secretary of the Interior Stephen Mather attended the meeting and took an active part in it. Outstanding workers in the organization in Wyoming were, in addition to the officers, M. R. Collins, James Christensen, Fred Holdredge, Judge Harry Illsley, Earl Warren, and W. J. Thom.

In this same year, according to Mr. Spaulding, "The Wyoming Good Roads alliance was formed for the purpose of going fifty-fifty with federal aid in western roads. The officers were: G. E. Parisoe, Laramie, president; W. L. Ayres, Wheatland, vice-president; P. C. Spencer, Lander, secretary; and W. J. Thom, Buffalo, treasurer. C. D. Oviatt of Albany county was also active."

At the election in the fall of 1916, the voters of Wyoming adopted a constitutional amendment making it possible for the state to participate in the federal aid. The legislature which convened soon afterwards passed the State Highway act on february 19, 1917, through which was created the State Highway department comprising a State Highway commission (bi-partisan with not more than three of the five members to be of the same political party), and a state highway engineer. The state highway engineer was placed in complete charge of the laying out and establishing of highways upon which any part of the state highway fund could be expended, except roads in the national forests.

The legislative act pledged funds sufficient to equal the sum apportioned to the state by the federal government. In order to start the state highway fund, a small legislative appropriation was made and a tax levy of a quarter of a mill was designated for the years 1917 and 1918.

From time to time, as circumstances have demanded, new laws have been passed providing for gasoline taxes, directing the diversion of a part of the license fees to provide a sinking fund for the retirement of state highway bonds, creating the office of state highway superintendent, and covering other important phases of highway development.

The State Highway department has done consistently efficient work through the years and has built up a primary highway system of four thousand seventy-six miles of road comprising a network of transportation lanes connecting all cities and towns. In many places the state highway is the only system for handling transportation between isolated communities scattered over a statewide area of approximately ninety-five thousand square miles. At the end of the 1942 biennium there were completed three thousand nine hundred twenty-six miles of oil-surfaced roads with only one hundred twelve miles of earth-graded road, and thirty-eight miles of gravel-surfaced road which had not been oil treated.

In 1942, 3,845,362 gallons of asphaltic road oil were purchased for maintenance work.

Since april 1, 1917, the State Highway department has expended on the state highway system $95,634,-127.93, of which $72,734,917.93 has been spent for actual construction. The income received during the period 1917 to 1942 has been $96,990,829.41 from the following sources: motor vehicle license tax, gasoline license tax, commercial vehicle compensatory fees, gasoline dealers license fees, oil royalties, federal aid, city, county and other aid, public service commission permit fees, bonds, bond premium, state appropriations, miscellaneous cash, trade-in allowances, offsets, and deductions.

According to a statement from the Highway commission in 1941, there were yet four hundred thirty miles of secondary roads that should be built, — all eligible to be improved with federal aid funds, but, "the federal aid funds are inadequate to make any kind of a showing on this system. Congress itself tells the states how much of the federal aid funds they can spend on the primary and secondary systems. The federal government has continually increased federal taxes on motor vehicles, by way of gasoline tax and other excise taxes, until now it is collecting over twice as much from the motor vehicle user as it is returning to the states for highway construction."

The Lincoln highway, the Yellowstone highway, and the Park-to-Park highway, connecting many Rocky Mountain playgrounds, have all been completed and all are surfaced with oil or concrete. The same is true of all primary roads in Wyoming.

During the biennium, 1940-1942, highway bonds totaling $2,520,000 were refunded. By refunding these bonds, the interest rate was reduced from four per cent to two per cent, thus saving the taxpayers, approximately $50,000 a year. This amount of road-use fees and other vehicle license fees, which would have been used normally for paying interest on these bonds, were made available for the construction of additional secondary or farm-to-market roads.

Every year because of the increasing volume of traffic and improvement in motor vehicles, more and more demands are made upon the department for betterments and for new and improved road designs to facilitate the movement of traffic. It is necessary that new ideas and new methods be used in the design and construction of the highways. The design department has kept step with this change in standards, and the highways constructed during recent years have been built to high standards, which minimize their danger of becoming obsolete before twenty-five years hence.

In 1942 a comprehensive grade-crossing program for the elimination of hazards at dangerous railroad crossings was completed.

Engineers and technicians of the Wyoming state

highway laboratory have accomplished much in the way of performing tests to determine which of the available road building materials are best suited for use in the construction of Wyoming roads. A policy of developing and promoting the use of local materials for road construction, whenever an economy can be made without sacrificing quality in construction, has been employed.

The statewide highway planning survey, in cooperation with the public roads administration, has been engaged in making traffic surveys and investigations, accident studies, and gathering statistics for making financial studies relating to highway problems as they affect the state of Wyoming. The main purpose of these investigations and studies has been to provide future highway administrators and legislators with detailed facts and data as they apply to Wyoming highway transportation problems.

On january 10, 1936, L. L. Newton wrote for the *Wyoming Tribune* a comprehensive story of Wyoming's modern highway system. He gave much credit to Warren Richardson, Frank L. Dildine, W. E. Dinneen, Harry P. Hynds, Ezra L. Emery, and W. C. Deming of Cheyenne. He recalled also that Governor B. B. Brooks, S. W. Conwell, George Nelson, Marion N. Wheeler, and C. H. Townsend of Casper; John B. Sloan of Cheyenne; Charles Maurer and M. R. Collins of Douglas; W. L. Ayers of Wheatland; A. L. Duhig and A. K. Lee of Thermopolis; L. A. Shawver and A. O. Heyer of Shoshoni; and C. F. Robertson, Dr. W. O. Grey, L. E. Laird, F. S. Coulter, and Ray Bower of Worland, took an active part.*

It is interesting to note that when the *Tribune* was

*For details regarding the State Highway commission *see* APPENDIX.

advocating good roads and emphasizing the fact that the auto business in Cheyenne was one of the city's biggest industries, Deming was looking far ahead. In an editorial, he wrote: "It will not be very long before the flying machine will be a factor in this community. It will be playing a part in both business and pleasure. It will become an asset without much of a community investment. Cheyenne must get ready for this new thing so marvelous in its results but so simple in itself."

Deming attended practically every republican state convention for years, frequently serving as chairman of the resolutions committee. Aided by others, he was able to put through platforms somewhat in advance of the views of the more conservative members of the republican party in Wyoming.

During this period, politics of the state and nation were upset by the progressive movement of Theodore Roosevelt in the nation and by Joseph M. Carey in Wyoming. The *Tribune* remained steadfast as a republican paper.

The eventual success of Mr. Deming in keeping on friendly terms with both Senator Warren and Senator Carey is worthy of comment.

"To my surprise," says Deming, "when Judge Carey became governor, he occasionally sent for me to discuss public state matters and said he desired to appoint me as a member of the Wyoming commission for an exposition in Philadelphia, which did not materialize because of the World war."

In 1897, Robert La Follette, of Wisconsin, had urged the direct primary.

Early in 1907 Governor Brooks of Wyoming expressed the opinion in his legislative message that "perhaps the time has arrived for the abolishment of the

old fashioned caucus and convention, and the substitu-
tion of a new primary election plan, which has been
adopted in many of the states. . ."

Mr. Deming thought so too, but was criticized by
a member of the old-line republicans because of his
work on behalf of the primary law. Although W. E.
Chaplin, of Laramie, was consistently against the law,
he defended Mr. Deming's independence in the matter
in an editorial written in 1918.

Said Mr. Chaplin: "Possibly in the matter of the
primary law, he did not go around and consult with
party leaders before advocating it in his paper. It must
be admitted that he is not built that way. But the primary idea was in the air throughout the union and still
holds in practically all the states. His advocacy of it
here in Wyoming was but following in the footsteps
of some of the greatest politicians of the entire nation.
. . If he was entirely responsible for it in the state,
and jammed it down the throats of legislators whether
they believed in it or not, then he must be given credit
for being a good jammer. There is one thing about
him – he will stick in the face of keen opposition. . .
He would make an exceptionally able official in any
position within the gift of the state and would hand
the trust to his successor untarnished and bettered by
his having held it. This is the simple truth."

Mr. Deming gave exceedingly careful consideration
to the legislation which he felt should come before the
twelfth legislature in 1914. In speaking before the
Young Men's Literary club in Cheyenne he said: "I
would have the Wyoming legislature reform its position in favor of the direct election of United States
senators . . . members of the legislature should be
elected with a view to their qualifications to make laws,

rather than as to how they will vote for United States senator."

At this time the *Tribune* advocated an appropriation for the building of a new library and supreme court building and favored child labor legislation; eight hour working days for laboring men; the extension of a pure food and drug act to include seeds, plants and trees; the licensing of dealers who sell guns and ammunition; employer's liability; registration fee for automobiles, the proceeds to be turned into a good roads improvement fund; and a semi-annual tax paying period.

Relative to taxation, Mr. Deming said: "Wyoming needs manufacturing, yet I am frank to say it will be very slow in coming, because of our small population and inadequate railroad facilities. The freight rate is against us. The best that we can hope to do for some years to come is the securing of small enterprises, like creameries, ice plants, packing houses, etc., for the product of which there is a local demand. . . It is possible, however, that we might hasten the investment of large capital in iron, steel and wool enterprises by granting immunity from taxation for a period of ten years."

He was strongly in favor of a blue sky law.

"Viewing the wrecks of the Penn Wyoming Copper company, the Hanover Canal, the North Platte Irrigation company and scores of others known and unknown, few states have suffered more from wildcat stock-jobbing than Wyoming," he said. "Kansas has met this situation by the enactment of what is popularly called a blue sky law. This means, of course, that under that law the proper officials will see that stock cannot be advertised and sold for something which is obviously a fake and a fraud. Wyoming has been the victim of get-rich-quick exploitation and the enactment of a practicable and effective law, putting a stop to obvious frauds would do much toward restoring confidence in Wyoming enterprises."

C. Watt Brandon, editor of the *Kemmerer Camera,* says of Mr. Deming: "I have been close to him in matters political. He was one of those newspaper men who worked willingly and happily to advance his friends along the political horizon, but seldom asked for anything for himself. I have always felt that Mr. Deming was worthy and entitled to any political honor his party could have bestowed upon him."

One of his strong political adversaries, S. G. Hopkins, former state land commissioner of Wyoming, says: "Between political campaigns, Mr. Deming's paper displayed an attitude of fairness on political matters both in its news columns and editorially. This policy gained for him the confidence and esteem of a large number of his readers of the opposite political party, for people, generally speaking, admire fair play. It was this policy that gave his paper so much influence in a campaign and which was so difficult to break down or overcome. As the campaign approached, Mr. Deming's paper swung into line with his party organization and carried with it a large following of liberal voters where confidence had been gained by the policy he had pursued. This demonstrated his political sagacity.

"At times I had doubts if the powers that be in his party fully appreciated the influence of Mr. Deming's paper during the campaigns. Perhaps they were not in a position to understand and feel it as I was. When I entered a campaign, I had no fear of the campaign managers of the opposite party, astute politicians though they were. There were generally too many of them and sometimes they worked at cross purposes, which led to mistakes which I watched for and took advantage of, but I did fear Mr. Deming's paper with its circulation extending to every hamlet in the state. How to break down that influence or offset it was my greatest problem. . . Mr. Deming's paper was ruthless in its aggressiveness during campaign periods. . . I regarded Mr. Deming as political enemy number one, because he was the most important factor in the opposition.

"Mr. Deming was a good sport politically. After the votes were counted, the campaign was over and politics were adjourned. If successful, he did not crow over much. If defeated, he took it with good grace and there were no recriminations or reprisals. He was tolerant of the opinions of others and magnanimous to his political foes."

When Mr. Deming was president of the United States Civil Service commission, he recommended Mr. Hopkins for a temporary appointment in Washington, with an opportunity to acquire a classified Civil Service status under the rules. Hopkins, being a lawyer, became a valuable member of the board of appeals of the Civil Service commission and served more than ten years.

In a letter to the author of this biography, Mr. Hopkins very frankly says, "Mr. Deming's action in assigning me to duty was purely voluntary. I had no claim personally or politically to consideration. More and more as the years go by, Mrs. Hopkins and I realize and appreciate Mr. Deming's kindness and our gratitude cannot be expressed in words."

President William Howard Taft, an advocate of world peace and an international court of arbitration, was having much trouble securing support in congress for these policies. On the spur of the moment, Mr. Deming sent him a telegram which was immediately used by the Associated Press the following day –

WASHINGTON, D.C., Jan. 9. President Taft has been asked to call a conference of the men who make the sentiment that makes and unmakes governors – the representatives of the press – to consider world peace. William C. Deming, prominent Wyoming editor, made the request in a telegram to the president, as follows –

Cheyenne, Wyo., Jan. 8, 1912.
HON. WILLIAM H. TAFT, President United States
The greatest world problem today is the prevention of war. The masses are with you in your efforts to bring about arbitration of all international differences, but public sentiment needs to be crystallized into effective form.
President Roosevelt's house of governors was a unique and worthy movement.
In dealing with state and national questions, it is bearing fruit, even if governors cannot make public sentiment.
You can go the ex-president one better by assembling the men who make the sentiment that makes and unmakes governors.
The press makes public sentiment, and most newspapers and magazines favor arbitration.
I hope you will call a meeting of the representatives of the press of the nation to be held in Washington at an early date to discuss the question of world peace and how to attain it. Arbitration of all differences between capital and labor should occupy an important place on the program.
WILLIAM C. DEMING, editor, *Wyoming Tribune*

This message resulted in an invitation to address the Lake Mohonk (N.Y.) conference on International Arbitration.

"I accepted, of course," said Mr. Deming, "although it required a great deal of assurance as Nicholas Murray Butler, president of Columbia University, was to preside over the meeting and the program listed speak-

WILLIAM HOWARD TAFT
the only man who has served as President and Chief Justice
of the United States

ers from Great Britain and a half dozen other important countries.

"I began immediately to prepare my address and feel that I gave it probably more thought and attention than any other effort in my experience. There were two results of consequence. First, an invitation from R. E. Olds, automobile manufacturer of Lansing, Michigan, to take charge of the *Michigan State Journal* at Lansing, with an option to purchase the same at a low price. The *Michigan State Journal* today is worth a half million dollars. Second, an award or honorarium of fifty dollars from the Carnegie Peace foundation which used the address in pamphlet form. It was also published as a congressional document."

Mr. Deming was unable to accept Mr. Olds's proposition because it would have necessitated leaving Wyoming.

"In most respects," he says, "I made more interesting contacts and friends in a short time at the Lake Mohonk conference on International Arbitration in 1912 and 1913 than upon any other occasion. My files show a large number of letters from prominent men and women, not only in this country but in other countries in the months following.

"I particularly recall the fine old Persian prophet, Abdul Bahai, whose writings and doctrines were much in vogue at that time. He was a delightful character and looked and acted as one might expect a prophet to appear. I received about two hundred calls for copies of my address. They came from Canada, Denmark, Germany, Argentina, Japan and other countries."

Mr. Deming attended the Lake Mohonk conference again in 1913. The meetings were discontinued later because of the World war.

A Trip to Europe

In the decade following his resignation from the United States land office (1913-1923), Mr. Deming's interests were widely varied. In addition to attending to his regular newspaper and real estate businesses, he continued to give liberally of his time to the promotion of civic and state improvements, and actively participated in politics. His relaxation came chiefly through his travels.

With a passport issued july 25, 1913 by William Jennings Bryan, Secretary of state, he set forth from Quebec on a journey to England and the Continent in the month of august.

In a booklet entitled, *Seeing Europe with the Editor of the Tribune,* he brought to his readers accurate and vivid word pictures of the places which he visited from Toronto to Rome and back to the New York harbor in october.

He was able to enjoy the ocean voyage through his characteristic tenacity which kept him "on deck." Over the north Atlantic strewn with icebergs "the ship rolled continually and pitched at intervals," he wrote. "Since we left the St. Lawrence and the Straits of Belle Isle and entered the open sea I have remained on deck in all kinds of weather and made the fight so far successfully against seasickness. There were vacant places at the table. By evening the ship's doctor said forty first-class passengers were sick. . . It has been a hard day to stay out because of the weather. . . All windows

and doors, even on the upper decks, are closed to keep
out the rain and spray which dashes over the decks.
I did not not put a piece of foolscap paper on my chest;
I did not take any anti-seasickness dope. I have simply
eaten judiciously and paced the deck, however difficult
to walk. On monday it was a great struggle. My head
at times felt as if it contained all the blood in my body.
I knew every minute I had a stomach and that it was
likely to get busy. Then I would find some place where
the wind was the strongest, fill my lungs and walk.
Fifteen or sixteen hours of that at a stretch on a heavily
rolling ship gets on the nerves, but the proper kind of
a fight will win and few men were sick because they
were willing to make the struggle and keep it up, hour
after hour. Many women stayed inside and were seasick.
Air and exercise are the best preventives."

Instead of the usual travelogue, overburdened with
detailed locations, dates, and names, Mr. Deming's
booklet stressed the people, their customs and habits,—
what they were doing and where they lived. Lights,
music, color, glamour, and human interest were woven
into the historical backgrounds of the various countries.
He made his readers hear with him the musical tinkle
of the bells and see the dipping of the flag in salute as
his steamer passed the boats, tugs, barges and rafts on
the Rhine; made them taste the juicy strawberries of
high Alpine valleys; and enabled them to catch the
strains of the municipal band playing in the public
square in Venice.

Soon after arriving in England, he wrote: "Warwick
Castle, right in the heart of this old city (Warwick)
overlooking the placid Avon river, gripped me as nothing else I have yet seen. It is the best preserved medieval
castle in England. When I was shown through this

mighty monitor of the past, this former habitat and ren-
dezvous of great lords and kings of England, I felt that
for the first time in my life I stood where Anglo-saxon
history was made. The castle was begun in 915 by a
daughter of King Alfred. The towers are more than
six hundred years old, and were built both for offensive
as well as defensive fighting. There are two acres in the
inner court, which is entirely surrounded by the castle
and turrets. Even as early as the Roman times, it is
believed, a fortress existed here."

In speaking of his visit to the Louvre in Paris and
other sites, he expressed the feeling that thousands of
travelers have experienced. "There is much that one
cannot remember or assimilate; he almost forgets where
he was yesterday or last week," Mr. Deming wrote,
"and at night would rather go to bed than anywhere
else in the wide, wide world. But in years to come as
he sees it in the books, on the stage, or at the biograph
show, it will all have a meaning and interest it never
had before. It creates a longing for knowledge."

A paragraph from his description of Venice says:
"Venice should not be judged by daylight. It is only
when the glimmer of the moon over the city and the
white light of electricity along the canals meet after
sunset that all imperfections vanish and Venice stands
forth soft, harmonious, insinuating and fascinating
beyond words."

From Pompeii Mr. Deming wrote: "Pompeii! At
last I am at the gates of this once buried city. All my
life, I think, I have looked forward to the day, and
like most Italian days in september, it is ideal, neither
too hot nor too cold and all around us except on the
old Pompeii side itself is evidence of business activity.
In front is the beautiful bay, dotted with boats, big and

little. On the shore I see them building a freighter or fishing boat of large dimensions, and building it in the open and building it all by hand, just about as I imagine the Pompeiians did two thousand years ago. Railway trains are dashing back and forth through the station, New Pompeii, outside the walls of the ancient city. Farms and truck gardens galore I noticed as I came in. It is about noon and strangely enough out of a party of fifteen no one rushed immediately to the gates of the excavated city, but went calmly to the hotel a few yards away, washed up, and got ready for an Italian dinner. For an hour we partook of this repast on the open portico of the hotel and listened to the American jazz of a rattling good Italian orchestra.

"And there was much finer music as well. No Italian orchestra would devote all its attention to ragtime. In the long waits between courses, American tourists did lively dances, much to the amusement, apparently, of the English and Germans who were also on pleasure bent but could not find it in their hearts to 'break loose' as the average American does when he is away from home.

"I mention all this as an indication of the seeming indifference of the tourist after he has been 'hitting the trail' for two or three months and gazing on a new film, as it were, every day. Why, the men even took time to smoke death-dealing Italian cigars before indicating to the guide that they were ready to step across the street and take a casual look at a former great city, which has been excavated from the ashes of Mt. Vesuvius. . . In one respect, at least, ancient Pompeii was ahead of Cheyenne. Its streets were all paved with blocks of stone and at all the corners there are adequate crossings made of higher blocks of stone. . . One of the most interesting sights now is to see the deep ruts worn in the street pavements by the continuous heavy wagon traffic two thousand years ago. . . There is evidence of communal or municipal housekeeping, as the bakeries, laundries, and other domestic utilities were elaborate with little or no facilities in the larger homes for these things. I imagine the saloons and soda fountains on the corners must have looked very much as they appear today, especially in Latin countries. . . One of the most remarkable things one sees in Pompeii is the evidence of an advanced knowledge of plumbing. They used lead pipe, and the stop-cocks and valves in the water fountains, park basins, and in their houses were very similar to those that we use today. One of the most elegant private buildings is the Home of the Tragic Poet, which, in the *Last Days of Pompeii,* is made the dwelling of Glaucus. On the threshold is a watchdog in mosaic, perfectly clear today with the inscription, *Cave Canem* (beware of the dog).

Mr. Deming concluded the account of his tour with: "There is something about the home-coming and docking of a ship after a long voyage that can only be felt; it cannot be described. The time seems interminable while the lilliputian tugs are swinging the big boat around to its pier. In the distance, the windows of your dock are filled with crowds of people waiting to receive friends or members of their family. Hundreds of hand-kerchiefs seem to be fluttering continually, and each one on the boat is endeavoring to identify someone in the composite throng. . . To the philosopher of life, the actual experience or the real trip abroad varies only from those in dreams from the fact that one results from the operation of the conscious mind when linked with the will and the way."

Mr. Deming's travels have at different times included Central America, Mexico, Cuba, the West Indies, and innumerable places and points of interest in the United States and Canada.

Political Reminiscences

In recalling various political events of the state, Mr. Deming says: "The Honorable Wallace C. Bond, president of the board of trustees, University of Wyoming from 1933 to 1941, came to Wyoming in 1896. When I reached Cheyenne in 1901, he was private secretary to Governor DeForest Richards. Mr. Bond served also as United States consul at Aden, Arabia, and Karachi, India, and was general-consul in Denmark.

"Mr. Bond probably has the best recollection of political events during the 1890's and later of any citizen of the state.

"Speaking of prominent republicans who practically dominated the situation for the most part during the first ten years of statehood, Mr. Bond would include Francis E. Warren, Joseph M. Carey, Clarence D. Clark, Frank W. Mondell, Willis Van Devanter, John A. Riner, William A. Richards, John W. Lacey, Timothy F. Burke, Benjamin Fowler, Richard H. Scott, J. A. Van Orsdel, Charles W. Burdick, Charles N. Potter, Otto Gramm, J. M. Rumsey, Jack Davis, and William E. Chaplin.

"According to Mr. Bond's memory, the defeat of Senator Warren for reelection to the United States senate resulted from the disaffection of senator DeForest Richards, of Douglas, representative Bryant B. Brooks, of Casper, and senator Fenimore Chatterton, of Rawlins. The reasons were rather more political than personal, Mr. Bond thinks, because Richards,

Brooks, and Chatterton were all prominent men and probably had not been included as fully in the inner councils of the republican party as they felt they should be. Inspection of the above list of republicans will show that practically all of them became very prominent in the higher elective and appointive offices of the state.

"DeForest Richards and B. B. Brooks in time joined the Warren organization, while Fenimore Chatterton remained a close friend and follower of Joseph M. Carey.

"Perhaps Mr. Bond's most interesting recollection is of an incident that occurred at the time of the Wyoming Industrial convention in Casper in 1904.

"A. J. Mokler of Casper, was owner and publisher of the *Natrona County Tribune*. He and Mrs. Mokler had invited Mr. and Mrs. M. C. Barrow of Douglas, Mr. and Mrs. Wallace C. Bond and W. C. Deming to become their guests during the convention.

"According to Mr. Bond, a short time prior to the meeting, Barrow, editor of *Bill Barlow's Budget* of Douglas, had written articles concerning gubernatorial candidates then in the field, including Acting-governor Fenimore Chatterton and the Honorable Bryant B. Brooks. Barrow was particularly caustic in dealing with Chatterton and some of his appointees. One scathing article which he wrote was about the state militia and particularly Adjutant-general Frank A. Stitzer, whom Barrow described as wearing 'celluloid cuffs that rattled when he walked.'

"At the time of the convention, the state militia was encamped in Casper for training. One day about the noon hour, a number of the militia men, forming a noisy and threatening group, came to the Mokler residence and demanded that 'Bill' Barrow be turned over to them. They proclaimed that they were going to toss him in a blanket and then duck him in the Platte river.

"This aroused the fighting spirit of Mr. Mokler, both because Barrow was his friend and his guest and because he believed in the old Anglo-saxon theory that a man's house is his castle.

"Mr. Mokler took from his gun cabinet a thirty-thirty Marlin rifle and, standing on the porch of his home, announced in a firm voice that he would shoot the first person who dared to enter his gate.

"The invaders hesitated, but did not immediately disperse. In the meantime, the news of the riot had spread and about half of the convention, headed by Francis E. Warren and the Honorable Patrick Sullivan, came to Mokler's house to help quiet the throng.

"Mr. Bond says, 'My recollection is clear on this matter because Mr. Deming and I stood beside Mr. Mokler during the incident, not because he needed any backing, but as a matter of courtesy to our host. Moreover, we both knew a number of the young men in the militia and felt that our presence there might have a calming effect.'

"In the first decade of this century, there were three brothers at Rawlins who had had unusual success as sheepmen, merchants, and bankers. They started from the scratch. Their names were Thomas A. Cosgriff, John B. Cosgriff, and James Cosgriff. The last named had become ambitious for political recognition.

"As the Cosgriff business interests throughout the state were large, young Cosgriff received considerable encouragement to become a candidate for governor against B. B. Brooks who had been elected for the unfinished two-year term of DeForest Richards, deceased. He entered the convention in 1906 but was defeated by Governor Brooks, whose administration had been creditable and who had a larger personal following.

"Mr. Bond says, 'My recollection is that the *Cheyenne Leader* supported Mr. Cosgriff and Deming's *Tribune* supported Governor Brooks.' "

Early in 1914, there was much speculation in the newspapers of the state as to the various candidates for state offices. On march 28, 1914, John W. Cook of Lander suggested that Deming run for governor. Other newspapers, including the *Hulett Globe,* took up the suggestion, and Mr. Deming received many letters urging him to enter the race. He did not have the desire and, moreover, thought all signs pointed to the election of state Senator John B. Kendrick of Sheridan by the democrats.

However, he did believe he could defeat Frank L. Houx, democratic secretary of state, then a candidate for re-election. The Honorable Charles W. Burdick, L. C. Hinkle and the republican organization generally thought so, too. They argued that Deming, having the *Tribune* as a spokesman, and being a good campaign speaker, would have Houx at a disadvantage, especially since the latter's cause had been weakened by certain criticism of his office and his policies in land and oil matters. The place on the ticket for secretary of state was held open for Deming until noon of the last day for filing.

When Deming finally decided against it, Birney H. Sage, a local contractor, filed. He was defeated.

From a personal political standpoint, Mr. Deming says, "It was the mistake of my life. I feel I could have won, and become acting-governor in 1916 when Governor Kendrick, who had defeated H. S. Ridgely, went to the senate. The fact that a republican secretary of state would become acting-governor would not have deterred Kendrick from running for the senate against the incumbent, the Honorable C. D. Clark. In politics it pays to enlist when the party organization and your friends are for you and wish you to enter, especially when all the circumstances are favorable. More than once I have failed to act along this line.

"One of the outstanding achievements of the legislature of 1915 was the passage of the Public Utilities bill and the independent judiciary law. Senator Ralph Kimball, now on the supreme court bench, took off his coat and pushed the entire republican platform or program through."

Under date of february 16, 1915, George E. Brimmer of Brimmer and Brimmer of Rawlins, Wyoming wrote Mr. Deming:

"I learned this morning that senate file number 5, Public Utilities bill, passed the house last evening. Too much credit cannot be given to you for the work which you did in behalf of this bill, and I feel that you are entitled to the thanks of the republican party for the earnest effort made by you through the *Tribune* to secure fulfillment of the platform pledges of the two parties."

After Europe became embroiled in war in 1914, Mr. Deming became more than ever an advocate of world peace, and he received nationwide recognition for his writings on the subject.

Although much opposed to war, he did everything in his power to assist his country when the United States entered the great conflict in 1917.

He was not, on account of his age, eligible to enlist for immediate active military service, but he applied through Senator F. E. Warren to the adjutant-general with the hope of being able to be assigned to duty in some capacity. His application was placed on file in the War department.

Having been so closely associated with Senator Warren and his family in Cheyenne, he knew personally General John J. Pershing, who had married Frances, the senator's daughter. While on a visit in Washington, Mr. Deming wrote on may 20, 1917: "I have never seen anything more unanimous or popular than the selection of General Pershing to lead the first expeditionary forces to France." And he predicted that General Pershing would be made a general of high enough rank to place him upon equal footing with Haig and Foch.

It may be of more than passing interest here to mention that while Senator Francis E. Warren was living and active in politics, his critics sought to discredit Pershing and incidentally reflect upon former President Theodore Roosevelt by asserting that Captain John J. Pershing's rapid promotions in the army were the result of political influence and favoritism.

Senator Warren felt very keenly such attacks and addressed a letter to former President Theodore Roosevelt when Roosevelt was doing magazine editorial work in New York for the *Outlook*.

Colonel Roosevelt answered promptly. The body of the letter was typewritten, followed by an emphatic, characteristic, final punch in Roosevelt's hand-writing. The reply speaks for itself:

November 18th, 1910

DEAR SENATOR WARREN: It does not seem to me that the quotation in question is capable of misconstruction, whether taken apart from its context or not. Your son-in-law was promoted so strictly on his own merits that I had absolutely forgotten that he was your son-in-law until I received your letter.

Even now, I cannot remember whether he was married to your daughter or engaged to her at the time he won the victory because of which I promoted him.

My impression is that he was not yet married to her. In any event, the promotion was made purely on the merits, and unless I am mistaken, you never spoke to me on the subject until I had announced that he was to be promoted.

The article that you enclosed from the *Washington Herald* is a tissue of malicious falsehoods. It is not a case of a man writing under an erroneous impression, it is a case of a man being guilty of malicious and wilful untruth. Faithfully yours,

THEODORE ROOSEVELT

(To promote a man because he marries a senator's daughter would be infamy; and to refuse him promotion for the same reason would be an equal infamy. T.R.)

General Pershing's fine record in the World war and his dignified conduct since amply justified President Theodore Roosevelt's judgment many years before Pershing was in command of the American forces in France.

With his usual foresight, Mr. Deming also said while in Washington: "Congress has a big task on its hands, and now thinks in terms of millions and billions instead of thousands as heretofore. . . The people of the nation should begin to realize that they are going to be taxed as never before . . . Perhaps we shall never return to the old schedules for raising revenue or to old standards of living."

Although not called to active service, Mr. Deming entered local war activities and assisted generally in Wyoming, with both Red Cross and Liberty Loan drives.

He took much pride in the *Tribune's* Service flag and through his editorial columns praised his staff members who were cruising the high seas or were in training camps. Upon the resignation of Fred L. Babcock from his staff, he wrote: "Next week, Fred L. Babcock, reporter and general news man, will proceed to some training camp, probably at American Lake, Washington. Babcock is going to be profoundly missed in the *Tribune* office and on the street. He is a star reporter and has a way of making everyone his friend. . . His smile is perennial and probably has a great deal to do with his success as a news gatherer."

Upon the insistence of friends in many parts of the state, Mr. Deming decided to enter the race for congress in 1918 to succeed Frank W. Mondell, who had decided to run for the senate, Senator Warren having considered retirement.

The following letter shows that Senator Warren really desired to retire at the end of his fifth term:

United States Senate, Committee on Engrossed Bills
Washington, D.C. April 2, 1917
Hon. Patrick Sullivan, Chairman, Wyoming Republican Central
Committee, Casper, Wyoming.
Dear Senator Sullivan: I regret extremely my failure to see you during my brief visit in Wyoming.

You were East and I was almost immediately ordered back in public duty, thus a personal interview was impossible, hence this letter to advise you of what I then desired to say.

To be so soon summoned back to Washington after my arrival in Cheyenne emphasized and strengthened my decision not to be a candidate in the next election to succeed myself as United States senator.

For the last few years, Washington has claimed so much of me that my business interests and I have been almost strangers, and what has grieved me far more has been the scant time and opportunity afforded me for cultivating old, and making new, friendships and acquaintances among the rapidly increasing Wyoming constituency; and for making of more frequent tours throughout all of the magnificent Wyoming, of which I have so long been proud to be an humble part.

I feel I owe to you as chairman of the republican party of Wyoming this early announcement so that the ball may be set rolling and that party organization and endeavor may not await, but instead, may push forward in earnest an early effort to select, and elect, not only my successor but an entire ticket from its abundant number of patriotic, loyal, deserving members.

Wyoming in electing me five times to the United States senate, and also to various other positions and offices of honor and trust, has honored me far beyond my deserts. This I freely acknowledge and I wish I might adequately express how profoundly grateful to legions of valued friends I am, and shall always be, for this trust and confidence reposed in me.

In return for this generous preferment, I have ever striven to do my best for our commonwealth and country, under all conditions and circumstances, and my determination is to continue to do so, not only during the remainder of my term of office, but as a private citizen thereafter.

I feel that I have now reached a time of life when I have earned the privilege of enjoying some rest and recreation, and of being able to devote more time to my private business, family, and friends which constantly increasing public duties have forced me, in a measure, to neglect.

Let us nominate and put to the front in the contest of 1918 a selection of our best material, those who will give the best that is in them of continuous energetic, efficient statesmanship. If we do this, success will surely be ours at the polls, and what is still more important than party success, we shall have the honor and just approbation which always follows industrious, intelligent and honest effort. Yours sincerely,

F. E. WARREN

When the possibility of Mr. Deming's becoming a candidate was mentioned, the *Cody Herald* said of him:

Without doubt, he has a wider state and national vision than any other man within our borders. His intimate knowledge of the needs as well as the opportunities of Wyoming is so accurate and his interest so keen and ability so marked that he stands head and shoulders above his peers. He is the logical successor to Mr. Mondell . . . for twenty years Wyoming has benefited and will continue to profit by the progressive and constructive policies of W. C. Deming. His work as a live newspaper publisher as well as the patriotic service rendered on various state boards which have functioned acceptably will be lasting.

A. G. Spillman of Burns on january 22, 1918, expressed the sentiment of hundreds of Wyoming citizens when he said:

Mr. Deming has the interests of the entire state at heart and always works fearlessly and faithfully for the upbuilding and advancement of the peoples' interests. He advances more ideas, advocates more reforms and improvements than any other man in the state. He has done more than any other one man toward settling up and developing the great resources of the state. Especially the agricultural interests. He knows the needs and requirements of all the people, therefore is better qualified than any other man in the state to represent you, regardless of your business, vocation, or location.

In urging Mr. Deming to run in the primaries for congress, the *Laramie Republican* said:

Mr. Deming's training in the law, and his experience gained in the United States land office at Cheyenne at a time when that office was not only very busy but had an almost endless variety of problems presented to it, is of the utmost value for such a position. . . Mr. Deming has been very successful as a man of affairs, all his business ventures having turned out well . . . his friends have always pointed with pride to the fact that every board on which he has ever served, or any public enterprise with which he has been connected, has never had a deficit . . . his newspaper, although always staunchly republican, has ever been progressive in its tone and it has many reforms to its credit, perhaps the biggest one being the sentiment that it built up for the present state depository law. . .

Robert D. Carey, the gubernatorial candidate, also thought Deming would strengthen the ticket, as Cheyenne was entitled to a place.

With the stage seemingly set for a successful campaign for the house of representatives, Mr. Deming learned that Senator F. E. Warren, who had hoped to retire, had, upon the insistence of many friends, announced his intention again to become a candidate for the United States senate and that Frank W. Mondell had withdrawn from the senatorial race and would again run for congress. Immediately Mr. Deming withdrew from the race.

Many of the state editors commented upon the withdrawal and praised Mr. Deming for his unselfishness. Said the *Basin Republican:* "Mr. Deming can wield a great influence for good in the state by giving his personal attention to the management of the *Tribune* which is one of the leading exponents of independent journalism in the state."

Mr. Deming threw his whole hearted support into the campaign for the election of Warren and Mondell, and Robert D. Carey, with successful results.

In 1922 there were only two leading republican candidates for governor – the incumbent, Governor Robert D. Carey and the Honorable John W. Hay, of Rock Springs. It was an ardently fought contest and Mr. Hay won.

In the general election which followed, by reason of some temporary split in the party, William B. Ross, democrat, a young attorney, was elected. Governor Ross did not live to complete the first half of his four year term. Secretary of state, Frank E. Lucas, becoming acting-governor.

At a special election in 1924, the republicans nominated the Honorable E. J. Sullivan of Casper and the democrats nominated Mrs. Nellie Tayloe Ross, widow of the deceased governor, William B. Ross. Mrs. Ross was elected.

In 1926 among those more actively mentioned as republican eligibles were the Honorable Frank C. Emerson, state engineer, and the Honorable Frank F. Lucas, secretary of state. Others who received some consideration by their friends were the Honorable William

E. Chaplin, who doubtless could have been nominated and elected, and likewise the Honorable George E. Brimmer, the Honorable Patrick J. Sullivan, the Honorable J. M. Schwoob and the Honorable J. C. Underwood.

Mr. Emerson was nominated and elected. Governor Emerson served four years and was reelected in november 1930, but died in february 1931. Secretary of state, Alonzo M. Clark, became acting-governor until january 1933 when the vacancy was filled by the election of Leslie A. Miller, democrat. Governor Miller served efficiently for a period of six years until january 1939.

"Over a period of nearly thirty years," says Mr. Deming, "I rarely missed a republican state convention. It was my privilege, on many occasions, to serve as chairman of the resolutions committee. During the troublesome days from 1908 to 1920 when the party was more or less divided or in a process of liberalization, so-called, I made an effort along with many others to keep a bit ahead of public sentiment or, at least, to go along with it in order to deprive the democratic party of the advantage which would accrue by its advocacy and origination of progressive legislation.

"This was particularly true of conventions held in Casper, Sheridan and Cheyenne. Doubtless the 1914 convention in the Knights of Columbus hall in Cheyenne took the prize for voluminous and liberal proposals. J. Ross Carpenter had constituted himself a local leader and Governor John B. Kendrick's political star was in the ascendant. They set a very lively pace, so much so that many republicans thought it folly and dangerous to attempt to compete with them.

"However, as chairman of the resolutions committee,

supported by men like Attorney A. H. Maxwell, of
Lander; Editor C. Watt Brandon of Sheridan, now of
Kemmerer; L. L. Newton of Cody, now of Lander;
George E. Brimmer, then of Rawlins; S. H. Sibley, of
Burns; and Charlie Harkins, of Worland, I brought
in a list of resolutions suggesting certain legislation,
that seemed to stun the delegates.

"I recall particularly the expression on the face of
my highly esteemed friend, John W. Hay of Rock
Springs, as the resolutions were reeled off one by one.
Mr. Hay stood somewhat on the border line between
progressivism and conservatism, but the committee's
proposed program was almost too much for John. He
once told me in his courteous manner: 'Deming, you
are going in the right direction but why travel so
damned fast. Leave something for the future.' However, after he had become the republican candidate for
governor in 1922, I am sure he was glad that matters
like an independent judiciary, a public utilities bill,
workmen's compensation, and various other regulatory
acts were already upon the statute books."

In february 1919, Governor Robert D. Carey announced the appointment of the following new members
of the board of trustees of the University of Wyoming:
Mrs. Mary Brooks of Casper, Dr. E. W. Croft of Cow-
ley, the Honorable W. C. Deming of Cheyenne, and
the Honorable C. P. Arnold of Laramie. Holdover
members of the board were: L. H. Brooks, C. S. Beach,
Doctor A. B. Hamilton, C. D. Spaulding, and Katherine Morton, superintendent of public instruction,
ex-officio.

This appointment was a worthy tribute to Mr. Deming's interest in education, his fine business judgment
and his high standing in the state.

In making the announcement of the appointment, the *Laramie Republican* said:

Mr. Deming is a man who believes in doing things and doing them in a big way. He has had much experience in educational matters and will give the university the benefit of rare business training. He belongs to that class of business men who are of the opinion that trustees have a responsibility to perform and that if they fail to exercise their powers they render themselves liable to severe public criticism. . . The Wyoming State University owns a million dollars worth of lands, some of them producing oil, and able men are needed on the board.

Mr. Deming was elected vice-president of the board and was placed at the head of a committee charged with getting at the bottom of university business and with recommending the most approved methods and the best possible means of getting the highest efficiency out of the institution.

The proposed law school received his earnest support and it was opened in september 1920, with a complete three-year course beyond the pre-legal work leading to the L.L.B. degree. Harrison C. Dale (now president of the University of Idaho), was in charge of the new school.

Later as president of the board of trustees, Mr. Deming, with others, was active in bringing about the acquisition of lands adjoining the university grounds in order to enlarge the campus and straighten its boundaries, as urged by President Crane. He recognized the need of a fiscal agent and assisted in creating that office, which has proved of tremendous value. He urged and helped bring about the adoption of a general building plan, including symmetrical beautification of the grounds, and assisted in the building of the gymnasium-armory.

As president of the board, Mr. Deming was assisted by Dean Prosser of Tie Siding, vice-president; Fred Geddes, Deerwood, treasurer; and F. A. Holliday of Laramie, Mrs. Avery Haggard of Cheyenne, J. A. Elliott of Wheatland, Governor Ross and Katherine A. Morton.

During Mr. Deming's regime President A. G. Crane was selected to head the institution, and the University of Wyoming "Cowboys" gave the new president and his family a wild and woolly welcome. Upon the invitation of Mr. Deming, the Crane family left the Union Pacific at Cheyenne to make the last fifty-one miles of their journey in Mr. Deming's automobile over the Lincoln highway. About four miles out of Laramie, an avalanche of students dressed in cowboy attire swept down upon the auto, held up the passengers and commanded them to dismount. The surprised newcomers were then escorted to an old Overland stage coach in which were seated Doctor and Mrs. Aven Nelson, the retiring president and his wife. Shouts of "Powder River, Let 'er Buck," rent the air. The new arrivals were escorted to the County Fair grounds on the east edge of Laramie where the grandstand was filled with Wyoming citizens. There a six-gallon hat was presented to the new "King of the cowboys."

Mr. Deming says, "President Crane, in twenty years, accomplished more than all his predecessors had achieved, but they had laid an excellent foundation."

Upon his appointment as president of the Civil Service commission in Washington, early in 1923, Mr. Deming presented his resignation as a member of the board of trustees. The resignation was not, at that time, accepted. Instead, he was urged to wait until june before resigning – to return for commencement and then to announce his intentions.

Doctor Crane said of him: "Mr. Deming's ability and public-spirited interest in the welfare of the young people have made him a dependable friend of the institution."

One of the most eminent alumni of the University said upon his resignation: "If he is as good in the new job as he was a trustee of the University, he will be a credit to Wyoming. I think he was the best trustee the University ever had."

The late Charles Maxwell, dean of the department of education, said he expressed the opinion of his associates in the faculty in commending Mr. Deming's sound judgment and keen insight into the problems of the University.

Mr. Deming has often remarked that of the honors and recognitions accorded him in Wyoming, he really enjoyed most his work as president of the board of trustees of the University of Wyoming. He values highly his election as an honorary member of Alpha chapter, Phi Beta Kappa of the University of Wyoming.

The interest in the welfare of the University of Wyoming, which was aroused through his active membership on the board of trustees, has continued through the years.

Mr. Deming felt that the University was fortunate in finding so worthy a successor to Doctor Crane in the selection of President J. L. Morrill, former vice-president of Ohio State University. Doctor Morrill came to the campus in 1941, during strenuous times. With an unusually fine personality, with much ability as a public speaker and editor, and being, to use a popular term, an all-round mixer, he has won a place of high esteem among the students, the alumni, and the people of the state.

Cowboy Reception to Dr. Crane

By Alice E. Wright

Escorting Dr. Arthur Crane and his family into Laramie, Wyoming.

Presentation of the "Six Gallon Hat" to Dr. Crane.

Dr. and Mrs. Crane in the old Overland Coach.

Arrival of guests at Fair Grounds, W.C. Deming at right. University of Wyoming Cowboys "Holding Up" the New Prexy.

Soon after being chosen a member of the board of trustees at the University of Wyoming, Mr. Deming was elected to the board of trustees of the Frances Warren Pershing Memorial hospital of Laramie county, of which John W. Lacey was president, and John A. Martin, Samuel Corson, and James Dolan were members.

Under a law of the state of Wyoming, counties are authorized to build at the county seat memorial hospitals when as much as twenty-five thousand dollars has been raised by donations. By a popular vote of the people, bonds may be issued to be used in erecting such a hospital.

The board of commissioners of Laramie county, acting under such authority, accepted from the Honorable Francis E. Warren and his son, Fred E. Warren, a gift of twenty-five thousand dollars to be used for a memorial hospital. In recognition of the gift, the hospital was christened the Frances Warren Pershing Hospital to honor the daughter and sister of the donors.

At a special election held april 21, 1919, a bond issue of seventy-five thousand dollars was authorized. The remaining funds were solicited as memorial gifts by the board of citizens. Some of these gifts were acknowledged by metal door-plates in the hospital. William R. Coe, then of Park county, gave fifty thousand dollars. In all, the board raised more than three hundred thousand dollars and turned over a modern hospital, well-equipped, and with no indebtedness except the county bond issue.

Mr. Deming remained a member of the hospital board until he took up his duties with the Civil Service commission in Washington in 1923.

The Purchase of the Cheyenne Leader

In the summer of 1920, The Tribune company began negotiations for the purchase of the *Cheyenne Leader,* Wyoming's oldest newspaper. On july 12, Leslie A. Miller, one of the owners, telegraphed Mr. Deming, who was in the East, as follows: "Am now in position to make offer to you of franchise subscription list and good will of *Leader* at six thousand dollars, this based on theory you would not need the physical equipment stop if you need any machinery make an offer on same please wire at once your disposition toward above offer and when you will be home."

From Chicago Deming wired, "Am interested in buying *Leader.* Will see you Wednesday morning at ten o'clock."

July 15, 1920, the *Tribune* purchased the *Leader* from its officers, Leslie A. Miller, Thomas Hunter and Randolph Leigh, and announced that the: *"Cheyenne State Leader* will continue to be operated from the *Tribune* office as a morning and sunday newspaper."

The *Leader* had been published continuously since september 19, 1867 when Cheyenne was a boom settlement in a wild and woolly period. The Union Pacific railroad, building westward to a junction with the Central Pacific, had not yet reached the townsite. This region was then in Dakota. There were only provisional town and county governments, set up by serious-minded persons who realized the necessity for some measure of enforcement of law and order. The railroad did not reach the settlement until november 13, 1867.

Before the end of the year, three hundred commercial enterprises, representing every branch of business and supplying all demands of this great human herd, were operating in Cheyenne. The population in 1868 was six thousand – grown to that number in less than a year. The appellation Magic City was apt.

It was in such a place and atmosphere that N. A. Baker set up the newspaper which was purchased by Mr. Deming. Writing of this pioneer venture, Mr. Baker said:

On saturday morning, july 6, 1867, at Denver, the first number of the *Colorado Leader* was issued. This was by the writer. Business conditions then not being promising, the plant was transported by wagons to the site of Cheyenne, four assistants and the writer arriving there early in september.

The conditions on our arrival were these: A young city in the feverish excitement of early making. The Union Pacific road had not yet reached Cheyenne, but was there a few weeks later. Building of stores and shops was very active, and for many days was carried on days, nights, and sundays.

There was but one building in town that yet had a floor in it. This the writer was able to secure for the *Leader*. This was a log building with a store front in it belonging to E. A. Allen.

On thursday, september 19, 1867, we were able to issue our first number of the *Cheyenne Leader*. There were on the street opposite the postoffice, which was on Eddy street, fully three hundred men, all eager to get a copy of the first paper, for each of which was paid twenty-five cents.

This was a fine thing for the writer, as it had taken all his money to pay for his team transportation to the Magic City. He could now pay for his board, at the Bell House, and pay his assistants on the paper.

The *Leader* prospered from that time on, and was soon able to increase its facilities for business.

In 1869, Baker suffered the loss of his printing plant by fire, and shortly thereafter he sold the *Leader* to

Major Herman Glafcke. In the 1880's, Glafcke sold it to Morrow and Sullivan. In 1890 it was sold to John F. Carroll and Joseph A. Breckons, who in 1895 sold the *Leader* to E. A. Slack, Carroll going to the Denver *Post* and Breckons becoming Senator Warren's private secretary. Shortly after the turn of the century, Colonel Slack sold the *Leader* to Wallace C. Bond, his son-in-law, and Harry Clark. In 1909, W. S. Edmiston purchased the *Leader,* which in time was acquired by a democratic syndicate. In 1920, the *Leader* was bought by William C. Deming and merged with the *Tribune*.

The names of the *Tribune* and *Leader,* also that of *Cheyenne Sun,* appeared at the masthead of the new *Tribune-Leader*.

In 1920, the predictions about air service which the *Tribune* had made a decade before came true. Cheyenne became an important port on the transcontinental air line.

A municipal airport, of several acres, north of the city, was laid out. Cheyenne erected the original hangars, which in time were replaced by substantial brick buildings. The Boeing company was succeeded by the United Air Lines, which with the Inland Air Lines for north and south traffic, now has modern equipment and housing at the port.

On august 19, 1920, Victor B. Smith, managing editor of the *Omaha Daily Bee,* sent the following letter by air to Mr. Deming:

The *Omaha Bee,* upon the occasion of the inauguration of air mail service between Omaha and Cheyenne, felicitates its Wyoming neighbor upon this new application of science which brings the two cities so much closer together. Scarcely more than fifty years ago, it was a week's journey from Omaha to Cheyenne; the Union Pacific railroad reduced the time until its fast trains now carry the mail in twelve hours; the air mail will now cut this to five or possibly four hours. This, coupled with the general growth and development of both Nebraska and Wyoming, will undoubtedly bring the two states closer together as the years go by.

On september 7, 1920, the second assistant postmaster-general sent a letter to Mr. Deming by the first dispatch over the Trans-continental air mail which conveyed the appreciation of the postmaster-general and himself for "the assistance that you have been in making effective this great forward step in expeditious transportation of the mails."

On the same day, Mr. Deming sent a message by the first mail airplane to be dispatched from Cheyenne to Salt Lake City. In his letter to A. N. McKay, general manager of the *Salt Lake Tribune,* he said: ". . . I trust that we shall both live to see the day when I shall receive the *Salt Lake Tribune* through the air, and you in turn shall receive our paper in the same manner."

The plane which was scheduled to leave the airport at Cheyenne at 5:30 A.M. was scheduled to arrive in Salt Lake City at 9:55 A.M.

A letter sent from Cheyenne to Mr. Deming on the first trip involving night flying left Cheyenne july 1, 1924, at 7:10 P.M. and arrived at Washington july 3, at 4:00 A.M.

Today, Cheyenne has one of the finest airports in the United States, with passenger and mail planes flying day and night, east and west, and north and south. The repair shops are large and modern, employing several hundred men and women. They are used also by the U.S. Army bombers.

Mr. Deming served at various times on many of the

important Cheyenne reception committees for visits of dignitaries, including President Wilson, General Pershing, and others.

When General Pershing returned to Wyoming in 1920, after the close of the World war, Deming was one of a committee that met him in Greeley, Colorado, and escorted him into Cheyenne. On this committee were: H. S. Ridgely, J. W. Hammond, B. B. Brooks, C. B. Richardson, Mayor Ed. P. Taylor, W. C. Deming, Curtis Hinkle, John W. Hay, E. W. Stone, C. L. Rigdon, W. E. Chaplin, Fred E. Warren, John Boyd, D. A. Preston, Charles Irwin, William Jeffers, Harry Fisher, Colonel M. O. Bigelow, T. B. Kennedy, Randolph Leigh, Harry P. Hynds, W. C. Johnson, and Charles E. Lane.

Some Early Romances[6]

I scarcely can remember when my heart was not alive to sentiment and my mind filled with romance — if such a distinction is permissible.

The summer of 1886 marked an epoch in my life. I was preparing in various ways to enter college in september, but there was one welcome and pleasant interruption. In july an attractive and mentally-alert girl, of my own age, arrived from a far-away state to spend the summer with an aunt, who was a close friend of our family. The young visitor was hardly settled when I was invited to call and help make things pleasant for her.

I had enjoyed passing, youthful flirtations with some of the home girls, but nothing serious. Even then I had conceived the idea or adopted the theory that opposites in eyes and hair and complexion were most likely to find common ground for interest and enjoyment.

Lo and behold! The visitor was exactly all I had felt an opposite should be. Moreover, she had a spritely mind and a magnetic personality. The result — I saw her every day, usually in the evening, for long strolls or driving in my side-bar buggy through quiet lanes.

The day for leaving home and entering college arrived. Very tactfully, but firmly, it was hinted by my parents that I should spend the last evening with them or at least return very early after bidding my brown-eyed girl friend goodbye. I promised, no doubt, but

6 Upon request, Mr. Deming has written this chapter. A.W.S.

completely lost track of time. Perhaps I did not have a watch. The hours fairly flew. More likely because her name was Bird. At any rate, when I reached home the house was absolutely dark. All members of the family had retired – unduly early, I thought.

I rapped at my parents' door and found them, especially my father, very much aggrieved. He stated briefly that all plans for leaving on the morrow for college were cancelled and suggested that I unpack my things and look for a job at home. The situation was embarrassing, especially as he had not yet handed me the necessary funds for a railroad ticket, and other expenses incident to entering Allegheny college. I went to bed, got some sleep, arose very early, called the family, carried my bags to the front veranda, ate breakfast, and began my au revoirs. By this time my father had relented somewhat, aided no doubt by a word from my mother. The cash was forthcoming and I started on my journey with high hope, ambition, and determination to devote all my time to my studies.

At least, I reasoned there must be no love affair. The school was co-educational, so there was safety in numbers.

Fraternity life, the debating society, an occasional good show or opera adequately supplemented my studies. Frankness impels me to say that I was not a great student outside of the lines which most appealed to me, to wit, literature, languages, debating, and political economy. The sciences and higher mathematics were more or less difficult.

The second year found me adhering to my program – for a time at least.

Strolling down Highland avenue with a breezy co-ed on a beautiful october afternoon, suddenly something happened.

As if she had seen a specter or an angel drop from the sky, my companion rushed across the street and beckoned for me to follow.

"This," she said, "is a friend and chum, Ellen Bowman, who has just returned from a year abroad."

We were near the sorority house of the girl who had interrupted my stroll with the buxom sophomore. Mostly I stood on the side lines and listened while the two girls chattered. I also made a survey. The returned friend or chum was about the most attractive thing in skirts I had ever seen. Her voice was soft and musical, she was slender and graceful and most divinely fair.

Indeed, she was a blonde, with eyes of blue, as light as my own.

Just how or why or under what circumstances I saw her again soon I do not now recall. But all my theories as to contrasts were upset, and my resolution not to become interested in any woman while in college was demolished.

I must here crowd two years of romance into a few lines. The long time I would have to wait before being able to support a wife would not appeal to any girl, it seemed to me. I could not, therefore, conscientiously monopolize her time, even if she were willing, although I made a pretty good hand at the job. She was too fine in every way to escape other admirers. In due time she married one of them and carried with her my sincerest wishes for a long and happy life. Today in the fullness of her motherhood and widowhood, she is still a splendid example of womanhood – happy and healthy as anyone might wish to be.

Even now, I am not forgetful of my first real college romance, which was almost as much spiritual as otherwise in its influence upon my youth and my outlook on the years to come.

The eldest in a family of children enjoys certain advantages as well as disadvantages. I sensed very early the deep affection of parents for offspring and vice versa. As I grew older, I observed a subtle distinction – the father's pride in his sons and daughters when they merited it and a mother's love under all conditions.

Being more in the company of the maternal ancestor, I think we almost took our mother and her ministrations for granted. She read our minds, understood our emotions, and enveloped us at all times with affection and understanding.

Father, aside from being frequently detained all day in court or his office, often did not come home for the noonday meal. Moreover, he was a great traveler, sometimes with members of his family and at other times alone. A result was, we did not see him as many hours of the day as we saw our mother and I recall, as if it were yesterday, the sensation of pleasure and satisfaction experienced as I saw him approaching the home at the end of the day or upon his return from a long journey.

Then, too, it was apparent that my sister, as she developed, probably understood our parents better than the brothers did and was in a way nearer to them, if that were possible. All this accentuated in my mind the thought that without children and family interest and affection, life is incomplete.

For a few years out of college, I kept myself well in hand, devoted my time largely to my work, though feeling in the very nature of things I would meet my fate.

In the old aristocratic Ohio town to which I had migrated, I soon acquired quite a circle of congenial friends – even among the young ladies. They were of the best families and best minds of the community and I spent many congenial hours with them. However, I remained heart-whole and fancy-free.

The early association with Zell P. Hart in the *Tribune* office was stimulating because of her intense interest in our mutual problems incident to a growing business. Occasionally, I called at her home, at first to discuss and complete some new plan for improving the paper. Her baby daughter, Helen, a sweet blonde child, was cared for during the day by her grandmother, Mrs. Mary Douglas Smith. Mrs. Smith's unselfish devotion to her daughter and granddaughter was no small part of Zell's life, for without the knowledge that Nannie (Helen's childhood name for her grandmother) was there at home with Helen, Zell would not have been able to go out and make her place in the business world. I became very fond of Helen, more so, I think, because I had seen comparatively little of young children in recent years. It was apparent that her mother, who was so businesslike in the office, changed to a more feminine role at home. Her common sense heels for walking and her skirts shorter than those in vogue at that time were exchanged for slippers and becoming house gowns.

During our business talks, she rarely failed to pick up her mending or do some exquisite needlework. As time passed, she understood my interest in books and desire to improve my mind along cultural lines. She also did pastel sketching. In fact, it seemed, she excelled in anything to which she turned her hand.

She was among the first in her community to become interested in Bernarr MacFadden and his magazine *Physical Culture,* and later in life visited his popular sanitarium in Dansville, New York. He became the publisher of *Liberty* and other magazines.

Being a lover of good poetry, art, and books, some of which I had not had time to read or study, without special effort she introduced all of these into our evenings at her home. She rarely sat with idle hands.

It was her way. She had a strong will and indefatigable energy. I had been accustomed from my college days to taking the lead in many things. While there was much she could contribute to my welfare and enjoyment, she frequently and frankly stated I had not only given her an opportunity to do much for herself, but, out of my experience, had shown her how to do it. She was always deeply appreciative.

Thus the long hours and hard work at the office were relieved by these weekly or sometimes semi-weekly exchange of ideas. Yet for a long time no suggestion of sentiment entered in. When it was introduced, it was analyzed and questioned by reason of our somewhat contrasting temperaments. I had not known a woman quite so independent, quite so self-assertive, and quite so capable, and withal so attractive as she. My acquaintances and friends in Kentucky, in college, and even in Warren had been more of the conventional type and few of them had ever done anything outside of the home.

Our lives presented striking differences, and that very fact began to influence our feelings and sharpen our mutual interest. Perhaps it was in keeping with the theory as to the positive and negative poles of a galvanic battery, except that I was sometimes on the positive end and she the negative, while at others these viewpoints were reversed.

Her sense of humor was very keen and enlivened our labors. Years before congress enacted a pure food and drugs act, when reading proof, she laughed heartily at the extreme claims of the patent medicine advertising and said there should be a law against such misleading statements. Her smile was effective with everyone who came to the office. The ensemble embraced an unusual coordination of her very dark brown eyes, black hair, and full lips, which at times took on something of a gentle curl.

Zell Hart and I continued to discuss our problem, but reached no conclusion. That was about the situation when I decided to accept the offer to edit the *Tribune* in Cheyenne, Wyoming.

She evidenced much interest in my enterprise, though somewhat doubtful of its wisdom and desirability, except possibly from the standpoint of my health.

Naturally, because of our mutual business interests, we corresponded frequently. In order to keep in touch with the Ohio paper, in which I had a controlling interest, and to see my relatives in the east and south, I returned about twice a year.

I had found many attractive friends in Wyoming. Zell Hart grew with her responsibility and I was absorbed with mine.

During a trip to Warren in 1906, I was especially impressed by her poise and charm, whether in the office or in her home. Nevertheless I did not propose. Returning to Cheyenne, it occurred to me if I expected to marry and enjoy children before long past middle age, I should think seriously about it now. I spent days and nights wrestling with the subject. At last the die was cast.

A short time later I proposed by letter but somewhat to my disappointment, she did not accept by return mail, but took some days for consideration.

Her reply was delicate and appropriate, setting forth

the pros and cons, many of them repetitions of my own doubts through the years. From her position, the chief hurdles were leaving her mother and Helen, even temporarily, placing responsibility of the growing *Tribune* in less experienced hands, and, lastly, her intuitive feeling against the far West. Her every instinct was a product of the New England spirit transplanted in the Connecticut reserve of Ohio.

She urged me to return to Warren, which I could not do, as I had been promised a well-paid federal position, the *Tribune* was developing rapidly as an influential state paper, and I had made considerable progress as a political factor in the state.

She at last agreed to come to Cheyenne, but asked for several months to prepare for the change of residence and adaptation to new circumstances.

A few years before, Griffin Cochran, news editor, and James H. Walton, business manager of the *Tribune,* and I had purchased a house at 216 E. 21st street. We furnished it simply and enjoyed our bachelor quarters there.

We had entered into a gentleman's agreement that the one who married first would be given an opportunity to buy the interest of the other two. To the surprise of both Mr. Walton and myself, young Cochran, after a few months, announced his engagement and took over the home.

After Zell and I had decided upon our future, I did not relish the idea of beginning housekeeping in a rented place. Furthermore, I was naturally inclined to begin paying for a home of my own.

I bought a modest, six-room, one story house on Van Lennen avenue. I sent Zell the measurements of all rooms and she began at once buying or having made

In her early twenties

Society editor of the Warren (Ohio)
Tribune

At the time of her marriage to
William C. Deming

ZELL HART DEMING

suitable furniture. All these and other preparations extended our engagement to nearly one year. In my opinion, long engagements are not desirable.

However, the time passed and we were wedded in Cleveland june 14, 1907. The Reverend A. A. Abbott, D.D., a former Episcopalian minister in Warren and special friend of Zell Hart, performed the ceremony. We enjoyed a brief honeymoon trip to East Aurora, N.Y., and an opportunity to become pretty well acquainted with those unique characters, Mr. and Mrs. Elbert Hubbard, who conducted the attractive Roycroft Shop and Inn and published a tabloid magazine of national and international fame called *The Philistine*. The Hubbards were lost when the "Lusitania" was sunk by the Germans in the World war.

While our house in Cheyenne was old, I doubt whether there was another home in the community furnished in better taste, most of it being solid mahogany and the floors were covered with oriental rugs. Curtains, draperies, and pictures were in harmony with the general plan.

We kept a maid, who came in mornings and remained until after the evening meal.

The result was Mrs. Deming was not very busy. She made friends easily, but found difficulty in passing the time, as Cheyenne offered little in the way of amusement or diversion from day to day. We entertained some and enjoyed our friends.

Among the families prominent in Cheyenne at that time were the Hunter, Abbott, Brewster, Boyd, Johnston, Kinkead, Burdick, Kennedy, Matson, Boice, Walton, Clark, Burrage, Conway, Marble, Warren, Whitaker, Freeborn, Smith, Carey, Van Tassell, Ross, Henderson, and Richardson.

Zell urged me to permit her to come into the *Tribune* office in some capacity. I did not think it advisable for many reasons, as I had sufficient help and there might arise the question of rank and authority. I continued to edit the *Tribune* while performing my duties as receiver of public moneys in the United States land office. The local land boom and homesteading era was on and we were very busy.

When summer came in 1908, we both went east, I to attend a national republican convention, and she and Helen to see her mother. Zell put in considerable time in the *Warren Tribune* office, and found much to do, as the general management had been left in the hands of a young man who had not had very complete experience.

In the fall she returned to Cheyenne and Helen entered a girls' school in Denver. About the same program was followed the second winter. We read books, attended the few road shows at the Capitol theater, went to Denver occasionally, and to all intents and purposes led a satisfactory life. She was always interesting and always eager to travel or do something worth while. She resisted idleness and detested indolence.

When summer came again, the lure of the elms and oaks and maples of Ohio called. She never quite adjusted herself to a treeless country. She said something was missing in nature. Each year she prolonged her visits in the east and each year I made fewer trips to Warren, although I still owned a controlling interest in the *Warren Tribune*.

In 1913 we agreed that it was not an altogether satisfactory way of living, especially as I was keeping up a home in Cheyenne and she one for her mother in Warren. We abandoned housekeeping. Zell moved back

about 1920

about 1930

to Warren and I took an apartment in the Deming building, reserving only my books and enough furniture for the purpose. We maintained a regular correspondence and I visited Warren from time to time.

The World war and the United States participation later absorbed much of our thought, as every business was directly or indirectly affected. She developed rapidly as a newspaper publisher and my responsibilities in Wyoming increased at a rapid rate. In time, we both came to feel that our married life under such circumstances, she living in Ohio and I in Wyoming, was difficult in various ways.

In the early part of 1918, while on a visit east, the question of a divorce was raised. I felt she might wish to marry again and there was yet time for me to do so if fate should decree such a thing. Neither of us, however, had any such plan or purpose. It was just the prospect that both might improve upon the existing situation and be relieved of certain restrictions which hampered our goings and comings which influenced us. There had never been a divorce in her immediate family nor in mine, hence neither fancied the new role, but finally accepted it, although she remarked that she would be willing to go on as it was. As I see it now, she probably was right and it might have been better to preserve the status quo.

Fortunately, Ohio permitted annulment of marriage on the grounds of willful absence for three years. She had been living in Warren since 1913 and I had continued my residence in Cheyenne, Wyoming. So that part was easy.

I had so much confidence in her sense of fairness and abstract loyalty to me that I did not even engage a lawyer.

Considering our somewhat extensive mutual interests in two newspapers and in real estate in both Wyoming and Ohio, the settlement of our affairs was not difficult. She neither expected nor asked alimony.

However, with a smile and touch of humor, she said, "Unless we can make some satisfactory exchange of stock in the *Wyoming Tribune* and the *Warren Tribune,* I shall be placed in the position of working for my divorced husband. That might be embarrassing or seem odd or unusual to others, even though we understand it ourselves. I know your deep feeling for the *Warren, Ohio, Tribune* and want you to retain a substantial interest and, of course, I desire that your brother, Tom, shall remain as editor."

Incidentally, she preferred to retain her present married name, because it involved fewer complications, and I had no objection.

We reached an agreement without controversy, she relinquishing all her stock in the *Wyoming Tribune* and Deming Realty company and taking *Warren Tribune* stock in return. She made the *Tribune* one of the outstanding papers of its class in the United States and acquired a circle of friends among publishers that was nation-wide. Our respective families remained on good terms. We corresponded occasionally, exchanged Christmas presents regularly, and she consulted me on important matters concerning the *Warren Tribune* and our real estate in Ohio.

We both were members of the Associated Press and the American Newspaper Publishers association. She was the first woman admitted to the floor of the Associated Press. She appealed to the national association for a franchise for the *Tribune* over the protest of S. S. McClure of the *Youngstown (Ohio) Telegram*. Mrs.

Deming, who had been connected with the *Tribune* for many years, presented her case as if thoroughly accustomed to such environment. She became a world traveler and saw about everything worth seeing on four continents.

She was much pleased with my appointment as president of the United States Civil Service commission, and the news story was given a conspicuous place in the *Warren Tribune*.

I experienced no envy or jealousy concerning her prominence in journalism and success in business generally.

Thus, the years from 1918 to 1936 seemed to "tread upon each other's heels so fast they followed." We both prospered and found plenty to keep us busy. Moreover, there was variety, truly called the spice of life.

In the early spring of 1936, she visited Florida and was a guest of the Pancoast hotel at Miami Beach, while I stopped at the Roney Plaza. She was planning to leave in a few days on a trip to the West Indies with some friends. She dined with me one evening, and for the first time I realized that she was not very well. She said her blood pressure had been coming down very rapidly, that she tired easily, and her doctor had told her she must not over-exert herself at any time. She was planning to construct an electric elevator in her home, when she returned, in order to be spared the effort of climbing stairways.

The sea trip apparently was restful and, a short time after her return in april, she attended the annual meetings of the Associated Press and American Newspaper Publishers association being held in New York.

I had been in Washington for a few weeks and went to New York on sunday morning in order to be present at the opening meeting monday morning. On previous similar occasions we had usually attended one Theater Guild performance together. I phoned her, asking if there was anything at the theater she wished to see. She said, H. G. Wells's new picture "The Shape of things to come" or some such name, was on. We attended in the afternoon and had dinner together. Strolling up Park avenue, we looked in the shop windows. I saw a tie that pleased me. In pursuance of her thorough way of doing things, she insisted that I write down the number so I could find the store easily later. I did so and bought the tie. She remarked, "Before I go home, I am going to buy a summer ermine coat. Do you think that would be extravagant?" I smiled and replied, "Of course not, as you can easily afford it."

I did not see Zell at the monday or tuesday meetings, but we had planned to enjoy a stage show tuesday evening. It proved to be a subtle romance, with a bit of tragic marital mystery, but done so artistically that one's feelings were not harrowed. Between acts and scenes she would tell me how she thought it would end, and her analysis proved correct.

I attended the wednesday morning meeting. About eleven o'clock she came in and, strangely enough, sat in the same row in which I was seated, though at some distance away. When the session adjourned for luncheon, I had a passing impulse that I should walk over and exchange a few words with her, for appearance sake, if no other, as we had many mutual friends in the meeting. But I did not do so. I left by one door and she by another exit, a short distance away. From her position in the hall or lobby, she looked across and smiled very naturally, as I had seen her do thousands of times. The remainder of the day I felt a vague sense

HELEN HART HURLBERT
daughter of Zell Hart Deming

ZELL P. HURLBERT
granddaughter of Zell Hart Deming

of remorse or regret in not approaching her for a few words or possibly inviting her to luncheon if she was not otherwise engaged. The thought seemed to haunt me.

Thursday morning I returned to Washington, as I was preparing to start for Cheyenne soon and had several matters to look after in the national capital.

Sunday morning I was packing for my trip, having already secured my railroad ticket and berth, expecting to leave that evening.

The phone rang and I recognized my brother Tom's voice. He was calling from Warren, Ohio, and said, "Have you heard about Zell?"

"No, what is it?" I replied.

"She was found dead in her room at the Waldorf Astoria by a maid at nine o'clock this morning. Helen and her husband are motoring somewhere in Florida and we have not been able to locate them yet. You must go to New York and take charge."

The shock was terrific, so great that the news was almost unbelievable. Its very suddenness steadied me, however, for I had no time to lose. There were trains to New York every hour.

In a short time I had changed all my home-bound traveling plans. I left my ticket with the porter to be redeemed and soon found myself on the most trying journey of my lifetime.

In New York it was necessary to act promptly, because it seemed best to get started for Warren on a midnight Erie train. The hotel management, the funeral director, and Zell's faithful chauffeur-secretary, George Farmer, made everything as easy as possible.

From them, I learned she had been stricken with acute indigestion wednesday night and had called the house physician. A nurse was secured, and Zell seemed to improve and dismissed the nurse saturday morning. Sometime saturday night or early sunday morning, a heart attack occurred and the end of her busy life came with the close of a newspaper meeting she so much enjoyed.

My strain grew when once en route. I slept but little and we arrived at mid-afternoon on monday. Relatives and friends were at the station. Helen had been reached and asked that the funeral be set not earlier than thursday.

It was a period of suspense for all. The out-pouring at the obsequies at the Episcopal church which followed the services at her home was almost unprecedented and the floral tributes were countless. When we returned to her Elm street home from the cemetery, her close friends and relatives were kind enough to remark that although it was a strange coincidence that I was the only one of her near associates, relatives, or friends available in the emergency, Zell probably would have had it that way, as Helen could not be there. I was glad to be of some service at such a time.

The press the country over was unanimous in its tributes to her genius and success as publisher and as a woman, and I contributed, emphasizing the fact that she had not only unusual gifts as a business woman, but highly developed literary qualities, a rather unusual combination.

Her warm friends, Mr. and Mrs. Ogden Reid, owners of the *New York Tribune,* devoted a beautiful editorial to Zell Hart Deming.

In her last will, drawn a year before, she expressed a desire that her daughter, Helen, should succeed her in the *Tribune* office, and that her granddaughter, Zell,

COMMANDER AND MRS. GRISWOLD HURLBERT IN 1943

should, in time, also interest herself in newspaper work.

Helen, both before and after her marriage, had worked at times in the *Tribune* office, including four years as society editor. Keenly appreciative of her "Mother Zell" both as a woman and mother and as a newspaper publisher, she is today president of the Tribune company with the ideal and example of Zell before her as she carries on. And Zell Hart Hurlbert, studying for the newspaper business, spends her summer school vacations working in the *Tribune* office.

Zell Hart Deming enjoyed good poetry and perhaps it is fitting to close these references to her life with a passage from Kipling of which she was always especially fond:

When Earth's last picture is painted and the tubes are twisted
and dried,
When the oldest colours have faded, and the youngest critic
has died,
We shall rest, and, faith, we shall need it—lie down for an
aeon or two,
Till the Master of all good workmen shall set us to work
anew.

Of a Personal Nature

"Fortunately, in my boyhood I was a regular attendant at church and sunday school," says Mr. Deming. "My mother was a remarkable Bible scholar. The combination gave me a rather wide interest in the scriptures from a literary standpoint, as well as otherwise. It seemed to me when I read Shakespeare and other classics that most of them had their foundation in Holy writ. The New Testament, particularly, entertained me as a source of literature and common sense as well as gospel, as set forth by the Apostles and the Master. I found all of this very helpful in my newspaper work and other activities where a medium of expression was required.

"When I left home for Ohio, I took with me a letter from the Methodist Episcopal church, but do not find that I ever officially used it, although I attended services from time to time. The same was true when I came to Cheyenne. Through my position as editor of the *Tribune,* I became well acquainted with the various ministers and found many of them congenial as well as somewhat gifted in their profession. I have contributed to a number of denominations.

"Just why I do not now remember, but I dropped in to hear the Reverend Harmon McQuilken occasionally at the Presbyterian church. He was young, tall, cheerful, and a good preacher.

"After a few weeks, he seemed to assume that I was a member. If I failed to attend and met him on the street the next day, before he was within a block, he would raise his long right arm, with his index finger pointing at me, as if pronouncing judgment. Then, with an expansive, forgiving smile, as he approached me, would lower his arm and exclaim, 'Deming, you were not at church yesterday.'

"Therefore, during his pastorate, I attended with some regularity, partly because it was easier than finding an alibi.

"While heartily in sympathy with all church movements, regardless of creed, and deeply appreciative of the important place they play in every community, I have been woefully negligent so far as individual church relationship is concerned."

"I have never been superstitious," Mr. Deming said, "and probably have started more journeys on friday than any other day in the week and never yet had a mishap. I have, however, observed many interesting coincidences throughout my life and have sometimes had remarkable intuitions and premonitions as to what might or might not happen.

"I have no faith in horoscopes or fortune telling, yet it has been interesting to observe how often the following worded weight tickets have come out of penny scales, whether in Wyoming, California, Florida, or elsewhere: 'You have a wide variety of interests but are by no means a jack of all trades.'

"About the only significance in this is that the statement is one of a large number of stock appraisals used by manufacturers of these public weighing machines. In the very nature of events, some of these were bound to fall my way. All seers find it pays to flatter."

As this biography was resolving itself into a personal or intimate story, the author asked Mr. Deming about

his habits in relation to smoking and drinking. He said:
"My father was a regular cigar smoker all his life but
urged me not to take up the habit until I was of age,
if at all."

"In college I smoked an occasional cigarette but no
cigars. After I graduated I began smoking cigars, a
custom more popular among young business and professional men then than today. Strangely enough, I did
not like the domestic product, although born and reared
in a tobacco growing state.

"Only the dark cigars made in Key West or Tampa,
Florida, or imported from Havana satisfied me.

"I was able to keep the cigar habit under control by
suspending my smoking from time to time, and gave
it up entirely before I was fifty years of age. I can't say
that I ever fully enjoyed the habit. In the first place,
I was a nervous smoker. I would exhaust two cigars
while the average person was smoking one. Furthermore, I could not read, write, work, play, drive, or do
anything else while smoking. I was like an old fellow
of my acquaintance who said, 'When I smoke I have
to tend to it.' Therefore, it was a great loss of time.

"For sociability largely, I substituted cigarettes, but
did not inhale the smoke.

"After ten or fifteen years of intermittent cigarette
smoking, I gave it up, because it raised my blood pressure and left me with a generally uncomfortable feeling.
The smoke also irritated my eyes.

"As to liquor, it is a mistake to assume that only the
young of the present generation ever indulged. Many
of my youthful companions in Kentucky did drink
beer, whisky, or brandy. The same was true in college.
The girls, however, did not drink and very few smoked
cigarettes, and then very privately.

"Personally, I never had to adopt any fixed rules as to total abstinence. I did not particularly like the taste of hard liquor or its effect. Very little of it left me in an abnormal condition mentally and physically. The reaction was not pleasant.

"Instinctively, I wanted to be myself so far as possible. Otherwise I did not think that after drinking I was as efficient or capable of enjoying life or even a social gathering.

"Hence, I rarely took a cocktail or high ball and but very little wine with a meal.

"I was neither a teetotaler nor a drinker. I do not deserve any credit for my moderation.

"Let me record here that practically every friend of my boyhood, whether in Kentucky or in college, who drank regularly or to excess died before he was fifty."

When asked if he had ever had any serious illness, accident, misfortune, or disappointment, Mr. Deming replied lightly, "The question is certainly comprehensive; however, I have had none from which I failed to recover.

"During one of my summer vacations," he continued, "when a college student, I was stricken with fever, either malarial or typhoid, I do not recall which. A college friend from a neighboring town and I, being 'fed up' with trips on the old Erie railroad to and from Meadville and Cincinnati, took a steamboat at Pittsburgh and traveled to Maysville, Kentucky. It was in the latter part of june and the weather had become very hot. No doubt, I picked up a germ of some kind, as river boats in those days were not very sanitary and much natural ice was used in drinking water. Soon after arriving home, I became ill and spent several weeks in bed. I realized for the first time what it meant to be more or less helpless physically and sometimes within signaling distance of the Valley of the Shadow.

"Better still, I learned of the amazing skill and resourcefulness of our family physician, Dr. Luther B. Holmes; and of the patience and knowledge of nursing possessed by my mother. I would sometimes wonder when she found time to sleep. The combination brought me through in good shape.

"There were minor operations for hernia when an anaesthetic was administered. I took it easily and when I awakened marveled, in retrospect, at the mysterious sleep, and welcomed the good cheer of the smiling young woman in white who stood at the foot of the bed. Jokingly, she remarked, 'It was not so bad after all.'

" 'No,' I rejoined, 'it never touched me.'

"I had an unusual experience in this connection when my tonsils were removed by a famous surgeon, Dr. Charles W. Richardson, of Washington, D.C., in his private hospital. After an attendant had begun giving me the ether, or whatever was used, someone rushed in and excitedly halted the performance, saying the patient ahead of me was suffering from a hemorrhage and Doctor Richardson's attention was needed. I was asked to rise from the table and wait a half hour or more before the anaesthetic was resumed. Apparently, the incident made no particular difference with either me or the surgeon, for I was out of the hospital in about four days.

"About ten years ago in Washington, during an early spring epidemic of influenza, I took cold. It grew rapidly worse during the day. At six o'clock I experienced a severe chill, the first in my lifetime. Being unable to control my muscles disturbed me very much. Soon I was conscious of a rising temperature and in two or three hours of very severe aches and pains in all my muscles.

"The hotel physician had closed his office and gone home. Believing sleep a pretty good remedy for almost anything, I went to bed. All my symptoms grew worse. I not only could not sleep but could not rest in any one position. Excruciating pains enveloped my legs and arms and my heart beat so rapidly and noisily I could hear as well as feel every pulsation. My only relief came from arising and standing on my feet, but that surcease lasted only a few seconds, the pain returning when I again lay down. I did not have a sedative of any kind. About three o'clock in the morning, alarmed by my rising temperature and tumultuous heart action, I began to wonder whether that delicate organ could continue to function. I rose again, put on my bath robe, sat down at the desk and wrote some directions to one of my brothers and then returned to bed. After another hour of pain, exhaustion followed and I went to sleep for about two hours. It required a good doctor, a cheerful nurse, and ten days time in a hospital to put me on my feet again. Anyone else, no doubt, would have had judgment and decision enough to call a physician the evening before.

"As to ill luck, adversity, misfortune, etc.," Mr. Deming says, "there were losses of deposits in at least four banks that had failed in Wyoming and Ohio, and also the payment of one hundred per cent assessments on stock in some of those institutions. I suppose these would be called misfortunes, but they, also, like chills and fever, were not fatal.

"Of course, there were other bad stock investments, such as the Baltimore and Ohio railroad, Auburn Automobile company, and certain oil stocks.

"Fortunately, the new act regulating stock exchanges and issuance of securities has minimized such an evil. I congratulate Franklin D. Roosevelt on putting it through.

"As to accidents," remarks Mr. Deming, "I have frequently said that I have probably seen several million automobiles in my lifetime, but never was near enough to observe a collision or an accident. Occasionally I have happened along soon thereafter.

"About fifteen years ago, while traveling over the Blue Ridge mountains in Virginia with two friends, on a rainy day, the car began to skid as it moved down the mountain side. The road was a bit slippery and the tires were no doubt worn. I was sitting in the back seat alone. The driver was one of the best and safest I have ever known, yet when he lightly placed his foot on the brake, the skid began. I had such confidence in his judgment and skill that I felt no anxiety, but he was unable to straighten the car out as it moved down the crooked highway. None of the three of us made any remarks or attempted to leave the car, although that might have been possible. I recall my reaction was that the driver would eventually bring the automobile under control, or, if he did not, that it would turn over on the upside and not the precipitous side of the highway. When we reached a wide, flat point, flanked by soft Virginia red mud, the car gently and comfortably rolled over on its side. My companions were H. G. Porter and Cecil E. Custer of the Civil Service commission.

"Before attempting to get out, each asked the other if he was all right and the answer was in the affirmative. By that time a number of tourists had stopped and helped right our machine, which had suffered no damage except a smashed fender and broken glass. We

turned around and went back to the Hill Top house
for luncheon and then resumed our journey to Monticello, the beautiful home and shrine of Thomas Jefferson. I jokingly told my friends it was a case of mind
triumphing over matter – in that the automobile did
not upset until it reached a safe place to land."

Thirty years ago, Mr. Deming having contracted a
severe cold, visited the Seventh Day Adventist sanitarium at Boulder, Colorado. He was so much impressed
with the diet, which included all vegetables, fruits,
cereals, milk and its compounds, but excluded coffee,
tea, and meat, that he has consistently followed up his
acquaintance with these institutions in different sections
of the country.

It was not alone the diet which he found helpful, but
the hydrotherapy treatments and massages which ac-
company a stay in the Seventh Day Adventist hospitals
or sanitariums. Hydrotherapy, of course, in a broad
sense means hot water, applied through external hot
packs in various forms. In addition there are salt rubs,
electric baths, Russian steam baths, and many other
treatments.

From time to time, especially when he needed a rest
or a quick recovery from a cold, Mr. Deming has spent
from two weeks to a month at the Porter Sanitarium
in Denver; in sanitariums at Hinsdale, Illinois; Glendale, California; and Orlando, Florida; the Washington sanitarium, District of Columbia; and Dr. John
H. Kellogg's beautiful new place at Miami Springs,
Florida.

The Seventh Day Adventists use what is popularly
known as The Battle Creek, Michigan, treatment. As
a matter of fact, the Seventh Day Adventists initiated
the sanitarium at Battle Creek, which was later devel-

opened as a great national and international institution by Doctor Kellogg. During his life, Doctor Kellogg, a bachelor, has adopted and educated forty boys and girls. Two of the daughters manage the Florida place.

The doctor, in his eighty-seventh year, spent his winters at the Miami Springs institution and lectured at least twice a week to his guests, as they were called. Many of them were leading business men, who came for rest and rexalation. Since the above was written the federal government has taken over the Miami Springs place as a hospital. Doctor Kellogg died at the age of ninety.

Mr. Deming said, "I have met some most interesting characters at Doctor Kellogg's sanitarium, among them, Admiral Richard E. Byrd; Sidney Hillman, president, Amalgamated Clothing Workers of the United States and a power in the labor movement; Roger W. Babson, the statistician and financial wizard; Dr. Alexis Carrell, the famous biologist and surgeon, who was a delightful companion and reminded me somewhat of an old fashioned country doctor; and Mr. Foster of 'Ask Mr. Foster' fame. Foster, in reply to a question as to his career, said: 'When a young man, in my twenties, I was timekeeper or assistant foreman during the construction of the old Ponce de Leon hotel in St. Augustine. Henry W. Flagler's railroad had reached that point and there was a demand for a large winter resort. St. Augustine was then a comparatively small city. In one way and another, I bumped into nearly all the tourists. I noticed that most of them wrote souvenir postal cards, that they bought trinkets, and that every last one of them asked questions, particularly about travel schedules, hotel accommodations, and rates, and many others too numerous to mention. From that idea,

I started my first business of selling souvenirs and offering a free information bureau. I selected attractive young ladies who needed work and put them behind the counters, usually in hotels. Today I have about one hundred such places scattered throughout the United States and its possessions.'

"Foster lived in a beautiful apartment on the top floor of a tall building in New York where he entertained his friends and exhibited moving pictures that he had taken throughout the world. Ward G. Foster died in Coral Gables, Florida, march 16, 1940, after more than fifty years of active business life."

Publishing Activities

In looking back over his experiences, Mr. Deming said in later years, "I have had many contacts in my life – social, political, commercial, religious. None has offered so many opportunities to study human nature as has my newspaper work, and none has afforded more thrills, greater satisfaction, or better chance to achieve results."

He was always earnest in his advocacy of those things most important to the development of the state of Wyoming. Many of the members of his staff remained with him through loyalty and a keen desire to assist in the building up of the *Tribune*.

He encouraged young men and women to stick to their jobs and not to become rolling stones. "The executive of practically all concerns," he said, "whether business or professional, changes within a period of thirty years. Keep in line of promotion and be ready when the opportunity arrives." It is worthy of note that John Charles Thompson, who was a young reporter on the *Tribune* in 1901 was made editor by Mr. Deming when official duties took him to Washington years afterward and he is still holding that position.

Although the *Tribune* opposed Judge Joseph M. Carey for governor in 1910 when he ran on the democratic ticket, Judge Carey once said of Deming: "He is a man of ability and integrity. I wish we had more newspaper men like him." Judge Carey probably recalled that Deming, fearing a party split, had urged

the republicans to nominate him (Carey) for governor
at the state convention in 1902, and also put up a good
fight for Carey's friend, Secretary of state and acting-
Governor Fenimore Chatterton in 1904 when the Honorable Bryant B. Brooks was chosen. The *Tribune* did
splendid work for Brooks in the campaign, however,
and the Casper statesman became a warm friend of
Deming. Judge Carey was elected on the democratic
ticket in 1910.

An insight into his newspaper experience is obtained
in an article published in the *Independent Magazine*
of New York City in 1913 entitled, "Buying a Newspaper and paying for it by Hard Work." The article
written under the *nom de plume,* Burn Brunk, was a
slightly disguised account of Mr. Deming's own experience. The editor of the *Independent* prefaced the
article with this remark: "It would make a good object
lesson for students in our schools of journalism if journalism were, like law, taught by the 'case method.' "

The following extracts from an address given by
William C. Deming before the Wyoming Editorial
association give a vivid picture of many of the basic
principles upon which his newspaper work was so
successfully built up:

"WHAT IS NEWS: Every newspaper man not only
asks himself, but is frequently asked by others, 'What
is news?' I doubt if this has ever been answered more
completely than by Horace Greeley when he said:
'A newspaper should embody in a single issue the information daily required by all those who aim to keep
informed on every important occurrence, so that the
lawyer, the merchant, the banker, the economist, the
author, the politician, etc., may find whatever he needs
to see, and be spared the trouble of looking elsewhere.'

"Any matter of legitimate and public nature, as for instance, the result of an election, the enactment of a general law, the decree of a court, the destruction of property by fire, cyclone or earthquake, a new invention, the discovery of a mine, the promotion of new enterprises, the incorporation of industrial, commercial, or transportation companies, athletic contests, forthcoming community affairs, marriages, births, and deaths of local or national note – these are essentially of public interest and no person can expect a publisher to withhold them. Such events are news per se.

"Of less important, yet of more frequent occurrence, is the grist of personal and, in a measure, private happenings, which make up the human interest side of the newspaper and touch a chord of sympathy, arouse the curious impulse or provoke the reader to laughter or tears. The divorce court grind, the engagement of well known people, the society dinner, the surgical operation where the victim is a magnate or a statesman, and a thousand and one other personalities not necessary to name – these are not essentially public matters and yet the newspaper of today gets them, as a rule, and the public enjoys reading them just so long as the affair is not theirs personally.

"Herein lies the field for judgment and diplomacy on the part of the reporter and sound discretion on the part of the management of the paper.

"Every news item published should tell the what, the where, the when, the how, and the why. In short, it should answer briefly and clearly every question that will arise naturally in the mind of the reader.

"The reporter should avoid superlatives in his descriptive matter, always seeming to hold something of kind, quality, or degree in reserve. He should omit fulsome praise, but should scatter a flower here and there, when the opportunity is properly presented, and wherever possible, indulge within bounds a humorous strain. Next to making the reader think and talk, and act if necessary, make him smile and laugh, and your periodical may become the family paper of the town.

"There should be absolute divorcement of editorial and news columns. The newspaper, through its editor, becomes the mouthpiece, as it were, for the entire community. If the editor is fortunate enough to remain free of any political, commercial, or social interest which might attempt to restrict or modify the free exercise of his views and opinions, his paper becomes a tower of strength in the community. . . While I have never been of the school that believes that to preserve and manifest independence of spirit and thought and action it is necessary for a newspaper owner and editor to be a complete hermit and dissociate himself from every other activity – social, political, or commercial – I have felt that he should never become so ambitious for position or wealth that he puts himself within the power of any interest.

"A newspaper, whether big or little, has a right to be prosperous, and the more prosperous it is, the more powerful it may become; because there is nothing like dependence to sap strength and will power. But success cannot be attained at a sudden bound; it comes through the progress of years and it is merely relative. The editor of the weekly in a town of twenty-five hundred can hardly hope to attain the same degree of financial success as the editor of a daily in a town of twenty-five thousand; but he can become relatively as influential and quite as happy. I have doubted the wisdom of the chain ownership of newspapers as it is being carried out in this country today. The most influential editor is the man who owns his own paper, edits his own paper, and lives among those he serves year after year.

"The editor imported from the main office of the syndicate can have only a superficial grasp of the problems of the community, and no editor-in-chief in San Francisco or Chicago or New York can properly appraise the conditions in the small city hundreds of miles away.

"The man who edits his own paper for twenty years in a given community is in a position ordinarily to act intuitively and instinctively on almost any problem affecting his neighborhood that may arise; and if he is the right sort, there will be many times when it will be necessary for him to take direct issue with his neighbor with whom he plays bridge or golf, with the political leader of his own party, or with the president of the town's biggest bank. My thought is that the newspaper, not the changing head of a political organization or chamber of commerce, or civic club, should lead; because the newspaper man is on the job in civic matters every day, the others only casually and occasionally."

One of Mr. Deming's regrets in his newspaper career has been that he was not able to do actual mechanical work. This phase, however, was left to his brother, Tom, in the early days of their training in Kentucky, and to his cousin, C. B. Rigg.

There was a neighboring newspaper man named Bell who, as a hobby, took great delight in working in the composing room and making up the last forms, which included, of course, the first page with the latest news.

After visiting him and seeing him in action, Mr. Deming said: "I envied that newspaper man his versatility, ability, and efficiency, and if I had my newspaper life to do over again, I certainly would learn to set type and make up the forms."

M. C. Barrow, of Douglas, whose newspaper was called *Bill Barlow's Budget,* did not like Deming's independence and free and easy way of treating all subjects, particularly politics. Barrow was an able writer and at times a bitter critic, with whom most Wyoming editors hesitated to engage in controversy. He tried to laugh Mr. Deming out of court, but had no luck.

"Cognizant of the fact that western people generally liked a scrap, Mr. Deming gave Barrow punch for punch, with now and then an extra clip," said W. E. Chaplin. On more than one occasion Barrow found it necessary to retract statements and to apologize to the new editor, one instance being when he accused the *Tribune* of willfully omitting one of the resolutions passed at the Woolgrowers association meeting. Barrow did not realize that he was helping to put the *Tribune* on the map. In time Deming and Barrow became excellent friends and Bill frequently entertained the Cheyenne editor at his home in Douglas.

The following tribute written by Mr. Deming upon the death of Barrow struck a popular note:

> Life is not as we take it,
>   This wonderful life of ours,
> But life is as we make it,
>   A garden of thorns or flowers.

"Merris C. Barrow was the author of his own philosophy, the creator of his own religion. To him the world was a great, moving, living thing. As he passed through it, he gathered incense from every flower and plucked pleasures from every friend. Even his enemies furnished exhilarating diversion and his work was the galvanic battery that stirred his emotions and kept his blood tingling through his veins.

"His newspaper, the *Douglas Budget,* was not so much in his eyes, a purveyor of the news of the vicinage, as a medium through which he breathed his theories of life and speculated on the meaning of death. When his wit and humor, satire and sermons, sought a wider field, an extended horizon, he established his magazine *Sagebrush Philosophy,* and reached many widely scattered thousands who sympathized with his soul longings and reechoed his original and sometimes daring appeals to the human instinct, which many feel but try to conceal. 'Bill' was honest with himself and his readers, for he spoke what he felt and felt what he spoke.

"What warnings he had of his early demise we do not know, but his last utterance in his magazine was prophetic and indicated that he sometimes mused on death and contemplated the end.

"At times his prose took on the rhythm of poetry and he carried his readers along unconsciously into realms of the life eternal, which to him was the love everlasting.

"He was an optimist and a master of written emotion as well as a maker of idle satire that ripped the mask from many worldly shams.

"But he is gone and the hour hand is set on his going. In this world it will never be changed. He was generous and kind to his family and friends. He would divide his last dollar with the lowest and never feared the highest.

"He lived his creed."

His remains were interred in the cemetery at Douglas, but his grave was unmarked until 1935 when his old-time friend, A. J. Mokler, induced the Masonic grand lodge of Wyoming to purchase and have erected at the head of his grave an appropriate monument.

Other editors who enjoyed battling with the *Tribune's* editor were J. Ross Carpenter and Alex Hastie, both of whom were associated with the *Leader,* before it was purchased by Deming.

Mr. Deming thought that the small homesteader, the settler on an irrigation project, the sheep man or cattle man who grazed in the national forests, the prospector or operator of a mine on the public lands were all concerned as much with the policies of the federal government as with those of the state. He, therefore, printed important national and international news, as well as state news, with good heads. His editorial articles were always carefully and forcefully prepared. Fair play was paramount in every matter of local importance.

Commenting upon Mr. Deming as an employer, Fred Babcock, travel editor of the *Chicago Tribune* (1937) said:

"I worked for him, and traveled over Wyoming with him, as his city editor for five years, and in that time I came to know him and appreciate him, as I have known and appreciated few persons. I should say, off-hand, that the three qualities that have impressed themselves upon me are Mr. Deming's fairness toward everyone, his determination to keep his paper free and independent, and his loyalty toward men working under him. In my five years with him, I had plenty of opportunities to test out all three of those qualities, and I never knew him to fail.

"In those days (1918 to 1923), I was young and bumptious, and I was always getting into hot water. Mr. Deming invariably pulled me out.

"I recall that once, soon after the World war, when

the troops were still being brought to what was then
Fort D. A. Russell (now Fort F. E. Warren), for
demobilization, some army officer came along and announced that unless certain moral conditions were
cleared up, there would be no more troops. In Mr.
Deming's absence. I ran the full story under the front-
page streamer: 'Purge Cheyenne or Lose Soldiers –
Which?' Whereupon a group of business men called
down the wrath of the gods upon me and convened a
meeting of the Chamber of Commerce to say what they
thought of a newspaper that dared to print the truth.
And they said it a-plenty. But when my boss returned,
he backed me to the limit. On another occasion, when
an evangelist was holding forth under the auspices of
several of the leading churches of the city, I went to
hear him and gave my resumé of his sermon under the
heading: 'Bulgin Promises you Heaven and then Gives
you Hell.' There was hell to pay that night, with boos
and hisses for the author of such a sacrilegious screed,
and, the following day, a storm of letters to the editor,
demanding that I be fired instanter. Mr. Deming
consigned the letters to where they belonged.

"He was always like that. He could and would, when
necessary, tell the advertisers or the church people or
the gangsters, or anybody else, where to head in. Once
convinced that he, or one of his subordinates, was right,
his stand never wavered. In the last quarter century,
I have worked on papers all the way from Chicago to
the Pacific coast. I wish I could say for all of my editors
what I can conscientiously say of Mr. Deming: 'He
doesn't pass the buck; he can take it, and the men under
him don't have to stand the gaff. He doesn't repudiate
them even when they make mistakes.'

"One of the finest tributes I ever heard paid to an

editor was given by James M. Cox when he visited
Cheyenne as the democratic candidate for president in
1920. In his address at the Princess theater, Mr. Cox
roundly scored the republican press of the country for
its treatment of his campaign, but he stopped in the
middle of his speech to explain that there was one
exception. As I remember them, his words were something like this: 'In all this there has been one republican paper – *The Wyoming State Tribune* – that has not
distorted the issue or sought to mislead its readers.
It has printed the truth. It would be ungracious and
unsportsmanlike of me if I did not make this statement.'"

Deming gave ardent support to his friend, Warren
G. Harding, but did not close the news columns of the
Tribune to the democrats.

John Charles Thompson said when the new building
was erected:

"When William C. Deming came to the *Tribune* a
year after the turn of the century, Cheyenne was a town
of perhaps six or seven thousand population with many
of the raw edges of its frontier period still untrimmed.
The *Tribune* had a precarious circulation of perhaps
five hundred copies, virtually confined to this community. A couple of typesetting machines, a rickety flat-
bed press capable of printing two pages at a time, a
mere 'shirt-tail' of type, constituted its plant. The editorial, business, and mechanical staffs combined numbered six persons. There were six carrier boys. It was
a sick newspaper with a discouraged personnel, housed
darkly in a dank basement. From the unpromising
beginning, by patient, sagacious effort, he developed
The Tribune-Leader of today with its statewide circulation exceeding ten thousand copies and a plant which
is most complete among those of newspapers of com-

parable circulation anywhere, housed in a spacious building which is envied by every publishing enterprise in the Rocky Mountain region.

"While he was so building materially, William C. Deming was accomplishing, too, his ideal of producing a high-grade newspaper devoted to the promotion of development of Cheyenne and Wyoming that never subordinated principle to commercial or political expediency."

James H. Walton, long associated with the *Tribune,* said:

"Mr. Deming was the ideal newspaper publisher and editor. As the publisher of the *Wyoming State Tribune* in Cheyenne for more than a third of a century, he held, in my opinion, first place of influence in shaping the policies of both the capital city and the state of Wyoming.

"During all this period, Mr. Deming's influence was behind every movement for the betterment of Cheyenne and Wyoming, and many were initiated and brought to completion through his personal and editorial influence.

"As an editor and publisher, Mr. Deming always had certain carefully worked out constructive objectives for the betterment of his community and state which he kept constantly in mind and toward which he directed his own energies and those of his associates and friends.

"Although he published the *Tribune* for profit and as a politically republican paper, he never allowed financial returns or political expediency to sway him from a course which he considered for the best interests of the republican party or the state of Wyoming."

As early as 1901 the new *Tribune* editor became a member of the Associated Press. This was soon after its reorganization as a great world or international news gathering agency. He remained a member until february 1, 1937, when he retired from the newspaper publishing business.

During his active affiliation with the Associated Press and the American Newspaper Publishers association, he acquired a large acquaintance and made many friends among publishers throughout the country by his brief addresses and committee work at annual meetings in New York.

He continues as a non-resident member of the National Press club in Washington, D.C.

Mr. Deming says: "I regret now that I did not keep a detailed record of editors and publishers, young and old, whom I met from time to time during my thirty-six years membership in the Associated Press.

"Melville E. Stone was general manager when I was elected to membership and Frank B. Noyes of the *Washington Star* was president from 1900 to 1938 when he retired.

"They were complete opposites in personality and appearance. Stone was democratic and unconventional, while Mr. Noyes was reserved and was an aristocrat in every sense of the word.

"It was with much interest that I observed Mr. Noyes's method of dealing with the membership in annual meetings. I have never known a presiding officer who was so exact in his rulings. He wasted few words and his decisions were usually accepted without protest.

"The Associated Press probably made its greatest progress under his regime. There were many difficult problems, including the purchase and financing of the wirephoto rights, costing nearly a half million dollars, and the long-drawn-out contest in more recent years with William R. Hearst over matters of policy in the association. Robert McLean is now president and Kent Cooper general manager.

"About 1913 or 1914," says Mr. Deming, "A. J. Mokler of Casper, for some reason, desired to retire from active work, perhaps in order to devote time to his historical writings. He asked me if I would be interested in buying the *Casper Tribune* and placed a tentative value of sixty-five hundred dollars upon the plant. I regret to say that I did not interest myself in the proposition. A few weeks later, a gentleman, probably forty years of age, called upon me at the *Tribune* office and asked me if I knew of a good weekly paper in Wyoming which might be bought at a reasonable price. The visitor was James E. Hanway,[7] then of Colorado.

"I told him there were a few papers, which probably could be purchased, and in my judgment the *Casper Tribune* had the best future. When I gave him the figures, sixty-five hundred dollars, which Mr. Mokler had suggested to me, he said, 'I haven't that much cash. I could make a down payment of about twenty-five hundred dollars.'

"I then suggested, 'If you will go to Casper with twenty-five hundred dollars and satisfy Mr. Mokler as to your standing, experience, and good intentions, I believe you can buy his paper.' Mr. Hanway proceeded to Casper the following day, that is tuesday, and by saturday had closed the deal with Mr. Mokler.

"Within a few months, active oil drilling development began in the Salt Creek field and Mr. Hanway began publishing a tabloid daily paper, stating that it was an experiment. Affairs moved so rapidly during

---

[7] James E. Hanway is now practically retired from active work. His son, Earl Hanway, a fine citizen, able newspaper man, and delightful companion, is now manager of that publishing business.

the next ten years that Casper for a time outstripped Cheyenne in population and the *Casper Daily Tribune* became a voluminous and prosperous daily newspaper.

"Mr. Hanway not only made money publishing the *Tribune,* but also some profit, I believe, selling the paper and taking it back. Upon one occasion, Charles Barton, a brother of Bruce Barton, famous writer, and later a member of congress from New York, was the purchaser and it was reported that he made a down payment of fifty thousand dollars, which he failed to follow up."

In view of the preceding paragraphs it is interesting to refer to page 106 of *The Memoirs of J. Edwin Hanway,* published in 1942, where Mr. Hanway says:

In Cheyenne, my first act was an immediate call upon Mr. William C. Deming, then the owner and publisher of the *Wyoming State Tribune,* at that time the largest newspaper in Wyoming. Through the years I had formed acquaintance with Mr. Deming at Press association meetings, and on other occasions, and my admiration for him inspired my confidence in him. I felt that he not only was well informed on Wyoming and its opportunities in general, but that he would take a personal interest in helping me to find the right location for my future endeavors.

In this conclusion I was not disappointed, and we engaged in a long discussion. He seemed to believe that Casper, located in the center of the state, in Natrona, was the most favorable spot in the whole country at that time.

Oil in quantity had been struck in Salt Creek field and was an important factor relating to Casper's future, he pointed out, and also he understood that Alfred J. Mokler, publisher, for eighteen years, of the *Natrona County Tribune,* a weekly newspaper, was desiring to retire.

He also remarked that as the leading republicans of Casper were anxious that the newspaper remain a republican publication they undoubtedly would be glad to extend any assistance which might be needed.

His words were as music to my ears, and as though the Big Rock

Candy mountains were just around the bend. I felt that no time should be lost! In my haste to arrive in that Promised Land at the earliest moment possible, I straight-way stored the old jallopy in Dineen's garage and boarded the first train north for Casper.

Aside from his newspaper work, Mr. Deming has written upon a variety of subjects for magazines, books, and pamphlets. His best known work, entitled *Roosevelt in the Bunk House,* is a detailed human interest story of Theodore Roosevelt's three visits to Wyoming, the only complete account under one cover.

One of the high spots in President Theodore Roosevelt's career was his horseback ride from the University of Wyoming in Laramie, Wyoming, to Cheyenne, may 30, 1903, at the end of which he made an exhaustive Memorial day address. Weary as he must have been, the following day he found time to write a chummy letter to his friend Henry Cabot Lodge, longtime senator from the state of Massachusetts and grandfather of the second United States senator of that name from the old bay state. Teddy said:

Yesterday was a day on which I wish you could have been around. It did not start out in any unusual manner. We breakfasted at half past seven, at eight we left the train at Laramie and indulged in a small procession, and then I made a speech. [From the steps of Old Main.] But immediately afterwards the fun began, for we started on a sixty-two-mile ride across the plains, and one low mountain ridge, to Cheyenne.

Doctor Rixey, who is a first class horseman, went with me together with the marshal and his deputy, and Senator Warren, and three or four others — of the latter party we shed three by the way, including Warren. We changed horses five times and took two hours for lunch at the Van Tassel ranch.

We went a good fast gait, one place for five miles on a downright run, old Van Tassel being bent upon finding out how fast I could ride; and as the horses were his I let them go as fast as they could stretch themselves.

At half past five we struck the army post three miles out of Cheyenne, and I reviewed the troops.

Then I rode in, heading the procession to the grandstand, and there I made a three-quarters of an hour speech as the closing incident for the Memorial day services.

Altogether it was great fun. But I am heartily glad that the trip is now nearly at an end. I have three fearful days to look forward to in Iowa and Illinois, and then I go home.

In *Roosevelt in the Bunk House* Mr. Deming describes in reverse order three visits which Roosevelt made to Wyoming: one in september, 1900, when he was governor of New York and was campaigning for the vice-presidency; one on Decoration day, 1903, while at the peak of his popularity as president of the United States; and the last in the summer of 1910, after he had returned from Africa and was recognized as perhaps the strongest character upon the world stage. There are also included in the booklet a sketch of Roosevelt as Civil Service commissioner and several articles on the West.

"Theodore Roosevelt," said Mr. Deming, "retired from the presidency march 4, 1909, when he was only two score and ten years of age. Shortly thereafter, in order that his friend and successor, William H. Taft, might not be embarrassed by unauthorized gossip and speculation as to Roosevelt's influence upon the new administration, and in order to satisfy still further his taste and inclination for the strenuous life, Theodore Roosevelt made a hunting and exploration trip to Africa.

"Emerging from the jungle, he was received and entertained with high honor in Egypt, France, Germany, and Great Britain. His trip homeward was a triumph, and his mail was burdened with hundreds of invitations to visit American cities and address private and public organizations. He returned to America in the summer of 1910. In memory and appreciation of old times in Wyoming . . . to the surprise of the effete east and the variegated interests of the country, his first extended visit was in Cheyenne, Wyoming, as the guest of honor at the annual exhibition of the Frontier association, which perpetuates for all comers the old life of the west . . . august 28, 1910, during this visit, Colonel Roosevelt was entertained at a sheep and cattle ranch fifteen miles north of Cheyenne, owned by Senator Francis E. Warren . . . If the visitors expected merely a dinner of black bread and bull beef, they must have been surprised when they saw the American Beauty roses, the unique leather-bound menu cards, and the choice viands and wines which were spread before them as the dinner progressed.

"James R. Garfield sat near Colonel Roosevelt. Some of the newspaper guests indulged in bits of quiet humor because so few members of Roosevelt's 'tennis cabinet' had connected with the Taft administration.

"Roosevelt's autograph was, of course, much in demand. When I approached the colonel I remarked, 'Colonel Roosevelt, I have your signature on a commission as receiver of public moneys in the United States land office at Cheyenne.' Whereupon Mr. Roosevelt, with great alertness and, I trust, accuracy, said, 'That's so, that's so. I remember, I remember.' Then I added, 'And I have been reappointed by President Taft.' Quick as a flash, looking at Garfield with a squint in his eye, he replied, 'Well, that's better than Jim has done.' This provoked general laughter at the former secretary of the Interior, who had failed to succeed himself.

"After the dinner was served, in order that the tables

might be prepared for the second setting, which included neighbors and employees, who seemed to be coming from the four corners of the surrounding country to see the greatest rough rider of them all, we adjourned to the bunk house . . . there we began to feel the presence of the master and to acquire true glimpses of the weird, inexplicable character of the man.

"In the center of the main floor was a long table, on either side of which were benches in lieu of chairs. One lamp dispelled the darkness of the hour and the fragrant smoke of havanas. Gathered in groups about the room were ex-cabinet officers, senators, newspaper men and magazine writers, governors, city officials, chauffeurs and ranchmen. The cowboys, sheep herders, and ranch hands of the Warren Livestock company came and went in the discharge of their duties, now and then lingering to catch a word from the old cowman whose range was the universe, and who had roped and hogtied every important honor within his native land.

"In the midst of the smoke and babel of tongues sat Roosevelt, surrounded by eager listeners . . . He is a veritable torrent of conversation, an overflowing reservoir of experiences, a restless, rolling sea of thought. He talks like a whirlwind, shows his teeth like a bull pup, shakes his head like a buffalo, and threshes around with his arms and legs like his unconquered bucking prototype of the now famous Frontier Field . . . In that hour in the bunk house on sunday evening, august 28, 1910, he fought over again the battles of San Juan Hill and El Caney; he recalled conversations with Hamilton Fish the night before the young New Yorker was killed; he talked of Buck O'Neill, and the magnificent work of the colored regulars of the Twenty-fourth United States infantry, and quoted a Spanish prisoner who said of the Americans, 'They kept pushing forward as if they were going to take us with their hands.' Roosevelt intimated that he 'got a Spaniard.' He discoursed on the present peace of the world, and any possible future war, relating his plans to raise volunteers if the opportunity comes in his lifetime.

"He tramped through Darkest Africa, described the big game, and paid tribute to the native tribesmen who accompanied him. He sailed down the Nile, affiliated with savants in Cairo and Alexandria, hobnobbed with scholars in Europe, dined with kings, discussed royalty and philosophy, compared monarchs and republics, and said there is a place and a work for each and all.

"One tired cow-puncher who had slept all day sunday came shambling down the stairs – the bunk-house is a two-story affair – and rubbing his eyes and surveying the unusual visitors remarked, 'I thought I heard a strange hoss in the corral.' . . . For the time being, this first citizen of the world permitted nothing to raise a barrier between him and those who were intent on seeing him and on hearing him talk.

"The newspaper men desired to hear him talk particularly about himself and asked many questions to gain an understanding of this human dynamo, this composite man of the North and South, the East and West, whom all respect and none quite comprehend. He was just as approachable on that subject as on any other. When Roosevelt's attention was called to the fact that the *New York Sun* had characterized his speeches as 'commonplace' and 'platitudes' he gritted his teeth and asserted, 'But I live them.' He is just as ready to challenge criticism of himself as to fight the battles of his country.

" 'I do not pretend to be an orator,' he said, 'but what I say is true, and finds an echo in the hearts of the common people. As I said in my address, "beauty is fine, but strength is finer" . . . the strength of character and of mind and the body that enables a man to subdue a wild horse or conquer these broad plains.'

"A comparison between him and Emperor William of Germany, his recent host, was naively suggested, whereupon Roosevelt remarked, 'The Kaiser inherited his place – I made mine.' This was spoken with considerable emphasis, accompanied by vigorous striking of his chest with his hand. It was a choice epigram, apparently impromptu, and expressed with a note of finality which settled the question.

"Taking up another suggestion, and the audience was presumptuously frank, personal, and inquisitive, he replied, 'Oh, I know they say I am not a scholar, but the great universities of Europe were willing to take a chance on that,' coloring his answer with a bit of American slang, as he referred to his lectures at the Sorbonne in France and at Oxford University in England.

"In this connection, he also remarked, 'I presume there are those who will criticize me for leaving the stand at Frontier park and riding around the arena, but I felt there were several thousand people who were curious to see me and that it was as little as I could do to give them the opportunity.' Then, with his natural sense of humor, he continued, 'An American crowd always likes a parade. Barnum learned that years ago and profited by it.'

"He was as exuberant as a schoolboy who had won first prize and as joyous as a bird out of a cage. Roosevelt was so thoroughly unaffected that he did not even

THEODORE ROOSEVELT AND EX-GOVERNOR BARBER
at Frontier Days celebration, Cheyenne 1903

affect modesty. He was far too earnest and honest to allow mere convention to interfere with a character study of himself on the part of those whose sympathy and friendship he felt he understood. The psychology of the situation, the dim light of the room, the unique gathering and setting on the great plains placed all *en rapport* as our thoughts and interests centered upon the leading figure of the evening.

"And who knows but, as he looks back over thirty years and tries to follow his own spectacular career as a cowboy from the bad lands of Dakota, to Washington as United States Civil Service commissioner, to New York City as police commissioner, back to Washington as assistant-secretary of the Navy, to Cuba as lieutenant-colonel of a rough rider regiment, to Albany as governor of New York, and to Washington as vice-president and president, and then to Africa with big game and a royal tour across Europe, that Roosevelt is a study and a problem to himself.

"Theodore Roosevelt is the strangest man America has produced, a greater enigma than any statesman of the period, a leader whose past is secure and whose future is yet to be determined.

"He is a rare combination of originality, unconventionality, candor, self-confidence, alertness, fearlessness, aggressiveness, positiveness, and nervous energy, and it is is no doubt this combination which has made him the popular hero he is today."

The eighty-page book written by Mr. Deming relative to the great rough rider attracted much attention. Excerpts from it were printed in the *Literary Digest* in 1919 and brought letters of praise from many sources.

The Roosevelt House library and museum requested autographed copies of the book and in acknowledgment said: "It is a very real addition to our library and a valuable addition to the history of the colonel."

The Congressional library in Washington, noting that the author used United States Senator Lodge's personal tribute as a fitting close, wrote saying various readers had not been able to find the original author; neither had the library, and was still interested. Mr. Deming then asked through the *New York Times* for the information, but the mystery was never solved. The lines were:

> "He dwelt with the tribes of the marsh and moor,
>   He sat at the board of kings;
> He tasted the toil of the burdened slave
>   And the joy that triumph brings.
> But whether to jungle or palace hall,
>   Or white-walled tent he came,
> He was a brother to king and soldier and slave;
>   His welcome was the same."

Possibly some reader of this book can supply the author-poet's name.

After reading Mr. Deming's sketches of Roosevelt, John Clay, chairman of the executive committee of the Swan company, wrote as follows:

Chugwater, Wyo. Sept. 26, 1930

DEAR MR. DEMING: I received your three pamphlets yesterday afternoon and last night and this morning have read *Roosevelt in the Bunk House* and *Balaam*. The latter is a fine literary production, a story that is always interesting, well told, and realistic.

But Roosevelt with the imagery of old days around him takes my fancy. I only saw him once in 1886 at the Montana Cattle Growers association meeting at Miles City, Montana. There, as usual, he took the lead and one of the incidents of the meeting was the manner in which he swept Secretary Russell B. Harrison [8] (son of the president) off the floor for some silly remark he made in his address to the audience.

---

[8] Russell B. Harrison was a lawyer and newspaper publisher also a civil,

THEODORE ROOSEVELT EN ROUTE FROM LARAMIE TO CHEYENNE, MAY 30, 1903

Left to right: Captain Seth Bullock of North Dakota; Surgeon General P. M. Rixey, Washington, D.C.; United States Senator F. E. Warren, Cheyenne; Hon. N. K. Boswell, Laramie; President Theodore Roosevelt; United States Marshal Frank Hadsell, Rawlins; Fred G. Porter, Cheyenne; Deputy United States Marshal Joe Le Fors, Cheyenne; Superintendent W. L. Park of the Union Pacific Railroad, Cheyenne; Hon. William Daley, Rawlins; Hon. Otto Gramm, Laramie; and John Ernest, Laramie

These sketches are intensely interesting to me. I have travelled this West over fifty-six years, have known practically all the characters that ran through the narratives, have enjoyed their acquaintance once again.

I thank you for including my short story about the Cheyenne Club. Yours truly,

JOHN CLAY

mining, and electrical engineer. He was inspector-general of volunteers in the Spanish-American war. During his residence in Montana in the eighties he published a newspaper at Helena and was also superintendent of the United States Assay office.

On the Way to the Terry Ranch, southwest of Cheyenne, May 31, 1903

President Roosevelt *in the foreground;* former Senator Joseph M. Carey *on left white horse;* Dr. George P. Johnston *near center on dapple grey;* R. S. Van Tassell, *center, on big bay;* Acting-governor Fenimore Chatterton *in rear of Roosevelt,* and United States Marshal Frank Hadsell, extreme right

On the Lecture Platform

Next in importance to his interest in his newspaper work and writing, a survey places his work as a public speaker. As a youth he studied his father's manner and method on the platform and endeavored to follow them. He received outstanding recognition as a debater while in Allegheny college, and in the years following, devoted much time and effort to the preparation of public lectures.

His speaking was based largely upon his reading, observation, and historical research. Justice Willis Van Devanter, a member of the United States supreme court, said of him: "Mr. Deming is a man exceptionally well read along many lines. His studies were such as would help a man to know his own government and its people."

As to platform oratory and eloquence, Mr. Deming says, "I think the best examples were the lectures of General John B. Gordon on 'The Last Days of the Confederacy'; United States Senator Albert J. Beveridge's addresses on Lincoln and John Marshall; the elder Senator Robert M. LaFollette on 'Good government,' and Booker T. Washington (colored) on 'Up from Slavery'—the story of his own life."

Mr. Deming's own favorite themes have been the lives of great Americans—Lincoln, Franklin, and Washington constituting his most popular subjects. "In my opinion," he says, "the most potent influence, the most effective lesson, the greatest inspiration, the most thrilling thing in all this world is the life of a human being who has risen to heights of fame and usefulness by his own efforts and well ordered ambitions."

As an illustration of his vivid method, in lecturing on Washington, Mr. Deming said: "An aristocrat by environment, he became a revolutionary by instinct and patriotism; a lover of justice, he hated shams and denounced cowardice wherever he found it, yet he held his fiery temper subject to his will. Able, sedate, resolute, courageous, earnest, honest, patient and industrious – homely qualities which place him on a footing with all mankind, yet so rarely blended in one man – have fixed him upon a pedestal of posthumous glory, memorable and immortal."

In addition to his historical lectures, Mr. Deming has for many years been in demand as a speaker at banquets, conventions, and innumerable gatherings in the state. His mind, according to press comments after some of his lectures, "was full of charming anecdotes and logic, philosophy and history were at his command. Above all, he possessed the countenance and general appearance of an honest, sincere man, which always carries so much weight with any public assemblage."

When queried how he could and did speak and write upon such a variety of subjects, Mr. Deming said it was not so difficult as it seemed.

"Someone has stated that the next best thing to having knowledge is to know where knowledge can be found, or words to that effect. Upon accepting an invitation to speak, I immediately started a file on the subject. Everything I saw, thought, read, or heard that was pertinent went into the grab bag. In due time I sorted it out, used what was to the point, elaborated and polished it all, and then in two or three hours I could dictate a speech that needed but little changing.

President Chester A. Arthur and party in Yellowstone National Park, 1883

Standing: (*Left to right*) Col. Mike Sheridan, U.S.A.; Gen. Anson Stager; Capt. Philo Clark, U.S.A.; Judge Rawlins; Col. J. F. Gregory, U.S.A. Seated (*Left to right*) Gov. Schuyler Crosby, Montana; Gen. P. H. Sheridan, U.S.A.; President Chester A. Arthur; Secretary of War Robert T. Lincoln; Senator George G. Vest

"At times there was but little or no notice. Such was the case when my colleague, Mrs. Gardener of the Civil Service commission, died and conduct of the obsequies fell to me.

"Of course, I had to prepare, yet I could use no notes. It was necessary to be as natural as if speaking extemporaneously. The situation was new to me."

THE WASHINGTON STAR said: "The funeral services for Mrs. Gardener were held in the afternoon of tuesday, july 28, 1925, at her late home, 1838 Lamont street, N.W., Washington, D.C. She had requested that there be no religious ceremony, and the services were in charge of William C. Deming, president of the United States Civil Service commission."

MR. DEMING: "FRIENDS: We have assembled here to pay a last tribute of love and respect to Mrs. Helen H. Gardener, a member of the United States Civil Service commission. This informal ceremony is in accord with the written request of the deceased. She expressed a wish that her colleagues upon the commission and her close personal friends, Mrs. Carrie Chapman Catt and Mrs. Maud Wood Park, make a few remarks.

"I first met Mrs. Gardener when I became a member of the Civil Service commission. Her kindly, genial companionship and her willingness to assist me placed us upon a very easy footing, and that companionship and friendship grew and strengthened each day. I recall how naturally she said to me after I had become a member, 'The public does not discriminate between a new commissioner and one who has had experience. There is a great code of principles and precedents, so if I can give you the benefit at any time of my own efforts and observations, it may save you some anxious hours.' Her advice and cooperation were cheerfully given and as cheerfully received.

"Mrs. Gardener's long experience as an author, lecturer, student, and laborer for the common good, and especially in the cause of women, qualified her for high duties and responsibilities. She was both generous and just. She possessed one of the best minds I have ever known. She reasoned with great accuracy, and was resourceful in any situation. Her memory for details, even to the closing days of her life, was remarkably clear. Her sense of humor was spontaneous.

"I think I have never known anyone who with so little ostentation did so much for others. She believed in the Oriental motto that 'He who gives has all things, and he who withholds has nothing.' To the many women of the commission, and others who called on her, she was a mother, sister, and friend. She devoted her public life to the cause of women and her immediate personal activities to her family and friends.

"Her selection as a member of the United States Civil Service commission by President Woodrow Wilson, abundantly justified the precedent then set of choosing a woman to occupy a place upon that high body.

"Her years rested so lightly upon her shoulders that she had up to her last serious illness the vigor of a woman of fifty and the enthusiasm and interest in life of a schoolgirl. Around the conference table of the Civil Service commission, she was an interesting study, because when the occasion demanded, she could be a stern as well as just judge. She had little or no patience or sympathy with chronic offenders against the civil service law. It sometimes seemed to me that she could add six inches to her short stature when she lifted her shoulders and raised her head in asking a pertinent question. Withal she brought to the commission a woman's tenderness and a woman's intuition.

"She exercised great breadth of vision, and there was an entire absence of prejudice in the discharge of her official duties. She made no distinction between North and South, East and West, or between parties or factions; but she was especially alert in seeing that no rightful opportunity belonging to women was over-looked in the service and that the under dog, regardless of his creed or color, had his day in court.

"Her home, as many of us know, was a perpetual delight and she made it cheerful even in her illness.

"Of her it may be said, 'She lived in deeds, not words; in heart throbs, not in figures on the dial.' Her courage and optimism abided through her long illness. Her last words saturday evening to her niece, Miss Helen Crane, to her secretary, Miss Rena Smith, and to our librarian, Miss Anna Holdridge, when they were leaving her, were 'Goodnight, children.' She said it as naturally and as happily as if she would see them again. That was her way. She always made things easy for those around her.

"Just as she was courageous in life, she faced bravely the great unknown. In keeping with the eternal fitness of things, the end did not come to her in the dark, still watches of the night. She passed away peacefully in her sleep after a glorious sunrise.

"If, in the unrevealed scheme of the universe, there is yet service to be rendered and good cheer to be spread, the dauntless, diligent, and generous spirit of Helen Gardener will go marching on."

Washington Days and Ways

On february 23, 1923, the following telegram was sent from Washington, D.C., by Senator Francis E. Warren:

WILLAM C. DEMING, Cheyenne, Wyoming. Following nomination has just been sent in by President Harding for action of Senate. "I nominate William C. Deming of Wyoming to be member of the United States Civil Service Commission *vice* John H. Bartlett resigned." I expect early confirmation please accept congratulations and all good wishes. When are you coming down.

F. E. WARREN

On march 1, 1923, a second telegram followed:

Your nomination confirmed. Congratulations. F. E. WARREN.

Mr. Deming's appointment to the Civil Service commission, one of the most important divisions of the United States government, brought forth favorable comments from every section of the country. The commission was the first independent administrative agency, except cabinet departments, under the president. This seniority gave the commission many advantages in official and social life in Washington.

Every newspaper in the state of Wyoming carried an announcement or an editorial article relative to the appointment.

The following excerpts from some of these editorials give a cross-section of the high respect in which Mr. Deming is held by his fellow citizens:

CODY HERALD: Mr. Deming is one of Wyoming's best thinkers and constructive builders; has been a forward thinker and his keen insight and rare judgment have kept him in advance of the crowd in any proposition of moment in the State . . . Like any newspaper-man who does his own thinking, Deming has been cussed and discussed more than any other man in the State and time has proven many times the logic of the position he has taken.

GREYBULL STANDARD: Mr. Deming has conducted a real news-paper in which the news was printed without color. Columns of the *Tribune* have been open to the public, and if Deming disagreed with the views expressed, he did it in a fair manner in the editorial columns under his own name.

DOUGLAS BUDGET: The appointment will meet with the approval of Wyoming people . . . (Mr. Deming) is a believer in the civil service principle, with high ideals of public service and with the ability to give practical application of the things he believes.

BURNS HERALD: Mr. Deming is so well known and so highly respected that our citizens not only rejoice in his recognition but also claim a share of honor in his appointment. His influence has been state-wide.

WYOMING LABOR JOURNAL: The appointment of William C. Deming, editor of the *Wyoming Tribune-Leader,* to the federal service commission, conferred an honor on one of the constructive citizens of the state. Editor Deming has been a sincere booster for what he believes to be the best interests of the state; as an employer, he has always held the friendship of those associated with him, as evidenced by the resolutions adopted by the local Typographical Union.

Careyhurst, Wyoming, march 5, 1923
HON. W. C. DEMING: I congratulate you upon your appoint-ment as a member of the Civil Service commission.

While I appreciate the importance of this position, I feel you are well qualified to fill the place creditably. I can say quite frankly that I am sorry to see you leaving Wyoming, but I presume you will keep in touch with things here and will retain your interests in this State.

I will take this occasion to thank you for the help you have given me during the time that I was in office as governor not only in your capacity as editor of the *Wyoming Tribune* but also as a member of the board of trustees of the University. Sincerely yours,

ROBERT D. CAREY

Warren G. Harding,
President of the United States of America.

To all who shall see these presents, Greeting:

Know Ye, That reposing special trust and confidence in the Integrity and Ability of ———— William C. Deming, of Wyoming, ———— I have nominated, and by and with the advice and consent of the Senate, do appoint him ———— William C. Deming, of Wyoming, ———— a Civil Service Commissioner, ———— and do authorize and empower him to execute and fulfil the duties of that Office according to law, and to have and to hold the said Office, with all the powers, privileges and emoluments thereunto of right appertaining unto him, the said William C. Deming, during the pleasure of the President of the United States for the time being.

In testimony whereof, I have caused these Letters to be made Patent and the Seal of the United States to be hereunto affixed.

Done at the City of Washington this first ———— day of March, ———— in the year of our Lord one thousand nine hundred and twenty-three, ———— and of the Independence of the United States of America the one hundred and forty-seventh.

By the President:
Charles E. Hughes
Secretary of State.

Warren G. Harding.

Previous to Mr. Deming's arrival in Washington, his fellow commissioners, George R. Wales and Mrs. Helen H. Gardener, sent the following telegram of greeting: "It must be a special gratification to you to be a successor of Theodore Roosevelt[9] on the commission. We have preserved the desk and chair which he occupied and have placed them in the room prepared for your occupancy."

And thus, with the inspiration of a predecessor whom Mr. Deming so highly honored and respected, he prepared to take up his duties in the nation's capital. Just before leaving Cheyenne, he summarized his experiences in Cheyenne under the caption: "Twenty-Two Years of the Tribune."

". . . Without missing an issue, the *Wyoming Tribune* has undergone complete destruction by fire in 1902, has moved three times in each case into larger quarters, now owning its own building, . . . was able in 1920 to purchase the *Cheyenne State Leader,* the oldest continuous newspaper in the state, and consolidate it with the *Wyoming State Tribune*. . ."

A *Tribune* cartoon of William C. Deming with a huge pen in his hand announced that the skipper of the *Tribune-Leader* craft, who was going to Washington as Civil Service commissioner, "promises to throw out a 'line' in the form of a Washington letter."

These letters, "As Seen in Washington," which were published in the *Tribune* gave illuminating insight into the official life at the capital for eight years. Other captions were "Notes by the Way," "Casual Cogitations," etc.

Owing to the illness of Commissioner Wales, the official ceremony of presenting Mr. Deming personally

---

[9] Theodore Roosevelt was a member of the Civil Service commission from may 13, 1889 to may 5, 1895.

to the three hundred office employees was postponed. He was sworn in on march 31, 1923, by John T. Doyle, secretary of the commission, in the presence of Senator Francis E. Warren, Judge Charles E. Winter, congressman-at-large, former representative Frank W. Mondell, and immediate staff members.

President Harding's commission appointing Deming a commissioner to fill the post vacated by John H. Bartlett, former governor of New Hampshire who became first assistant postmaster-general, was presented by Commissioner Helen Hamilton Gardener.

Mr. Deming was formally elected president of the commission on april 9 by his colleagues and continued the duties which he had been discharging since march 31 because of the illness of Commissioner Wales.

The next day, april 10, he accompanied Senator Francis E. Warren to call upon President Harding to pay his respects and to thank him for the appointment. During the call, Commissioner Deming, on behalf of the Cheyenne chamber of commerce, presented to President Harding a formal written invitation to attend the Frontier Days in Cheyenne in july.

Immediately upon taking office, Mr. Deming issued a bulletin saying that he hoped to meet all of the employees of the service soon. "That we shall work together in harmony and continue to secure practical results is my hope and wish," he said.

The United States Civil Service commission, created in 1883, and composed of three members, "not more than two of whom shall be adherents of the same party," then had jurisdiction over more than 600,000 employees in the United States, Porto Rico, Alaska, Hawaii, and the Phillippines. At this time (1943) the number of employees includes more than 3,000,000 men and women.

With the responsibility falling upon the shoulders of Mrs. Gardener and Mr. Deming during Mr. Wales's illness, Mrs. Gardener became of inestimable help.

Born in Virginia in 1853, the daughter of a minister, Alice Chenoweth later took the legal pen name of Helen Hamilton Gardener and from 1875 to 1900 made her home in New York City where she wrote magazine articles, stories, and books. It was her conviction that a woman should take sole responsibility for her work and achievement and not lean upon family name or connection for recognition. . . Her whole life conformed to her conviction that a woman should "stand on her own feet."

In 1902 Mrs. Gardener married Colonel Selden Allen Day of the United States army. Upon Colonel Day's retirement from active service, they spent six years making a tour of the world. She was invited to lecture at many of the universities in Japan, France, England, and Italy and visited twenty countries collecting pictures and data. After returning to the United States, she gave university extension illustrated lectures under the title, "Ourselves and Other Peoples."

Mrs. Gardener was closely associated with Susan B. Anthony, Anna Howard Shaw, Elizabeth Stanton, and Carrie Chapman Catt, leaders in the suffrage movement. When she moved from New York to Washington, the equal suffrage leaders grew to look upon her as the diplomatic corps of the organization. She was credited with having done much toward securing the amendment to the Constitution giving women the franchise.

Mrs. Gardener was appointed by President Woodrow Wilson as the first woman member of the United States Civil Service commission. She took office april

13, 1920, and was instrumental in changing the president's opposition towards woman suffrage.

She died at Walter Reed hospital, Washington, D.C., july 26, 1925, at the age of seventy, although she appeared much younger.

Immediately upon being notified of his appointment to the commission, Mr. Deming was advised that soon after his arrival in Washington there would be a conference of a representative of the Civil Service commission, of the Budget Bureau, and the Bureau of Efficiency for the purpose of carrying out the provisions of the Reclassification act which would become effective in 1924.

Although the principle upon which the act was founded had been used in the postal service and in other countries and had made considerable progress in grading and systematizing duties and wages, the act was not well understood by the general public. It required much consideration and elucidation and much attention as to its purpose and its safeguarding provisions which took a great deal of the commission's time and thought.

Two months after he had assumed office, Mr. Deming received the following letter from President Harding:

The White House, Washington, may 29, 1923

MY DEAR CHAIRMAN DEMING: A question was raised in the cabinet meeting this morning relative to the physical examination of applicants for certification to government employment.

I am writing to inquire whether the commission demands any more than the certificate of the family physician.

If no more is required than the friendly certificate of the family physician, I wish you would arrange to have an interview with the chairman of the Federal Employees' Compensation commission and inquire into the abuses of the compensation service which develop out of the admission to public service of federal employees who are not physically fit for service.

May 29, 1925.

My dear Chairman Deming:

A question was raised in the Cabinet meeting this morning relative to the physical examination of applicants for certification to government employment. I am writing to inquire whether the Commission demands any more than the certificate of the family physician. If no more is required than the friendly certificate of the family physician I wish you would arrange to have an interview with the Chairman of the Federal Employees' Compensation Commission, and inquire into the abuses of the compensation service which develop out of the admission to public service of federal employees who are not physically fit for service. Perhaps it is desirable to formulate an Order requiring employees to be examined by a physician and surgeon who represents the public service.

Very truly yours,

[signature]

Mr. William C. Deming,
Chairman, U. S. Civil Service Commission,
Washington, D. C.

June 2, 1925.

My dear Mr. Deming:

Thank you for your letter of June one, in which you make reply to my inquiry relative to the physical examination by government physicians of applicants for government employment. Whatever action is necessary to hasten the reply of the Executive departments heretofore addressed I will be glad to have you take. I wish you would invite a conference with the Acting Surgeon General of the Health Department and get from him information relative to the ability of the Department to make these examinations without increase of appropriation. I am well convinced that the Health Department is not overworked, and I believe there is a possibility of the Department taking on this additional service without added expenditure. If you do not find such a disposition I should like to be informed so that I may interest myself in the matter in a becoming way.

Very truly yours,

[signature]

Mr. William C. Deming,
President, U. S. Civil Service Commission,
Washington, D. C.

Perhaps it is desirable to formulate an order requiring employees to be examined by a physician and surgeon who represents the public service. Very truly yours,   WARREN G. HARDING

Mr. Deming replied at once as follows:

June 1, 1923

THE PRESIDENT: Your letter of may 29 relative to the physical examination of applicants for certification to government employment has been received and I would respectfully report that the present situation in regard to this matter is as follows:

For a number of years this commission has believed it to be desirable that persons entering the federal service should be given a physical examination at the time of appointment, so that there might be on file a record for future comparisons. This examination to be uniform in character and without bias should be made by a federal physician. There has been, however, no force of federal physicians so distributed and sufficient in number to make such examinations, except the medical corps of the Army, Navy, and Public Health Service, and these have already duties occupying their full time.

Some months ago, however, the Employees' Compensation commission, together with this commission and the Public Health Service, held a conference to ascertain what action could be taken toward diminishing the number of claims under the Employees' Compensation act, which were believed by the Employees' Compensation commission to be consequent upon admitting to the service persons who had some physical condition predisposing to injury. As a result of this conference, a joint letter, of which a copy is attached, was forwarded to the executive departments and the independent establishments. Replies have been received from most of the independent establishments but from only three of the executive departments, the departments of Justice, Agriculture, and Commerce. These replies almost uniformly agree that it is desirable to have a physical examination at the time of appointment by a physician in the federal service. The commission has been waiting until replies have been received from a majority of the larger executive departments before actually formulating any definite plan, and it is believed that it would be desirable to defer such a plan until these larger departments have been heard from.

The War and Navy departments, having the necessary medical corps, have within the past two years, in their arsenal and yard

PRESIDENT HARDING VISITS YELLOWSTONE NATIONAL PARK, 1923

Left to right: Secretary of Agriculture, Henry C. Wallace; President Warren G. Harding; Secretary of Interior,
Dr. Hubert Work; Director of National Park Service, Stephen T. Mather; and Superintendent
of Yellowstone National Park, Horace M. Albright

services, installed such an examination. The Public Health Service has been making these examinations where requested to do so by the commission, but inasmuch as the appropriations for this service are made on a basis of the work already assigned under various statutes, it would be necessary to secure additional appropriation for this new duty.

An executive order at this time, requiring employees to be examined by a physician or surgeon who represents the Public Health Service, would be very desirable were it not for the fact that there is no appropriation available to make payments for a sufficient force of physicians to do the work. This commission has in mind, if the departments are uniformly agreed that such an examination is desirable, of submitting, jointly with the Public Service and the Employees' Compensation commission, a recommendation to you that an appropriation be secured to provide the necessary force of medical examiners to extend the systems at present in effect in the War and Navy factory services to the rest of the federal employees.

In connection with this subject, there is at present under consideration with the Post Office department a somewhat similar action which, however, has not reached a definite form as yet. Very respectfully, W. C. DEMING, Commissioner

The White House, Washington, June 2, 1923

MY DEAR MR. DEMING: Thank you for your letter of June one, in which you make reply to my inquiry relative to the physical examination by government physicians of applicants for government employment.

Whatever action is necessary to hasten the reply of the Executive departments heretofore addressed I will be glad to have you take.

I wish you would invite a conference with the acting Surgeon-general of the Health department and get from him information relative to the ability of the department to make these examinations without increase of appropriation.

I am well convinced that the Health department is not overworked, and I believe there is a possibility of the department taking on this additional service without added expenditure.

If you do not find such a disposition, I should like to be informed so that I may interest myself in the matter in a becoming way. Very truly yours, WARREN G. HARDING

This was the inception of the present system of physical examinations for government employees in the classified service.

The much needed reform was put into effect under the authority of an executive order of june 18, 1923, one of the last official acts of President Harding before he left for Alaska. He died in San Francisco in august.

On september 8, 1923, the commission issued the order which for the first time in the history of the federal government inaugurated a system of physical examinations for employees in the civil service.

With the view of promoting health and efficiency and of minimizing accidents among federal employees, the surgeon general of the Public Health Service was authorized and directed to make such physical examinations of applicants and employees as might be requested by the Civil Service commission. It was also his duty to keep the commission advised of the localities where medical officers were available for duty.

The new order made it possible to provide against the entrance into the service of persons whose physical condition might be a menace to their fellow workers. Employees also would be guarded against the danger of assignment to duties not in keeping with their physical limitations, and it would safeguard any future pension system.

In view of the fact that he had been working so recently with President Harding relative to the physical examinations for service employees, the news of the president's death in San Francisco on august 2, 1923, came as a distinct shock to Mr. Deming.

In answer to a telegram from the *Wyoming Tribune* for an editorial on the president's death, Mr. Deming wrote:

"The country has lost a great leader, a man of warm

PRESIDENT HARDING BIDDING FAREWELL TO ALASKA
IN 1923
made a short time before he went to California
where serious illness resulted in his death

sympathies. . . The naval conference and treaties
will stand everlastingly to his credit. His world court
stand will be vindicated. The budget bureau was a great
step forward in government financing. His advanced
position for law enforcement, especially as to prohibition, brought to him millions of new admirers and
friends. He had to meet many trying and discouraging
problems following the war and he was solving them.
He was big in mind and body and heart.

"I am glad I heard his magnificent speech renom-
inating Taft. I am glad I heard his address at the
unveiling at the Alexander Hamilton statue in Washington in may. I am glad I saw him at his best soon
after his return from Florida and felt his arm upon
my shoulder when I attempted to thank him for the
honor he had conferred upon me. I am glad I have
official letters written only a few days before his departure for Alaska showing keen interest in and clear
grasp of official affairs.

"He rose nobly with his opportunity and grew with
every serious demand made upon him. He had caught
the true vision of his position and of his country and
was walking in the light.

"His entire career from printer to president is an inspiration and the world is better for his having lived."

With characteristic thoroughness, Mr. Deming fa-
miliarized himself with every phase of the commission's
work and wrote many constructive articles and delivered a number of addresses relative to the history, the
aims, and the accomplishments of the Civil Service
system.

The demand for material of this kind from educators,
officials, civic and other organizations, students, and
others interested in the merit system was so great that

it was decided to publish it in convenient and comprehensive form.

Captioned, "Application of the Merit System in the United States Civil Service," a one hundred twenty-four page booklet was printed by the government printing office, Washington, in two editions, 1925 and 1928.

Mr. Deming's article "They would Work for the Government," published in a number of sunday newspapers on may 17, 1925, and crammed with human interest, was widely read. Said the article, in part:

"All roads lead to Rome, and also to the information bureau of the United States Civil Service commission at Washington. The travelers are of every race, color, creed, age, and station in life. They represent the polyglot citizenry of the United States and most of them seek work. A former Russian prince, fused in the great American melting-pot, was a recent caller. He got a job, not because he was a Russian prince, but because he possessed technical knowledge valuable to our government.

"In an ordinary day's work, when no exceptionally popular examination has been announced, about five hundred men and women present themselves at the commission's bureau and ask for information about government employment. No stage ever presented a greater variety of comedy, pathos, or even tragedy. There is tragedy in the faces and in the stories of those who have met with reverses in fortune, have suffered family losses, or have suddenly been thrown out of employment.

"One would be more than human if he did not find comedy in the appearance of a six-foot woman from the South, who proudly displayed a certificate of graduation from a detective school and proclaimed that she was now ready to 'capture.' He would be less than human if he did not find pathos in the plight of this ignorant, trusting dupe, who had spent her last dollar to come to Washington and had to ask the aid of charity to get back to her home.

"When a seeker of information tiptoes into the bureau, sidles over to a far corner, and asks for a confidential interview, the clerk picks up a record card and writes detective at the top. Usually that designation is correct. The information bureau now has on file more than three thousand cards, all dated within a year, and representing that number of persons who wish to be informed of the next examination announced for the Secret Service. Many of the cards which have been filled out by the applicants themselves appear to be specimens of ability to construct cryptograms, for they are scarcely decipherable. . . A son of Erin sought employment as a policeman, naturally. He found that he was an inch and a half below the specified height. He underwent a course of physical training designed to stretch him to the required height. But the difference was too great. He could not be stretched an inch and a half, so he had to content himself with a letter-carrier examination.

"Every possible kind of employment is sought, even as guard in a leper colony. A recent applicant said that he wished to be informed of the next examination announced for positions of interpreter. When asked to list the languages in which he was qualified, he wrote down twenty-three languages, including Icelandic.

"Among the hundreds of thousands of applications that poured into the commission's offices some were responsible for much amusement. On august 7, 1924, a bureau chief brought a lady to the commission. He had been trying to obtain a civil service status for her for ten years. . . For some reason he asked her age. She refused to give it saying: 'Why, there are a lot of men in Washington that want to marry me. There is one lawyer here that has proposed six times in the past two years. Anyhow, you don't have to worry about my age. I am well under the requirements.'

"One applicant gave a false statement as to her date of birth. On the application for steno-typist she gave the date as september 28, 1903, and her age as eighteen, whereas it now appears that she was actually born on september 28, 1904. In explaining this discrepancy, she wrote:

" 'At the time I filed application for examination, I was under the honest understanding that the date of my birth given by me was correct. This date was given to me by my parents, who had always figured my birthday in accordance with the Jewish calendar. The Jewish calendar year starts in the month of september and according to this calendar, my birthday falls upon a different date each year.' "

In one year the names of eight hundred thirty-five persons were added to the commission's "barred list" of those who by their own dishonesty had forfeited the right to compete in civil service examinations.

Mr. Deming wrote the following about some of his civil service experiences:

"When one considers there are nearly a million men and women now employed in the executive branch of the United States government, and four or five hundred members of congress seeking jobs in or out of the classified civil service for a multitude of constituents, the marvel is that the standard of efficiency is as high as it is. Naturally, some misfits will find a place in the service, especially in positions exempt from the merit system.

"One of the branches which requires constant vigilance is the Customs Service under the Treasury department, because of the number of men and women in the United States and in foreign countries who are professional smugglers of valuables.

"It is not so difficult to detect these violators when they attempt to bring in pictures, furniture, clothing, and rugs, but when it comes to jewelry, especially diamonds, that is a different proposition.

"Several years ago, a young man who desired a place in the Customs Service, with assignment to Paris or Antwerp, through friends prevailed upon the Treasury department to request the president to issue an executive order for the appointment which would have exempted him from competitive examination.

"It was alleged in his behalf, among many other qualifications, that he was an expert, by reason of sixteen years' experience in the handling, judging, and sale of diamonds and other jewelry. It was further claimed by his endorsers that he spoke several languages.

"Perhaps his friends or his congressman, who made the original request to the Customs Service, did not know that the president, regardless of the sponsors, would refer the matter to the Civil Service commission for recommendation.

"The White House, however, did send the request of the secretary of the Treasury for the executive order, containing the name of the applicant, to the Civil Service commission, asking for a report and recommendation in duplicate.

"An investigation followed. It developed that if the

alleged expert had sixteen years' qualifying experience, he must have begun when he was about fourteen years of age. Furthermore, he had jumped from pillar to post in the government service and in private employment. About his only preparation for the responsible duties of a custom agent, who was to detect smugglers of diamonds in Europe, was that he worked for short periods in a few jewelry stores in America. Also, his knowledge of languages was confined to English and a smattering of French.

"Witnesses stressed his good looks, his agreeable personality, his war record, and the fact that he needed the position. These, however, in the absence of bona fide experience and ability as a diamond and jewelry expert, would not qualify him for the position.

"The request for an executive order was withdrawn by the secretary of the Treasury.

"A subordinate called upon the Civil Service commission and admitted there had not been due diligence in investigating the alleged qualifications of the applicant before the first request was made. There was renewed pressure upon the bureau and it seemed willing to again consider the case of the applicant. The bureau wished to know, in advance, if another executive order was requested whether the Civil Service commission would regard it favorably.

"By this time, the file had assumed quite voluminous proportions."

Henry A. Hesse, chief of investigations and review, then considered the entire case carefully and reported against further action, whereupon President Deming of the commission wrote:

January 18, 1929

COMMISSIONERS WALES AND DELL: The attached file in the ....
case speaks for itself. I agree with Mr. Hesse that it would not only

be an impropriety to make another investigation suggested, but that it would be setting a dangerous precedent.

In the instant case, reduced to a practical proposition, if the Civil Service commission should make a gratuitous, advance investigation looking toward another executive order which has not been requested, and should report that .... is worthy and well qualified, and it should follow after his appointment that he had failed in his duties, the entire responsibility would be ours.

It almost looks as if we are being asked to give the young man a complete bill as to qualifications in advance, in order that the Treasury department may be practically relieved of any responsibility.

. . . .

The proposition made to us might be compared to that of an attorney who wished to present a hypothetical case to a court in order that he might be able to determine whether to bring suit.

W. C. DEMING

"Members of the commission all agreed to close the case," continued Mr. Deming.

"It was then that my colleagues, Commissioners Wales and Dell, suggested that I present the whole situation to the Honorable A. W. Mellon, secretary of the Treasury, in a personal interview, who apparently was not familiar with the case.

"I did so and nothing further was heard by the commission of efforts in behalf of .... for the position of customs agent.

"I have recalled the above case chiefly for the benefit of any others who may hold official positions requiring care and discrimination in protecting public service against incompetents and from political influence in behalf of unworthy applicants for favorable consideration and appointment.

"The commission did not imply or suggest that there was intent to defraud or weaken the Customs Service, but it did feel that friends of .... showed too much zeal in his behalf considering the exaggerations and misrepresentations relative to his experience as a diamond expert."

Requests made to the president of the United States for executive orders originate in many ways.

For instance, when an applicant for eligibility in the United States civil service fails, he occasionally attempts to circumvent the result through an appeal to his representative in congress or United States senator.

Failing in that, he or his friends may appeal directly to the president for an executive order.

The following is a diplomatic and effective reply to the White House asking for information when an executive order had been requested:

[The applicant did not receive the executive order.]

January 13, 1930

HONORABLE LAWRENCE RICHEY, Secretary to the President.

DEAR MR. RICHEY: A few days ago you phoned me concerning the rejected application of X for examination Metropolitan police department, District of Columbia. Mr. X's application having been rejected because he is under the minimum height requirement.

If I understood you correctly, you stated that the president had been requested either formally or informally to issue an executive order waiving the requirement in the case of Mr. X, thus permitting him to enter the examination. Your thought was that that would be setting a troublesome precedent and would in effect open the way to similar requests and in the final analysis place the president in the position of selecting applicants at least for the Metropolitan police force.

You asked if there was any way that the Civil Service commission could properly exercise its functions for the relief of Mr. X and at the same time spare the president such responsibility.

I stated that I recalled the case generally, but not all the details, and would look into it carefully and report to you later. I had a brief history of the case made which is enclosed herewith. You will see that Mr. X has filed three applications and each has been rejected because he did not meet the minimum height requirement of 5 feet 8 inches. You will further see that the commission's measurements have been confirmed by the Public Health Service and by the Board of Surgeons of the police department. Mr. X does not question the accuracy of the figures, that is five feet seven and one-half inches. It is probably natural for an applicant unfamiliar with the rules and regulations and the manner in which such qualifications are arrived at to feel that it is a mere technicality which could be or should be waived in worthy cases.

As you will observe in the brief history enclosed, the height requirement is that established by both the commission and the District of Columbia, and is an important competitive feature of our examination. If such a requirement can be waived in an individual case in the matter of one-half inch, it could be waived just as consistently in the matter of an inch or any other figure and, therefore, the standard would be completely destroyed. No exception has ever been made in behalf of an individual in a competitive examination for the Metropolitan police force. Such a waiver would be contrary to the spirit of the civil service law. It is just as necessary to fix a minimum height standard as it is to apply a minimum and maximum age standard. These limitations are arbitrary just as age qualifications for suffrage in various states are arbitrary.

The commission feels that you wish a perfectly frank statement of the situation, especially as Mr. X has made efforts previously through the office of the late United States Senator Francis E. Warren of Wyoming, through G. L. Collins, Surgeon, United States Public Health Service, through Mr. ...., a business man of Washington, D.C., and possibly others who have called or written in Mr. X's behalf.

I agree with you that if the president should issue an executive order, it would be a precedent that might frequently arise in similar cases. Furthermore, should Mr. X or any other applicant who failed to meet such a minimum requirement, secure a place on the Metropolitan police force by executive order, I fear it would be only human if at times he sought to capitalize that fact whenever it appeared to his advantage to do so.

If the foregoing point is well taken, I think it would be conceded also that if Mr. X or any other applicant should be able to prevail upon the commission to waive a competitive requirement, it would open the entire field to all comers similarly situated, and if an exception could be made for one-half inch, it could be made for three-quarters inch or any other height deficiency.

For the same reason above stated, if Mr. X by persistent effort of friends or members of congress finally secured a place on the police force through a waiver by the commission, it would be only natural for him, from time to time, to capitalize that fact while on the force perhaps to the embarrassment of his superiors.

The moral effect on others who had attained eligibility under the complete requirements might be prejudicial to the service.

I feel very sure that if Mr. X's friends and sponsors who are urging favorable action in his behalf either by executive order or waiver of a competitive requirement by the Civil Service commission fully realized all the circumstances and consequences, they would gracefully accept the situation as it now stands.

He seems to be a worthy young man and should be able to find a suitable place somewhere in the government service.

Begging your pardon for this lengthy letter, and trusting that it gives you sufficient information upon which to reach a conclusion, I am, Very sincerely,   W. C. DEMING, President

Mr. Deming applied the same character and degree of industry and resourcefulness in his new responsibility with the Civil Service commission that he had always shown in previous experiences.

After he had assumed his Washington position, the *Washington Post* carried a two column write-up by Lee Lamar Robinson entitled "Expert Workers for Uncle Sam – William C. Deming" from which we quote:

. . . the mere mention of printer's ink brings a rapturous smile. The taint is in his blood . . . he added largely to his experience and strengthened his foundation for work in after life by editing a weekly newspaper . . . after doing many things, he still clings to the newspaper business as the beacon light of a busy life.

There is a suggestion of a parallel in the histories of the new Washingtonian and the late President Harding, by whom he was appointed to his present post, in that both got their real start in the grueling work of keeping a struggling country publication on its feet, and the inspiration for their future successes in making good at this task . . . one at Warren, the other at Marion, Ohio. . .

Mr. Deming compiled a list of DO'S and DON'TS for government clerks which elicited commendation from business executives, as well as from government employees. Some of them were: "Don't expect to get more

out of your job than you put into it." "Don't be in too
much of a hurry about leaving at quitting time. A little
added to your day may add a little to your pay."

In commenting on this helpful list, the press added:
"Honorable W. C. Deming, in the short time since
becoming president of the United States Civil Service
commission, has won high praise from his associates
and from others for the conscientious interest he has
taken in the work of his office. There is praise particularly for the spirit of service with which he has enthused
the personnel of the Washington organization."

Mr. Deming's work brought him into contact with
the members of congress. "With rare exceptions, I
found members of both houses of congress most courteous in their relationship with the United States Civil
Service commission," he says. "After the natural timid-
ity and hesitation or embarrassment accompanying my
first appearance before the appropriations committee,
and later appearances in response to requests for information touching the merit system, or pending bills, I
really enjoyed the committee hearings."

Mr. Deming said: "The business of the federal government is administered by the executive department
now including nearly one million persons, of whom the
president is the chief. It might be said that almost any
high administrative or executive official may be called
before a committee of congress to give evidence for or
against a proposed measure or to stand investigation
upon some question.

"In many instances, when not called, chiefs of bureaus, commissions, and cabinet departments volunteer
in order to get their views clearly in the record.

"Even the military establishment is not immune from
such responsibility. Therefore, in my judgment, a man

or woman who accepts an important position in the government service should thoroughly acquaint himself with the law affecting his office, its rules and regulations, and his duties thereunder. Otherwise, he may find himself sometimes in an embarrassing and helpless position.

"As an example of the technique in congressional hearings, I am going to quote very briefly from certain extended hearings before committees.

"Either the budget officer, fiscal agent, or chief of an organization, is frequently called upon to justify its demands before an appropriation committee, or in the case of a deficiency bill.

"In 1929 William R. Wood of Indiana, a typical Hoosier, who always reminded me of Will Rogers, was very active upon the committee on appropriations and frequently presided in the absence of Daniel R. Anthony of Kansas. Wood's long service and familiarity with various departments made him a very useful member.

"In february 1929 the Civil Service commission submitted a supplemental estimate of fifty thousand dollars. I appeared before the committee in behalf of the request.

"The following is taken from official records:"

MR. WOOD: The budget estimate here is for only $50,000. How much do you need?

MR. DEMING: Our deficiency estimate with the bureau of the budget was $118,000 on an annual basis for salaries, counting expenses and contingent funds.

MR. WOOD: And you are allowed how much?

MR. DEMING: We are allowed $50,000.

MR. WOOD: The request for $118,000 was upon the basis of your employing how many more special examiners?

MR. DEMING: Twenty-seven more field investigators or special examiners.

MR. WOOD: If you get only $50,000 how many can you then employ?

MR. DEMING: I assume it will be proportionally reduced.

MR. WOOD: You would employ only half of twenty-seven.

MR. DEMING: Yes, sir, approximately.

Members of congress frequently are misled by applicants or eligibles as to why there is a delay in certification or appointment. Usually these criticisms are exaggerated and easily explained. However, Mr. Wood switched the line of questioning as follows:

MR. WOOD: Why does it take so long to determine whether or not a man who is an applicant is eligible?

MR. DEMING: Because it is necessary to go into an average of at least two different communities and investigate his personal life for at least five years back. The Secret Service of the United States investigates clear back to the applicant's school days. Economy has made it necessary for us, as a rule, to investigate for an average of only about five years prior to his application.

MR. WOOD: If you had the $118,000 would that permit you to go ahead as fast as would be practical and possible?

MR. DEMING: I am rather inclined to think so. It should be borne in mind that since we made our original estimates, there are certain new positions that have been brought in requiring work on the part of the Civil Service commission; for instance, the positions of distilled spirits clerk, storekeeper-gauger, and customs patrol inspector, for which we are holding examinations now.

During Mr. Deming's incumbency as president of the Civil Service commission, there were in the departmental service in Washington about seventy thousand employees, which, under the law, were presumed to be apportioned among the states so far as it was practicable to do so – provided the various states furnished eligibles.

Inasmuch as several hundred, possibly several thousand, of the minor positions, such as those of messenger boys, low grade clerks, common laborers, custodians, etc., did not pay large salaries, it was usually difficult to obtain applicants and eligibles from remote districts or states.

Therefore, almost from the beginning, the near-by states, especially Maryland and Virginia, showed a large excess of employees on the rolls in Washington. In other words, they had more than their quota under the apportionment act, because citizens of delinquent states did not apply and, of course, the position had to be filled.

Mr. Deming, being a newspaper man, decided to give wide publicity to this fact, in addition to the conventional statements made from time to time. He prepared for the *Washington Post* an article, in a light vein, so worded and so publicized by the newspaper that it attracted wide attention and aroused keen interest in the condition of apportionment.

It is no reflection upon the average member of congress to say that he is not familiar with the Civil Service law, in all of its ramifications, because it is technical and he has so many other things to do. He does know, however, that the folks back home want jobs, or think they do – preferably one requiring no preparation or examination.

This is one reason that members of congress strive so diligently and sometimes successfully to exempt employees in new activities and agencies from the operation of the United States civil service law.

There always are members of both houses who are looking for an opportunity to attack or criticize a public official in order to gain some publicity, both in Washington and among their constituents. That is an old practice and common to both parties. Newspapers will carry a bit of censure and ignore a compliment.

Mr. Deming's article on the apportionment supplied two of the senate's explosive members, the Honorable Smith W. Brookhart, of Iowa, and the Honorable J. Thomas Heflin, of Alabama, with an opportunity to be heard.

Therefore, Senate resolution 154, seventieth congress, first session, contained the following preamble to a resolution for a committee on investigation of appointments and dismissals in the civil service since july 1, 1919. The opening paragraphs were:

APPOINTMENTS AND DISMISSALS IN THE CIVIL SERVICE
FRIDAY, JUNE 15, 1928

United States Senate, Select Committee on Investigation of Illegal Appointments and Dismissals in the Civil Service. Washington, D.C.

The committee met (pursuant to call of the chairman) at 11:30 a.m., in room 250 Senate Office building, Senator Porter H. Dale (presiding).

PRESENT: Senators Dale (chairman), Brookhart, and Heflin; the Honorable William C. Deming, president Civil Service commission; C. W. Bartlett, chairman special committee, assistant chief, division of appointments; Miss Vivian Carlson, assistant chief, division of appointments; Mrs. Amy A. Harradon, congressional correspondence clerk, division of appointments; Ruloff R. Stratton, statistical clerk, division of appointments; H. E. Morgan, director of public information and recruiting; and John T. Doyle, secretary, Civil Service commission.

THE CHAIRMAN: The committee will be in order.

The committee had under consideration Senate resolution 154, which is as follows:

WHEREAS: William C. Deming, President of the Civil Service Commission, admitted in an article published in the *Washington Post* of march 6, 1927, that the Civil Service Commission had appointed in excess of quotas over ten thousand persons from the District of Columbia, Maryland, Virginia, and other states whose quotas are in arrears, and many ex-service men and women have been illegally separated from the service, and much suffering and hardship caused thereby, terminating in some cases in commitments to Saint Elizabeth hospital, and in other cases of suicide; . . .

THE CHAIRMAN: Will you tell the committee your name and position, Mr. Deming?

MR. DEMING: William C. Deming, president United States Civil Service commission.

SENATOR HEFLIN: Mr. Deming, have you got a copy of the resolution there before you?

MR. DEMING: I have read it, Senator; yes, sir.

SENATOR HEFLIN: I think, Mr. Chairman, we might permit Mr. Deming to make a statement orally, if he wishes to, before we begin.

THE CHAIRMAN: All right. Mr. Deming, if you will.

MR. DEMING: Now, Mr. Chairman, as I understand this proceeding and the resolution, they originated primarily from an article published by me in the *Washington Post,* march 6, 1927, concerning the status of the apportionment of positions in the classified service among the states and the District of Columbia.

If it pleases the chairman and the committee, I believe it is only fair to correct what seems to be an erroneous inference in the resolution concerning that article.

The use of the word "admitted" seems to imply that there has been some secrecy about the apportionment situation. Quite the contrary is true. The article published in the *Washington Post* of march 6, 1927, was given out for publication voluntarily for the information of the public, and for years the commission has published twice a month an apportionment table, available to the public, giving the exact distribution among states and territories and the District of Columbia of appointments to the departmental service at Washington.

The use of the words "Civil Service commission had appointed" indicates a possible lack of understanding of the commission's power in the matter of appointments. This office makes no appointments except in its own organization. Under the law and rules, the commission certifies eligibles secured through open competitive examinations for filling vacancies in the various departments and independent establishments to the appointing officers, who in the exercise of vested constitutional authority make the appointments. The commission has no jurisdiction in appointments except to see that the requirements of the civil service law and rules are met.

The limitations placed upon the power of the commission in removals have already been discussed. This office is not aware of any breakdown of morale and efficiency, or of any injustice, discrimination, intimidation, or illegal dismissals. It should further be stated that the power of removal is incident to the power of appointment, and that both powers rest in the departments and not the commission.

So far as the disparity of the state apportionment of appointments is concerned, the commission is able and ready to state the full reasons why the disparity exists, to point out its constant efforts to maintain approximate equality in the apportionment, and, of course, to give to the committee of the senate any other information regarding its work that is available or can be made so.

The Civil Service commission is not interested in the residents of one state above those of another. The commission is wholly in favor of the apportionment provision of the civil service law. It is beyond the power of the commission, however, to create eligibles from the states that are in arrears under the apportionment. If the residents of states in arrears are not sufficiently interested in positions in the departmental service at Washington to apply for them and become eligible for appointment, after having had due notice of examinations and full opportunity to enter them, they cannot reasonably object if residents of other states who have applied are examined and appointed. The vacancies must be filled. The Civil Service commission has no alternative, but is required to certify for appoinment the available eligibles, regardless of their residence.

The purpose of government employment is not to provide places for individuals, but to transact the public business. If some states do not supply the workers, others must.

SENATOR HEFLIN. Thousands of people do not know anything about these places being here; they do not know anything about these quotas, whether they are full or not.

MR. DEMING. That is the very reason I have been emphasizing this fact and working on it for six years.

I wish to say for the record here that we send to every postmaster and our local secretaries, where we have local boards, copies of announcements to be posted in the post office or in some public place, with a request – and we especially request this – that they leave copies with the newspapers; but we have found, generally speaking, that the newspapers of the country do not give that as much publicity as they should. We have gone to the point of making a news item out of these coming examinations, and still we are not able, except in a comparatively few cases – that is, a minority of the cases – to get the publicity we should.

SENATOR HEFLIN. I have had complaints made to me that there are eligibles already on the list, but they are far removed from here, and they are waiting for action to be taken, and these people who are here in the District and in Virginia and Maryland are forever and eternally dogging the commission to give them these places, and that they yield to that pressure frequently, instead of picking out the people who are on the eligible list and bringing them in here. Is there anything to that contention?

MR. DEMING. There is not, Senator; and I assume what you wish here this morning is accurate, detailed information and not discussions that go too far afield.

SENATOR HEFLIN. Yes. Would you suggest that the law be changed so as to specifically set out that certain states should not have more than a certain number?

MR. DEMING. I doubt the wisdom and practicability of that. But, to my mind, the most immediate method of starting in to equalize it would be to close the examinations, possibly, to applicants in the District of Columbia, Virginia, and Maryland, and one or two of the other states that are in excess of their quota, until such times as the apportionment is equalized. But then we are face to face with the probability that we would not have enough eligibles to carry on the business of the government.

SENATOR BROOKHART. Well, now if the examinations were closed as to the District of Columbia, and an effort was made in Iowa and Alabama and these other states, they could easily fill this quota?

MR. DEMING. That would depend who made the effort and how much of an effort was made. Up to this time it is not our experience that it can be done.

SENATOR HEFLIN. My suggestion is to fix the law so that a certain state cannot have more than a certain number. You stop when you fill that number. That might be a good provision.

The resolution provides, Mr. Deming, that we shall investigate and report on illegal appointments and dismissals from the civil service. What do you understand that to mean?

MR. DEMING. I am sure, Senator, I don't know just what you had in mind.

SENATOR HEFLIN. What we meant were those people that you have appointed above the quota in Maryland, Virginia, and Washington.

MR. DEMING. No; that would not be illegal, Senator, because of this fact —

SENATOR HEFLIN (interposing). Does it not violate the spirit of the Civil Service act?

MR. DEMING. No, sir. The Civil Service act of january 16, 1883, provides in section 2, paragraph 2:

And among other things, such rules shall provide and declare, as nearly as the conditions of good administration will warrant, as follows:

. . . Third. Appointments to the public service aforesaid in the departments of Washington shall be apportioned among the several states and territories and the District of Columbia upon the basis of population as acertained at the last preceding census. Every application for an examination shall contain, among other things, a statement, under oath, setting forth his or her actual bona fide residence at the time of making the application, as well as how long he or she has been a resident of such place.

Now, our construction of that is that it is not mandatory. It simply directs what the rules to be promulgated by the president of the civil service shall contain. In other words, the statutory directions are to be followed as nearly as the conditions of good administration will warrant. There is a discretion, therefore, left to the president to modify the statutory direction if in his judgment such action shall be requred for the purposes of good administration.

SENATOR BROOKHART. I have a complaint of this kind, that in july 1926, a reduction was made in the public debt and income tax divisions of the Treasury department, and that several hundred employees from states whose quotas were in arrears were discharged from these two divisions, while more than that number from those above their quota were retained in those two divisions.

MR. DEMING. But that is an administrative matter within that particular department, under the law, as the apportionment applies, as I said before, to the original entry into the service, and not the retention in the service.

SENATOR HEFLIN. As you said a while ago that the act did not seem to be mandatory. What is the reason for that? Why is not the act mandatory?

MR. DEMING. The very language of the act seems to imply that. The second paragraph of section 2 says: "And among other things, said rules shall provide and declare, as nearly as the conditions of good administration will warrant" –

It being foreseen that there would be instances or contingencies in which the exact application of the rule, particularly the apportionment rule, would obstruct the orderly conduct of the business of the government. For instance, in the condition we have before us now, of the states not supplying sufficient eligibles, we cannot stop the machinery of the government until such time as we get the eligibles.

Nothing ever came of the Brookhart-Heflin resolution as it was based on an entire misconception of the apportionment provision of the Civil Service act.

ATTORNEY GENERAL MITCHELL AND MR. DEMING EXCHANGE VIEWS

Following the adoption of the Eighteenth amendment, congress enacted a prohibition enforcement act and eliminated a large portion of the employees for the enforcement of the act from the operation of the United States Civil Service law.

In january 1930, the house of representatives had under consideration H.R. 8574, a bill to transfer the enforcement of the prohibition act from the Treasury department to the department of Justice. In the course of the resolution, it was provided that "the attorney-general is authorized to appoint, without regard to civil-service laws, an assistant director of prohibition and such attorneys as he deems necessary."

A hearing was held before the committee on expenditures in the Executive department of which William Williamson of South Dakota was chairman.

Attorney-general William D. Mitchell, together with a number of his legal staff, appeared in behalf of the transfer and the exemption of attorneys from the classified civil service. The round table was on a dignified plane and the attorney-general, an able lawyer and a pleasing gentleman, set the pace for frankness and courtesy. Mr. Deming says, "I felt honored to participate in such a discussion." On monday morning, january 27, 1930, the proceedings opened as follows:

THE CHAIRMAN. The committee will please come to order. We have with us this morning, gentlemen of the committee, the attorney-general of the United States, who has kindly consented to come before the committee and give his views with reference to the bill. After he has concluded his general statement, he will be glad to reply to any inquiries that members desire to make.

Will you proceed, Mr. Attorney-general, in your own way?

MR. MITCHELL. In a general way, as expressed in a letter addressed to the president by the attorney-general, the pending bill (H.R. 8574), is favored substantially as written. The attorney-general is also in accord with the recommendations made by Secretary Mellon and the reasons he gave for them.

THE CHAIRMAN. There are one or two matters, Mr. Attorney-general, that I should like to inquire about. Questions regarding them were raised from time to time during these hearings. In a general way, are you in favor of the bill substantially as written?

MR. MITCHELL. Yes.

THE CHAIRMAN. The Civil Service commission and others have raised objection to the provision in section 2, subdivision B, reading as follows:

"The attorney-general is authorized to appoint, without regard to the civil service laws, an assistant director of prohibition and such attorneys as he deems necessary."

The Civil Service commission appears to think that it would be in the interest of the service in the selection of a better type of man, if these attorneys were brought within the civil service laws and regulations. What is your opinion with respect to that?

MR. MITCHELL. We cannot have two classes of assistant United States attorneys. The assistant United States attorneys have never been under civil service, and I think it is inadvisable to put them there. That means that the lawyers now in the prohibition unit who are transferred to the department of Justice to aid in the work of prosecuting these cases and working up evidence would have to go to the United States attorneys' offices just on the same basis as any other assistant, except that their present salary and compensation would probably be retained.

STATEMENT of WILLIAM C. DEMING, President, United States Civil Service Commission

The bill under consideration (H.R. 8574) is a serious departure from present law, inasmuch as it places the assistant director of prohibition and such attorneys as the attorney-general may deem necessary outside the jurisdiction of the civil service laws. All attorneys in the bureau of prohibition in the Treasury department are now under civil service. The Civil Service commission has demonstrated that it can supply satisfactory attorneys by competitive examinations.

Further objection is raised to the phraseology of section 2. The attorney-general has the power, peculiar to him alone, to exclude from examinations those positions that he deems legal or confidential. Under the present wording, he could declare any position in the department as confidential and withdraw it from open competition. In this way agents, inspectors, and investigators who had been declared ineligible by the Civil Service commission could be appointed.

Our only reason for being here today is to preserve, if possible and proper, whatever ground has already been gained for the merit system. After having given you the benefit of our experience and observation covering two years of intensive work, we shall, of course, abide gracefully by your judgment. Under the act of march 3, 1927, all positions within the newly created prohibition bureau were classified in the Treasury with the exception of the position of prohibition commissioner. Under the bill now before you, section 2-a makes no change with respect to the head of the prohibition unit except in name. Section 2-b from our standpoint makes some rather important and, we believe, serious departures from the existing act. For instance, the attorney-general is authorized to appoint without regard to the civil service laws an assistant director of prohibition.

Our thought is, that it is unnecessary for the reason that the Civil Service commission has already demonstrated that it can prepare an examination for such a position, and that it can secure eligibles for such a position, because we have done so.

THE CHAIRMAN. How many attorneys are now in the prohibition bureau under the civil service?

MR. DEMING. My recollection is that there are now about one hundred eight, who have been taken from our registers.

MR. BEEDY. Out of a total of what?

MR. DEMING. Out of a total of several hundred on the register.

Attorney-general Mitchell has very considerately stated that he would hope to transfer those available who could be used to advantage, but at the same time, they would lose their classified status.

THE CHAIRMAN. I just want to ask you this question. Under the existing law, you may transfer an employee from the Treasury department to the department of Justice, and so remove him from the civil service against his wishes.

MR. DEMING. They could take the man, but if under the law, as now proposed, you have eliminated the position from the operation of the Civil Service act, he would no longer have a classified status.

MR. MITCHELL. I may clear matters up a little by saying that the only people we have intended to take outside of the civil service are lawyers, and it has been our intention all along that agents who are not lawyers and other people in this prohibition unit remain just where they are under civil service, and there is no disposition on our part to do otherwise. If there is anything about the details of the working of this bill that might produce a different effect, we have not been aware of it.

THE CHAIRMAN. Take the words "and in accordance with the civil service laws." If you would say, "and, in accordance with the competitive provisions of the civil service laws," I think it would meet the objection raised on that particular point.

MR. DEMING. I will offer a suggestion to cover that point presently. I am sure, Mr. Attorney-general, you are correct as to what the present thought or scope of this act is, but as it now stands, it could be construed as giving you authority to make any selections outside of the competitive examinations.

MR. SCHAFER. If the department of Justice wanted to discharge crooked prohibition agents, the ones that violate the sections of the law that they are supposed to be enforcing, they would have to run to the Civil Service commission in order to throw them out, would they not?

MR. DEMING. I am very glad you asked me that question. There is nothing in the operation of the Civil Service act that prevents an administrator from removing an inefficient employee or a crooked employee without going to the Civil Service commission. He cannot remove him for a political or religious reason, but he can remove him for causes satisfactory to himself.

MR. DALLINGER. Does he not have to give a hearing?

MR. DEMING. Not necessarily. He supplies the employee with the reason. The employee is entitled to have the reasons in writing.

MR. MITCHELL. Would you classify men eligible for the service in the enforcement of the national prohibition act without any information as to what his attitude is toward the law – that he would have a very earnest interest and good will about going at it – or is not that fact considered in your examination?

MR. DEMING. In all positions for the prohibition bureau we have held personal interviews and character investigations that were most sweeping. We have in our files probably the greatest anthology of crime that could be gathered.

MR. MITCHELL. I do not mean character. I mean something different from that.

MR. DEMING. That comes out in the personal investigations by our examiners, who find out practically everything about the applicant, and whether he is in sympathy with the law.

MR. STONE. In regard to age, the attorney-general might find men who are beyond age, and yet be efficient and have had a lot of experience, but this prevents the attorney-general from selecting that man.

MR. DEMING. It depends on the position. We fix the age limits on agreement with the department.

MR. STONE. Is it not a fact that some of the best attorneys would not want to take an examination of that kind?

MR. DEMING. That might be, but one answer to that is that the Interstate Commerce commission has demonstrated for fifteen years that it can get the class of legal ability that will fulfill its purpose through our examinations. The same thing would apply to the department of Justice.

THE CHAIRMAN. You suggested that you intended to propose an amendment. You have not done that yet. Would the language I suggested meet the objection you raised to subdivision (b)? With this language incorporated, it would read like this: "and, in accordance with the competitive provisions of the civil service law."

Would that cover the matter you have in mind?

MR. DEMING. I think I have substantially the same thing. If the committee believes the recommendations of the Civil Service commission should be approved, it might be accomplished by changing the first sentence of section 2-b of H.R. 8574, at the top of page 2, to read as follows:

The Attorney-general is authorized to appoint, in accordance with the competitive provisions of the civil service laws, an assistant director of prohibition and such attorneys and other officers and employees as he deems necessary.

And eliminate under section 3-a at the bottom of page 2: "but such attorneys shall not be subject to the provisions of the civil service laws."

If, however, the committee desires to withdraw from the competitive civil service the positions of assistant director of prohibition and attorneys, as proposed in H.R. 8574, but desires the other positions to remain in the classified service, that can be done by changing the line 4, page 2, in section 2-b, to read: "In accordance with the competitive provisions of the civil service laws, such other officers."

In order to make doubly sure and to bring the proposed bill within the spirit of the civil service laws as we see them, I would like to submit an amendment C, because it would precede the amendment just handed to you, at the end of section 2-a, for your consideration, as follows:

Every position in the prohibition bureau now subject to a competitive examination under the Civil Service act, rules, and regulations, and every new position which may be hereafter created for the administration of the prohibition law shall be and shall remain subject to the competitive provisions of the Civil Service act and rules.

I have been asked this question since these hearings began: "Would it be possible under the wording of section 2-b as it stands, giving the attorney-general the right, 'in accordance with the civil service law, to appoint such other officers and employees as he deems necessary,' for him to select agents, investigators, inspectors, or attorneys who have been found ineligible as the result of your character investigation?"

Under our construction of the act as it reads, we believe that it would be possible, but not probable, of course, if the department of Justice were familiar with the facts in the individual case. Now, having made more than ten thousand character investigations and having those records all on file in our office, we believe that the government is entitled to whatever protection our experience and observation and those records afford. Therefore, I submit amendment D, as follows:

No person shown by the records of the Civil Service commission to be ineligible as the result of a character investigation shall be appointed by the department of Justice to any position in the prohibition bureau.

The first two amendments should be designated as amendments A and B. I think those amendments will get our case before you.

. . .

MR. DEMING remarked, "The same quality of courtesy toward cabinet officers and their opinions obtains in congress as is found between members of that body, especially the senate. Therefore, congress permitted the department of Justice to have its way and appoint attorneys in the prohibition service without a competitive examination.

"At this time, 1940, the United States Civil Service commission, however, holds competitive examinations for attorneys in the Federal Communications commission, the Veterans' administration, the Interstate Commerce commission, the Civil Service commission and the Employees Compensation commission.

"In the Treasury department, when the Honorable Carter Glass was secretary of the Treasury under President Woodrow Wilson, he proposed certain minimum standards for attorneys and the Civil Service commission passed upon the qualifications of applicants in the light of the standard agreed upon.

"There is no reason, except one of patronage and prejudice of some heads of departments, why the Civil Service commission should not supply eligible attorneys for all these places.

"It is hoped the president's committee on Civil Service Improvement will make such a recommendation in its report."

During Mr. Deming's service with the commission, John T. Doyle was secretary. Mr. Doyle, the first employee of the Civil Service commission, accepted a clerkship in the New York post office in 1878. On march 9, 1883, he received an appointment as stenographer to the new Civil Service commission (in President Arthur's administration), and recorded the minutes of the first meeting. He was appointed secretary of the commission by President Cleveland on september 16, 1886. Mr. Doyle, who remained in active service until july 1, 1932, when he retired because of age, was the one administrative officer who made a life work of developing a merit system, replacing the old spoils system. For many years he was chairman of the committee on standard civil service law for states and cities and secretary and treasurer of the National Assembly of Civil Service commissions. He was in the United States service fifty-four years.

The *United States Civil Service Commission News,* in its november 1939 issue, pronounced John T. Doyle the outstanding individual on the commission's rolls, over a long period of years. His signature, always like a copper plate engraving, appeared on millions of documents. In the commission's entire history of fifty-six years, there have been only thirty-seven commissioners and Mr. Doyle served as secretary under twenty-eight of them.

Mr. Doyle relates an interesting episode which took place in 1926 during which Mr. Deming acquitted himself with due credit. Says Mr. Doyle:

Dr. Ellery C. Stowell, a distinguished professor of international law, was to speak at a luncheon meeting of the City club of Washington. I was a member of the club and, being fearful that the good professor would be critical of the commission and the bureau of efficiency, I invited Mr. Deming and Judge Warwick of the bureau of efficiency as my guests to answer him. Professor Stowell is a most delightful gentleman and of the best intentions, but unhappily was convinced that the federal personnel system could not be made to work with a high degree of effectiveness because of what he regarded as its bureaucratic attitude. He formed the Better Government league, of which he was president, and issued a number of pamphlets, "The Public Business," urging reforms of the federal service and particularly aimed to secure public access to personnel records which had been denied him.

Mr. Deming was seated next to Dr. Stowell at the speaker's table, and they conversed most amiably. Dr. Stowell's address, however, was directed mainly to the public school system in Washington which was crippled for lack of funds, and his attack upon the commission and other personnel bureaus which followed did not elicit much apparent interest, as Washington audiences are inclined to be blasé on that subject. Mr. Deming replied in the most happy vein and elicited applause at Dr. Stowell's expense.

The professor later brought a court proceeding upon the refusal of the Civil Service commission to furnish him a list of temporary employees. The court of appeals of the District of Columbia, however, in an elaborate opinion decided that a sufficient legal or legitimate special interest was not shown . . .

Later, in Philadelphia, before the Civil Service Reform association of that city, Professor Stowell renewed his attack upon the commission, to which Mr. Deming replied that Professor Stowell should direct his energy and ability, of which he had both, to something constructive instead of attempting to injure the only official body that stands between the merit system and the spoilsman. Mr. Deming added that the commission was "too busy to participate in Professor Stowell's hobbies."

Mr. Doyle describes Mr. Deming's service on the commission in extremely flattering terms. "He was highly esteemed by all who came into official association with him. He was generous and kindly to the force of the commission and appreciative of their loyalty and ability."

A Washington newspaper man said Deming was one of the few Civil Service commissioners who dared answer criticism by members of the house and senate in the press. He did it effectively and diplomatically, and retained the respect of congress generally.

After the adoption of the Eighteenth, or Prohibition, amendment to the United States Constitution, congress passed legislation and made an appropriation for enforcing the act. However, disregarding warning of the Civil Service commission, arguments by Senator Morris Sheppard, of Texas, and many others in the house and senate, the majority refused to place all the employees of the new prohibition bureau under the classified civil service. Appointments were left to the politicians throughout the country generally, with the result that hangers-on, ne'er-do-wells, racketeers, and even bootleggers, in large numbers, were placed in charge of the enforcement of the prohibition law — not all of course, but enough in time to discredit the movement.

Public sentiment eventually forced congress to change its view-point and give the United States Civil

Service commission jurisdiction. The examinations were open to incumbents and any others if they could qualify as applicants. More than half of the existing members of the prohibition bureau employees failed ignominiously. Naturally, a loud howl went up from them and their sponsors. A subtle campaign was started through the press to ridicule the civil service examinations, the major note being that prohibition enforcement officers were not supposed to analyze sentences, prepare a thesis upon agriculture or art, nor were they presumed to understand Einstein's relativity and explain it to a class of subordinates, etc.

The Civil Service commission anticipated just this kind of an attack. With his knowledge of publicity and the power of the press, President Deming, of the commission, recommended to his colleagues that they give wide publicity in newspapers to the questions in the various examinations. This was a precedent. The newspapers grabbed them as a real news item and the result showed that there was not a single academic question among them. They were merely tests of intelligence, in which the applicant, after reading or studying alternate answers, voted one of them with an X in a square.

Of course, those who passed the mental test had to run the gauntlet of a character investigation. Between the two, there was a terrible slaughter of politically appointed prohibition agents and employees in general.

"After the publication of the questions," says Mr. Deming, "the funny men in congress and in the prohibition bureau shut up like clams."

In 1928, Matthew F. Halloran, who had spent forty-five years in the Washington office of the United States Civil Service commission, wrote a book under the title, *The Romance of the Merit System.* He not only dealt with the factual history of the movement, but assembled a most interesting collection of reminiscences, including the period when Theodore Roosevelt, later president of the United States, was a member of the commission. Mr. Halloran asked William C. Deming, then president of the United States Civil Service commission, to prepare the foreword of this volume, which he did as follows:

"This book is called *The Romance of the Merit System,* by Matthew F. Halloran. By all the rules of realism and fancy, the romance of the federal merit system is Matthew F. Holloran. From messenger boy to chief of an important section, and today liaison officer between the Civil Service Commission and all of the government departments – a concrete example of the possibilities of the 'service.' It should be an inspiration to every American boy and girl who may start out alone to make a place in the world.

"If we may call the Declaration of Independence our great charter of liberty, and the Constitution the compass by which the Ship of State is held to its course, we may designate the Civil Service act the ballast which preserves an even keel in the stress of political storms.

"Many volumes have been written on the merit system, but they are mostly essays and treatises on isolated phases and features of the civil service law and its administration. No one except Mr. Halloran has attempted to tell the story from its conception, birth, and development to the present day when the classified service moves forward of its own momentum.

"*The Romance of the Merit System* is a splendid contribution to the epic of popular government."

In the course of his book, Mr. Halloran said:

William C. Deming of Wyoming, succeeded Governor John H.

Bartlett of Connecticut as president of the commission march 31, 1923. Mr. Deming is of medium size, smooth shaven, with a fine, scholarly face and pleasing personality. He is agreeable and congenial, but firm when the occasion demands. Among his conspicuous traits of character is the element of human sympathy, which is typical of the broad-minded, frank citizen of the West.

Thoroughly imbued with the spirit of the merit system and respectful at all times of the law, rules, and regulations, Mr. Deming is not bound by mere autocratic methods of procedure or form. He is entirely without prejudice, fair and impartial in all matters under consideration, bringing to the commission the benefits of long and successful experience in private business.

Having been admitted to the bar before entering the newspaper business, he shows a great interest in all matters involving questions of law, equity, and fact, but has sought to familiarize himself with the commissioner's work generally. During his regime, the work of the commission has received wide publicity in newspapers, magazines, and by addresses before various organizations. His suggestions for improving and clarifying certain methods of procedure have been valuable to the commission. He has steadfastly insisted that the same standards of fitness be applied in cases of reinstatement as in original appointments and that investigations be instituted at the source, if necessary.

Mr. Deming spoke upon so many phases of the commission's work and before such a variety of organizations that the commission published his addresses in booklet form entitled, *Application of the Merit System in the United States Civil Service.*

Some of the leading topics were, "A Panorama of Uncle Sam's Big Family," "Postal Service, 2,500 Years Ago and Now," "How Federal Employees are Selected," "Early Days of the Civil Service," "Reform in the Civil Service," "Progress of the Merit System," "The Veteran and the Government Service," "Women in the Government Service," "The Federal Service Viewed from the Inside."

"The senior commissioner, when I became a member," says Mr. Deming, "was George R. Wales, a native of Vermont. He was a farm boy who had lost his right arm in his early youth, but acquired a substantial education and a strong physique. He entered the United States Civil Service as clerk in 1889 at one thousand dollars a year. He was transferred to the commission in 1894 at fourteen hundred dollars per annum, becoming chief examiner on december 6, 1908. After serving eleven years, he was promoted to the position of Civil Service commissioner by President Woodrow Wilson. He was receiving about nine thousand dollars a year when he died.

"Mr. Wales had studied law, and having grown up, as it were, with the Civil Service commission, practically absorbed through preparation, contacts, and experience most of the rules and regulations. He was a man of pleasing personality, a good story teller, and popular throughout the commission and with the departments.

"Commissioner Gardener's successor, Miss Jessie Dell, came to the commission after more than twenty years service in the War department, a part of which time she served under General H. M. Lord, former director of finance and later director of the budget.

"Commissioner Dell possessed remarkable industry. She worked unceasingly to master the complicated technique of civil service administration and became an enthusiastic commissioner.

"When Franklin D. Roosevelt became president, he appointed Lucille Foster McMillin, of Tennessee, widow of a former governor of that state, to succeed Commissioner Jessie Dell, who returned to a position in another department of the federal government.

"I regret, more than I can express, that limitations

of time and space will not permit me to mention by name all the various chiefs of division, sections, and units with whom I served on the Civil Service commission. No more able and loyal organization of men and women could be found anywhere, and it was a pleasure to work with them. It was as interesting as it was remarkable, that such a variety of questions and interpretations, practice, and policies, could be constantly arising and requiring consideration and solution.

"When there was difference of opinion among chiefs and subordinates concerning the more important questions, the commission gave them an opportunity to express themselves around the conference table.

"On lesser matters, perhaps equally pressing, I was able to form a better judgment by listening to each one separately, after which I would make up my mind and pass judgment. I do not recall a single case in which those with whom I disagreed ever manifested any feeling of resentment."

While in Washington, Mr. Deming received word that Joseph M. Carey had passed away on february 5, 1924. Judge Carey, an empire-builder, statesman, and philanthropist, was for more than half a century as prominently identified with the development of Wyoming as any other man. He left the impress of his work and influence upon the history of the state.

William C. Deming, who had come to Wyoming in march 1901 to take charge of Judge Carey's newspaper, said: "My esteem for him was deep-seated and never shaken by any passing political difference. I recall with keenest pleasure and abiding satisfaction many pleasant hours spent at his home, always the center of genuine hospitality. He was a great reader and delighted to discuss books, particularly biography and history. His sense of humor was highly developed. He enjoyed a good story and was always able to tell one. He combined the traits of sociability and kindness with a willingness to fight for a principle. He stood for the best in public and private life. He had ideals and lived them.

"What the Mormons had accomplished in Utah he believed the pioneers of Wyoming could do, hence his early efforts to establish the Wheatland colony. He was always opposed to wanton waste and carried this policy of saving and reclamation to the realm of public lands.

"As mayor of Cheyenne, delegate in congress, United States senator, and governor, he left his impress upon the state but his most enduring material monument is Wheatland, with its beautiful homes and fine farms, which will proclaim his foresight, faith, and works until the end of time."

In this same year – 1924 – on october 2, occurred the death of Governor William B. Ross. In a tribute to him, Mr. Deming said: "Governor Ross was a typical exemplification of the oft-repeated statement that in this republic any citizen may have reasonable aspirations to a position of prominence. Born in a southern state, he was educated in the public schools and came to Wyoming a young man without acquaintance, influence, or money. He became the nominee of his party for governor in 1922 and was the only state officer elected by the democrats. All of his political successes have been made without the expenditure of large means. He did not have the money to spend. Character and some elements of good fortune were his sole political assets, for from the very beginning, his party was in the minority . . . He was a loving husband, an affectionate father. His character is a priceless heritage that will endure through the years."

Mr. Deming entered into the social life of Washington and thoroughly enjoyed it. He was entertained extensively. He was a guest at White House events during the administrations of Presidents Harding, Coolidge, and Hoover. These affairs varied from dinners, garden parties, receptions, and teas to musicales.

He belonged to the Washington Bachelors Cotillion and joined the Friday Evening Dancing club whose membership included among others: Senator and Mrs. Henry J. Allen, Mr. and Mrs. Julian B. Bolling, Senator Arthur Capper, Senator and Mrs. Royal S. Copeland, Mr. and Mrs. Fayette Dow, Commander and Mrs. Harvey Delano, Justice and Mrs. Peyton Gordon, Senator and Mrs. Walter F. George, Doctor Stanley Hornbeck, Mrs. Ollie James, Senator and Mrs. William H. King, Mrs. Jacob Leander Loose, The Honorable and Mrs. Frank W. Mondell, Senator and Mrs. Tasker L. Oddie, Senator and Mrs. Lawrence C. Phipps, the Honorable and Mrs. Fred Purnell, Mr. and Mrs. Stanley Reed, Senator and Mrs. Morris Sheppard, Mr. and Mrs. Everett Sanders, Mr. and Mrs. Arthur Tirrel, Mr. and Mrs. Sidney F. Taliaferro, Madame Karl von Lewinski, Colonel Eugene R. West, Mrs. Mable Walker Willebrandt, the Honorable and Mrs. Adam M. Wyant, Senator David I. Walsh, and Minister Senor Alfara and Senora Alfara of Panama. Mrs. Robert W. Imbrie, Miss Evelyn Weems, now Mrs. W. E. P. French and Mrs. Georgia Berry, now Mrs. Daniel H. Hudson.

Among those whose hospitality he shared at box parties at the opera, theatre parties, dinners, a society circus and informal affairs were Mrs. Horace G. Macfarland, Mrs. Bessie Brueggeman, Senator and Mrs. William Calder, Senator and Mrs. F. E. Warren, Mr.

and Mrs. Stanley Reed, the Honorable and Mrs. F. W. Mondell, Mr. and Mrs. Charles W. Burdick, Senator and Mrs. Kendrick, Commander and Mrs. Cecil Sherman Baker, Justice and Mrs. Willis Van Devanter, and Mrs. Nellie Tayloe Ross.

During his Washington residence, Mr. Deming lived at the Cairo hotel, the hotel Roosevelt, and the Mayflower.

He was a member of the Federal club, the National Press club, the National Geographic society, the Congressional Country club, and other outstanding organizations.

Mr. Deming delivered one of the main addresses at the Allegheny Alumni of Washington reunion and banquet in 1923, and spoke in a humorous vein about early day campus incidents.

He was a guest of honor at the twentieth annual banquet of Gamma Eta chapter of Delta Tau Delta at which the Honorable Henry C. Wallace, later secretary of agriculture, and the Honorable E. J. Henry, assistant secretary of labor, also were guests. Mr. Wallace is now vice-president.

He attended innumerable events of importance, such as the presentation to Doctor Hugo Eckener of the National Geographic's special gold medal, on march 27, 1930, and wrote about them for his *Tribune* readers. Eckener had brought over the first big German dirigible air ship. He also heard the Honorable J. Ramsey MacDonald, the great commoner, speak at the Press club.

Mr. Deming was invited by the Navy department to visit Panama for the naval maneuvers, but was unable to accept on account of his official duties. The return trip was scheduled to include stops at the Virgin

Islands, Porto Rico, and also at some other points.

On Easter monday, march 28, 1925, he was a patron of the Dixie ball given at the New Willard by the Robert E. Lee chapter, United Daughters of the Confederacy.

On february 19, 1925, Mrs. Nellie Tayloe Ross, governor of Wyoming, wrote that she was to be in the inaugural ceremony of the president and said: "I am asked to furnish names of aides and staff. Inasmuch as I shall have no aide except Colonel Davis, the adjutant-general, I am wishing you were going to be a member of my party. I suppose, however, there is provision made for your commission."

"Opportunities for meeting and hearing outstanding men and women in Washington were very numerous. In addition to those I have mentioned," says Mr. Deming, "I recall Gilbert K. Chesterton, brilliant and erratic English author, and dramatist, in a joint debate on the subject 'Is Psychology a Curse?' Chesterton had the affirmative and Cosmo Hamilton the negative. It goes without saying it was a unique and entertaining discussion. Both are brilliant English writers.

"Judging from the standpoint of vim and vigor, courage and character, sincerity without snobbery, all clothed in humor that amused or entertained but never hurt, I would place Will Rogers at the top of the list. He came nearer being the Abraham Lincoln type than any other American. His untimely death in an aeroplane accident off the coast of Alaska was an irreparable loss to millions of his countrymen.

"Ed Howe, of Atchison, Kansas, author and editor, called the Sage of Potato Hill Farm, resembled Rogers in some respects, both as to appearance, manner of speaking, and quality of his wit.

"In his later years, Mr. Howe's daughter, Adelaide, traveled with him. I saw them occasionally in Florida and both had visited the Richardson family in Cheyenne. Eugene Howe, owner and publisher of two newspapers in Amarillo, Texas, is a son of Edgar W. Howe and is considered a very fine business man as well as a leader in Texas state affairs.

"Some of the most diligent and accomplished public officials in Washington were those who were not much in the public eye.

"Herbert Putnam, librarian of congress for many years, was among that number. He was a highly educated and cultured gentleman and an experienced librarian even before coming to Washington.

"For some reason, from time to time, he invited me to have luncheon with him and discuss matters in general. I always enjoyed these informal visits because there was nothing in the nature of politics or partisanship or even personalities to mar the occasion.

"Sometimes I think Marc Antony's characterization of Julius Caesar is well adapted to Herbert Putnam, although Putnam's conquests were not in war but in the realm of peace and books:

> "'His life was gentle, and the elements
> So mix'd in him, that Nature might stand up
> And say to all the world, 'This was a man!'

"I wish to recall also Stephen J. Mather, who was director of national parks. He was a man of wealth and position, who gave time to the public service because he felt that it was his duty as a citizen. As a host, he was without a peer and his enthusiasm for his work was only exceeded by his modesty."

Ulysses S. Grant the third was in the same category of sincere public servants.

"A dinner given by United States Senator Robert D. Carey and Mrs. Carey in honor of Senator and Mrs. Charles L. McNary, of Oregon, and Senator and Mrs. A. H. Vandenberg, of Michigan, to which I was invited," says Mr. Deming, "stands out very clearly."

"It was a most delightful occasion and during the two hours which followed the repast many subjects of current interest were discussed. McNary was leader of the republican forces; Vandenberg, somewhat liberal, had become a power in debate and Carey was being recognized as a very strong member, more or less conservative, and an authority upon all subjects pertaining to the West. There was practically no restraint in their remarks, whether in approval or in criticism of legislation or individuals.

"It would be difficult to find three more brilliant and more attractive women than the wives of these three senators upon that occasion. I was so impressed with the resourcefulness and general knowledge of affairs shown by Senator Vandenberg of Michigan that I recognized he might some day become president of the United States, or at least a candidate or eligible. I have maintained correspondence with him for some years."

Among the Wyoming citizens, both men and women, who have made good in responsible positions in Washington, D.C., is Claude L. Draper, a native of Cheyenne.

After years of service with the Union Pacific railroad, with the Bennett Livestock company, and with R. S. Van Tassell, also serving as a member of the Wyoming house of representatives, he was made chairman of the Wyoming public service commission.

In 1930, Mr. Draper was appointed a member of the Federal Power commission by President Herbert Hoover.

Mr. Draper married Isabel Campbell Snyder, a member of one of Cheyenne's pioneer and highly respected families.

Not all of Mr. Deming's friends in Washington were republicans. He was an admirer and friend of Judge Hatton Summers, bachelor congressman from Texas, who now is considered the best legal authority in the house. They were often together and became quite chummy.

In Washington, not all plans, policies, and preparations for action are made in the department offices or even in committee rooms or on the floor of the house or senate.

According to Mr. Deming, "The best place and time to get the low-down, as it were, is when a few members of congress get together for a social evening, particularly following a good dinner. Sometimes they are very frank, even when both parties are represented, as occurs almost every evening during the session in the lobby of the Wardman Park hotel during the two hours, from eight to ten, that the official residents there gather for exchange of news and views. I have heard some pretty plain talking, always good humored, however, and if some enthusiast became a bit violent in his statements, the unofficial moderator of the evening cautioned him with a single word 'Tolerance, my friend, tolerance.'

"The Dean of the Wardman Park round-up is United States Senator Ellison D. Smith of South Carolina, known as Cotton Ed. Representative Bulwinkle of South Carolina is also a regular member. The late Rudolph Forster, long-time executive clerk, who lived at the Wardman Park many years, frequently sat in as a listening member only. Forster, a native of the District of Columbia, was a stenographer when he was

called to the White House in President William Mc-
Kinley's administration to help out for a few days. That
was march 5, 1897, and there he remained until his
death july 7, 1943. When he reached seventy, in october
1942, President Roosevelt issued an executive order
exempting him from retirement for age and sent a note
to him saying: 'This is permanent, I don't want you to
leave me as long as I'm here. F.D.R.' Forster probably
heard more conversation through various administrations, without breaking confidence, than any other man
in Washington. He took administrations as they came
without worry and retained the respect of every one
who knew him. His motto seemed to be, 'Give every
man thy ear, but few thy voice.' "

In discussing politics, Mr. Deming said:

"I have noticed two contrasting results of political
preferment. First, that a man of moderate ability may
be chosen to high office if a few circumstances run his
way.

"Even some trifling incident may be capitalized. For
instance, as in the case of a certain state auditor, who
rejected an item of forty cents for a ham sandwich and
twenty cents for a cup of coffee on the expense bill of
a state employee. His reason was that the price was too
high. Of course that was before World war II.

"The publicity surrounding this official act contributed toward making the auditor a governor and his
gubernatorial organization later made him United
States senator.

"W. Lee O'Daniel, a general salesman for a popular
brand of flour or bread, used the radio very effectively.
His entire family was musical and all participated,
from time to time, in the broadcasts. He further popu-
larized his salesmanship by using a Hill Billy band.

"His singing and his original poems struck a popular chord and there was a suggestion that he become a candidate for governor.

"He did so. Despite the fact that he was from Kansas originally and was charged with being a carpet-bag republican, his general appeal to the common man and woman brought success.

"After two years' controversy with many conservative leaders of the democratic party and with the Texas legislature, he was again nominated and re-elected.

"The fortunes of politics continued to favor him.

"Soon after his second inaugural, United States Senator Morris Sheppard died and Governor O'Daniel dug back into the past and appointed Andrew Jackson Houston to the temporary vacancy.

"Houston was an aged son of General Sam Houston, Texas patriot.

"This was a good stroke of politics and while Andrew Jackson Houston was able to proceed to Washington and qualify and sit in the body, in which his distinguished father had once sat, he lived only a few weeks.

"Governor O'Daniel became a candidate in a large field for the senate and was elected by a small margin.

"He was succeeded as governor by the Honorable Coke R. Stevenson, lieutenant-governor, whom many people consider the ablest public official in Texas. I met him frequently during a winter spent in Austin.

"The majority of public officials who attain high rank are deserving and enjoy all the public acclaim such positions bring. At the same time, many useful contemporary citizens, successful in business and the professions, die unhonored and unsung.

"Second, I have been amazed at the number of men in various states who, having been governor, member of congress, or United States senator, when defeated have sometimes become practically helpless, and penniless, unless they have secured some kind of consolation job upon the public payroll. I have met them repeatedly in my travels.

"Despite this, in a vague way, I harbored some ambition to be governor of Wyoming, both because I felt I might be of service and possibly influenced by the thought that it would complete my record as a citizen of my adopted state.

"When William B. Ross, a lovable character, died in the midst of his four-year term, sentiment crystallized quickly in behalf of his widow, Nellie Tayloe Ross, as his successor and she was easily elected. She was a credit to womanhood and to the state.

"In 1926, however, it was quite apparent that the majority of Wyoming voters felt they had discharged their obligation to this fine woman and would elect not only a man, but a republican.

"I was then pretty well immersed in my work as president of the United States Civil Service commission. Many letters came to me from influential republicans suggesting that I return to Wyoming and make the race. I was practically assured that an informal republican convention would endorse me, thus, no doubt, eliminating opposition in the primary. I gave the subject serious thought. The conditions appeared highly favorable, but I felt I had not sufficiently completed my program in Washington.

"Nevertheless, I took a short vacation and came to Cheyenne for consultation. The nomination was going begging for some reason. Aside from enjoying my work with the Civil Service commission, I recalled that I had known two governors of Wyoming who had died

in office, largely from the strain and demands upon
their time from many parts of the state. Hence, I
abandoned the idea.

"However, it was decided to send up some trial bal-
loons through the *Wyoming Tribune* with a subtle
emphasis upon the ability and availability of State-
Engineer Frank Emerson. A good follow-up system
was inaugurated by Cheyenne republicans and Emerson was nominated. He was a member of an important
commission to study and report upon the inter-state
controversy over the water of the Colorado river. In
Washington, I had heard his remarkable testimony
before a congressional committee and sent the *Tribune*
a signed editorial under the caption 'A Master Among
School Boys,' used later as a campaign document.
Emerson was elected.

"In the fall of 1929, Senator Warren died and it fell
to Governor Emerson to appoint his successor. My
name was presented to the governor – also that of the
Honorable George E. Brimmer, the Honorable William E. Mullen, and possibly Fred E. Warren (without his consent). I was in Washington.

"The Honorable G. R. Hagens, the Honorable E. J.
Sullivan, and C. L. Hinkle, chairman of the state republican committee, were also urged by their friends.
The governor referred the choice to the republican
state central committee, which, by vote, recommended
the Honorable Patrick Sullivan of Casper, who was
appointed and filled the place acceptably. He was not
a candidate for election in 1930 when Robert D. Carey
was chosen.

"Governor Emerson, no doubt, harbored a natural
ambition to be United States senator some time in the
future.

"These bits of political history are of no particular value, but may interest those not familiar with all the facts."

On october 7, 1924, Allegheny college conferred upon William C. Deming the honorary degree L.L.D. The ceremony was held in the college chapel and was one of the last official acts of President Fred Whitlo Hixson, who passed away in november of that year.

His address at Allegheny college was only one of many which Mr. Deming made while carrying on his duties as a commissioner. The following list is indicative of the number and variety of audiences which he addressed:

1923: MAY 24, Kiwanis club, Washington, D.C.
    OCT. 11, National association of postmasters, Washington, D.C.
    DEC. 6, National Civil Service Reform league, Washington hotel, Washington, D.C.
1924: Chamber of Commerce of the United States.
    Alumni of Delta Tau Delta, Philadelphia, Penn.
    Sons of the Amer. Revolution at Pittsburgh, Penn.
1925: APRIL 30, Council Dinner of the National Civil Service Reform league, New York City.
    MAY 21, Virginia Federation of Women's clubs, Richmond, Va.
    JUNE 2, Spanish American War Veterans, Camp Henry W. Lawton, 921 Pennsylvania Ave. N.W., Washington, D.C.
    JUNE 17, National spelling bee.
    OCT. 7, American Legion convention, Omaha, Neb.
1926: MAY 19, Illinois Federation of Women's clubs, Chicago, Ill.
    DEC. 14, Federal Club, at the University club, Washington, D.C.
1927: MARCH 16, Public Service Institute, hotel Somerset, Boston, Mass.
    JULY 20, Tri-State Postmasters' association, Indianapolis, Ind.
    SEPT. 15, Postmasters of the United States, Niagara Falls, N.Y.
    SEPT. 16, Assembly of Civil Service Commissions, Buffalo, N.Y.
1929: JULY 17, Tri-State Postmasters' convention, Columbus, Ohio.
    AUG. 28, Assembly of Civil Service commissions of the United States and Canada, Ottawa, Canada.
    SEPT. 18, National Association of Postmasters, Sacramento, Calif.

Mr. Deming made regular trips to Wyoming from Washington and kept in close touch with his business and his friends.

Among the outstanding things accomplished in Wyoming during this period were the building of Summit Inn on the Lincoln highway and the erection of a new building for the *Tribune-Leader* in 1928-29 on Seventeenth street in Cheyenne.

While a member of the board of trustees of the University of Wyoming, Mr. Deming usually made the trip in his automobile from Cheyenne to Laramie to attend to university business. On one of these journeys (about 1922), he observed a wooden sign at the summit, forty miles west of Cheyenne, giving the elevation eight thousand, eight hundred thirty-five feet and containing the legend, "Highest Point on the Lincoln highway."

Since the highway did not reach the highest point of the hill, Mr. Deming and a friend one day climbed to the peak where they found a weather beaten triangular structure, ten or twelve feet high, that appeared to be at least sixty or seventy years old. Under it was a stone to which was attached a bronze plate, marked with the four points of the compass, evidently placed there by a United States surveying party.

Because he knew that the pass over Sherman hill, on the route of the Union Pacific railroad, had been discovered by General Grenville M. Dodge, while on an exploratory tour in this region, Mr. Deming thought this high point which had been known up until 1920 as Crow Creek hill, should be dedicated to the general. Dodge, it seems, had reached the headwaters of Pole creek and had then made the short ascent to the top of the hill known as Cheyenne Pass. He then crossed the summit, and in trying to evade a band of Indians,

followed down the slope which he immediately recommended for the proposed route of the Union Pacific.

The *Tribune* began to advocate the erection of a
memorial to General Dodge, and succeeded in interesting the Union Pacific railroad in the matter. For a
time the railroad seriously considered the erection at
the summit of a statue of heroic proportions to the
memory of its early engineer and builder, but did not
do so.

The Honorable Leslie A. Miller, however, joined
Deming in a plan and together they erected a log-cabin
or lodge on the highest point of the Lincoln highway.
They called it Grenville Dodge Summit Inn, and
placed a corner stone in the fireplace chimney which
read:

Grenville Dodge Summit Inn/erected by WILLIAM
C. DEMING/and/LESLIE A. MILLER/in honor of/
GENERAL GRENVILLE DODGE/The Pass Finder.

On august 17, 1926, they announced that "Our plan
is not merely to attract tourists to the spot, hold them
a few hours, perhaps a day, maybe two days, and sell
them supplies and such. We hope to make the highest
point on the Lincoln highway, or Sherman hill, the
outstanding memorial site in the United States."

In august, 1926, a reporter of the *Tribune* who
visited the Summit wrote: "To the east of the Grenville
M. Dodge inn there lies a deep wooded valley, bounded
on the east by the ragged skyline of Ragged Top and
Pole mountain, to the south, in the immediate foreground, lies the ridge which is now the route of the
Union Pacific, beyond is a wide valley, purple in the
opalescent light of a noonday sun, with the majestic
Long's peak stabbing a hole in the sky for a far back-

ground. Turning slowly westward four main ranges of the Rocky mountains come into view. Just north of Long's peak is the snow-capped Mummy range, north of that, but closer to the foreground, appears Sheep Mountain, with the higher and snowy Jack Rabbit range beyond (Rabbit Ear). Here a sweeping view of Laramie Plains becomes the foreground of the picture with Laramie itself nestling in the middle distance, and the plains stretching away to Medicine Bow range and Elk Mountain, and the Snowy range making the extreme background."

Mr. Deming and Mr. Miller eventually sold the inn to Frank King, junior. The original building burned, but a second inn, erected across the highway from the original site, attracts many tourists both day and night and is patronized by university students from Laramie nearby. It also serves as a relief station for those caught on the hill in a blizzard.

Mr. Deming spoke before luncheon clubs and suggested through the columns of his newspaper that a joint committee be appointed by Laramie and Cheyenne Rotary clubs to take up with the commissioners of Albany and Laramie counties the subject of the improvement of the Happy Jack link of the long circle drive on the summit and the short circle drive by the way of the Cheyenne Mountain club.

This Pole Mountain area, now a part of the Medicine Bow national forest, has become one of the finest playgrounds for both winter and summer sports in southeastern Wyoming. Veedauwoo Glen grows more popular each year, and the roads are being improved from year to year.

Realizing that his newspaper had outgrown the Keefe hall quarters on Federal street, and desiring to keep step with the growth and development of Cheyenne, Mr. Deming began to plan in 1925 for a modern fireproof home for the *Tribune-Leader,* the oldest paper in Wyoming.

This building, a fine two-story brick, on Seventeenth street between Central and Warren avenues, was formally dedicated by the National Editorial association in 1929.

Visiting editors were amazed at the character of the structure, both as to arrangement, material, and contents of the plant. Throughout the interior, the building was finished in birch, beautifully polished. The basement, or press room, which is eight feet in the ground and four above, is almost as light as an ordinary ground floor. The composing room is a model of convenience, light, and ventilation. A second floor was added largely for present appearance and future contingencies. It houses two beautiful, modern apartments. The Deming Realty company still owns this structure, as it was not sold when William C. Deming retired and disposed of his paper in 1937.

Resigns from Civil Service Commission to Campaign for the Senate

William C. Deming was continued in office as commissioner of the United States Civil Service commission by President Coolidge and by President Hoover, and continued to serve as president of the body.

On november 24, 1929, occurred the death of Senator Francis E. Warren, eighty-five years of age, called the "Grand Old Man" of Wyoming. The senator had been ill three weeks with pneumonia and bronchitis. His passing was deeply felt by Mr. Deming, as the two had been close friends and coworkers for many years.

Deming paid a warm tribute to the senator through his papers, the *Wyoming Tribune* and the *Wyoming Stockman-Farmer* as follows:

"FRANCIS E. WARREN: Foursquare to Every Wind that Blew and Met Every Struggle Courageously. After more than twenty-five years of close personal business and political association with Senator Francis E. Warren, I am too depressed by his death to do him justice in a few words.

"Our correspondence and conferences for a generation cover such a wide range they would fill a book.

"This much I would record here and now – they have been for the upbuilding of the high principles to which his life was devoted, the improvement and development of a community and state we both loved.

"He met every struggle courageously and overcame obstacles with the skill of a military genius.

"His followers and friends were confined to no one party or creed and his memory will endure in the hearts of his countrymen.

"That I shall see him no more grieves me beyond adequate expression. Truly it may be said of him, 'Seest thou a man diligent in his business? He shall stand before the kings.'

"Senator Warren's life was replete with personal achievements and no man has done more for his friends.

"He was tenacious in reaching an objective and resourceful in any situation.

"Whether as a farmer-boy in Massachusetts, a young soldier in the Civil war, or United States senator from Wyoming, he stood foursquare to every wind that blew."

When asked to give his opinion of Senator Warren's outstanding qualities, Mr. Deming replied: "First I would say his business acumen. He started in the early seventies in Cheyenne with nothing, and in fifty years became probably the richest man in the state. His ranch and sheep interests were so large in Wyoming and Colorado that his colleagues in the United States senate called him 'The Greatest Shepherd since Abraham.'

"He understod the value of city business property and erected many of Cheyenne's best buildings. The last, the Montgomery Ward store on Central avenue, was under construction when he died.

"Politically, he was the best organizer I ever knew. His system was very effective. First he declined to acknowledge that a man, even of opposite politics, was his enemy. Second, he kept in touch with every section of the state and all classes of people. Though spending many months in every year in Washington, he made it a habit to read regularly all the weekly and daily papers promptly or have clippings from these papers placed upon his office desk. This was supplemented by a large list of friends in every county who looked after his interests and advised him concerning conditions, economic, political, social, and otherwise. For example, the Honorable Charles W. Burdick, of Cheyenne, and the Honorable George E. Brimmer, of Rawlins, both before and after he came to Laramie county, were probably his principal Wyoming correspondents. There could have been none better, because both were loyal, enthusiastic, alert, and aggressive. And speaking of loyalty, that probably was Senator Warren's crowning characteristic, as he stuck to his friends through thick and thin, and through good and evil report."

The following letter, one of a great many written by Senator Warren to Mr. Deming over a long period, is an example of the senator's caution and thoroughness in political matters, however unimportant.

Committee on Appropriations, United States Senate, Washington, D.C.

May 21, 1912

HON. W. C. DEMING, Warren, Ohio

DEAR DEMING: I am enclosing herewith the first page of a letter from .... of ...., which kindly read and return in your next letter to me. The second page of this communication was about another matter which would not interest you.

We had the promise, last year, of a place for .... in the .... service at probably $100.00 per month.

I am asking you to advise me, either in a letter or when you see me, as to ....'s condition and habits just now. Is he any good? Is he drinking, and grouchy, and scolding all of the time, or only once in a while?

What was the inwardness of his selling to .... some property, an account of which I saw in a newspaper, that put him in an unfavorable light?

I suspect his usefulness would not amount to much politically.

March 18, 1929

Hon. Wm. C. Deming
Civil Service Commission
Washington, D. C.

My dear Mr. Deming:

I wish to thank you for the courtesy you have shown me in tendering your resignation as Civil Service Commissioner. I am returning it to you without acceptance as I am anxious that you should continue in the service for the present.

I do wish to express my appreciation for your thoughtfulness toward me.

Yours faithfully

[signature: Herbert Hoover]

February 5, 1930

Hon. William C. Deming
Civil Service Commission
Washington, D. C.

My dear Mr. Deming:

I have your letter of resignation of January 28th which, of necessity, I must accept. I would, however, like to leave the precise date of such acceptance open to further agreement between us.

I should like to take this occasion to express my sincere regret that you feel you cannot continue as Chairman of the Commission. The long and effective service you have given has contributed to the upbuilding of the Civil Service, and your conduct of the office has won the full esteem of all members of the Government as well as the public at large.

I am in hopes that the time may come when your personal affairs will permit of your return to public service.

Yours faithfully,

[signature: Herbert Hoover]

Can he be used to any advantage worth while now and in the coming campaign? And if so, how? Yours very sincerely,

F. E. WARREN

After careful consideration, Mr. Deming, in january 1930, resigned as Civil Service commissioner, and in march announced his candidacy for the United States senate to succeed Senator Warren.

President Hoover did not accept Mr. Deming's resignation by date, but asked that he leave the date open and serve until relieved of his duties, several months later.

On august 8, 1930, after T. E. Campbell, former governor of Arizona, had accepted the appointment as commissioner to succeed Mr. Deming, President Hoover wrote:

"I should like to take this occasion to express my sincere regret that you feel you cannot continue as chairman of the commission. The long and effective service you have given has contributed to the upbuilding of the civil service, and your conduct of the office has won the full esteem of all the members of the government as well as the public at large.

"I am in hopes that the time may come when your personal affairs will permit of your return to public service."

C. C. Hathaway, personnel officer of the commission, said upon the resignation, "Few have had a longer period of service as commissioner than Mr. Deming, and none have done more to further the cause of the merit system."

Employees of the service presented to Mr. Deming a large silver plaque and a cane in appreciation of his splendid work as commissioner. At the presentation, which was in charge of commissioner George R. Wales, were colleagues, chiefs of divisions, and a large number of employees of the commission. The plaque was a most exquisite silver plate mounted tastefully and appropriately engraved. The cane had a beautifully finished silver handle. These gifts were accompanied by an elaborate bouquet of flowers.

The *Federal Employee,* official magazine of the National Federation of Federal Employees, in its april 1930 issue said:

". . . Throughout his service on the commission, Mr. Deming has shown a genuine spirit of friendliness and solicitude for federal workers, and it was with deep regret on the part of government employees generally as well as official Washington that his severance took place at this time."

Many things were accomplished during his service in Washington, which improved general working conditions. For instance, in reduction of force, it was customary to separate employees, old and young, without notice. An agreement was secured from nearly all departments, bureaus, and commissions to give at least thirty days' notice.

The commission prepared for President Coolidge's special committee, of which he was a member, the recommendation that the names of disabled veterans go to the top of the register, thus securing an actual preference in appointments. President Coolidge issued an executive order embodying that idea into civil service practice.

"My observation was," says Mr. Deming, "that the Civil Service commission experienced a keen disappointment when a veteran applicant failed to make a passing grade. The commission was even more disappointed when a veteran eligible failed to receive an appointment. In fact, if an appointing officer passed over the name of a veteran eligible, he was required to make a written record of the reason for his refusal to appoint."

In making his first announcement to run for the senate, Mr. Deming said: "There is an unexpired term from december 1930 to march 4, 1931, to be filled, as well as a full term. There is strong sentiment in Wyoming in behalf of the incumbent, the Honorable Patrick Sullivan, for the short term. If Senator Sullivan can be prevailed upon to make the race, that will be agreeable to me and I shall confine my activities to the long term."

In announcing himself as a candidate for the United States senate, Mr. Deming said in part:

"Inheriting from my father, a Union veteran of the Civil war, republican protective tariff views, I have never found any good reason for abandoning those principles. Study and observation of the United States under a protective tariff and under a tariff for revenue only, have convinced me that the country has been prosperous under a protective tariff and has suffered reverses under a tariff for revenue only or a tariff too low to protect American industries and American workmen from foreign competition.

"Wyoming is peculiarly interested in a protective tariff because of the very nature of our livestock, agricultural, mineral, and other basic industries, and the fact that we are a young and more or less undeveloped state.

"The preponderance of lands in Wyoming still under federal ownership and control is very large. Most careful attention should be directed toward a system by which such lands now free of all taxation may be made a part of our commonwealth. In cases where the recent policy of the secretary of the Interior with respect to oil exploration has worked an injustice upon permittees who have acted in good faith, proper modification should be forthcoming.

"Twenty-five years ago the people of the state assumed that the construction of the Pathfinder dam and reservoir in Wyoming meant reclamation of lands in central and eastern Wyoming. Too late we found that the reclamation was mostly in Nebraska. It is not too late, however, to offset that injustice to some extent, and for that reason, I favor the Casper-Alcova project and the Saratoga project. . . It is not sufficient to urge that reclamation has not paid for itself directly, because the indirect benefits are beyond estimation. . . The federal government should be able to finance projects in a manner and under a system that will make it practicable for the settler to own and cultivate such land as would be available under the Casper-Alcova and Saratoga proposals.

"As to other candidates or eligibles mentioned for the republican nomination, I have the kindest personal feeling toward all of them. I trust our pleasant relationship may continue. Furthermore, each is entitled to and will receive a square deal in the columns of the *Tribune-Leader.*"

When the Honorable Patrick J. Sullivan telegraphed from Washington to Cheyenne in 1930 that he would not be a candidate for the United States senate, Mr. Deming filed for both terms, and began his campaign in earnest. With his entrance, the race became a three-cornered one. Robert D. Carey, of Careyhurst, former governor of Wyoming, and Charles E. Winter of Casper, formerly representative in congress, had previously tossed their hats into the ring. Later W. L. Walls also became a senatorial candidate.

"As a matter of fact," Mr. Deming said later, "at no time did I feel confident of success, but realized the need of returning to my business and renewing my acquaintance throughout the state after eight years of absence. The primary election was very helpful to that end."

In line with this statement was the following which appeared in the *Laramie County News:*

"Mr. Deming is rather unique as a candidate, judging by the average political tactics. He does not campaign, merely renews old acquaintances and makes new contacts. . . His ability, integrity, and steadfastness of purpose cannot be questioned."

He toured the entire state and wrote extensively for the *Tribune* under the caption, "Highlights of the Campaign." In these columns he told of the people he met, and gave detailed descriptions of the various localities. These "Highlights" columns are a distinct contribution to Wyoming's history, as they contain references to many prominent families who have been connected with the state's development. For instance, Deming wrote of meeting Napoleon Bonaparte Kinnear and O. F. Poppenberg at Riverton. "Kinnear," he said, "married a daughter of Jim Baker and was a government packer; Poppenberg had been a cook in the army packer's outfit." At South Pass he found the Peter Sherlock family; at Eden Valley, the Arnott family. From Crook county he called attention to C. F. (Chris) Holley, one of the few contemporaries of Jim Bridger, General Custer, General Charles Francis King, Buffalo Bill, and other pioneers of the Fort Laramie days.

At Chugwater he met many farmers and their families who came to hear his Memorial day address. Many of them he recognized by name or face, as he had met them when they homesteaded during the period that he was receiver of public moneys in the United States land office.

He renewed his acquaintance with prominent men and women all over the state, including Dave Thomas, a magistrate in Rock Springs. "Judge Thomas still finds time to reel off a bit of Scotch verse," he said.

"John Hay, old-time railroad man, now banker, sheepman, and coal operator," he commented," typifies the opportunities for success in Wyoming." At Rock Springs, too, were John Parks, B. J. Corolla, and the Facinellis.

There was William L. Simpson in the Jackson Hole, Clarence Gardner, in Star Valley; C. Watt Brandon, then in Sheridan; the Danas, at Parco; Doctor Horton, at Newcastle, and many, many others.

Of Brandon, he wrote: "Speaking of Pinedale – twenty-five years ago C. Watt Brandon, now a successful publisher of Sheridan, was pioneering at Pinedale. He edited the *Roundup,* and incidentally corresponded for the *Wyoming Tribune.* We gave Watt carte blanche. In a word, Brandon found more material for good stories, and more charm and more romance in and around Pinedale than most people thought existed in the entire state of Wyoming."

As he went about the state, Deming's interest in good roads was paramount. "I was pleased," he wrote after visiting Cody, "to see the progress that had been made in the road building mostly through national forests at Uncle Sam's expense. . . All that Jake Schwoob, Gus Holm's, and L. L. Newton had claimed for the Cody way twenty years ago had come to pass."

In writing of Cody, he also mentioned Director Mary Jester Allen of the Buffalo Bill museum, Dr. Frances Lane, Senator George T. Beck, Caroline Lockhart, Jacob Schwoob, Tex Holm's, and Major E. S. Hoopes, official greeter for Cody.

Bryant B. Brooks, C. H. Townsend, and Patrick J. Sullivan were among the many warm friends he met while in Casper; in the Big Horn country were P. P. Anderson and A. W. Coons, and at Worland C. H. Harkins, a long time friend.

In completing his tour of the state, Mr. Deming said: "I can state frankly that I have a better and broader conception of the resources of Wyoming than I ever had before. I have been much impressed with the high average intelligence and good citizenship of our people. They are of the fiber of which strong states are made. It is no exaggeration to say that I have not had one unpleasant experience or regrettable contact."

The results of the primary election in august were: Robert D. Carey, first; Judge C. E. Winter, second; W. C. Deming, third; and W. L. Walls, fourth.

No higher praise could be given a man in politics than that which appeared in the *Wyoming Eagle,* democratic weekly published by Tracy McCraken, under the caption: "Deming's Clean-cut Campaign given Approval in State."

"For the clean-cut campaign he waged in his race for the Republican nomination for the United States Senate, real credit is due to William C. Deming, Cheyenne publisher. This does not mean that Mr. Deming was the only political contestant in the recent primaries who fought a clean and above-board battle. There were others whose performance was equally as commendable. Because of a series of circumstances, however, it does seem as though the campaign of the Cheyenne man is among those which stand out as particularly exemplary.

As soon as the final result was evident, Mr. Deming dispatched the following telegram to the successful candidate:

August 19, 1930

ROBERT D. CAREY, Careyhurst, Wyoming

Accept my hearty congratulations on your decisive and clean-cut victory. You may be assured of the full support of myself and the Tribune-Leader in the fall campaign.

W. C. DEMING

At the request of a majority of candidates on the republican state ticket and the congressional ticket, Mr. Deming was drafted by the republican party to direct publicity in the campaign. After being appointed publicity director by the Honorable L. C. Hinkle, chairman of the republican state committee, Mr. Deming chose R. E. Evans, managing editor of the *Casper Tribune-Herald,* as his assistant. Mr. Evans had obtained a state-wide reputation as an editorial writer in his conduct of "Brass Tacks," an editorial column in the *Tribune-Herald.* Wyoming republicans were mostly successful.

On november 7, Postmaster-general Walter F. Brown thanked Mr. Deming for his telegram reporting the good news from Wyoming concerning the election victory. "It was a curious election," Mr. Brown said, "One that seems to defy analysis. I assume that the opposite verdicts rendered by the voters of Wyoming and Colorado are due to the fact that republicans of one state were united and in the other were divided."

On november 8, letters were received from Robert D. Carey and Frank C. Emerson, successful candidate for the United States senate and the governorship of Wyoming, respectively.

Robert D. Carey sent his thanks "for the fine spirit which you have shown in the campaign and the hearty support you have given me. You may be certain that I am most grateful for the same."

Governor-Elect Emerson's letter read: "May I take this opportunity to thank you heartily for the fine support given my candidacy during the recent campaign by *The Tribune*. It surely was most helpful in bringing the result in my favor."

Following the election, Mr. Deming returned by automobile to Washington for the winter. In characteristic fashion, he put aside his personal feeling relative to the results of the primary and was quoted in the Washington newspapers as being extremely proud of the fact that Wyoming re-elected its G.O.P. governor and all other state officers as well as a United States senator.

Business Interests

With the exception of the winter seasons, Mr. Deming spent most of the time between 1930 and 1937 in Wyoming, publishing the *Tribune*.

During the winter 1930-1931, while in Washington he entertained *Tribune* readers with many additional columns called "As Seen in Washington."

At this time, through the editorial columns of the *Tribune,* Mr. Deming endorsed a number of progressive movements such as the construction of a rail line from Sheridan through Buffalo to Casper; the building of a new veterans' hospital; the restoration of federal lands to oil exploration; and the construction of landing fields at all of the major towns and cities in Wyoming.

He joined Paul J. Paulson in presenting a triangular park on Randall avenue, to the city of Cheyenne, to be used only for a park or for recreational purposes.

After spending the winter in Washington, Mr. Deming returned to Cheyenne, accompanied by C. C. Hathaway, personnel officer of the Civil Service commission, who was on leave of absence from official duties. En route westward, Deming and Hathaway visited many historic sites, among which was the Lincoln Memorial near Hodgenville, Kentucky, a beautiful temple housing the one-room cabin in which Abraham Lincoln was born. They also inspected the Old Kentucky Home at Harrodsburg, Kentucky, in which Stephen C. Foster wrote his immortal "My Old Kentucky Home."

At this time, there occurred the death in Cheyenne of the Honorable L. C. Hinkle, chairman of the republican state central committee. Mr. Deming had worked closely with him in campaign matters and wrote in the *Tribune* as follows: "Mr. Hinkle was a self-made man, in fact one of the many old-time Union Pacific railroad employees who attained success and distinction in other lines of work. He was a telegrapher and train dispatcher. If one were searching for a single word which would depict Mr. Hinkle's personality, it would be the term 'dynamic.' He was positive in his opinions and frank upon all occasions. . . Mr. Hinkle was a consistent and intense republican and has probably given as many years of his active life for advancement of his party as any man in the state. He did it with little or no hope of personal reward, but because he loved the party and because he loved a contest. He will be missed socially as well as politically."

Mr. Deming was appointed by acting-governor A. M. Clark as chairman, in charge of the matter of arranging for patriotic meetings in Wyoming for the coming year – 1932 – the celebration period of the two-hundredth anniversary of the birth of George Washington. As chairman, he put considerable thought, energy, and time into this work. Appropriate meetings and exercises were held in every Wyoming town and city. Mr. Deming prepared an elaborate address on Washington which he delivered in Cheyenne and published in book form.

During the summer, he felt increasing concern over the constantly growing problem of relief, and on august 29, suggested in a letter to the American Red Cross society that it distribute checks to hotels and restaurants by which diners would pay an extra ten per cent of their bills to the society, on a voluntary basis, making it up by ordering less.

He also wrote Walter S. Gifford, national director of the unemployment relief organization at Washington, complimenting him on the survey of the situation that he was making and suggesting that "in some manner, the point should be emphasized repeatedly until it becomes a nation-wide slogan that idle men and women should remain at home. The situation is only aggravated," he said, "by large numbers of unemployed traveling from place to place."

For a number of years William C. Deming has been exceedingly interested in the so-called park extension controversy of Teton county, which began over a proposed extension of the southern boundary of the Yellowstone National park and involved the acquisition for donation to the government of lands by John D. Rockefeller, jr.

As a result of the original agitation for extension, the Grand Teton National park was created in 1929, comprising an area twenty-seven miles in length and from three to nine miles in width, including the scenic Tetons.

The idea of park extension, however, did not cease with the creation of the new park and intermittently for fourteen years the question has claimed the attention of Wyoming's citizenry.

The matter reached a climax on march 15, 1943 when President Franklin D. Roosevelt by executive order number 2758, set aside an area comprising 221,610 acres as the Jackson Hole National Monument, under the Antiquities act.

Wyoming officially has refused to acknowledge the existence of the National Monument and refers to it as the "pretended" monument. The state has filed suit to restrain the superintendent of the Grand Teton National park from carrying out the provisions of the presidential proclamation.

To review all of the details of the controversy thoroughly would require a book in itself, but we shall endeavor to give a brief summary of the situation and to quote from the antis and the pros.

In 1926 John D. Rockefeller, jr., with members of his family, made a vacation trip to Yellowstone National park and the Jackson Hole region of Teton county, Wyoming. At that time, Horace Albright, superintendent of the Yellowstone National park, did everything possible to make the Rockefeller visit to that section one of more than ordinary pleasure.

Mr. Rockefeller was deeply impressed by the outstanding beauty of the Tetons and the possibilities for recreational development of the area and he was also interested in the fact that many elk in the Jackson Hole had died a short time before from starvation, due largely to the fact that the fences of settlers had taken away their natural winter feeding grounds.

Later, when persons who were familiar with the Jackson Hole country approached Mr. Rockefeller on the subject of preserving the area in a more or less primitive state, his approval and support were quickly forthcoming.

Mr. Rockefeller had already set a precedent in contributing more than two millions of dollars for the purchase of lands to be included in the Smoky Mountains National park in North Carolina and Tennessee. He also had purchased and donated the big trees in California and an extension to Yosemite park, California. Perhaps his most popular and colorful project is the restoration of Williamsburg, Virginia, to a colonial setting, which attracts thousands of visitors annually.

Elaborate developments were visioned by Rockefeller, Horace Albright, and interested friends and the formation of what was known as The Jackson Hole plan resulted. According to the plan, all of the Hole from a point just south of Jackson to the southern boundary of the Yellowstone park, was to be made into an extension of the park, with Mr. Rockefeller purchasing privately owned lands to present to the government. The town of Jackson was to be rebuilt in strictly old-time western style and so retained. Nothing was to be allowed in the park proper which would be of a nature to detract in any way from the scenic beauties of the area.

For the purpose of acquiring ranch lands and other private holdings in Teton county, the Snake River Land company was organized in 1927, to act as agent for Mr. Rockefeller. This company at once set about to purchase the contemplated property, and to remove from the landscape all advertising signs, hot dog stands, and other works of man that might offend the eye.

Such features as the Jackson Lake lodge, the Sheffield Tourist camp at Moran, and the like which were already established were taken over in the general scheme with the understanding that they were to be retained and expanded for the accommodation of visitors. Such facilities were leased to a private corporation for operation.

Mr. Deming states that when the general plans of the pro-park extension first became known to the public, they were widely approved and it was said that seventy-five per cent of the citizens of Jackson Hole favored the idea. But before the plan could be developed to any great extent certain influential people of the area outwardly turned against the scheme and sought to place obstacles in the paths of the promoters. They took advantage of the fact that considerable jealousy existed between the National Forest and the National Park departments of the federal government and enlisted the sympathy of the local officials of the Forest service. One or two of the men who had been instrumental in assisting Mr. Rockefeller in the initial purchases, changed their minds and joined the opposition. A newspaper known as *The Grand Teton* was established, with the apparent purpose of fighting the extension. Cooperation was sought from the livestock interests outside of Jackson Hole and this was more or less successful, inasmuch as the majority of stockmen in Wyoming are, whether logically or otherwise, constitutionally opposed to any further increase in public domain whether by extension of national parks, national forests, or otherwise.

The opponents of the Jackson Hole plan took the position that withdrawal of so much land would reduce the assessed valuation of Teton county in a sum approximating one-third of a million dollars, and would thus leave the county with a large deficit for fixed expenditures every year. They claimed it would also reduce the population.

Those favoring the plan asserted that whatever might be lost directly through taxes upon private land holdings would be more than compensated for by the development of Teton county as a great recreational and tourist center, comparable with the Swiss Alps.

The assessed valuation, it was claimed, decreased little more than thirty thousand dollars after title passed from the former individual owners to and was consolidated in the Snake River Land company. The company paid about seven thousand dollars a year in taxes annually.

Two additional causes of opposition to the plan were the dreaded prospects of further federal control of Wyoming lands, and the disapproval of the fact that private enterprise would be permitted to direct activities of a commercial nature in the Teton Mountain area.

In september 1931, Mr. Deming visited Jackson in order to obtain first hand information concerning the controversy.

The article which he later wrote, in which he discussed the Rockefeller plan for Teton county, was considered a real masterpiece of fair-mindedness. He was highly complimented upon it by men from all parts of the country, among whom were Secretary of the Interior Ray Lyman Wilbur and Superintendent Roger Toll of the Yellowstone National park.

The article, which appeared in the *Tribune-Leader* on september 30, 1931 follows:

"From time to time during the last six months, the press of Wyoming has carried a large number of articles pro and con, mostly 'con,' about the so-called Rockefeller plan looking to the purchase of more than 30,000 acres of land in Teton county, to be donated to the federal government as a reserve for the propagation and preservation of big game and for general recreational purposes.

"However, the assessed valuation of this property, it is claimed, has decreased but little more than $30,000 since title passed from the former individual owners to and was consolidated in the Snake River Land company. While about two-thirds of the land has been acquired, perhaps it is too soon to get a fair line on the ultimate result of lessened revenues. Thought should be given to taxing private property in any new park or preserve created as a result of any of the various plans.

"It appears that in numerical strength in the county at large, the pros are in the majority. On the other hand, it is equally clear that the antis have been the most active and most effective in getting their arguments and reasons for opposition into the press of Wyoming.

"For some purpose or other, the pros have not resorted to the public press. Perhaps one reason is that there is no law, federal or state, which prevents a private land owner from selling his land to Mr. Rockefeller or to anyone else if he wishes to do so. Likewise, there is nothing to prevent Mr. Rockefeller from buying private holdings if he is willing to pay the price.

"It seems that Mr. Rockefeller, through the Snake River Land company, has not counted his pennies when dealing with the ranchmen. In fact, it is freely stated that in many instances the ranchmen have been able to sell out for two, three and four times the assessed value of the land. Much cash has been brought into the country.

"Underlying the whole controversy, and possibly a primary if not the fundamental cause thereof, is the elk question. This question is: Shall the state of Wyoming retain jurisdiction over the southern elk herd? This herd, as winter approaches, moves southward, along the eastern slope of Jackson Hole, toward the winter feeding ground just north of the town of Jackson. The region traversed during this movement is that in which the elk are hunted during the open season.

Wyoming has jurisdiction over the hunting ground.

"But if federal authority were extended to this region, or to the greater part of it, then the state of Wyoming would be divested of authority to regulate hunting.

"Whether citizens should or should not hunt, and to what regulations as regards licensing, etc., hunters should be subjected, would be wholly in federal control.

"In such circumstances, it would be possible to make the heart of Wyoming big game country in effect a preserve for the benefit of outsiders or non-residents, with the regulations so drawn and applied that home folks would be virtually excluded. The spectre of this situation intrudes whenever the Jackson Hole question is discussed understandingly. It is especially significant when the phrase 'park extension' enters into discussion, as almost invariably it does.

"The adjustment of this phase of the question will require the best thought of the Interior department, of congress, of the Wyoming delegation, of the state of Wyoming and of the citizens of Teton county in putting this plan into effect. They claim full faith and credit should be given their position.

"As evidence that a large percentage of citizens are friendly to the park plan, they say that hundreds of them have signed letters and petitions commendatory of the project and that among them are the names of officers of Teton county and good citizens of Jackson.

"Friends of the new preserve refer to prolonged opposition to creating a park of the Grand Teton area. In time a compromise was effected by making it a national park distinct from the Yellowstone park and now Jackson points with pride to a beautiful new playground at its very portals.

"Thus it will be seen that so far as making heads or tails out of the real sentiment on the question, 'you pays your money and takes your choice.' It is claimed further that some citizens who one week oppose the Rockefeller plan may favor it the next week and vice versa. In other words, they do not stay put.

"To make things worse from the standpoint of arriving at a correct judgment, it is even intimated that opinions upon the questions as expressed by certain local people from time to time vary according to those with whom they are conversing.

"In other words, they can be very bitter when being interviewed by opponents and conciliatory when discussing it with friends of the proposal. That probably means nothing more than indifference on the part of a few such citizens.

"Out of all this turmoil, there has grown gradually a spirit of compromise. Senator Robert D. Carey, who visited Teton county in the latter part of august, sought to pour oil upon the troubled waters by having the Snake River Land company donate the lands in question to the state of Wyoming, to be maintained as a recreational and big game preserve. As to the proposed reimbursement for lands taken out of taxation, it is not clear where this reimbursement would come from, but presumably from the federal government if it took over the Rockefeller purchases and other privately owned properties to be eliminated from taxation.

"The Jackson Hole plan also contemplates the preservation of certain grazing rights and the maintenance of certain hay lands, etc., for the protection of any remaining stockmen and for the raising of food for big game during the severe winter. This latter compromise is an elaboration of the Rockefeller plan, the provisions of which are to be safeguarded in the act of congress creating the recreational area.

"The most reasonable conclusion from all of the foregoing is that both the pros and the antis seem to realize that the Rockefeller project has gone too far to be stopped. In fact, there is some doubt that any large number of people wish it entirely stopped. But all, both pros and cons, wish the present and future material interests of Jackson and Teton county adequately safeguarded. The opponents are willing to compromise by making it a state park and a state game preserve, with all of the rights of Wyoming citizens preserved, as well as the game, while the proponents of the general scheme now offer the Jackson Hole plan with its provisions for reimbursement to Teton county for loss of taxable wealth. They assert that Wyoming should not shoulder the burden of a state park.

"Representative William Deloney, a master of Jackson Hole problems, is said to be one of the fathers of the latest solution. Thus it will be seen that what a few weeks ago promised to blossom into a bitter sectional and political issue, instead of boiling up is now boiling down to a matter of certain details necessary for the welfare, stability and the future of Teton county upon the map of Wyoming.

"Whatever the result, I feel very sure the future of Jackson as a popular gateway to the lovely Grand Teton park of Wyoming and to the greater and more elaborate Yellowstone is secure. Farsighted pioneers have established an abiding place in a bejewelled setting. What Nature has so majestically provided, no man will be able to destroy."

The question of feeding the great elk herd mentioned by Mr. Deming in his article has gradually been solved.

The elk refuge in Jackson Hole which was first established under an act of congress in 1912 and enlarged through subsequent acts and executive orders now includes approximately twenty thousand acres owned and four thousand acres under lease. It is administered by the United States biological survey. The refuge now, according to the biological survey, can support the herd of twenty-five thousand elk easily. Many federal and national sporting organizations contributed to the feeding of elk, until the biological survey in cooperation with the state of Wyoming shouldered the responsibility. The refuge also has been made a bird refuge.

Because of the continued bitter opposition to the extension plan, three congressional hearings have been held, the last one being in Jackson in august 1938.

Says Mr. Deming: "Efforts to investigate the matter officially proved fruitless by reason of the methods of the opposition, who in many instances contrived to color and to govern testimony offered at the hearings.

"Senators Kendrick and Carey and Representative Carter apparently joined the antis in opposing the creation of additional federal parks or playgrounds in that vicinity.

"The matter became more or less a political football. In at least two political contests, it is said, the Rockefeller plan was made an issue.

"Friends of the Rockefeller plan reiterated the sincerity of Mr. Rockefeller and his desire to keep the beautiful recreational area in its primitive state and they pointed out that the housing facilities in the region were deplorably deficient.

"As a consequence of so much adverse publicity to his plans, Mr. Rockefeller became somewhat discouraged and ceased to push the matter. The officials of the National Park service, however, continued in their efforts to bring about the extension.

"In november 1937, Congressman Paul R. Greever took up the matter of completing the program for acceptance of lands of the Rockefeller interests and setting up reservations to protect Teton county and the grazing interests using the national forests.

"At the congressional hearing which followed in august 1938, the leading business interests in Jackson, dominated it is said, by past and present officials of the forest service, were led by William L. Simpson, an able pioneer lawyer. The sentiment expressed at the hearing was decidedly against extension."

Many presumed that the matter of further park extension had been dropped at least for the duration of the war.

In march 1943 the news of the creation of the Jackson Hole national monument by executive order, burst upon the people of Wyoming like a bombshell as no prior notice of such contemplated action had been given to the congressional delegation, the senate public lands committee, the governor or the people of Wyoming.

According to a statement of the county commissioners of Teton county, the so-called national monument included the total of 221,610 acres in which are 32,117 acres owned by the Rockefeller interests, 1400 acres of state-owned land, approximately 17,000 acres of privately owned lands in addition to the federal land of which 100,000 acres were under the administration of the Forest service.

In the area are one hundred forty-seven homes, including operating ranches, residences, and dude ranch properties. There are also six post offices, five hotels and cabin camps and ten dude ranches.

It seems that the action of the president was taken after a letter had been sent by John D. Rockefeller, jr. to the Interior department in which he stated that he did not feel that he could maintain his holdings in Jackson Hole much longer. He explained that he was reducing his obligations and burdens and felt it necessary to dispose of his Wyoming lands in some way.

Government officials evidently felt that the government should not lose the gift of the Rockefeller lands, and having failed to accomplish the park extension through congressional approval, sought presidential assistance.

Secretary of the Interior Ickes is credited with saying before the Public Lands committee hearing: "I saw a way to do this. I did it, and the people of Wyoming be damned."

The result of the presidential order has been an unprecedented arousal of interest in the matter of state's rights, not only in Wyoming but throughout the country.

Many who evidently were not particularly interested one way or another in the park extension itself, have been aroused and have joined the opposition because of what they term a subterfuge in method.

Governor Lester C. Hunt immediately vigorously protested the creation of the monument without the knowledge or consent of the people of the state or the congressional representatives and wrote to President Roosevelt as follows:

My Dear Mr. President: The far reaching effects on the economy and the people of our state, and particularly on that section of our state included in Teton county, of your proclamation dated march 15, 1943, creating the Jackson Hole National Monument commanded me to trespass upon your time, even during these strenuous days to protest the creation of the monument, and, in justice to you and to the people of Wyoming, I feel my protest should no longer be delayed.

The reservation of the area south of Yellowstone National park for park or other restricted use has been the subject of controversy and has made uncertain the future of this area for the past twenty-five years. Two congressional hearings have reported adversely and twice our national congress has withheld approval of the enlargement of Yellowstone or Grand Teton National parks and on two occasions the Wyoming state legislature has memorialized congress protesting such extensions. Your recent proclamation is now strenuously objected to by people living in the area affected, by officials of Teton county, by myself, by our congressional delegation, and by the entire citizenry of the state of Wyoming.

As a result of these combined protests, congress has taken no action, but the secretary of the Interior now attempts to justify the creation of the monument without considering the protests because those protests were lodged against the enlargement of Teton National park. It is true the protests were against the enlargement of the park because such use was the only use contemplated, but it must have been apparent to him and everybody else that the objections were directed against the reservation of the area outside of either Yellowstone or Teton National parks which would restrict its use more than that of the forest reservation.

Mr. President, let me state that much of our prosperity is derived from the livestock industry and the success of that industry depends to a very large extent upon the use of forest areas for grazing and upon feed produced in areas in the vicinity of the forest reservations. Any curtailment of the use of such areas, as eventually happens when parks are extended or monuments created, results in a serious curtailment of livestock production which now has such a vital place in our war effort.

A more direct local effect of the establishment of the monument will be the loss of more than one-third of the taxes of Teton county to say nothing about the indirect effect through loss of population.

Reliable figures indicate that that county and the schools will not be able to operate with such reduced revenue. The loss of taxes in Teton county also affects state revenue derived from taxation.

It may be argued that all privately owned lands, which will eventually be acquired in the Jackson Hole area, will be paid for without loss to the owners. No doubt this is true, but those people who must remain, people who have established homes, raised their families on what they had a right to believe would be a permanent home, will not be reimbursed although they will be most seriously affected and may have to leave. Businessmen in the town of Jackson and other parts of the area will also be seriously affected, if not completely ruined. In fact, a large community will be disrupted and many people compelled to start anew in some other place.

There is another feature of the monument which I feel obliged to stress and that is the inclusion of thousands of acres of land which by no stretch of imagination can be considered as containing historic landmarks or objects of historic or scientific interest, or lands which are necessary to the administration of the monument or to protect its valuable part. I base this statement upon personal familiarity of the area and upon reliable information I have assembled. This area could, and in my judgment, should be eliminated. The facts at my command show that if the area were confined within the limits of the boundaries indicated on the attached map, all the part of the area which prompted the establishment of the monument would be retained and the injury to public and private interests reduced to a minimum, and Wyoming's wild life conservation program could continue without interference, to the advantage of the entire nation.

The above and other facts could and would have been submitted had the secretary of the Interior seen fit to consult with me prior to presenting the proclamation to you. In ignoring me in the matter, I believe he has departed from a precedent which has been long established and should not be passed over lightly.

A fundamental principle of democracy is involved, namely, that by virtue of the proclamation, American citizens are dispossessed of their homes on the recommendation of a bureau and this principle, I am sure you will agree, is not in harmony with your views and my views of democracy and americanism.

President Roosevelt replied to Governor Hunt that benefits to be derived by the nation were the compelling reasons for establishment of the Jackson Hole National Monument.

THE PRESIDENT CONTINUED: In issuing the proclamation (creating the monument area in western Wyoming), I was careful to protect all private interests now established in the monument area.

Existing grazing rights will not be interfered with and there will therefore be no adverse effect upon the production of livestock, now so vital to the war program.

I am aware that national forests, wildlife refuges, federal grazing districts and other forms of federal land reservations, except the national parks, return a portion of their revenues to the counties in which the lands are situated.

Uniformity of practice in this regard appears to be desirable and I would favor some equitable means by which a portion of the revenues of Yellowstone, Grand Teton and Jackson Hole could benefit Teton county.

There is an indirect benefit, of course, in the resulting increase in local business and assessed valuations which experience has shown to follow the establishment of parks and monuments as tourist attractions.

I am informed that in 1941 your own state of Wyoming collected more than $151,000 in taxes from Yellowstone National park alone. This was due in no small measure to the federal developments that made the area available and added to the possibilities for human enjoyment.

I honestly believe that the resumption of tourist travel, which will undoubtedly follow the war, will result in a great deal more money flowing into Teton county and the state of Wyoming than if the federal government had not established the Jackson Hole National Monument."

Former Governor Leslie A. Miller of Wyoming, regional director of the WPB, issued a vigorous thirteen-page statement in support of President Roosevelt and Secretary Ickes in which he stated that "had I been confronted, in official position, with the necessity to deal with a similar set of circumstances, confronted by the same type of opposition, I would unquestionably have been moved to adopt a like course. There are times when self-respecting public officials must be resolute and quite definitely this was one of the occasions."

Mr. Miller states that he knows "there are many in

that region (Teton county) who believe that the ultimate destiny of Jackson Hole is recreation. By one means and another, however, people of influence, for reasons of their own, have managed to intimidate many of those who would like to speak out and consequently the voices of proponents have been stilled."

He quotes various petitions and other documents to show the interest of the people who have favored the extension plan, and agrees with Albright that along about 1930 and 1931 some opposition appeared emanating chiefly from past and incumbent forest officials. Mr. Miller summarizes as follows:

The grazing rights heretofore enjoyed by the cattle men will be continued.

Fishing rights are not disturbed.

Only eight per cent of the lands in the monument are privately owned and the rights and privileges of the owners are not disturbed.

Ninety-two per cent of the lands, including the Rockefeller gift, are merely changed from one federal jurisdiction to another.

The national park management is pledged to a program of promoting the advertising of the area and the attracting to it of more and more vacationers – that they can succeed is attested by the record of increasing numbers into Grand Teton National park up to the year of the war emergency.

Also says Mr. Miller: "The State of Wyoming and individual communities therein have expended hundreds of thousands of dollars advertising for tourist trade and always the great lure – the attraction *par excellence* – has been the Tetons. Can any reader recall a piece of literature printed in the state in recent years which has not carried a picture of these magnificent mountains? . . . The writer . . . wants, oh so much, to have the people of Wyoming live up to the reputation he has claimed for them for fairmindedness, generosity, for appreciation of the better things of life. It grieves him deeply today to have fellow citizens cast aspersions upon the deeds and motives of Mr. Rockefeller in the matter here discussed. In all this land of ours there is no work of nature to equal the beauty and grandeur of the Teton mountains, no waters to compare in attractiveness of surroundings to the lakes of Northern Teton county. To protect and preserve these lands and waters from commercial exploitation, to maintain them for the enjoyment of the millions of people of America who appreciate that we have sufficient land and water in the country outside of this area to support all our economic needs, is a praiseworthy, a generous, a patriotic thing to do. Mr. Rockefeller, in his attitude and his actions, deserves not criticism and condemnation, but the gratitude of the people of Teton county and of Wyoming.

"So deeply do I feel that a great mistake may be made today if the opposition to this project succeeds in its will to defeat the purpose of Mr. Rockefeller, the president, and the National Park service in the enlargement of Teton National park, and as a result the area shall once again be claimed for commercial purposes, the lakes made into irrigation reservoirs and the tourist traffic be utterly unguided and unprovided for, I predict and utter the prediction in all sincerity that the day will come when Wyoming will hang her head in shame and regret the act as she will regret nothing else in her proud history.

"If the action of the president shall by congress be allowed to stand, a great blessing indeed will be vouchsafed the people of Teton county and of Wyoming. The controversy, stirred primarily by personal motives and a feudal jealousy of one federal bureau toward another has served for many years to set friend against friend, neighbor against neighbor, has caused endless waste of time and energy in wordy arguments and public oratory. The project has been a football of hypocritical partisan politics in every recent election. What peace of mind, indeed what great profit to all concerned would quickly ensue if all this were ended and Teton county could settle down to the business of working out her destiny as host to the vacationers of all the land!"

Those who know former Governor Miller best say he has never hesitated to speak out in meeting even against strong opposition if convinced his views are sound.

While there have been some bitter criticisms of Mr. Miller for his position in the present controversy most Wyoming citizens give him credit for being fearless and sincere.

Governor Hunt issued instructions to the state Fish and Game department to disregard a letter written by Superintendent of Grand Teton National park, Charles J. Smith, concerning regulations regarding bear hunting on the monument. Immediately Assistant-secretary of the interior Oscar Chapman stated that Smith had no authority to issue the order. Thus the confusion continues.

In may 1943, the attorney-general of Wyoming filed suit in the United States district court in an attempt to prevent the federal government from taking over the major part of the Jackson Hole region as a monument. The petition asked the court to restrain Superintendent Charles J. Smith of Grand Teton National park from carrying out the provisions of the presidential proclamation and from interfering in the state's jurisdiction over the area involved.

Representative Frank A. Barrett introduced H.R. 2241 in the house of representatives to annul the order

creating the monument. A Public Lands committee
hearing on the bill followed at which Mr. Barrett said,
in part:

Numerous and varied proposals for new park boundaries and extensions have been made from time to time and I submit herewith a
brief summary of the bills which have been introduced in congress.
The very fact that none of these bills passed is the best evidence that
the congress and the people were unalterably opposed to any extension
of the park area in the Jackson Hole country. It evidently was because
of this universal opposition that the monument law was resorted to.
It was apparent that neither the consent of the people nor the consent
of congress could be obtained to set aside for park purposes, the area
now embraced within the Jackson Hole National Monument.

. . . In order that you may be fully informed as to the attitude
of the people, I might say that in all the letters, telegrams, resolutions, etc., which have come to my desk, only one citizen of Wyoming
has indicated that he might favor the creation of the monument. To
the best of my knowledge, sentiment is almost one hundred per cent
against the extension of the park area in Wyoming.

I will briefly call attention to various documents now in my files
and will submit them to you for your consideration.

I have received numerous resolutions protesting the creation of the
monument. These come from about every kind of organization in the
state, and from all parts of the state. They express the sentiment and
feelings of thousands of people from every walk of life. They represent the sportsmen's organizations, Lions clubs, Rotary clubs, Real
Estate boards, town councils, county commissioners, women's clubs,
American Legion, Chamber of Commerce and livestock interests.
I have not received one resolution favoring the creation of the monument.

. . . To create a national park by subterfuge destroys our sense
and feeling of security. . . This is probably the most outstanding
example of government directive that has occurred to date. . . the
people had a right to believe that if further attempts were to be
made to extend the park, they would have opportunity to be heard
and protest. When they awoke to what had happened they were
stunned. . . The creation of the national monument by proclamation is a usurpation of the powers and prerogatives of congress.
It is a circumvention of the orderly process of government."

In speaking of the people of Teton county, Mr. Barrett continued:

"One morning they awoke to find themselves in the middle of the Jackson Hole National Monument. At first they were stunned and shocked. It was almost impossible to believe that, without notice or hearing, their government could, by executive order, set aside so vast an area for park or monument purposes. It mattered little what you called it. It was in fact, an extension of the Grand Teton National park. After their minds cleared and they realized what had happened to them, they reacted naturally as any human being would react under the circumstances. They were resentful. They were fearful. Their boys were away on the battle fronts of the world fighting to preserve and protect their home. And now their government, without resorting to the orderly process of constitutional government, had suddenly taken action that would ultimately deprive them of their homes and their means of livelihood."

A telegram from Governor Hunt to Representative Barrett said:

Strongly urge House Public Lands committee report favorably your bill H.R. 2241. Every newspaper in this state, every county, state and national elective official and our citizens 100 per cent resent action sponsored by National Park service through the Interior department and accomplished by presidential proclamation No. 2578. I strongly protest Park service in accomplishing its objectives by secret means, knowing as they did that the creation of the monument could not be had in an open and above board manner in the usual democratic processes, namely action by congress. . .

Secretary of the Interior Ickes asked to appear before the Public Lands committee and in his testimony said: "Basically the controversy over Jackson Hole is essentially a row between the Forest service and the National Park service."

Former superintendent Horace Albright also stressed the fact that the Forest service was at the base of much of the opposition to the extension. He declared that the creation of the monument was the finest thing that ever happened to Wyoming.

The Wyoming Stock Growers association in convention at Lusk, Wyoming in june 1943, passed a resolution demanding the removal of Secretary of Interior Ickes, saying: "The national monument steal in Teton county is an attempt to do by executive act what could not be done in the open and this act, together with Ickes' unfair and dishonest methods in connection with the establishment and enlargement of the King river canyon and Olympia national park, makes him unfit to hold an office of trust. . ."

Said J. C. Thompson, the editor of the *Wyoming Tribune* on march 22:

The Japanese pulled a "sneak play" when, on that "day of infamy," dec. 7, 1941, they gave America, a friendly nation, "a stab in the back" with their blitz of Pearl Harbor. The quotations are words of Franklin D. Roosevelt, president of the United States. The effectiveness of the yellow barbarian's strategy and tactics, it appears, was not lost in Washington – the demonstration that, when you design to give a friend "a stab in the back," a "sneak play" is advisable. Witness – the Jackson Hole Monument.

From far and wide have come expressions of opinions relative to the creation of the monument. In the main the early objections have been ignored and the well-organized opposition is based on extended federal control of state lands.

Says the editor of the *Arizona Farmer:* "That Jackson Hole squabble up in Wyoming isn't something that affects Wyoming alone. It involves a principle that affects every state, and especially Arizona."

The Idaho Wool Growers expressed concern over the method in which the monument was created saying: "With amazement and concern . . . a constrained construction has been placed upon the powers delegated to the president and a subterfuge has been resorted to

famous artists. Some of the paintings are of heroic proportions, covering the entire side of huge rooms.

"I may add that possibly because of the western atmosphere in which I live, one of the most interesting paintings in the gallery, in my opinion, is a large canvas by the famous French painter, Rosa Bonheur, showing a number of cattle being used for plowing in the field. It is one of the best works of the woman who produced the 'Horse Fair,' which was purchased by Cornelius Vanderbilt and which hangs in the Metropolitan Museum in New York.

"All told, there are hundreds of beautiful paintings, representing many different schools. In addition, there are a number of handsome tapestries and in the large courtyard, between two wings of the building, a collection of works of sculpture, including a copy of Michael Angelo's 'David' . . . It is worth a trip to Florida merely to see this unusual collection."

While in Florida, Mr. Deming was asked to make addresses before civic and luncheon clubs, and on february 8, 1932, spoke before the Great Miami Airport association on the importance of the Cheyenne airport.

In the spring he left Florida for Washington in order to participate in the annual meeting of the United States chamber of commerce. His route took him past Stone mountain in Georgia, to the Biltmore estate in North Carolina, and then north through Virginia, to his destination. His description of the visit to the Biltmore estate shows vividly his keen appreciation of art.

On the estate, located about a mile from Asheville, North Carolina, on beautifully wooded hills, George W. Vanderbilt, in 1890, began the erection of a magnificent home. When it was completed five years later,

it had three hundred sixty-five rooms and had cost
several million dollars. . .

Concerning it, Mr. Deming wrote:

"Entering the estate, I drove for about two miles
through the grounds. The roadway is lined with trees,
a small stream running nearby; and the wooded hills,
said to be well stocked with game, stretch as far as the
eye can see. Suddenly, the trees open and the castle
is in sight at the right. The first impression is of an
unusually long stone building, with a central turret,
and with a multitude of windows. It looks solid but not
cold, or impressive. It is almost friendly.

"Entering the main hallway, I was pleasantly greeted
by the woman attendant in charge and invited to take
my time in inspecting the premises. Not all of the three
hundred sixty-five rooms by any means are open – only
the main rooms on the first and second floors. The first
object of interest is the grand stairway of beautiful
white stone supporting itself without any columns and
winding gracefully up, floor after floor to the roof of
the tall building. Seldom have I seen a staircase so
charmingly combine beauty of design with the impression of dignity and strength.

"Before ascending to the second floor, I turned to
the hallway and there saw the first of the building's
splendors. Spain and France have made their contributions here, the former in a steel treasure chest of
the sixteenth century; France, by a tapestry that once
belonged to the famous Cardinal Richelieu.

"Next came the oak drawing room, panelled in
Norwegian oak, with bronzes over the fireplace and
eighteenth century furniture here and there. On the
walls hang engravings from many of Landseer's well-
known animal paintings.

"But perhaps the most impressive room was yet to come. It was the banquet hall, an immense room seventy-two feet in length and seventy-five feet high. As I entered it, I could not but wonder how many regal banquets had been held within its walls. It would truly be a fit meeting place for kings, ancient or modern.

"The object which perhaps calls forth the greatest interest of visitors is found in what is called the print room. In it are the chess table and set of chess men which once belonged to Napoleon Bonaparte and which he used while imprisoned at St. Helena. It is said that when the Little Emperor died, his heart was placed in the drawer of this selfsame table. If the chess men could talk, what stories they could recount.

"Here and there throughout the huge mansion are objects of interest or beauty, usually both. In the dining room, looking out upon the North Carolina wooded hills, is a fireplace by Wedgwood, in the characteristic white and blue.

"Upstairs is a bedroom suite that once belonged to Louis XVI of France, furnished all in red damask. Here and there are paintings by famous artists. Just as I entered the banquet hall, two small children in charge of a middle-aged woman entered and, after looking about a moment, disappeared through a side door. When I was about to leave the mansion, the attendant said: 'Did you notice those children? They are the Vanderbilt boys, little George and William. To my knowledge, you are the first visitor who has ever seen them here. They have a new nurse and she did not get them out of sight at the proper time, for they are never allowed to be seen by the public.' Although they are the heirs to a great and famous fortune, so far as I could observe they looked no different from any ordinary Americans of the same age. While these youngsters are commonly spoken of as the Vanderbilt children, they are the offspring of Mr. and Mrs. John Francis Amherst Cecil, owners of the Biltmore estate. Mrs. Cecil will be remembered as the attractive young daughter of George Vanderbilt, who startled society of two continents many years ago by marrying an English lord much older than herself."

Although busy with official affairs in Washington, Mr. Deming was ever alert to the needs of his own home vicinity.

When the water supply of Cheyenne, in 1932, was being rapidly depleted and there was no check upon the amount being used in the homes and on the lawns, Mr. Deming took a strong position in favor of water meters, although he knew it would not be popular with the property owners generally. His files show that although he was in Washington part of the time, he kept in close touch with the situation.

A note to Charles Thompson, editor, and W. I. N. Cox, business manager of the *Tribune,* ended with: "Please arrange a conference soon upon the subject with members and officers of the Chamber of Commerce, City commissioners, and State Public Service commission. There will be technical and legal objections raised, also questions of policy. . . We should face the situation as it is today and forget any differences between Revis and True or Allison, Holliday and Weybrecht. . . Don't let any former mayors interfere with the meter program by dragging out old fights and past controversies between city engineers. . . I think the *Tribune* can push it through – that is, the purchase, financing, and installation of meters before april 1, 1933."

Mayor Weybrecht acted promptly and cooperated fully, and meters were installed. No doubt meters were absolutely necessary to avoid waste of water and a critical shortage.

Through the years, Mr. Deming's interest in good roads continued, and when a special dispatch in 1932, from Fort Collins, Colorado, to the *Denver Post,* stated that thirteen miles more were to be oiled on the Fort Collins-Laramie road or cut-off, he realized the disadvantage to Cheyenne. Immediately he urged a meeting of a strong committee with the Colorado state highway commission in Denver, with a view to having the Fort Collins-Cheyenne road recognized as a part of the federal system, and therefore eligible for assistance from the United States, as well as from Colorado and Wyoming.

"If the states of Colorado and Wyoming would eliminate curves, cut down grades, and complete an oiled highway from Fort Collins to Cheyenne," he said, "a large number of autoists going from Cheyenne to Denver would use both the Greeley and Fort Collins routes for the sake of variety, if nothing else."

Many articles for the road appeared in the *Tribune.* Wyoming took the lead and completed an excellent oiled road to the Colorado line in order to show the contrast. Fort Collins then cooperated with Cheyenne in extending it to that city. Alfred G. Hill, of the Fort Collins *Express-Courier,* did yeoman service in making sentiment and bringing the Colorado highway commission into line.

James H. Walton, Archie Allison, W. J. Dinneen, and Mr. Deming appeared before the Colorado Highway Advisory board, the United States bureau of Public Roads, and Governor Edwin C. Johnson in Denver.

The interest which was aroused at this time brought final results in 1936 in the completion of the oiled highway between Cheyenne and Fort Collins, designated as part of United States highway 87, despite the prolonged opposition of Chairman Vail of the Colorado commission. Governor Johnson, now United States senator, favored the project and stood with the Larimer county, Colorado, sponsors and the Cheyenne, Wyoming, advocates of the road. All hands gave the *Wyoming Tribune* credit for success in its long-drawn out campaign for a hard-surfaced road from Cheyenne to Fort Collins.

In august 1932, W. H. Jackson, pioneer Union Pacific photographer, came to Wyoming to visit and accompanied Mr. Deming and John Charles Thompson on several trips, including one to the Ames monument and the Summit, which he first saw in 1868. Despite his ninety years, Jackson could pace his companions in climbing the hills.

Mr. Jackson first came west at the age of nineteen, after serving in the Civil war with a Vermont regiment. He reached St. Louis from New York in 1866, and headed west as a bullwhacker over the Oregon trail. After spending the winter in Salt Lake City, he went on to California with a mule train. In the spring of 1867, he bought a herd of one hundred fifty mustangs and drove them back to Omaha, where there was an active horse market.

At Omaha, he began his photographic career. He followed the Union Pacific west in 1868 and 1869, making interesting and historic pictures en route. His work attracted national attention, and he was engaged by Dr. F. V. Hayden, then geologist of the geological survey, to make pictures of the public domain – moun-

John Charles Thompson, William H. Jackson, and William C. Deming in 1932
at the Ames monument near the Summit between Cheyenne and Laramie

tains, valleys, and all unusual features in the then little known Rocky mountain West.

Outfitting at Fort D. A. Russell (now Fort F. E. Warren), in 1870, he gave ten years to this work. He took the first photographs of the Yellowstone National park in 1871, and the first of the Tetons in 1872. He has done more than any other man to preserve the history of the West through painting and photography. Many of his photographic plates are in official files in Washington; hundreds more are being preserved in the Dearborn institute, owned by Henry Ford. More than two thousand of his photographs are in the Western history department of the Denver (Colorado) Public Library.

After he returned East from his visit in 1932, Mr. Jackson wrote Mr. Deming as follows:

"Wyoming – Cheyenne particularly, will always have great attraction for me. In Cheyenne I first set up my 'dark box' in a room above John Sumner's store for the preparation and development of my negatives in beginning my 1869 series of U.P. views; meanwhile living at the Tin restaurant on Eddy street. . . My occasional visits to Cheyenne have been something to remember and be thankful for, chiefly through your interest in the work I am engaged in for our old West – a matter of mutual concern."

Jackson died on june 23, 1942 in his ninety-ninth year.

During his later years he spent a great deal of time making water color sketches of the old West as he had seen it. Many of these sketches were used in connection with Wyoming historical events, including the Covered Wagon centennial celebration.

Says Mr. Deming: "On february 21, 1930, President

Hoover issued a proclamation commemorating the one hundredth anniversary of the departure of the first wagon train from St. Louis, Missouri for Oregon and the Northwest.

"On the twenty-third day of june following, Governor Frank C. Emerson, of Wyoming, issued a proclamation designating july third, fourth and fifth, as dates for an observation of the Covered Wagon centennial at Independence Rock, Wyoming.

"Robert S. Ellison, then of Casper, prepared an interesting history called *Independence Rock, the Great Record of the Desert.* It was illustrated by William H. Jackson, of New York, pioneer artist and photographer. The foreword was written by the late Daniel W. Greenburg. Mrs. Addie E. Homberg, of Lander, contributed a poem for the occasion.

"Active interest in the program was taken by the Natrona County Historical society led by the following: Thomas Cooper, president; D. W. Greenburg, secretary-treasurer; G. R. Hagens, first vice-president; C. E. Winter, second vice-president; B. B. Brooks, third vice-president; Mrs. W. H. Winter, curator of museum; Albert Park, Otto Bolln, Lew M. Gay, R. S. Ellison, W. S. Kimball, S. W. Conwell, C. F. Shumaker, C. E. Hoffhine and H. A. Wagner.

"Independence Rock attracted attention early in the last century because of its unique formation and has been marked by the Wyoming historical landmark commission, because the names of hundreds of emigrants are carved upon the face of the rock. Hence the designation 'Record of the Desert.'

"Independence Rock is located in Natrona county, a short distance east of Devil's Gate, and is visited annually by large numbers of tourists.

Devil's Gate on the Sweetwater river near Independence Rock
reproduced from an original painting by William H. Jackson

"The completion of a modern highway from Casper to Lander and over Togwotee pass to the Jackson Hole country has contributed much toward popularizing the many historical points in central and western Wyoming.

"The program celebrating the centennial was participated in by the Oregon Trail Memorial association, the Boy Scouts of America, the Knights of Columbus and the Ancient, Free and Accepted Masons.

"Father De Smet had named the rock, 'The Great Record of the Desert' as early as 1840, and posterity has named a lake in Johnson county in honor of the distinguished Catholic missionary.

"The relationship of the Masonic order arose from the fact that the first lodge of emigrant masons in this section of the Rocky mountains was held july 4, 1862 on the top of Independence Rock.

"The entire program in 1930 was carried out according to schedule, closing sunday, july 6, with early devotional services, a complete record of which may be found in the files of the Wyoming Historical society.

"Hundreds of those present at the exercises camped in the vicinity and carried away pleasant recollections of the occasion."

The question is frequently asked, "How did Wyoming handle the relief situation before President Franklin D. Roosevelt was inaugurated president?"

Following the boom in the early part of 1929, the Wall street crash, october twenty-fourth the same year, and the business collapse in 1930, 1931, and 1932, unemployment became quite general throughout the United States. Conditions were particularly acute in the cities. President Hoover, alive to the situation, appointed Walter Gifford, president of the American Telephone and Telegraph company, director of a national organization on unemployment and relief, during the winters of 1931 and 1932. Mr. Gifford lost no time in organizing groups throughout the country.

The Honorable George E. Brimmer was named chairman for the Wyoming state organization and George W. Hewlett was chosen the head of the Cheyenne relief committee. Associated with Mr. Hewlett were Charles D. Carey, William C. Deming, Warren Richardson, Edward T. Storey, Archie Allison, James Buckley, and James H. Walton.

This committee proceeded at once to gather information as to the unemployed and needy, regardless of the cause, in Cheyenne, and Laramie counties. Cash subscriptions, voluntary and solicited, were received, and the work and efforts of the committee were coordinated with the commissioners of Laramie county, the mayor and commissioners of Cheyenne, the Salvation Army, the Red Cross, the Help One Another club, and other similar local associations.

Ample funds and supplies were available at all times. Fearing, however, that some deserving person or family might be overlooked, the committee periodically asked for confidential information through the Cheyenne newspapers. There was never a time, so far as known, when anyone was neglected.

Nevertheless, the national depression got into politics to some extent and was the subject of discussion in congress, in the concluding days of Mr. Hoover's administration and the opening months of President Roosevelt's regime.

Aroused by statements made on the floor of the United States senate, Senator Hiram Bingham, of

Connecticut, wired Acting-governor A. M. Clark of Wyoming, "How many people are starving in Wyoming?"

Governor Clark consulted Chairman Brimmer and others and replied promptly, "No one is starving in Wyoming. This state has been caring for its unemployed, its aged and its needy liberally and systematically. We need no outside help."

That was the situation when all local organizations in Wyoming were dissolved and succeeded by the paid, political set-up under the New Deal.

Under local, unpaid administration only those actually deserving applied for assistance. Millions, no doubt, received aid from relatives, as had always been the custom in the United States. That was all changed when the Roosevelt administration centered activities in Washington and left the impression that unlimited federal funds were available for the asking.

On november 22, 1932, Deming was present at the dinner in honor of Governor Franklin D. Roosevelt, president-elect of the United States, given by the National Press club in the club's ballroom. Special guests were Speaker John N. Garner, vice-president-elect of the United States; James A. Farley, Frank C. Walker, Louis McHenry Howe, Raymond Moley, and Eddie Dowling. The entertainment was under the personal direction of M. H. Aylesworth, president of the National Broadcasting company, and son of a former president of Colorado State college at Fort Collins, Colorado.

When asked, "What was your experience or observation during the Franklin D. Roosevelt bank holiday, so-called?" Mr. Deming said:

"I was in Washington throughout the winter of

1932-33 engaged chiefly in writing for the *Wyoming Tribune* and doing special articles for eastern papers and magazines.

"The unemployment situation had grown steadily worse for more than a year. The Hoover volunteer agencies functioned well for the most part, but after the election the previous november, the Democratic national committee and other leaders in that party intimated that President Roosevelt would propose a more comprehensive and efficient system under government control with a salaried setup, but presumed to be only an emergency measure.

"During the weeks preceding march 4, economic and financial conditions were delicate and more or less alarming. Day after day, in january and february 1933, I saw men and women carrying away gold from the banks and Treasury department, for hoarding, no doubt. Some of them used small satchels or traveling bags. The country was still on a gold standard and the public put it to the test.

"It is reliably stated that President Hoover requested a conference with President-elect Franklin D. Roosevelt on the entire financial situation, particularly with respect to bank withdrawals, but Mr. Roosevelt declined a meeting.

"In Washington, many of us heard an intimation that there would be some kind of a bank moratorium when Roosevelt was inaugurated. If not, it was believed many banks would have to close. All over the country depositors were withdrawing funds and placing them where they would be most accessible. I had personal accounts in the Riggs National bank of Washington and in the Cheyenne banks. The *Tribune* and the Deming Realty company likewise had deposits in the

Stock Growers National bank and the American National bank.

"At that time, Robert L. Bailey of the Civil Service commission and I were living in an apartment in the Westchester and we frequently discussed the situation. Bailey was a man who attached little or no importance to the value of money, believing that it was made principally to spend, so he did not worry. He was a brother-in-law of Robert V. Fleming, president of the Riggs National bank, and doubtless could have any reasonable accommodation when the banks opened, if he needed it.

"Mr. Bailey's parents lived for many years at Monticello and his brother Ernest, of Charlottesville, was born in the room in which General Lafayette was entertained by Thomas Jefferson. Mr. Bailey inherited Jefferson's beautiful gold watch and is a collector of time pieces. He is now Civil Service contact representative at the capitol and has an office with the Civil Service committee of the house. Energy, ability and popularity have contributed to his success.

"On march 1, I had sixty-five dollars in cash in my pocket. I declined to withdraw any additional funds, largely because I wished to see how I could and would meet an emergency if it came.

"After the inauguration of Roosevelt, a bank holiday was declared and bank doors were closed throughout the country. Everybody was on the same footing and that made it easier all around.

"The sixty-five dollars served all my purposes for spending money during the moratorium and I divided with some of my friends. Of course, my rent was easily handled and I could sign meal checks at a number of places and had charge accounts at several stores. Hence, I saw no reason for becoming panicky or doing anything out of the ordinary. I had some cash left when the banks opened about ten days later.

"It may be most financial panics, so far as they affect bank withdrawals, result from a state of mind. If there were no newspapers, no radios, and no politicians and public speakers, many of our worries would not be recognized.

"Indeed, had Hitler, Mussolini, Deladier, and Chamberlin not made any speeches in 1939, I doubt whether there would have been a second world war, at least so soon.

"Shakespeare understood all of this when he wrote:

> Tell me where is fancy bred,
> Or in the heart or in the head?
> How begot and how nourished?
> Reply, reply!"

While absent from Cheyenne, Mr. Deming learned of the deaths of two prominent Wyoming citizens, both friends of his – Judge Roderick N. Matson, who died february 14, 1933, and Harry P. Hynds, who passed away on march 11, 1933. He wrote feelingly of both.

Judge Matson had just been appointed by President Herbert Hoover as Minister to Athens, Greece. He had served as judge of the first judicial district, and later had resigned to rejoin his law partner, T. Blake Kennedy, now United States district judge.

Harry P. Hynds, who began his career as a blacksmith on the Cheyenne and Black Hills stageline in the early eighties, was the first proprietor of the Plains hotel in Cheyenne, and in later years had been exceedingly successful in prospecting for oil. The Plains hotel was erected by a company headed by Senator Warren, Thomas A. Cosgriff, and Dr. H. M. Bennett. It is now owned chiefly by the Warren estate, but is under lease to a local operating company.

On february 21, 1933, Ray Baker, chairman of the committee on the reception of governors of states and special distinguished guests as a sub-committee of the Inaugural committee in Washington, asked Mr. Deming to serve on the committee.

During the inaugural period, Mr. Deming placed his car and chauffeur at the disposal of his friends in Washington, including Mrs. Nellie Tayloe Ross, who soon afterwards was appointed director of the United States mint by President Franklin D. Roosevelt.

Upon the invitation of the Hoover and Curtis Campaign club, he was present at the Union station to bid Godspeed and farewell to retiring President and Mrs. Hoover, when they left Washington shortly after 12:30 P.M. on march 4.

While residing at the Mayflower hotel, Mr. Deming frequently met Vice-president Curtis and his half sister, Mrs. Dolly Gann, his hostess, who won her struggle for social and official precedence over Mrs. Nicholas Longworth (Alice Roosevelt), wife of the speaker of the house of representatives.

"Vice-president Charles J. Curtis," he says, "was proud of the strain of Indian blood in his veins and gave much credit to his Kaw Indian great-grandmother. When a small boy, he was on the reservation, but the far-sighted old lady sent him to his white kin, saying 'This is now a white man's country. If you expect success in life, get an education and stay with your pale-face relatives.' "

After attending the spring meeting of the twenty-first annual session of the Chamber of Commerce of the United States, as a national councillor, Mr. Deming returned to Wyoming.

During the ensuing months, in addition to attending to his business interests, he made a number of addresses at important meetings. At a banquet in honor of Assistant-postmaster-general Joseph C. O'Mahoney, given at the Plains hotel on june 5, by the Federal Business association, he gave a short response in which he paid tribute to the civil service worker. In closing, he said, "Like my able friend, the Honorable A. D. Walton, retiring United States district attorney, I have had my day in court and at the federal pie counter. I am willing to stand aside for abler, handsomer, and hungrier men. Mr. Walton, however, will be heard from in the future. His elements of leadership will not remain dormant."

On june 10, he was a guest at the ninth annual reunion of Old Timers at Rock Springs; and on june 23, was one of the speakers at a dinner in Cheyenne, given by the Laramie county Bar association.

During the last week in june, Deming accompanied Warren Richardson of the Wyoming landmark commission, and John Charles Thompson, on a trip to Salt Lake City, Fort Bridger, and other historic points. They were among the ten thousand persons who witnessed the dedication of Old Fort Bridger as a landmark.

"The Fort Bridger State park," Mr. Deming reported to the *Tribune,* "is an inspiration to every man and woman who would understand the making of our commonwealth and the evolution of our nation.

"By tradition, illiterate and uncouth – yet James Bridger played a part in establishing American dominion over the West and Northwest. The most cultured and experienced statesman could not have done more.

"Fitted by training for the hazards and hardships of the period, he maintained a haven in the desert for the comfort and assistance of pioneers seeking the American promised land.

"Having approached this oasis at twilight last saturday evening, I can understand Bridger's emotion and why he might have said, 'This is the place. Here I'll pitch my tent.' Skyline, babbling brooks, rich grasses, and shady nooks,– it is fitted by nature for man's habitation.

"Fort Bridger, under the jurisdiction of Bridger, the pathfinder, followed by the Mormons, and then the habitat of the United States army, later the home of the Carter family, and now perpetually dedicated as a state park, is outstanding. I know of no other thirty-six acres endowed by history with such a lineage.

"Enough remains of their handiwork to carry the lessons of the fathers and mothers of the period down to posterity.

"Without sacrificing a stone of the old buildings from the Pony Express station and the United States army guard house, to the more pretentious officers' quarters and parade grounds, a bit of planning and a small appropriation from time to time will make Fort Bridger, Wyoming, an outstanding playground and mecca for generations to come."

As a member of a caravan, the Cheyenne party not only attended the dedication at Fort Bridger, but proceeded to Little Sandy creek, South Pass, Rock Creek Hollow, and Devil's Gate where monuments were also dedicated.

Mr. Deming's interest in marking the old Oregon Trail dates back to 1906 when he was among those who welcomed to Cheyenne a distinguished pioneer, Ezra Meeker, then seventy-six years old, who was retracing the old Oregon Trail with an ox team and prairie schooner.

Meeker was born december 29, 1830. In may 1851 he traveled by ox team to Iowa and in 1852 migrated to Oregon in a covered wagon.

When he was seventy-six years old he started eastward over the old trail, and when eighty miles north of Cheyenne, deviated from his route and visited Cheyenne, in order to interest the people of the capital city in helping to mark the trail.

Through the publicity given to Mr. Meeker's visit in the *Wyoming Tribune* and other newspapers, the attention of thousands of people in Wyoming was turned to the historic trail and to the necessity for marking it. Teachers and school children became more interested in the study of their local history; the good roads movement, in which Mr. Deming was so active, received an impetus; and in due time, the state legislature in 1913 created a Wyoming Oregon Trail commission and appropriated the sum of twenty-five hundred dollars with which markers were to be purchased under the supervision of a committee of three members.

An interesting story of Ezra Meeker's remarkable west-to-east journey and his arousal of interest in marking the course of covered-wagon travel to the Pacific-northwest, was described as follows by Harry L. Talkington:

"The trail was made by trappers and traders, missionaries and map-makers, worn deep and wide by the migration of three hundred thousand people, lined by the graves of twenty thousand dead, witness of romance and tragedy, unique in history, and will always be sacred to the memories of the pioneers of the Northwest."

Erza Meeker went to Oregon in 1852, with his young

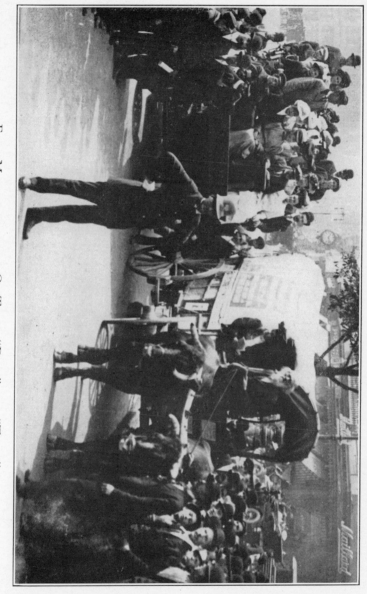

EZRA MEEKER WITH HIS OX-TEAM, "DAVE" AND "TWIST"

on trip in 1906

wife, in a prairie schooner drawn by oxen. He took up land, farmed, became the hop king of the Northwest, and later turned to banking.

At the age of sixty-eight he made four trips over the Chilcoot Pass and down the Yukon to the Dawson mines and at the age of seventy-six embarked upon one of the most noted expeditions known in the history of the United States. He retraced the steps taken by him fifty-four years before in the same manner as then.

After assembling an outfit, comprising a schooner-type wagon and two oxen, named Dave and Twist, Meeker began his memorable journey on january 29, 1906. He made his first talk and placed the first marker at Tumwater, several miles south of his home in Puyallup, Washington. Half of the sum of forty-two dollars, which he collected at Tumwater, was used to erect a temporary stone.

Proceeding eastward along the old Oregon Trail to Omaha, Meeker interested Chambers of Commerce, school children, women's clubs and other organizations which contributed pennies and dollars, in addition to time and materials.

In many places Meeker had no difficulty in recognizing the old landmark of emigrant days, but in other places the desolate plains had turned into fertile field. . . Then he might have to walk days with old settlers and those interested in possession of traditional information to locate the route. . . He met with all sorts of cooperation and the lack of it, from hearty enthusiasm to cold indifference.

From Omaha, the aged Meeker went to Indianapolis, Indiana; then to New York City by way of Hamilton, Dayton and Columbus, Ohio, and Syracuse and Albany, New York. In New York City he was detained a month until a new ordinance could be passed granting him the right to drive cattle on the streets. When at last he swung his oxen down Broadway, headed for Washington, D.C., police had to hold back the crowds that were eager to see Rip Van Winkle.

"A royal welcome awaited Meeker when he drove up in front of the White House," says Talkington. "President Roosevelt left cabinets and affairs of the nation and bareheaded came out to see him and his pioneer team and wagon. 'Well, well, well,' exclaimed the president. 'I am in favor of this work to mark this trail,' and addressing Senator Piles of Washington, 'If you will bring before congress a measure to accomplish it, I am with you and will give it my support to do it thoroughly.' "

In addition to the nearly two hundred markers which were erected through Meeker's direct efforts and later by others, about sixteen hundred miles of the Oregon Trail were sectionized.

In 1915 in order to demonstrate progress Meeker went over the same trail and highways in an automobile. In 1924, at the age of ninety-three he flew across the country in an airplane. Four years later at the age of ninety-seven he attempted another automobile trip across the country but was taken ill and forced to return to Seattle, where he died on december 3, 1928.

Today Meeker's wagon with Dave and Twist attached may be seen, encased in glass, in the rooms of the Historical society at Tacoma, Washington. Along the Oregon Trail are many fine markers, which not only do honor to the memory of the early emigrants, but stand as fit tribute to the efforts of Ezra Meeker — pioneer trail marker.'

In november 1933 occurred the death of United

President Coolidge greets Ezra Meeker
on the White House lawn

States Senator John B. Kendrick. In pursuance of a request by Governor Leslie A. Miller that memorial services be held throughout Wyoming on sunday, november 12, in honor of Senator Kendrick, Mr. Deming was invited to deliver the address at the First Methodist church in Cheyenne.

He traced the story of the senator's life and told how at age twenty-two, in march 1879, Kendrick began his long trek "northward, one of many Texas cowboys driving a herd of three thousand cattle from Matagorda bay on the Gulf of Mexico to the Running Water range in northeastern Wyoming." He told of Kendrick's splendid success as a business man, his life as governor, and as United States senator. "Nothing I have said and nothing that we can now do will add to the fullness of Senator Kendrick's life, an epic of the old and the new, the East and the West," the speaker said.

This splendid address was printed in the *Congressional Record* of may 14, page 9083, as part of the tribute paid to Senator Kendrick by his colleague, Senator Robert D. Carey. Congressman Vincent Carter in the house of representatives, speaking eloquently of the life, character, and public service of John B. Kendrick, also included in his remarks the address delivered by William C. Deming.

In december 1933 when the *Tribune* published in full Governor Leslie A. Miller's message to the legislature, other daily newspapers also decided that they, too, would print the manuscript in full. The governor later expressed his gratitude, saying the fact that the *Tribune* had published the message resulted in other papers doing likewise, thus giving the message splendid publicity.

On january 5, 1934, Mr. Deming sailed on the Grace

line steamship, Santa Paula, from San Francisco for New York via the Panama canal. Stops were made at Los Angeles, Mazatlan, Mexico, El Salvador, San Jose de Guatemala, La Libertad, Balboa, Cristobal, Cartegena, Puerto Columbia, and Havana. The ship docked at New York on january 23. Admiral Sims, of World War fame, also made the trip.

Before leaving Cheyenne for the journey, Mr. Deming said upon being asked about future plans, "I am interested in the United States senatorship or governorship only from the side lines. I have no aspirations, whatever, leading in either direction, and am satisfied that I can be happier, healthier, and possibly more useful as a newspaper man and as a private citizen in the ranks than in any political office. Freedom to go and come and speak one's mind freely without being misconstrued or misunderstood is a privilege which should not be lightly thrust aside."

At that time he reported that "The *Tribune-Leader* shows a constant growth in circulation both in Cheyenne and in Wyoming, notwithstanding the depression and has never been on a sounder foundation than it is today."

Following the voyage, which was delightful in every respect, he spent some time in New York, Washington, and Florida before returning home.

While in Washington, he attended a luncheon at the Metropolitan club on february 22, as the guest of Justice Willis Van Devanter, given for members of the Washington National Monument society and their friends.

On may 8, in answer to General Hugh L. Johnson's claim that only "Old Tories" and "pirates" were criticizing the New Deal, Mr. Deming presented a strong

Front view of William C. Deming's home
820 East 17th Street, Cheyenne

case against the Roosevelt administration and its policies and programs in a newspaper article. He called as
witnesses democrats, progressives, republicans, social-
ists, farmers, labor organizations, and editors, many
of whom had spoken against Roosevelt's policies. The
article was widely read and commended.

General Johnson subsequently quit the Roosevelt
official family and became one of the New Deal's
leading critics.

One reason Mr. Deming was able to disagree from
time to time with his party organization or with those
in high office in the state and nation, and retain their
respect, was that he placed principle above policy
and the good of his party above an individual or the
organization.

Not long before Deming's retirement from the newspaper publishing business, Senator O'Mahoney, who
always had the respect and personal friendship of the
Tribune proprietor, proposed that the United States
relinquish to the states all public lands within the
boundaries of the several commonwealths. Mr. Deming
took a position against Senator O'Mahoney's bill and
against similar views of the Honorable Charles E.
Winter, republican representative in the house of
representatives, on the proposition.

Mr. Deming stated that, notwithstanding resolutions
by the Wyoming legislature and certain organizations,
there had been no adequate discussion of the subject,
and that the question was too important to be closed
as a result of mere formal resolutions.

He stated further that "the homestead law, with
modifications from time to time (in the future as in
the past), served a useful purpose and will do so for
years to come. Wyoming needs and desires more people

than it now supports or has upon its tax rolls."

Former Governor B. B. Brooks, large land holder and livestock man, promptly wrote the *Tribune* publisher saying, "For many years I have been a subscriber to your paper and always have read your personal articles with great interest and pleasure. With respect to the public land situation, as contemplated in Senator O'Mahoney's bill, I think your position against such action is absolutely sound and correct."

The bill did not pass.

In june, the former commissioner was appointed a member of the Council of National Civil Service Reform league, composed of persons in various parts of the United States who, in some definite manner, had expressed an interest in the merit system or who had knowledge of its workings and were in sympathy with its purposes. Meetings of the council are held two or three times a year, usually in New York City.

Quite in keeping with his principal hobby – real estate – Mr. Deming in 1934 purchased the house at eight hundred twenty East Seventeenth street, one of the historic residences of Cheyenne. It was erected by W. C. Lane of the firm of Sturgis and Lane, early cattlemen of southwestern Wyoming. Later it was owned by the Peters family. The lot, one hundred thirty-two feet square, is bounded by fine trees and the house contains fourteen rooms.

For many years it was the property of the Union Pacific Railroad company, during which time it was occupied by a local superintendent or some other high official. Interesting Union Pacific families who have occupied the Lane house include those of W. L. Parks, Harris, E. R. Breisch, Mullen, and N. A. Williams. Mr. Williams, prior to his death in 1940, was general

Side view of William C. Deming's home, Cheyenne

manager of the Union Pacific system. Mr. Deming had the exterior of the house decorated in brown, and remodeled the interior, until today it is one of the finest homes of the city,– spacious, dignified, and furnished in splendid taste. It is so arranged that the house manager has ample, modern quarters.

Mr. Deming spends seven months of the year in Cheyenne, entertains his friends, and enjoys visits from relatives. A great variety of flowers, including roses, are grown on his property, and his vegetable garden has been a source of satisfaction.

Across Russell avenue, on the east, is the southern colonial home which William B. Ross, as a young attorney, erected for his bride, Nellie Tayloe Ross, who came to Wyoming from Memphis, Tennessee.

On the west is a large white house with spacious grounds, occupied for many years by William Myers and family. Mr. Myers was a pioneer dry goods merchant. The home is now owned by A. H. Read, prominent contractor.

The widow of R. S. Van Tassell occupies the commodious home facing Lake Minnehaha, while the Charles D. Carey place is now owned by Walter Flora and family.

In february 1935, W. C. Deming was reinstated in the Cheyenne Rotary club, at which time he spoke on the subject, "Mexico," having recently visited that interesting country.

He gave a similar talk on february 27 to the Cheyenne Kiwanis club, and in the same month was one of the principal speakers at the Knights of Pythias Castle hall at an Old Timers' night and annual reunion of Cheyenne lodge No. 2, of which he has been a member forty-five years.

When the Wyoming Reclamation association held its second annual meeting in Cheyenne, he presided at the informal banquet which was attended by more than one hundred persons.

One of his talks of the year was at the annual convention of the American Newspaper Publishers association held at the Waldorf-Astoria hotel, New York City, on april 24, 25, 26, and 27. Upon request, Mr. Deming selected two of the topics on a list and then led the discussion.

The New York Herald, in reporting the meeting, said: "The publishers discussed new methods of news handling which had been used successfully, and William C. Deming, of the Cheyenne, Wyoming, *Tribune-Leader,* said that a recent automobile trip from Cheyenne to New York City had convinced him that the newspapers of the country were too greatly standardized. He had read them, he said, in city after city, and had found them using the same Associated Press reports, the same comics, and the same features in about the same way. 'Local newspapers,' he asserted, 'should go in for local features and local pictures.' "

After the "Grass Roots" conference of republicans held at Springfield, Illinois, in the spring of 1935, he approved a similar meeting proposed for the Rocky mountain region. He had no serious objection to calling a new party the "Liberal Republican" or "Constitutional Republican party," or even the "Republican-Democrat" party. He suggested that the meeting could be known as the "Rocky Mountain round-up."

"The important thing," he said, "is the country and the constitution . . . When men of the caliber of John W. Davis, Bainbridge Colby, and Alfred E. Smith appear convinced that the Franklin D. Roosevelt administration has not only run counter to all the tenets

LIVING ROOM IN WILLIAM C. DEMING'S HOME, CHEYENNE

of the democratic faith, but has turned the party over, bag and baggage, to dreamers, theorists, and radicals, it is not the time to stand upon a question of party nomenclature."

A republican conference did convene at Salt Lake City on october 22, at which Mr. Deming was a member of the resolutions committee, which drafted a report assailing the present national administration for extravagance and broken promises.

In june he attended the annual meeting of the Wyoming Stock Growers association, which convened at Cody and when, at the closing session, he was asked to express the appreciation of the visitors for the splendid hospitality of the citizens of Cody, he said in part: "While science and invention will, from time to time add variety to Wyoming industry, nature has decreed that livestock and attendant agriculture will remain the basic resource. Hence, this association now in its sixty-third year will long continue to carry on."

"The Making of a Nation," was the title which he chose for a historic address delivered before the bar of Laramie county, Wyoming, the Larimer county, Colorado, association at Ft. Collins, and also the Western Nebraska Bar association in Sidney, Nebraska. The Honorable William O. Wilson and Harry B. Henderson, jr. participated actively in the Wyoming and Colorado bar meetings.

On november 1, W. I. N. Cox, business manager of the *Tribune-Leader* resigned his position to accept a better position in Utah. Mr. Cox wrote to Mr. Deming as follows: "I have been most happy in your service during the past five years. I have enjoyed working for you and have tried at all times to give you the best service possible under any and all conditions, and you have been very good to me. You have a fine, loyal organization, a valuable paper, and more than nine thousand paying subscribers who seem to swear by the *Tribune*. This is a wonderful combination."

In keeping with his usual custom, Mr. Deming went south for the winter (1935), making his headquarters at the Roney Plaza hotel in Miami Beach.

In april 1936 he attended the annual meeting of the American Newspaper Publishers' association and the Associated Press in New York City.

At this time, as has been related in a preceding chapter, there occurred the death of Zell Hart Deming, who was stricken suddenly while in attendance at the New York conventions above mentioned. After her funeral in Warren Ohio, Mr. Deming returned to Wyoming.

On september 8 he received the following invitation from Robert D. Carey, United States senator, written from Careyhurst:

"As you perhaps have heard, Colonel Knox, candidate for vice-president, will stop off here on friday, spending most of the day with me. While I am not inviting anyone outside of his party, the state chairman, and national committeeman, I would like very much to have you join us at lunch about one o'clock. Hoping you can come, and with best wishes, I am . . " Mr. Deming was much impressed with Mr. Knox's ability and virility.

The committee named to urge the presence at Casper, september 11, of the republican editors of the state, upon the occasion of the visit of Colonel Frank Knox, was: William C. Deming, James E. Hanway, and C. Watt Brandon.

Frank Knox is now secretary of the Navy in the cabinet of President Franklin D. Roosevelt.

Presidents I have Known

While political articles, speeches, and talks were being featured on every side, the Cheyenne Rotary club in 1936 took time from the stress and strain of the moment to feature a program during which Mr. Deming spoke on the "Presidents I Have Known." The speaker told of having served in some capacity under six presidents – Theodore Roosevelt, William H. Taft, Woodrow Wilson, Warren G. Harding, Calvin Coolidge, and Herbert Hoover. Incidentally, he held commissions under several Wyoming governors.

Concerning his first meeting with President Harding, Mr. Deming said he was accompanied to the president's private office by Senator F. E. Warren and former Congressman Mondell. President Harding "did not remain sitting, but met us halfway and then herded us all in a circle in the middle of the room," Mr. Deming said. "When he and Senator Warren and Representative Mondell had exchanged salutations and gibes, the President's arms being extended almost around all of us, I found an opportunity to begin my little speech.

"After about a dozen words, which indicated that I was about to thank him, President Harding said, in a happy, humorous, informal drawl, 'Oh, Deming, that's all right. If I hadn't appointed you, these Wyoming fellows would have boycotted me,' and changed the subject.

"I might add," Mr. Deming reports, "that my name had been mentioned to the president several months

before as a member of a certain investigating commission, authorized by congress. Mr. Harding very
wisely said, 'No, the work requires considerable expert
technical knowledge. I prefer to use Deming later in
a more important administrative position. I know him
and also his Ohio connections.'

"Soon after President Coolidge succeeded to the
presidency, I was the guest at a meeting of the famous
Gridiron club of Washington whose membership con-
sists of newspaper men.

"It was my good fortune to be present upon this
occasion, as the guest of Byron Price of the Associated
Press, and I wondered to what extent President Coolidge would 'break over' during the dinner hour. As a
matter of fact, I do not recall that he spoke a half
dozen words to the president of the club or any guest
during the dinner.

"He read his speech from manuscript, without any
effort at eloquence or emotion, but it contained the usual
Coolidge wisdom and occasional bits of New England
wit that struck home.

"Those nearest to President Coolidge say he was not
only reluctant to waste words in conversation, although
he spoke to the point when he was interested, but that
he rather disliked public speaking. A friend who was
calling upon Coolidge in 1927, found him wrestling
with an address to be delivered in Pittsburgh. He had
prepared about four pages and remarked, 'I wish somebody would kick me twice if I ever agree to make
another speech.' "

The following description of another occasion upon
which Mr. Deming was in a group of which President
Coolidge was a member should prove of interest to
Wyoming readers:

PRESIDENT AND MRS. COOLIDGE
on the White House lawn, september 1927

Says Mr. Deming: "President Coolidge's summer vacation in the Black Hills was such a success, both from the standpoint of personal enjoyment and good advertising for South Dakota, that Wyoming hoped to be next.

"Therefore, the various state officers, commercial clubs, sportsmen's associations, national park directors, and members of the Wyoming official family in Washington united in presenting a formal invitation to the president to visit the Jackson Hole country.

"Through Senators Warren and Kendrick and Representative Winter, an engagement was arranged at the president's office for ten o'clock. The plans had been carefully worked out, with Representative Winter as the speaker and about twenty daughters of Wyoming citizens, wearing western outfits, forming a half circle in the rear of the room.

"They displayed in front of them a long banner with some appropriate wording. At the close of Mr. Winter's remarks, they gracefully reversed the banner, showing on the opposite side these words, 'Mr. President, stop roaming – try Wyoming.'

"President Coolidge smiled economically, and we all held ourselves in readiness for a reply.

"He arose slowly from his chair, but never uttered a single word.

"He merely led the procession out of a side door onto the south lawn of the White House, where we all had our pictures taken.

"That ended the incident and the invitation."

The country at large, and Washington correspondents in particular, coined a great many jokes and bon mots at the expense of Coolidge's economy and so-called parsimony.

Says Mr. Deming: "Clifford Berryman, cartoonist for the *Washington Star,* said, 'On a trip to Florida, President Coolidge refused his second dish of strawberries, remarking that he did not wish to destroy his taste for prunes.'

"Also, that Coolidge was so honest he would not take a word from the dictionary unless he really needed it.

"There is always some speculation as to what presidents talk about when the out-going chief executive accompanies his successor to the capitol for the installation ceremonies.

"Woodrow Wilson asked President-elect Warren G. Harding which of the dumb creatures he most highly esteemed. Senator Harding replied, without intending to speak lightly, that the elephant had always seemed to him the most intelligent, the most human, and most kindly of animals. Then he related briefly the story of an old, domesticated elephant that had labored long for his owner in India. At last, the elephant was the victim of a great stack of teak logs, which fell upon him and crushed him to such an extent that death was evident and imminent. Harding said that the elephant, in an affectionate manner, reached out with his trunk to the native keeper, wound this strange appendage about his companion and held him gently for five hours until the end came."

"First, second and third class postmasters were not classified by law until 1938 in the Franklin D. Roosevelt administration, but each president since Wilson had, under some form of an executive order, used the Civil Service commission as a sifting process by holding examinations and having certified three eligibles," says Mr. Deming.

"This system served a good purpose and was the next

best thing to classification under the merit system, by an act of congress. For instance, the Cheyenne postmaster, William G. Haas, a former railway postal clerk, has come up through the ranks and has held his position as a result of such examinations and appointments under both republican and democratic presidents.

"President Coolidge, though a successful politician, as well as a statesman, was a good merit system man.

"If I wished to consult him, it was only necessary to phone his office secretary or drop a note, and an appointment would be arranged. When the president sent for me, as he did from time to time, particularly in the days when an effort was being made to place the Prohibition bureau under the Civil Service commission, I responded promptly.

"I cannot recall that any of the three presidents under whom I served in Washington, attempted to interfere with the orderly processes of the work of the commission, or influence its judgment. Conferences usually had to do with proposed legislation affecting the service.

"A president has an executive staff and a private secretary, who is his buffer between the public and the executive. He usually has also a personal secretary, whose duties are general and confidential.

"President Coolidge employed T. Edward Clark, generally known as Ted, for this delicate duty.

"Clark was a yankee, like his chief, and resembled him in more ways than one, except that he was a good mixer. Clark's methods were indirect, but very simple.

"If he sought information, he called upon an official, strolled up and down the floor, probably smoking a pipe, told a joke or two, asked a few questions, and went his way.

"In this manner, he was able to keep the president

informed of conditions and affairs not appearing of record.

"The four-year term of Roland M. Baker, postmaster of Boston, ended in 1929, about the same time President Coolidge was to be succeeded by Herbert Hoover.

"Mr. Baker had been an efficient postmaster, and apparently was in good standing with the republican organization in Massachusetts and the post office department.

"However, for personal reasons, not political, President Coolidge desired to appoint Charles R. Gow, a professor in Harvard University, provided the gentleman could meet the usual test of general experience, good character, intelligence, and efficiency in his own work, as set forth in the requirements and as brought out through personal investigation in the home of the applicant. There were thirteen applications received by december 31, 1928, the closing date for applications.

"For large cities, investigations are made by representatives of the Civil Service commission and the Post Office department, acting together and making a joint visit. J. H. Weiss representing the commission and John W. Johnston, the Post Office department, went to Boston and promptly began the work.

"In the natural course of events, it takes several weeks from the time the Civil Service commission is advised by the Post Office department that the term of an incumbent will expire on such a date, and completion of an examination.

"Of course, there may be a reappointment without further examination if the postmaster is satisfactory and the president desires to name him.

"It was rumored that someone in the Post Office department favored the incumbent postmaster at Boston, notwithstanding the president preferred the Harvard man. Thus, both sides were watching the progress of the investigation, which circumstances required should be unusually careful and complete. It was necessary to interview a large number of the patrons of the office, especially business men, and this took time.

"Early in january 1929, Ted Clark came to see me to inquire when a report would be made, indicating that the president had a great many things to clean up and wished to make the appointment before march 4, 1929, the end of his term. I assured him, that so far as I could survey the situation, there would be ample time. Meanwhile, the investigators were carrying on.

"Not because President Coolidge questioned the good faith of the Civil Service commission, but probably because some one had carried the suggestion to him, that Postmaster Baker was an influential politician, as well as a good postmaster, and that it might happen that the matter would be left open until the next administration, particularly if the Post Office department favored Baker's reappointment, he became impatient.

"The Civil Service commission had heard some of this gossip, but did not attach much importance to it. However, I was not surprised one evening, about eight o'clock, to receive a phone call, at my apartment, from Ted Clark, saying in effect, 'The Old Man is much disturbed over the Boston postmastership situation.'

"Why so," I asked.

"He is afraid a final report may not be made before march 4, and he wishes to see you at his office tomorrow morning at nine o'clock," was the answer.

"While I was familiar with the general situation, of course, I did not have all the data and steps in mind, so I immediately phoned H. A. Hesse, chief of the investigations of the Civil Service commission.

"I said, 'Mr. Hesse, the president has asked me to call tomorrow morning at nine o'clock to make an informal, advance report on the progress of the Boston postmastership examination and investigation.

"I wish you would prepare and have ready for me by eight-thirty tomorrow morning, a statement showing every step in the case from the time the Civil Service commission received a request to hold the examination. Bring it down to date if possible.'

"Although it was no small job, Mr. Hesse, always prompt, had upon my desk at the Civil Service commission office, as requested, a complete report, which showed not only diligence, but substantial progress, and a statement that the final report would be ready, probably within forty-eight hours.

"It was about the middle of january and Washington weather was not particularly genial. I entered Private-secretary Everett Sanders' room. Lo and behold! There was Postmaster-general Harry S. New, sitting in a big arm chair, and he had not removed his coonskin coat. Sanders was cordial as usual.

"I had known Mr. New as a newspaper man, as United States senator, and as postmaster-general, and he was always courteous and friendly.

"I said, 'Good morning, Mr. Postmaster-general, I presume we are here upon the same mission.'

"Mr. New responded somewhat gruffly, 'I suppose so.'

"Apparently, he had found it necessary to get an early start from his suburban home, quite remote from the White House and drive through early morning traffic on one of Washington's most inclement winter mornings. Perhaps he had not had his breakfast.

"After a few minutes, the signal came to show us in.

"The president was seated behind his desk. He nodded and spoke to us rather abruptly. Mr. New sat down in a big upholstered arm chair in the corner, immediately to the left of the president, while I took possession of a lighter chair, more directly in line with Mr. Coolidge and nearer his desk.

"Without any preliminary, the president, looking at Mr. New, said, 'Mr. Postmaster-general, what do *you* know about the progress of the examination for the postmastership of Boston?'

"Almost as curtly as the president had spoken, and with some emphasis, the postmaster-general replied, 'Mr. President, I don't know *anything* about it.'

"That was doubtless true, because, as a rule, such matters were handled by one particular assistant, unless for some reason it was brought to the direct attention of the postmaster-general.

"President Coolidge seemed a bit surprised at the short reply, and particularly its tone, but he did not lose his bearings and immediately turned to me and said, 'Mr. Deming,' with an emphasis on the name, 'What do you know about the case?'

"I replied, 'Mr. President, so far as the responsibility of the Civil Service commission is concerned, I know all about it.'

"Without waiting for him to say a word in response, I pulled my chair up to the end of his desk and remarked, 'If you will bear with me for a very few minutes, I shall read a written report and leave the same for your consideration.'

"I did so and that ended the interview.

"The investigation was completed within a very short time, and eligibles were certified january 26, 1929, which showed Roland Baker, the postmaster, the highest eligible by reason of his education, experience, good record and five points military bonus; Charles R. Gow, the professor, second; and Herman Hormel third.

"President Coolidge, exercising his right of choice, from a list of three eligibles, appointed his friend, Mr. Gow, the Harvard professor. I learned subsequently, that the Harvard man did not like the job, and resigned in january 1931, in order to return to his work as an instructor.

"The reader will understand, of course, that these incidents by no means present a true picture of Coolidge's temperament and character, only one phase, his abruptness at times, and his disinclination to carry on a conversation.

"It is said Mr. Coolidge followed this practice because of natural reticence and the more important reason that it conserved his strength and energy for the composite, serious duties of the various administrative offices he had held from mayor of Northampton to governor of Massachusetts, and president.

"In my judgment, the only satisfactory interpretation of all sides of Coolidge's remarkable career are found in William Allen White's book, *A Puritan in Babylon*. Apparently this quaint New Englander followed a very well defined course from the time he left college – and that was holding public office. He consistently refrained from opportunities and offers which might have taken him into a business or into the active, exclusive practice of law. I think he not only liked public life, but realized his capacity for careful administration, his absence of selfish interest, and sought opportunities along that line.

"The following is a true incident never before appearing in print.

"Alexander P. Moore, one time publisher of the *Pittsburgh Press and Leader,* and husband of the beautiful actress, Lillian Russell, was appointed ambassador to Spain in 1923 and served about two years.

"Sometime during that period, Mrs. Zell Hart Deming, publisher of the Warren, Ohio, *Tribune-Chronicle,* made a trip to Great Britain and the continent.

"Being the first woman member of the Associated Press, and having a large business and social circle of friends in her home country, she knew Mr. Moore personally, and paid her respects to him in Madrid.

"Before she left, Mr. Moore said, 'I have been engaged for some time with the king and his government in regard to certain reciprocal relationships which would be of advantage to the United States, if made effective; but for the most part, negotiations must be held in great confidence. Therefore, I desire to convey certain information to President Coolidge through other than ordinary diplomatic channels. I will outline the matters to you and hand you some notes, which I shall be pleased to have you deliver in person to the president, upon your return to America.'

"Upon her arrival in New York, Mrs. Deming proceeded to Washington, where through the president's secretary, she was accorded an engagement rather promptly. Having made a success as a writer and publisher she was more proud of her business card than of her formal calling card. Upon her arrival at the White House executive office her business card was placed upon the president's desk.

"Naturally in calling upon the president she was well groomed for the occasion and being a woman of poise and fine personality felt no trepidation in entering the presence of the master of the White House.

"President Coolidge remained seated at his mahogany desk when she entered. The nearest chair was some distance away. Without smiling he looked up and said, 'Well, what can I do for you?'

"Though somewhat surprised by the chilly reception the caller did not lose her self-control but responded somewhat firmly: 'Mr. President, there is not a thing in the world you can do for me. I came here to do something for you. I came because I was requested to do so by your representative in Spain, who wished to have me convey in person a message he preferred not to commit to writing.'

"President Coolidge was doubtless as much surprised at her reply as she was at his inquiry. The ice was broken.

"It was very interesting to hear Mrs. Deming tell how President Coolidge's manner immediately changed. Apparently he had assumed, from her card, that she was a professional or business woman seeking some favor for herself or a friend. When she turned upon him, in a manner unusual in the presence of the chief executive of the nation, Mr. Coolidge decided, apparently, that he had met his match. Henceforth they had a very pleasant visit. She disclosed the information and message conveyed through her by Alexander Moore, the American ambassador to Spain, and withdrew as graciously as was possible under the circumstances.

"I wish time and space would permit examples, indicating Coolidge's alert mind and consistent policies. He could say more in a few words, and have it remembered, than any other American statesman. His personal friend, F. W. Stearns, of Boston, says, 'Governor Coolidge conferred with only three men during the Boston police strike; myself, William M. Butler, and one other citizen. When a number of Boston business men and party leaders warned him that an election was only a few weeks away and he should compromise or be defeated for reelection, Coolidge replied, 'My election is not necessary.'

"The result is well known. Mr. Coolidge issued his famous manifesto, 'There is no right to strike against the public order by any man, any place, any time.'

"His fearlessness and independence made him vice-president and president."

"President Herbert Hoover," says Mr. Deming, "seemed to meet you psychologically and physically, at least, half way.

"When I called upon the president to tender my resignation as Civil Service commissioner in march 1930, the president was surprised, and . . . declared he regretted very much that I wished to resign. I felt that he paid me a very high compliment when he remarked, 'I never have lost any sleep over the administration of affairs in the Civil Service commission. . .'

"President Hoover asked that the resignation be deferred until he could find a successor for the commission, even though I should return to Wyoming.

"Talking as if we were just two private citizens, engaged in every day activities in life, he leaned over, and placing his hand upon my arm in a friendly, frank way, followed up by saying, 'So far as most business is concerned, your colleagues and staff will be able to carry on, and in case of disagreement between the two commissioners, the papers can be referred to you for final decision.' That happened a number of times after I returned to Wyoming.

"To my surprise, my successor was not named until july 1, 1930."

About two years later, while in San Francisco, Mr. Deming motored to Palo Alto in order to pay his respects to the Honorable Herbert Hoover, Leland Stanford's most notable graduate.

"We were admitted without ceremony," Mr. Deming says, "and as there were no other visitors, I did not feel I was transgressing upon his time. . . Of course, we both indulged in some reminiscences. . . In the course of the visit, I remarked that President Roosevelt had just requested another billion dollar appropriation for the New Deal.

"With a touch of quiet humor or sarcasm, with which Mr. Hoover is gifted, his brief comment was, 'It requires no ingenuity to spend money.'

"In the eight years since he left the White House, Herbert Hoover has become one of the country's most popular and able speakers. His audience is nation-wide and his influence grows from day to day. His grasp of domestic and international problems is unequalled by any contemporaneous statesman. Still comparatively young, he, no doubt, will continue to exercise a great influence, not only upon his party but upon the country at large.

"S. D. Warfield, chairman, board of trustees, Seaboard Air line, told C. W. Barron, publisher of the *Wall Street Journal* and *Boston News Bureau,* in discussing Harding and his secretary of commerce, 'Hoover knows something about everything, but nothing fully.'

"That was not a fair statement, but even if it were true, there would be some reason for the idea, because Hoover spent so many of his mature years preceding the World war in the Orient and was so occupied during the early days of the war in Europe and at

PRESIDENT AND MRS. HERBERT HOOVER

greet those who attended the annual egg-rolling festivities in the South grounds of the Executive Mansion, Washington, D.C., march 28, 1932

home as food administrator, that he had little time for general policies and economics.

"However, I think it is now conceded that no man in the country has a clearer idea of the philosophy of government, of the needs of agriculture, of economics and finance, than Herbert Hoover. Furthermore, he has become one of the country's most able and entertaining speakers.

"He may never be president again, but with his knowledge, experience and poise, he probably would be the best man available for the responsibilities of that great office.

"I would say one of the chief differences between Coolidge and Hoover was that while Coolidge was indifferent and retiring in his disposition and a man of few words, even with his best friends, Herbert Hoover was at ease and sociable among companions, but somewhat reserved, it seemed, in public contacts.

"This phase of his temperament was difficult to understand, in view of his world-wide travels, experience, and acquaintanceships. Many public officials are modest and self-effacing by nature, and Mr. Hoover is one of them.

"One day I received an invitation to attend dinner at the home of a friend, Mrs. Mable Walker Willebrandt, of California, an attractive and gifted woman, who then was assistant attorney-general.

"When I arrived and had exchanged greetings with the guests, I suspected the gathering was more political than social. Among them were Honorable Hubert R. Work, postmaster-general in the Coolidge cabinet, and a number of citizens prominent, not only in official life, but in business circles in California and elswhere.

"Well, it was soon apparent, during the dinner and

afterward, that the object of the meeting was to lay plans for the nomination of Herbert Hoover for president.

"If I made a list of those present, I have not been able to find it in my file. Ordinarily, I think I should have taken the precaution, in view of the importance of the meeting, to have recorded the names in my note book. However, I recall Dr. Hubert Work and the Honorable Stephen J. Mather.

"Dr. Work and his associates carried on a very effective campaign and Mr. Hoover was nominated and elected without difficulty.

"He gave me a commission for reappointment, and I found him a most satisfactory president under whom to have responsibility. He was thoroughly interested in the merit system and was always amenable to suggestions for enlarging its scope, and improving the service.

"My most recent contact with former President Herbert Hoover," says Mr. Deming, "was in the summer of 1939 when he spent a fishing vacation in the Jackson Hole country, Wyoming.

"Responding to urgent invitations, he met informally with republicans of Wyoming in four different cities. I attended the Casper meeting, august 21. There were two hundred guests at the dinner, after which it was announced Mr. Hoover would attempt to answer any reasonable or pertinent question or inquiry.

"Cards were distributed and at least fifty guests took advantage of the opportunity to interrogate Mr. Hoover.

"The questions covered the field of constitutional government, recent political history, New Deal legislative enactments, agriculture, economic subjects and everyday national and world finance; climaxed by the moral issues attending the ills and evils of an abortive effort to subsidize the electorate and blind the public generally to the failure of the administration's policies.

"For more than two hours, Mr. Hoover discussed these problems, never lacking for a word or thought, dismissing the lighter with a bit of humor and extending the more important into a thesis, sometimes approaching the eloquent, frequently the classic, and always direct and sincere.

"He said in part: 'The forefathers and the constitution never guaranteed anyone happiness or success – only liberty of thought and speech and action in their proper sphere and above all the right to work and achieve.

" 'We can never go through another great war without becoming a totalitarian state ourselves in order to effectively fight such a war. When we have finished we shall not have established peace in the world. We shall have sacrificed liberty for generations in the United States. By far the greatest service we can give to civilization is to hold the lamp of liberty alight on this continent.'

"He stressed the dangers from federal extravagance and continued deficits, especially in relationship to hospitals, colleges, universities and foundations generally, supported, in the main, by interest upon large bequests, as well as the effect upon millions of citizens with savings bank accounts and life insurance policies, the proceeds of which are affected by New Deal policies.

"Not a person left the room during the entire catechism; all sat charmed by his wide range of knowledge.

"It was the message of a master and a milestone in the lives of those who heard it.

"So far as I have been able to judge," Mr. Deming concludes, "presidents are much like successful men in other lines of business. Most of them, born amid humble surroundings, have proved that opportunity may knock at anyone's door; but the individual, through alertness, ambition, energy, industry and character, must be willing to meet opportunity half way."

Speaking of the governors of Wyoming, Mr. Deming said, "De Forest Richards, of Douglas, was chief executive of the state when I came to Wyoming. While he was a western sheepman and banker, he looked more like an English duke or French count than a long-time resident of the Rocky mountain section. In fact, he was one of the finest looking men I ever saw and dressed and acted the part of governor. I was indebted to him for my first official appointment as a member of the Louisiana Purchase Exposition commission and he also signed my certificate as a member of the lower house in the seventh legislature.

"I have known all the governors of Wyoming since and have found them, regardless of party, men of high character, much intelligence, and pleasing personality. They have all been mentioned from time to time in the course of this book.

"Among the most recent has been Governor Leslie A. Miller, a self-made man and a credit to his family and to the state. He was a Union Pacific railroad employe, held various important offices including state senator and has been a success in business and a good citizen generally.

"The Honorable Nels H. Smith was quite typical of the opportunities in the United States, and particularly in the West. He came of Danish descent and like many others who have succeeded in the livestock business and in politics, carved out his own career. Governor Smith's administration measured up well, in most respects, with those of his predecessors. Among the *errata* of his four years as governor, friends mention the veto of the school teachers' pension act, his alienation of leading republicans for personal reasons, and the methods used in terminating Dr. Crane's twenty-year tenure as president of the University of Wyoming.

"Dr. Lester C. Hunt, inaugurated governor in january 1943, is a staunch advocate of state's rights and is vigorously fighting to preserve those rights for Wyoming. He has a pleasing personality and much industry, both valuable assets in politics.

"The Memoirs of former Governor Bryant B. Brooks is a distinct contribution to the history of Wyoming. The achievements of Governor Brooks are an inspiration to every young man who has become familiar with the record of this remarkable citizen of Casper. He made the initial payment on his present valuable ranch with beaver pelts and has accumulated a fortune.

"Another illustration that the United States of America is a land of promise and opportunity is manifested in the life of United States Senator Edward V. Robertson of Cody, Wyoming.

"Mr. Robertson was born in Wales of Scotch parentage may 27, 1881. After passing through the grammar and high schools of his native country he enlisted in the third battalion, Welsh regiment, and served nearly three years in the Boer war in South Africa.

"He immigrated to the United States in 1912 where he entered the livestock business in Park county, Wyoming, raising both cattle and sheep. Mr. Robertson took an early interest in republican politics and was recognized as an indefatigable worker. He has served upon the Republican State Central committee, the Republican National committee, was vice-president of the Wyoming Stock Growers association, and is a trustee of the Cody General hospital. He is a thirty-third degree mason.

"At the general election in 1942 he was elected over the incumbent, Senator Harry H. Schwartz, to the United States senate, where he is recognized as a good speaker and a fearless advocate of republican principles."

In the following list the successful candidates for governor of Wyoming are given in the left-hand column, with the defeated in the right-hand column:

1902	De Forest Richards, R.	George T. Beck, D.
1904	Bryant B. Brooks, R.	John E. Osborne, D.
1906	Bryant B. Brooks, R.	S. A. D. Kiester, D.
1910	Joseph M. Carey, D.	William E. Mullin, R.
1914	John B. Kendrick, D.	Hilliard S. Ridgely, R.
1918	Robert D. Carey, R.	Frank L. Houx, D.
1922	William B. Ross, D.	John W. Hay, R.
1924	Nellie Tayloe Ross, D.	Eugene J. Sullivan, R.
1926	Frank C. Emerson, R.	Nellie Tayloe Ross, D.
1930	Frank C. Emerson, R.	Leslie A. Miller, D.
1932	Leslie A. Miller, D.	Harry R. Weston, R.
1934	Leslie A. Miller, D.	A. M. Clark, R.
1938	Nels H. Smith, R.	Leslie A. Miller, D.
1942	Lester C. Hunt, D.	Nels H. Smith, R.

In july 1936, Mr. Deming suffered his first serious illness in years and was in bed for a few weeks, resulting from high blood pressure, but recovered in time to take part in the fall campaign.

Although tireless effort and work were exerted on behalf of Landon and Knox and the republican candidates in Wyoming, an overwhelming tide swept the democratic candidates to victory in 1936.

On november 19, the Honorable Robert D. Carey wrote to the *Tribune* editor as follows: "I want to thank you for the excellent support which your paper gave me during the campaign. While it is possible our state organization was weak, I do not think the results could have been changed as too large a majority was for the New Deal. . . . I am not at all unhappy over my defeat as there were many reasons why I had no desire to go back to Washington. . ." Mr. Deming was then in California for his health. Attorney H. H. Schwartz of Casper succeeded Senator Carey.

A few short weeks after Senator Carey wrote this letter – early in 1937 he was stricken by death at the home of his brother Charles, in Cheyenne. Again, Mr. Deming realized the toll which the stress and strain of public life was exacting from Wyoming's eminent citizens. Robert D. Carey had the distinction of having served as governor and United States senator, as his father, Joseph M. Carey had done. He was Wyoming's first and only native son to rise to such dual eminence.

Mr. Deming, who was in Los Angeles, was much shocked by Senator Carey's death. He at once gave thought to retiring from active newspaper work, a step his brothers and sister had been urging for some time. Indeed, recalling that Senator Carey was ten years younger than himself, and that his own high blood pressure was keeping him at sea level, he suddenly decided to sell the *Tribune-Leader*. For five years he had hesitated because of his intense interest in the work and his sentiment for the paper.

Sale of Wyoming Tribune and Wyoming Stockman-Farmer

Returning from California about the middle of january 1937, Mr. Deming opened negotiations with Alfred G. Hill of Fort Collins, Colorado, who had sold his paper, the *Express-Courier* to Merritt C. Speidel, and had approached Mr. Deming on the subject of buying the *Tribune,* a few months before. Now, realizing that health considerations were more important to him than personal sentiment or party obligations, and desiring to spend the remainder of the winter in Florida, Mr. Deming reached an agreement without delay. In fact, in less than three days Mr. Hill purchased the *Tribune* and *Stockman-Farmer* and took possession on february first, following the deal.

When asked concerning his future plans Mr. Deming said: "Cheyenne and Wyoming will remain as my home base. I may go to Florida in march and later to Washington, D.C., and Ohio, but I shall return here in may because there is no better climate anywhere than Cheyenne in the summer and fall. My private business affairs, including the Deming Realty company will give me something to do. In my absence, Fred H. Ware and William H. Owens will look after my affairs."

Mr. Hill, the new owner, suggested that Deming continue his *Tribune* column "Casual Cogitations," from time to time, and he did so.

Alfred G. Hill completed his college education in the University of Kansas in 1917 and immediately entered service in the World war. Following his discharge in 1919, he returned to Kansas and accepted a position with the *Topeka Capital,* on which he had been employed as a reporter prior to attending the University of Kansas. From Topeka he went to the *Philadelphia Public Ledger* and later was a member of the Washington staff of the United Press. Next he accepted the position of alumni manager of the University of Kansas. In 1924, Mr. Hill was one of the purchasers of the *Arkansas City, Kansas Traveler* selling his interest in 1928 and immediately heading a company which purchased the *Fort Collins Express-Courier.* On january 1, 1937 the *Courier* was sold to Merritt C. Speidel and associates of Iowa City, Iowa. A month later, Mr. Hill purchased the Cheyenne publications. All of Mr. Deming's interests were in the best possible financial condition. There were no bonds or mortgages against his newspapers or real estate and he had no personal debts.

While no public statement was made as to the consideration, it is said Mr. Hill paid two hundred thousand dollars for the *Wyoming Tribune.* The *Tribune* had no accounts payable except first of the month bills, which were less than the earned bills receivable.

Mr. Deming agreed to leave a checking bank balance of eighty-five hundred dollars, and as a matter of fact left nearly ten thousand dollars, exclusive of some earned Cheyenne Building and Loan stock and *Stockman-Farmer* bank balance.

A large surplus in stocks, bonds and savings accounts, amounting to more than thirty-five thousand dollars, had been distributed a few weeks before as a New Year dividend for *Tribune* stock owners, W. C. Deming and Thomas H. Deming.

The paper had been purchased from Judge Joseph M. Carey for fourteen thousand dollars in 1904, the record shows. Mr. Deming had conducted the *Tribune* for Judge Carey about three years before buying it.

Following the sale of the *Wyoming Tribune-Leader,* John Charles Thompson, who had long served under the Deming banner, wrote:

"For the first time in more than the period of a generation, this newspaper is issued today without the direction of William C. Deming. The fact is difficult of realization for those heretofore connected with the paper; for those long associated with him it is all but incredible. For a third of a century the character of the man and the character of the newspaper have been essentially one and the same, the latter so molded upon and thoroughly conforming to the former's fine principles and high ideals that in the viewpoint of his assistants, and that of a notable part of its clientele, William C. Deming has been *The Tribune* and *The Tribune* has been William C. Deming. Today his ownership and direction have terminated, relinquished because the state of his health makes his retirement from the complexities and unremitting nervous strain of daily newspaper publication imperative. His character, the newspaper's reflection of his principles, however, remain an active factor. The man has been disassociated from the newspaper, but not the newspaper from his ideals; *The Tribune-Leader* goes on without his management, but with the inspiration of his character to guide and counsel the succeeding management.

". . . Happily, Mr. Deming's relinquishment of ownership of *The Tribune-Leader* does not have the corollary of his removal from Cheyenne. He has extensive property here, the city will continue his home, his interest in and devotion to the community are unaffected by the curtailment of his business activities made necessary by the state of his health. . .

"Mr. Deming has taken great pride in the fact that in the more than a quarter of a century of active newspaper work as editor, proprietor, and manager, he never had a strike, a lockout, or a libel suit that amounted to anything. Furthermore, he never failed to meet a payroll or discount all bills."

According to Kent Cooper: "Mr. Deming had been a true and loyal member in that fraternity of newspaper people who founded and advanced the Associated Press. His newspapers have reflected the work and spirit of the Associated Press, whether in the interests of his community and state or in behalf of the service at large. . . The Associated Press and its management have been proud to call him colleague and friend."

Of the various expressions of appreciation or regret over his retirement from the newspaper publishing business, Mr. Deming said: "There have been none that I appreciated more than a formal framed tribute from the Wyoming Typographical Union which was as follows:

APPRECIATION TO WILLIAM C. DEMING:
President and publisher Wyoming State Tribune-Leader: march, 1901 - february, 1937.

Through your many years of publishing *The Wyoming State Tribune,* later merged with the *Tribune-Leader,* it has been the privilege and pleasure of the membership of this union to know you intimately as employer, business man and friend.

The work you have carried on during these thirty-six years has been greatly responsible for the high standing

WILLIAM C. DEMING WHEN HE CAME TO
CHEYENNE, 1901

RELAXING AT MIAMI BEACH
after retiring as publisher of the
Wyoming Tribune-Leader

of the State of Wyoming in all lines of advancement. The success of your work is truly exemplified in the results shown.

For the same number of years our organization has had the finest relations with you. Discussions, yes, but dissension was never allowed to exist. The announcement of your retirement from the field of newspaper work leaves us with a great sense of loss, a feeling of emptiness that close relationship alone can leave.

We have a thought of happiness that you can retire from your arduous labors as publisher of the leading daily newspaper of the state of Wyoming, enjoying the fruits of a life of labor for the principles you held ever before you.

May our sincere wish to you, our employer, our friend, be for the success of your every undertaking.

Thomas H. Baker, Harland J. Bates, Thomas A. Boehler, Arthur C. Bolin, J. F. Purnell, Edward R. Caldwell, Edward A. Callies, Duncan Clark, Neil Clark, Jr., Richard A. Corbeil, D. S. Dean, T. A. Edmondson, Raymond D. Ellis, Thomas V. Fox, Charles B. Googer, Richard L. Guthrie, Walter C. Hardy, Alvan W. Harris, Robert V. Hawks, Charles E. Hawley, Charles W. Hoffman, Guy R. Hough, Matt Kinney, Clarence M. Lee, Arthur F. Lewis, Craig Lewis, H. N. Lewis, Robert Marsh, Andrew B. Martelon, B. C. Martin, Robert McClung, J. Wm. Moore, Charles A. Nichols, Paul J. O'Brien, Harry C. Purcell, Robert R. Quin, George G. Reed, Laura M. Sanborn, Jack L. Spicer, Ed P. Taylor, John P. Taylor, Earl Todd, Ernest L. Viner, Helene Wentzel, Arnold Wilson, Leonard C. Wood, H. J. Woodman, James H. Lee, L. Leroy Williams.

Cheyenne, Wyoming, february 1, 1937.

On february 22, Mr. Deming issued a card, "In Appreciation," which read: "The greatest satisfaction my active life as a publisher has brought me is the warm expression of friendship and good will my associates have manifested throughout.

"Let me repeat, for your encouragement, what I have said before and elsewhere,– there has been no magic about anything I have accomplished in my field of endeavor.

"Whatever success I may have had resulted from hard work, and, as many of you know, from a very modest beginning.

"You and those who have preceded you have rendered valuable assistance.

"Your delightful parting gift will be long cherished, and in bidding you farewell, I wish you health, happiness, and prosperity wherever your lines may fall."

Although his name no longer appears in the masthead of the *Tribune-Leader* and the *Wyoming Stockman-Farmer,* it is indelibly written into the history of Wyoming – not as the names carved on sandstone cliffs that are gradually being effaced by rain and wind – but as a deeply embedded part of the development and progress of the state. His influence as a newspaper man and citizen of Wyoming will remain.

Alfred G. Hill, new owner of the *Tribune,* and Tracy S. McCraken, owner of the *Eagle,* later in 1938, merged their interests, publishing both papers in the Tribune building, each retaining its political policy and staff.

In 1939, about two years after the sale of the *Tribune* by Mr. Deming, Merritt C. Speidel, of Palo Alto, California, owner of a large chain of papers, purchased Mr. Hill's stock in the two publications. Mr. McCraken became executive manager. Mr. Deming said: "Mr. McCraken,* starting about fifteen or twenty years ago with the weekly *Wyoming Eagle,* has had remarkable success. He is a clever writer, and a resourceful publisher. I wish the Cheyenne Newspapers, Inc., success."

Freed of exacting responsibility for the first time since his college days, Mr. Deming was now at liberty to come and go as he pleased. In company with his brother-in-law, W. H. Morrison of Wheatland, and his brothers, David S. and Thomas H. Deming, he made a trip through the Jackson Hole, Grand Teton National park and the Yellowstone park in the summer of 1937. They returned by the way of Moran, Dubois, Ft. Washakie, Lander, Alcova, Casper, and Douglas.

Soon after returning to Cheyenne from this trip, Mr. Deming received the following letter from Senator Joseph C. O'Mahoney, relative to the supreme court fight:

"I am most grateful for your letter of july 17. Certainly no one could have asked for more generous support than I have had from the people of Wyoming. I feel confident, as I dictate this letter, that the supreme court fight has been won. The news correspondents, who just left my office, are all carrying stories to that effect today. Your letter emboldens me to send you herewith an autographed copy of the judiciary report."

Mr. Deming had written Senator O'Mahoney a letter urging him to join in a fight against this bill, saying, "The efforts and the words of those who sustain the

---

*Mr. McCraken's progress in other lines of business has been rapid. He has acquired or established a chain of Wyoming daily newspapers.

At the same time he is the leading spirit in operating at least three large hotels, two in Cheyenne and one in Laramie.

As a side issue he controls the Cheyenne Radio Incorporated.

Mr. McCraken is of Scotch ancestry which may account for his acquisitiveness. His ambition and energy have brought success.

dignity and the independence of the supreme court, and not of those who would weaken the judiciary, will live in history."

The president had lost his battle to pack the United States supreme court, his first important defeat.

Earlier in the year, the *Washington Evening Star* had carried the following big headlines:

U.S. Shake-up hit by Former Head of Civil Service. Deming, 8 Years President of Commission, fights its Abolition

In an article, the *Star* said: "William C. Deming, for nearly eight years president of the United States Civil Service commission, today took issue with the plan for reorganizing the agency as urged on congress by President Roosevelt. 'The Civil Service commission is one official organization, so far as membership is concerned, deserving of confidence and also freedom from congressional puttering and attack,' according to Deming."

Two years of vigilance on the part of many friends of the commission saved the merit system from political attack. The president's plan proposed to abolish the long established non-partisan board of three and substitute a single administrator.

In november 1937, Dr. A. G. Crane, president of the University of Wyoming, announced a gift of one thousand dollars by William C. Deming to the student welfare foundation. This foundation was established in 1929 to provide loans to needy students, to establish scholarships, and to promote student welfare. Mr. Deming later raised the amount of his gift to five thousand dollars to be paid in annual installments.

In a letter accompanying the gift, the donor said: "I am generally interested in the cause of education, and particularly in the University of Wyoming. Furthermore, I am impressed by the practical value of your student welfare foundation fund in aiding needy boys and girls."

In appreciation of this worthy gift, the editor of the *Laramie Republican-Boomerang* said: "The town can well join the university in expressing thanks to W. C. Deming for his generous donation to the student welfare fund. Money could hardly be better invested than in helping deserving young people to obtain an education."

Later Mr. Deming also launched the WILLIAM C. DEMING scholarship fund at Allegheny college, Meadville, Pennsylvania, amounting to five thousand dollars, with an initial one thousand dollar contribution.

Having observed the transformation made in Denver by the improvement of Cherry creek, resulting in the Speer boulevard, and the Rock Creek park extension in Washington, D.C., Mr. Deming several years ago began a vigorous campaign for the construction of a drive from the Hereford ranch along Crow creek through Cheyenne to Fort Warren.

Under the Mayor Allison regime, the project was undertaken vigorously with the aid of W.P.A. funds. In the winter of 1937, the work was halted because of lack of city funds for material. Mayor Allison advised Mr. Deming, who was in Florida, of the cessation of activity. At once Mr. Deming contributed a carload of cement and the link under the Union Pacific railroad south of the Lincoln highway was finished.

This drive not only has great promise for the future but even now relieves the viaduct of much heavy traffic.

Commissioners A. W. Trout and Ed Warren worked whole heartedly with Mayor Allison in advancing the improvement.

The mayor and commissioners in formal meeting adopted the following:

RESOLUTION NO. 524. A RESOLUTION OUTLINING CERTAIN FEATURES OF FLOOD CONTROL AND DRIVEWAY CONSTRUCTION IN THE VICINITY OF CROW CREEK IN THE CITY OF CHEYENNE, ACKNOWLEDGING A GIFT OF ONE THOUSAND DOLLARS AND OTHER ASSISTANCE FROM WILLIAM C. DEMING, AND NAMING SAID DRIVEWAY "DEMING DRIVE."

Whereas, to prevent damage of property by flood, to provide a direct connection between the Lincoln highway at Dillon avenue and the Yellowstone highway at Third street, and in general to meet a public need, the city of Cheyenne has had plans prepared and surveys made for widening the channel of Crow creek, and raising and rip-rapping the banks of Crow creek, thereby reclaiming thirty or more city blocks from damage by flood, and for the construction of a driveway from the easterly boundary of the Fort Warren Military reservation, southeasterly along the creek to the point of its intersection with the Yellowstone highway; and

Whereas, this project was regularly and fully approved by the City Council of Cheyenne, Wyoming; and

Whereas, during the past two-year period, a considerable amount of construction work has been done on this project; and

Whereas, during the said two-year period, William C. Deming, a citizen prominent in the affairs of this community, has given assistance to the council in planning the project, and has at one time furnished a carload of cement for use in construction work on the project, and has at other times furnished cash for the purchase of rights of way and for other purposes in connection with said project; and

Whereas, the said William C. Deming has at this time presented to the City Council ONE THOUSAND DOLLARS ($1,000.00) in cash, to be further used for the purchase of rights of way and for construction purposes:

New, Therefore, Be It Resolved that, in appreciation of the lively interest shown by Mr. Deming in helping to plan and carry on the work of the project, the said driveway is hereby named DEMING DRIVE, and shall be so recorded on future maps of the city of Cheyenne, Wyoming.

Presented, read, adopted and passed by the City Council of Cheyenne, Wyoming this twentieth day of november, 1939.

CITY OF CHEYENNE, A Municipal Corporation, by
ARCHIE ALLISON, Mayor.

The compliment paid Mr. Deming in officially designating the Crow creek project as "Deming Drive" met with general approval.

At the 1939 election, Mr. Warren was chosen mayor; Mr. Trout was reelected commissioner; and Al Kay was made the third member of the commission. It is believed these men will carry on successfully and keep Cheyenne moving forward as the Magic City of the Plains.

The *Wyoming Eagle* said editorially:

"Government names parks, mountains, and lakes after citizens who have served their country or humanity in a big way. Smaller units of government too infrequently follow the same procedure in honoring distinguished homefolks. The designation of a municipal thoroughfare as 'Deming drive' in honor of a foremost citizen, W. C. Deming, is a step in the right direction. Similar recognition could well be given other public-spirited men and women who have served and are serving the community as he has done and is doing. Mr. Deming is one of many whom Cheyenne should be delighted to honor in this manner."

The *Wyoming Tribune's* editorial remarks were as follows:

"The Cheyenne city council becomingly extends deserved recognition with its order officially designating the motor road paralleling Crow creek in the western and southern parts of the town 'Deming drive.'

"This admirable civic improvement has been promoted for years by William C. Deming, who contributed to its development land, material, fiscal aid.

"When completed, Deming drive will extend from the boundary of the Fort Warren reservation on the west to United States highway 85 – the Denver-Fort Collins road – on the south; will be the local equivalent of Denver's Speer boulevard along Cherry creek.

"Mr. Deming's advocacy of the creek driveway, his moral and material assistance in its construction, constitute but a minor item of his interest in Cheyenne civic affairs throughout the more than forty years of his residence here, during thirty-seven years of which period he was publisher of *The Tribune* and constantly devoted editorial influence to the furtherance of civic improvements.

"The christening of a driveway with his name is for those familiar with his civic service a gratifying expression of public appreciation." Alongside the new drive in South Cheyenne Mr. Deming presented the city with land for a park and playground.

In an address before the Florida Republican league at the Robert Clay hotel in Miami, Mr. Deming expressed his views on the relief situation. "No person actually requiring food, clothing or shelter," he said, "should be overlooked in these trying times, but public benevolence should not be a partisan asset or football for any political organization."

While in Florida, Mr. Deming called upon Dr. Hamilton Holt at Winter Park. In describing his visit with this distinguished educator, he says: "More than twenty-five years ago, when Hamilton Holt was editor of the conservative New York *Independent Magazine,* he asked me to write two articles, one on 'The Operation of the United States Reclamation Service' and the other, 'What is Dry Farming?' Both were published and I received twenty-five dollars for each.

"About twelve years ago, Doctor Holt was made president of Rollins college at Winter Park, Florida, a co-educational institution of high standing and unique in many ways. Its students come from every state and Doctor Holt has been highly successful as the head of an educational institution.

"In the vicinity of the administration building, shaded by tropical trees as well as dignified by live oaks, Doctor Holt has established the 'Walk of Fame.' As one moves about over the pavements, on either side he sees irregular shaped stones from the homes of notables from all over the world. Each bears a condensed inscription. There are six hundred of them already in place and it is something of a test of one's knowledge, as he reads and remarks, to himself or companion, 'I am familiar with this one but not that one.'

"Well, to make a long story short, Wyoming is not

represented. Doctor Holt asked me for suggestions, stating that mere political prominence is not sufficient. Such recognition, he said, has to be accompanied by other achievements or something unusual in the individual's career.

"Nevertheless, I suggested the name of Francis E. Warren, who had been awarded a congressional medal of honor for distinguished service in the Civil war, who served both as territorial and state governor, and at the time of his death in 1929, had served longer in the United States senate than any other man.

"Also the late United States Senator Clarence D. Clark, of Evanston, who had helped write the constitution of Wyoming, who had served in the lower house of congress and who was United States senator for more than twenty years. He was an able lawyer and a Chesterfieldian gentleman, and became chairman of the judiciary committee of the United States senate.

"I included, of course, the Honorable Joseph M. Carey, who came to Wyoming as a young man in the late seventies, served upon the territorial supreme court, as mayor of Cheyenne, delegate to congress, United States senator and governor, and was author of the Carey Land act, one of the early important examples of reclamation legislation.

"Dr. Aven Nelson, for fifty years on the staff of the University of Wyoming and the leading authority on Rocky mountain flora, was another suggestion; also the late Grace Raymond Hebard, who wrote a number of important books including *The Life of Chief Washakie, sacajawea* and *Pathbreakers from River to Ocean.*

"I included Justice Willis Van Devanter of the United States supreme court, retired, and former Representative in Congress, Frank W. Mondell. Reference has been made elsewhere to Justice Van Devanter's fine record of achievements.

"Mr. Mondell was chiefly a self-made and self-educated man. He became identified with the construction firm of Kilpatrick Brothers and Collins, who had contracts for the extension of the Burlington railroad through western Nebraska and also into Colorado. When that work was completed, it appeared that the contractors would have to pull up stakes and move their heavy equipment back home, either to Omaha, or somewhere in Iowa. The Burlington officials, however, stated to the contractors that if commercial coal could be found in northeastern Wyoming, the line would be built into the new town of Sheridan and would later be extended to Billings, Montana. Although young Mondell was not trained as a geologist, a chemist, a civil engineer or a college man, the contractors realized that he was a student of nature as well as of books and they sent him over the proposed right-of-way to look for coal out-croppings.

"In a word, Mondell located coal mines in and around Newcastle and Cambria in Weston county and helped to lay out the town of Newcastle of which he later became mayor. He did so well as a public official that he was elected to the state senate and then to the national house of representatives, where he served for more than twenty-five years.

"When Mr. Mondell decided to make the race for the United States senate against John B. Kendrick, the incumbent in 1920, he was republican leader of the house and in direct line for succession to the speakership, instead of Nicholas Longworth, who attained that honor. Through more than thirty years close association, personally and politically, with Mr. Mondell, I would say he was the best authority in congress on legislation affecting reclamation, arid farming, homesteading and desert entries, general mining, and forestry administrations. He had them all at his fingers' tips.

"In my suggestions to Doctor Holt, I included Esther Morris, deservedly known as the 'Mother of Woman Suffrage' because of her work in securing equality for women in the territorial constitution of Wyoming; John Colter, who discovered Yellowstone National park; Chief Washakie, Shoshone Indian, always a friend of the whites, who fought under General Crook in the campaign against the Sioux and who is credited with saving the life of young Lieutenant Guy V. Henry, who later distinguished himself in the Spanish American war.

"Also mentioned were: Sacajawea, the Shoshone Indian woman who piloted Lewis and Clark in their great expedition to the Oregon country; Nellie Tayloe Ross, who succeeded her husband, Governor William B. Ross and who during her two years in the governor's office, reflected much credit both upon the state and upon womankind; and John B. Kendrick, a tall, typical cowboy who drove a thousand cattle from Texas to Wyoming in the late seventies (1879), laying the foundation for a fine ranch and a fortune, and who married one of the most charming women in the West and subsequently served Wyoming as state senator, governor, and United States senator with distinction.

"After brief consideration, Doctor Holt said that Nellie Tayloe Ross probably met the qualifications because she was the first woman governor in the United States. Sacajawea, he thought, might squeeze through. It is now up to their friends to contribute a stone to the Walk of Fame.

"There is a fine point involved, in view of the various and important activities and achievements of all those mentioned above, and that point is, 'What constitutes fame?'—a synonym for which is renown, reputation, and notoriety.

"It was my first opportunity for many years to renew my contacts with Doctor Holt. In order to show that 'Bread upon the waters cast shall be gathered up at last,' I gave him my check for fifty dollars, as a contribution to the college welfare fund, for which he was very grateful, even if I did not include interest on the two twenty-five dollar checks, which the *Independent* had sent me a quarter of a century ago."

In view of the fact that Doctor Holt hesitatingly thought that Sacajawea might squeeze through in winning a place in his Walk of Fame, it seems worthwhile to devote some space to this famous woman of history.

One of the most important Wyoming organizations, from the standpoint of the past, as well as the future, is the Historical Landmark commission.

The first commission, comprising R. S. Ellison, chairman, J. S. Weppner, secretary, and treasurer, Warren Richardson, was named by the late Governor Frank C. Emerson in 1927, and made its first report in 1929.

Mr. Ellison took a very active interest while a resident of Wyoming and was succeeded, as chairman, by Warren Richardson, of Cheyenne. Both Mr. Richardson and Mr. Weppner are still serving and John Charles Thompson has been made treasurer.

There have been more than fifty sites, monuments, plaques and other evidences of historical significance acquired, dedicated or erected, by this commission throughout the state of Wyoming.

Among the more important are the acquisition of Fort Bridger, Fort Laramie, Fort Reno, a monument to "Portugee" John Phillips at Fort Phil Kearny, fencing cliffs along the Oregon Trail (bearing names of pioneers), and more recently a monument to Sacajawea, the Shoshone Indian woman who accompanied Lewis and Clark through the Northwest to Oregon.

To quote from the *Annals of Wyoming,* October 1941: "While the afternoon shadows slowly slid down the eastern slopes of the Wind River mountains near Fort Washakie, on september 26, 1941, more than one thousand people attended the unveiling ceremonies of the bronze tablet, placed on a huge monolith of granite by the Wyoming Historical Landmark commission, as an additional tribute to the memory of Sacajawea, Shoshone Indian woman, who with her husband, Touissaint Charbonneau, accompanied the Lewis and Clark Expedition to the Pacific coast in 1805. The monument, erected on United States highway 287, points the way to Sacajawea's grave, two miles westward in the Shoshone burial ground.

"With all of the color and precision of a theatrical pageant, the program progressed under the able direction of L. L. Newton, of Lander, master of ceremonies. But this was not a rehearsed production – this was reality – for there were present Indians and white men who personally had known Sacajawea, 'Bazil's Mother.' Included among these were: Pandora Pogue, ninety-eight-year old Shoshone woman, arrayed in a bright shawl, beaded moccasins and leggings; Quantan Quay, stalwart one hundred-year old Indian scout; Mayor W. T. Jones of Lander, who at one time operated a meat business on the Shoshone Indian reservation and who knew 'Bazil's Mother' well; and the Reverend

GREAT-GRAND-DAUGHTERS OF SACAJAWEA UNVEIL MONUMENT TO MEMORY OF FAMOUS WOMAN

Left to right: Chairman Warren Richardson; Governor Nels H. Smith (with back turned); Master of Ceremonies L. L. Newton; Irene Large and Gloria Isis

John Roberts, beloved missionary among the Shoshone Indians, who performed the rites of the Episcopal church at the grave of the aged Indian woman on april 9, 1884.

"To the right of the monument were gathered direct descendants of Sacajawea's son, Baptiste, and of her nephew and adopted son, Bazil. To the left were members of the Washakie family and the Indian and white friends who had known 'Porivo' as Sacajawea was often called. To the rear on a raised platform Arapahoe and Shoshone warriors in full regalia added much color to the scene.

"Chairman Warren Richardson, John Charles Thompson and Joseph S. Weppner of the Historical Landmark commission, were introduced as the ones directly responsible for the erection of the beautiful memorial. Next, the Indian committee (composed of Charles Driskell, Mrs. Maud Clairmont, Mrs. Nellie Scott Thomas, Jo Durand and Gilbert Day, with Superintendent Forrest Stone and Engineer Space) was introduced and credited with the success of the celebration. Recognition also was given to the valuable assistance of the sub-committee comprising: The Reverend John Roberts, Mrs. B. B. Brooks, Mrs. Lenora Stone, John Charles Thompson, and Mrs. Inez Babb Taylor.

"Then came that part of the ceremony which gave proof to the reality of Sacajawea. Pandora Pogue . . . stood straight and proudly as Interpreter Compton repeated the interview that he had with her in which she told of knowing Sacajawea at Fort Bridger in 1868 and later at the Shoshone agency. Pandora Pogue was present when Sacajawea died and she saw her buried in the cemetery near the Roberts Mission.

"Quantan Quay, through the interpreter, stated that he had known Sacajawea or Porivo very well, also her sons, Baptiste and Bazil. 'I was at the council at Fort Bridger when this reservation was given to us,' he said. 'Sacajawea was at that meeting. I know she was there because I saw her. . .' He also told of attending her burial.

"The next speaker was the Reverend John Roberts, Episcopalian missionary on the Shoshone reservation for more than sixty years, who said: 'I want to say a few words to you especially concerning the burial of the heroine of the Lewis and Clark Expedition. I shall not trouble you with an account of that burial because it would take too long and the sun is going down. . . I wish to say to you that I did have the privilege and honor of leading the burial services of that great woman. . . She was buried in what is now called the Shoshone burial grounds as the monolith indicates which is dedicated and unveiled today. For us and for future generations to come it indicates that she was buried in the Shoshone cemetery . . . may the memory of that noted Shoshone woman live forever in the hearts of a grateful people.'

"Former Governor Bryant B. Brooks of Casper, as speaker of the day, lauded the young Shoshone woman for the important part she played in opening the great west to a new civilization. He paid a tribute to her loyalty and her willingness to do her task and do it well. . . He spoke of the Indians and the whites working together to build a home in the beautiful valley and of the historical significance of the day's celebration.

"In the formal ceremonies Warren Richardson, on behalf of the Landmark commission, presented the

REVEREND JOHN ROBERTS
Episcopalian missionary who buried
Sacajawea in the Wind river cemetery,
Shoshone Reservation, 1884

FORMER GOVERNOR B. B. BROOKS
at the unveiling of the Sacajawea monument, 1941

marker to Governor Nels H. Smith for the state of Wyoming. The governor, in turn, entrusted it to the care of the Shoshone and Arapahoe Indians.

"As the two great granddaughters of Sacajawea: Irene Large and Gloria Isis, lifted the American flag and unveiled the marker, the slanting sun rays made the plaque glow like molten gold.

"Chief Dick Washakie, in accepting the memorial, upon behalf of the Indian tribes, pledged his fidelity to the white people and confirmed the faith of his father, Chief Washakie, in his white friends."

Late in may, 1938, Mr. Deming, accompanied by his secretary, James Hull, completed a twelve thousand mile automobile journey to Florida and back, through a dozen states and the District of Columbia, without accident or unpleasant incident.

While in Washington, D.C., the following appeared in the column of Frederic William Wile in the *Washington Star*:

Renewing ties of official days in Washington this week is William C. Deming of Cheyenne, Wyoming, president of the United States Civil Service commission under Harding, Coolidge, and Hoover. Mr. Deming, Kentuckian by origin, succeeded in life concurrently along four lines. Over a period of thirty years, he made a state institution of his daily newspaper, the *Wyoming Tribune,* at Cheyenne. He also built up the *Wyoming Stockman-Farmer.* Then he organized his own realty company, owner and operator of office buildings and apartment houses. In his spare moments, he was a public speaker and lecturer and held various state and federal offices. Mr. Deming sold his Wyoming papers a year ago, but retains an interest in his first journalistic love, the *Tribune,* of Warren, Ohio.

On the return trip, Mr. Deming and Mr. Hull traversed Virginia and West Virginia over much the same mountain route followed by Daniel Boone and the pioneers who migrated west to Kentucky.

Stops were made in Kentucky and Ohio to visit relatives before heading west to Cheyenne.

"Discouraging contrast was observed," said Mr. Deming, "in the steel sections of Warren, Youngstown, and Cleveland, as a result of the strike and the depression which began last september. Whereas, formerly smoke from hundreds of stacks almost obscured the sun on a clear day, now idle chimneys, furnaces and mills act as a pall upon the communities, while relief kitchens and government food supply depots are doing their bit to relieve a distressing situation."

On june 14, he gave the principal address at the Flag day exercises of the Cheyenne lodge No. 660 B.P.O.E., in which he urged the American people to lead in a movement for a great international tribunal to supplant war among the nations.

On july 12, he gave a talk before the Cheyenne Rotary club called "Isms, and Schisms, Scrip and Scripture in California," which had to do with Upton Sinclair, Doctor Townsend, Senator Sheridan Downey, and the Ham and Eggs proposition in California.

The attention given by the author to the variety of activities in which Mr. Deming has been engaged, and the responses he has made in the way of public speaking since returning to Wyoming from Washington nearly ten years ago, are indicative of his ability to cover a wide range outside of the newspaper profession.

He maintains active membership as a Scottish Rite mason, a Knight of Phythias, a son of the American Revolution, a member of the Cheyenne Rotary club, and is an honorary member of the Young Men's Literary club of Cheyenne. Many years ago he was accorded a conspicuous place in *Who's Who in America*. His name has continued to appear there.

Winter Home of William C. Deming
at Redlands, California

During 1938 and 1939 he devoted much of his time to his real estate interests, increasing his holdings in Wheatland, in Miami, and in Cheyenne.

On march 20, 1939, occurred the death of his brother-in-law, William H. Morrison, an esteemed citizen of Wheatland. Mr. and Mrs. Morrison were well known in Cheyenne and were frequently guests of Mr. Deming. For many years, Mr. Morrison had managed the Wheatland Roller Mills and more recently had conducted a successful real estate and insurance business.

During the summer and fall of 1939, Mr. Deming gave considerable time to cooperating with the author of this biography. This proved a severe strain upon his eyes, especially in preparing so many reminiscences and reading proof on manuscripts. He went to California in december 1939 where a severe nervous attack followed, delaying the completion of the biography.

Gradually, however, Mr. Deming recovered and spent the winter of 1941 in Austin, Texas. In december of that year he was notified by Arthur T. Vanderbilt, president of Phi Beta Kappa associates, that he had been elected as one of two hundred founding members of that organization. One object of the association is the preservation of freedom on which both scholarship and civilization are dependent and the development of an informed leadership for democracy. Phi Beta Kappa was established at Williamsburg, Va., more than one hundred years ago and numbers more than ninety thousand members.

The winter of 1942-43 was spent by Mr. Deming in California, where he purchased an attractive home at Redlands, to be used for winter residence when desired.

As this biography goes to press Mr. Deming's name appears in many news releases as having made provision for six prizes annually totalling two hundred dollars, to be awarded to Wyoming farmers and ranchers for tree improvement.

These prizes will be awarded in 1943 through the cooperation of the University of Wyoming, based upon the best results from plantings of Clark-McNary trees since 1927.

Beginning in 1944, awards will apply to new plantings. The contest is to be open to adult farm and ranch people and to 4-H forestry and beautification club members.

Dr. J. L. Morrill, able young president of the University of Wyoming, calls this provision of Mr. Deming, a "far-visioned interest and generosity, which will help to build the beauty and agricultural productivity of our state." He also says, "The University is grateful for the opportunity to co-operate with Mr. Deming in encouraging the ranchers and farmers of the state to improve and enrich the countryside of their homes and the attractiveness of the Wyoming scene."

The awards will be fifty dollars for first, thirty dollars for second, and twenty dollars for third in dry land plantings; and similar amounts will be given for irrigated plantings. The awards made to winners in 1943 indicate success.

Provision has been made in his will by Mr. Deming for payment of these awards for twenty years, assuming, of course, that there is continued interest in the plan.

Judging will be by the county agricultural agent, and the commanders of the Veterans of Foreign Wars and American Legion posts which have jurisdiction in the entrant's region, and will be tabulated and completed by Professor W. O. Edmondson, extension forester and horticulturist at the University of Wyoming.

"The plan," says Professor Edmondson, "will be to carry along enrollments from year to year to insure replanting where necessary, and also to insure use of the best cultural practices."

Many winds have blown over the Wyoming prairies in the almost two score years since the young Kentuckian first glimpsed the blizzard-ridden West. Since then great dams have created vast lakes to irrigate myriad acres; deserts have bloomed; cities have thrived; towns have been created and have prospered; a net-work of oiled highways has covered Wyoming; silver-winged carriers have established transcontinental sky routes; the radio has brought the world within speaking distance; pioneers' sons have built up range stock into prize winning herds; fine stands of timber and tumbling waterfalls have been protected for posterity; a great state university has expanded; Cheyenne has become a modern, cosmopolitan city – and as William C. Deming looks back across the years, he must feel great satisfaction in knowing that he has been a part of all of this.

A new country needs its pathbreakers and its pioneers. It also needs its builders – and Mr. Deming has been one of Wyoming's many substantial builders. He still is. He has become as much a part of the state and as loyal to it as if he were a native son.

Through the *Tribune,* for almost four decades, he carried a varied message, but as he says, "It was the responsiveness of Wyoming men and women to any reasonable appeal that gave me courage to persevere and the will to achieve."

Among the Scrapbooks

William C. Deming has one of the most interesting sets of scrapbooks in the West – or in the East, too, for that matter, about twenty-five in number.

A collector of autographs would find them a veritable gold mine. There are many names of presidents, of White House secretaries, and of persons of official importance. There are signatures of Ed Howe, James R. Garfield, John Harvey Kellogg, Bainbridge Colby, J. Hamilton Lewis, A. H. Vandenberg, Reed Smoot, Fred W. Wile, Dolly Gann, Nellie Tayloe Ross, Mabel Walker Willebrandt, Carl Gray, Frank B. Noyes, Ulysses S. Grant, 3rd, Justice Stanley Reed, Adolph S. Ochs of the *New York Times,* and of dozens of men and women of note in Wyoming and elsewhere.

Back in the 1890's Mr. Deming began to write a special column for the *Warren Tribune*. This was before there were many regular columnists.

"I wrote columns," he said, "because I could get closer to people. They were not as formal as editorials."

Down through the years he has written under many captions. These have all been preserved in the scrapbooks and cover an amazingly wide field.

Lee Taylor Casey, columnist of the *Denver News,* said in his column: "Mr. Deming's column, 'As Seen in Wyoming,' is the most brilliant, entertaining, instructive and illuminating newspaper feature that has appeared in that state since the days of Bill Nye and the *Laramie Boomerang* – and before."

Let's turn the pages of the scrapbooks and pick at random some of the titles of articles, mostly in a lighter vein, which will give a glimpse of the compass of subjects upon which the *Tribune's* owner has written. For example:

Our Most Privileged Character – the telegraph messenger boy.

Why the Fair Lady Screamed – tootsies caught in the theater seat.

Is Apple Pie Extinct?

Is the Bath Brush Passé? (A friend tells me he went to four drug stores in New York before he was able to find a bath brush.)

America's Most Famous Shrine – the Lee Mansion and Cemetery at Arlington.

Grave of First Unknown Soldier buried in Arlington National Cemetery.

Ovidian Kisses Torrid but Expensive – a divorce case.

Behind the Scenes at the Flying Field.

Modern Girl is Industrious – the woman pays her way.

The Night Air Mail.

Reckless Auto Driving.

A Word about Labeling Pictures.

There's no Formula for Success – cited Lincoln's life and that of Calvin Coolidge.

The Gold Standard.

Women and Oriental Mysticism.

What do you know about Rainbows?

Chicago Brown Stone House yields Rare Art Treasure. An old family mansion.

The Ecstatic Adventure of Life. A story about Bishop Charles Edward Locke of St. Paul, who did not worry.

The Red Devils – advocated cutting down on the use of the auto horn.

Dying at Fifty-Seven – "Nobody but a harvest hand or hod carrier should consume the food that the average man tries to assimilate. Half the time the good wife is to blame for tempting him,– every person should know his proper weight for his height and train down to it."

Is Einstein only Joshing?

When Tragedy and Comedy Mingled – story of how Americans controlled themselves when a German submarine shot an English boat. "In times of great danger and distress, American people preserve their self-possession and whatever else they may show, they don't show the white feather."

What the Old Preacher Said.

The History of Money.

Colorado Injures Itself in Preventing Development of Wyoming's Water Resources.

Keeping Traffic Lanes Open should be required of Contractors.

Time for Wyoming Dry Farm Potatoes to Supplant Greeley Spuds and the Idaho Product.

Vote as you Please, Belong to any church you Like, But Don't Get Excited – "Personally, I have never been able to understand religious prejudice or race hatred. I have travelled in foreign countries, met people of various religions and found that human nature is much the same in all of them. If a Protestant is a good citizen he is respected and so treated, the same is true of a Catholic, or a Jew and any other. . . Vote for whom you please, belong to any church you like, but don't get excited."

Sarah, Abraham's Wife, not able to Conceal her age.

Al Smith Finds Fame Transient as Fleecy Cloud.

Retailer Gets 25 per cent of Tourist Dollar.

Babson – Right or Wrong, Still Guessing.

Renaissance of Empress Eugenie Hat brings Joy to Danbury, Conn.

Marathon Dancing.

Future Homes may be Heated from our Radios or Busted Atoms.

What is a Good Golf Score?

The Pickle Route to Fortune.

Trees do not Drink at Night.

No Main Streets in Washington.

Aphrodite without a Nightie, also Venus and Psyche – a humorous description of Greek and Roman statuary indiscriminately scattered over the grounds of the Southern home of an art collector.

The following are samples of the hundreds of articles in the scrapbook which have been selected without thought to chronology or continuity.

"Wyoming is entering the third generation from the period of first settlers who succeeded in establishing homes and habitations, in this Rocky mountain state. . . Timothy Dyer was a remarkable character in many ways. He passed the age of fourscore and maintained his interests here until he died. His ruddy countenance, pleasant smile and sympathetic voice endeared him to all those who had been favored with the opportunity of knowing him. . . While his name will be associated always with the birth and growth of Cheyenne, he probably will be remembered longest as the proprietor and owner of the first modern hotel of the period in the wide stretch of country from Omaha to Salt Lake City. The old Dyer house on Pioneer avenue played its part well and passed into history. . . Sometimes I wonder if the present is producing a race of men as vigorous as those who opened the Rocky mountain west to civilization. . . Timothy Dyer, with his great fund of humor and inexhaustible supply of optimism, was an outstanding example and worthy of emulation by those who have come after him."

"May 1917 – I have met Miss Rankin, the congress-woman from Montana. She is vivacious, modest and attractive. . . At the National Press club, I have chatted with 'Uncle Joe' Cannon and heard him make a good speech on the revenue bill. Though eighty-one years old he is still about the best talker in the house. He is very fond of Mondell, whom he calls 'Frank,' and takes pleasure in recalling that he helped Mondell get the three hundred twenty-acre law through when under the rules, as speaker, he had a good chance to lend assistance. Both sides pay great deference to Cannon and all old animosities seem to have passed. Age is a mellowing process and among its compensations is the inclination to forget or forgive one's enemies."

"My impression of woman suffrage, as I have seen it in Wyoming, destroyed and dissipated any lurking prejudice I may ever have had concerning this great national reform . . . contrary to the general impression, Wyoming women are not office-seekers – they are generally selected for superintendent of schools. While they take an interest in the primaries and may dominate them upon issues in which they are particularly interested, yet I have never seen them sit in a convention which preceded the Wyoming primary election law."

HOW WOMAN SUFFRAGE CAME TO WYOMING – "On feb. 19, 1935, the Honorable Leslie A. Miller, governor of Wyoming, issued a proclamation the first section of which reads as follows: 'In recognition of the first law found anywhere in legislative history which extends the right of suffrage to women, the tenth day of december of each year is designated as Wyoming day. Such a day shall be observed in the schools, clubs and similar groups by appropriate exercises commemorating the history of the territory and state and the lives of its pioneers, and fostering in all ways the loyalty and good citizenship of its people.'

"In pursuance of Governor Miller's proclamation Grace Raymond Hebard and Marie Montabe Horton prepared a one act play under the title, 'The Birth of Wyoming day – When Woman Suffrage came to Wyoming.'

"Anyone interested in the history of the woman suffrage movement in the United States will find both entertainment and instruction in this delightful bit of light literature.

"Brief quotations will serve to portray the atmosphere surrounding the first Wyoming territorial legislature and the procedure which finally realized the dream of Esther Morris, a pioneer woman, who is rightfully credited with being the mother of woman suffrage in Wyoming and incidentally in the United States.

"At the first election for members of the legislature in Sweetwater county (formerly Carter county), on the second day of september, 1869, Colonel William H. Bright, a democrat, and Captain H. G. Nickerson, republican, were candidates for the upper house, and called the council.

"A few days before the election Mrs. Morris, of South Pass, gave a tea party at her residence at which there were about forty ladies and gentlemen present.

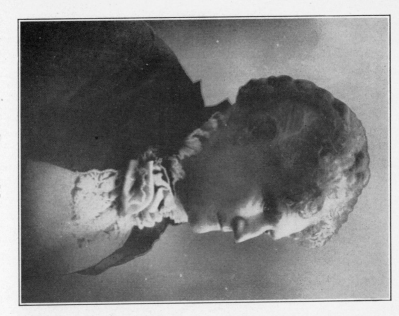

Mrs. Esther Morris
first woman Justice of the Peace;
mother of Woman Suffrage movement in Wyoming

Colonel William H. Bright
member of territorial legislature who introduced
the woman suffrage bill, 1869

Colonel Bright and Captain Nickerson were invited. While sitting at the table, Mrs. Morris arose and stated the object of the meeting. She said: 'There are present two opposing candidates for the first legislature of our new territory, one of whom is sure to be elected and we desire here and now to receive from them a public pledge that whichever one is elected will introduce and work for the passage of an act conferring upon the women of our new territory the right of suffrage.'

"Of course the two candidates pledged themselves as requested, and received the applause of all present. Colonel Bright, the successful candidate, true to his promise, introduced the woman suffrage bill and it ultimately became a law.

"As might be expected, the bill ran the gauntlet of the delays common to parliamentary procedure, where an active opposition knows what it does not want and is able to maintain a struggle. While there were a few serious speeches in behalf of the act, there were even a greater number which made Colonel Bright's bill the subject of humor, satire and sometimes bitter opposition. Among those who took a pronounced position against the woman suffrage bill was Ben Sheeks, in the lower branch.

"In one of his numerous efforts, Mr. Sheeks said, 'Mr. Chairman, Gentlemen. You cannot be serious. This question is vital to us, why the first thing you know women will want to be serving on juries, they will desire places upon the bench and heaven knows what they will be wanting next. Let us keep woman in her rightful place as a homemaker and mother. Mr. Chairman, I move that further consideration of this bill be indefinitely postponed.'

"Esther Morris, with a knowledge of human nature,

politics and mankind, had not rested when she secured the consent of Colonel Bright to father council bill number 70. There were only four votes for the Sheeks' motion to postpone.

"Thereafter each test vote showed that the suffrage advocates were holding their ground.

"In due time Speaker Curran announced its passage and the bill went to Governor John A. Campbell for his signature.

"The authors of the play have staged an appropriate setting, with Mr. Bright, the father of the bill, and Esther Morris, the mother, among others, present in the governor's office for the historic scene. Upon the suggestion of Mrs. Morris, Ben Sheeks, leader of the opposition, was also invited and proved to be a good loser.

"When the ceremonies were concluded Governor Campbell presented the pen to Mrs. Morris who responded as follows: 'Thank you, Governor Campbell, and may this new law pave the way to a greater freedom, a broader education and an advanced citizenry, not alone for Wyoming but for the entire world.'

"Mr. Sheeks then stepped forward and said, 'Governor Campbell, I have opposed this bill from the first, but it is now a law; therefore, I accept it. May I propose a toast? (Men all nod. Mr. Sheeks raises arm in grand gesture.) To Wyoming's lovely ladies, once our superiors, now our equals.'

"Had Esther Morris lived until august 1920 she would have rejoiced to see woman suffrage, once a joke and a by-word, and sometimes considered a bit of political gallantry manifested by a provincial body of territorial lawmakers, proclaimed as the nineteenth amendment to the United States Constitution.

WOMAN SUFFRAGE IN WYOMING TERRITORY
scene at the Polls in Cheyenne, november, 1888

"Esther Morris was the first woman justice of the peace in the world, it is said, and performed her duties with great dignity and ability.

"A half century later the leader of the opposition in the Wyoming council wrote as follows:

Montesano, Wash., Oct. 14, 1919

DEAR MISS HEBARD: Wise as I thought myself fifty years ago, I am willing to admit that I have learned some things since.

I have advocated and voted for woman's suffrage, and have no doubt of the wisdom and justice of my later action, whatever the good women of Wyoming may think of my former conduct. Yours truly,   BEN SHEEKS

"Gallant old Ben Sheeks might have mused, 'New occasions make new duties; Time renders ancient truths uncouth.'"

"The Tribune does not desire and will not publish scandal, nor will it permit its columns to be used to further the personal prejudices of correspondents. Any correspondent wilfully misrepresenting or falsifying from motives of personal dislike or spite will be summarily dismissed."

"The Suwanee river . . . I have read at various times that anyone filled with sentiment would be grievously disappointed in the Suwanee river in that he would expect too much. This afternoon when I drove over this famous stream, made famous by Stephen C. Foster's immortal song, I found the reverse to be true. It is not a very wide stream but the trees on the bank are beautifully reflected in its historic waters. The flow seems to have cut away the banks in many places until today a wall of rock-like substance several feet high appears on either side. Over the bridge spanning the stream is the simple but significant sign, 'Way, Down Upon the Suwanee River.' Far more than many other larger streams, this little body of water has won a tender place in the hearts of the Americans."

"I have frequently called attention to a movement looking to the union of various church denominations which were separated as a result of the long-drawn-out differences over slavery. The latest has to do with a proposed union of the Presbyterian church with the United Presbyterian church. It is expected that the two assemblies will meet separately in 1934 and later unite to form one body which shall be known as the General Assembly of the Presbyterian church in America. I note the same point with respect to the two branches of the Presbyterian church as with the Methodist and others, that the proposed date of union is always sometime in the future and the actual achievement has a string to it. In the present case it is said, 'ministers of the two negotiating churches will be asked to study the proposed plans in order that a joint committee might reach a complete agreement.' Here's hoping." [10]

"How many readers of this column have seen a night mail ship arrive and depart at the Cheyenne field? If you have not done so, you have missed a real thrill. You will observe a commingling of lights and shadows, shades and colors no artist can reproduce.

"The combination of border lights, flood lights, revolving light and moonlight merge into a marvelously fascinating effect. There are various shades of blue, pink, purple and green, and at times the field itself looks like water reflecting back the rays of the moon.

"Suddenly the stillness of the night is broken by the humming of the machine somewhere above and beyond the vision. Then weirdly out of the darkness two red-

[10] Such an agreement was effected.

BENJAMIN SHEEKS
leader of opposition in territorial legislature
to woman suffrage bill, 1869

JOHN A. CAMPBELL
Governor of Wyoming Territory, 1869

dish, lantern-like beacons appear in the distance. They gradually grow in size and come nearer and nearer; the big 'bird of paradise' dips its beak; sails slantingly toward the hangar. The pilot, heavily robed, alights. His buddies give him a hearty greeting and he is off for home, a warm fire and welcome dinner.

"It is a good picture, a big canvas and a free show.

"The editor of the *Tribune* desires to pay a personal tribute to the late Thomas A. Cosgriff. While I had met him casually and occasionally before he came to Cheyenne to enter the banking business, it was not until he became a citizen here that I came to appreciate his remarkable business ability and kindly personal qualities. From the day Mr. Cosgriff took up his residence in Cheyenne, he was a citizen in all the term implies. He knew the full responsibilities of citizenship and he new its duties well.

"Cicero said: *Civis Romanus Sum* (I am a Roman citizen). Thomas A. Cosgriff, from the day he came to the capital city, lived the part and gave fully and freely of his energies toward improving Cheyenne.

"He felt keenly the obligations incurred by business eminence and success. He believed in the future of Cheyenne and he was always eager to make it bigger, better and more beautiful. I often wonder that a man of his energy ever found time for the amenities and the gentler arts. Yet he was a man of literary tastes and a student of affairs.

"Mr. Cosgriff made money rapidly but his success was the result of his originality, his untiring industry and his superior methods of organization. He knew how to do things and his energy supplied the time and the will constantly to extend his field of activity.

"And yet, money to him was only a means, not an

end. He used it intelligently, liberally and well. The city of Cheyenne and the state of Wyoming have never yielded to the idea that he had severed his citizenship or changed his allegiance to Colorado. In his death we all mourn the passing of a very remarkable Wyoming self-made man."

A letter from Rick Ricketson, division manager of the Fox West Coast theatres, on november 14, 1935 said: "Your article of november 12 on 'Mutiny on the Bounty,' I believe, is one of the finest editorial appraisals of the subject that I have seen in my long connection with the motion picture industry. I am taking the liberty to send copies to the Metro Studios and to thirty of the leading showmen in this territory."

Mr. Deming not only has received hundreds of letters from well-known contemporaries, but has been a collector of original historic communications.

For instance, he once prepared an article concerning Horace Greeley and Nathan C. Meeker and the Union colony in Colorado, now Greeley.

The article was written for the *New York Tribune* and the original letter was presented to Mr. and Mrs. Ogden Reid, owners of that newspaper.

The important point in this incident is that Horace Greeley's foresight and interest in farming resulted in the rich Greeley colony. He had visited that section in 1859 by stagecoach, spending some time in and around the new town of Denver.

The article was as follows: "Horace Greeley, Nathan C. Meeker and the Union Colony in Colorado.

"A study of history shows that many important events have had very casual beginnings.

"For instance, when Horace Greeley, publisher of

the *New York Tribune,* sent his agricultural editor, Nathan C. Meeker, to Colorado, in quest of land suitable for a settlement, he gave Mr. Meeker the following letter:

COMMISSIONER, INDIAN AFFAIRS, WASHINGTON, D.C.

New York, Jan. 19, 1870

DEAR SIR: My friend, N. C. Meeker, who will hand you this, goes to the Rocky Mountains directly in search of land for a new colony. He desires the good will of the Indians of the plains and appeals to you for aid and counsel. Any favor you can do him will be gratefully appreciated by yours.   HORACE GREELEY

"Being curious as to the origin of the great publisher's interest in a farm settlement in the Rocky mountain region, I made some investigation and found that Arthur H. Carhart, in his book, *Colorado,* discusses the enterprise in considerable detail.

"In 1859, Horace Greeley, editor and principal owner of the *New York Tribune,* made a trip across the United States by stage. He visited the little city of Denver. Mr. Greeley was more impressed by the agricultural development in some sections of Colorado than by the gold-mining boom.

"Upon his return, he interested the agricultural editor of the *Tribune,* Nathan C. Meeker, and others in colonizing an agricultural district in Colorado. A committee came out in the summer of 1869, seeking land for the purpose.

"On december 23rd, the Union colony was organized. Mr. Meeker was president, General Robert H. Hammond, vice-president, and Horace Greeley, treasurer. Messrs. Meeker, Cameron and Fish came to Colorado in 1870 and in early april selected lands near the Cache la Poudre and South Platte rivers' junction. A small town called Latham was located here. Fort Latham was built later for protection against Indians.

"The above committee purchased about 12,000 acres of land from the Denver Pacific railway and took over provisional title to 60,000 acres of public land. For the entire 72,000 acres, the immediate total money outlay was not quite $60,000.

"Fifty families came to Greeley in may, 1870, and in a short time the present town was platted.

"Today, Greeley stands in one of the richest irrigated sections in the world. There are 300 irrigation projects in Weld county with more than 2,000 miles of main ditches and laterals, irrigating 400,000 acres of land. Greeley is a modern city in every respect, and the seat of a fine college. The property values in the town and county exceed $100,000,000.

"With all of his experience, intuition and knowledge of practical things, Mr. Greeley could not have anticipated the far-reaching results of his desire to aid agricultural development in the arid and semi-arid west. It is equally true that Mr. Meeker, with all of his background, could not have envisioned that which time would bring forth, nor the tragic end that awaited him.

"In order to complete this bit of history, I am appending some facts concerning Nathan C. Meeker. The reader will discern that Meeker, through his early reading and his efforts to establish a phalanx of the followers of Fourier in Ohio, was preparing himself for a more practical plan in the west.

"Furthermore, it will be seen that Carhart and the writer of the biography of Meeker differ slightly as to whether Greeley or Meeker really originated the idea of the Greeley colony in Colorado. My guess is that the honor goes to the publisher, Horace Greeley, because throughout his life he was a pioneer in thinking, in experimentation and in action. Greeley also had interested himself in a Fourier colony in Red Bank, New Jersey, as early as 1843. The combination of Greeley and Meeker was important and doubtless necessary for success. It does not occur always that the capacity to conceive and the ability to achieve are found in the same mind and body.

"According to the *Dictionary of American Biography,* Nathan Cook Meeker was born, july 12, 1817, in Euclid, near Cleveland, Ohio. He was the son of Enoch and Larana Hurlbert Meeker. He attended school in Overland and in Hudson.

"From his seventeenth year, he was a wanderer and a wayfarer, changing his home and vocation so rapidly that it has been difficult for his family and his biographers to fix very definitely all of his movements.

"He did newspaper work in New Orleans; taught school in Cleveland; engaged in special literary work in New York; was a school master at Allentown, Pennsylvania, in 1842, and at Orange, New Jersey, in 1843.

"The following year, he was conducting a small mercantile business at Euclid, where he married Arvilla Delight Smith, who survived him. While in Euclid, he became interested in the teachings of Francois Marie Charles Fourier, a French socialist. He joined the Trumbull phalanx at Braceville, Ohio, near Warren, where Fourierism was being practiced. There, he worked on a farm, lectured, taught school, prospered, and, as he said later, 'learned how much cooperation people would bear.'

"Three years experience sufficed, and in 1849 he reentered the business world in Euclid. Early in the fifties he was invited to open a store in Hiram, where a group of Campbellites were preparing to start a college. While there, he wrote a novel, *The Adventures of Captain Armstrong,* which was an interesting commentary upon the final phase of his own life, for the captain, wrecked on an island in the south seas, tried to educate the savages in the ways of civilized life.

"The panic of 1857 brought this Hiram venture to a close. He opened another store in southern Illinois, became a newspaper correspondent, and about 1865 joined the staff of the New York *Tribune.*

"As agricultural editor of Greeley's paper, he became a well known writer and his series of articles on the Oneida community in New York attracted attention.

"In 1869, he was sent west to survey the work of the Mormons. (Horace Greeley had visited Salt Lake City and interviewed Brigham Young ten years before.) While Meeker did not reach Utah, he learned much about the conditions in the territory of Colorado. 'Out of this trip grew his plan to organize an agricultural colony in the west,' says a biographer.

"With the support of Horace Greeley, and of the *Tribune,* he launched the Union colony in december, 1869. On april 5, 1870, he selected a site on the Platte river, north of Denver and on the Denver Pacific railway. His call for settlers proved successful. By may, land had been bought from the railroad and from individuals, while agreements had been made with the railroad and with the government to obtain much more. The colony was cooperative, yet not like the Oneida community. Instead, it recognized private ownership of land and individual control of activity. No saloons and no billiard halls were tolerated. A school was opened at once, a library started, and a lyceum founded. Colorado looked upon the colonists as dreamers, led by a crank, Meeker, tall, awkward, and slow of speech.

"On november 16, 1870, he published the first issue of his paper, the *Greeley Tribune,* in which his editorials were able admonitions to his followers. The *Greeley Tribune* is still going strong and is a valuable property.

"In 1878, however, Meeker accepted the appointment as Indian agent at the White River, Colorado reservation and proceeded to carry out his ideas in managing Indians. Like the Captain Armstrong of his novel, he believed in the civilizing effect of work. He endeavored to induce the Utes to live in log houses, to plow the fields, to raise crops, and to support themselves. His lack of understanding led him into difficulties. The Utes, hostile to his plans, rose and killed him with all the rest of the white men in the agency, september 29, 1879.

· · · · · ·

"The known gold-mines of Colorado, for the most part, have been exhausted, but the state's sunshine and showers, its fruits and its flowers, its mountain scenery and agricultural valleys are a rich and enduring heritage. It matters little whether Greeley or Meeker initiated the idea of a colony in Weld county, Colorado. Doubtless, it required the faith and efforts of both to make it a success. They had many views in common. The great publisher left splendid monuments to his genius, while Nathan C. Meeker, like many pioneers, sacrificed his life in a cause, but his work survives."

THE SET OF A SAIL

One ship drives east, and another drives west;
With the selfsame winds that blow;
'Tis the set of the sails and not the gales
Which tells us the way they go.

> Like the winds of the sea and the ways of fate
> As we voyage along through life;
> 'Tis the set of the soul that decides its goal,
> And not the calm or strife.—*Selected.*

The above lines were a favorite quotation and appear prominently in one of Mr. Deming's more serious efforts. Also the following:

> I am weary of planning and toiling
> In the crowded hives of men;
> Heart weary of building and spoiling
> And spoiling and building again;
> And I long for the dear old river
> Where I dreamed my youth away;
> For a dreamer lives forever
> And a toiler dies in a day. – *John Boyle O'Reilly.*

Mr. Deming says: "As I look back over the years and recall the many choice spirits that have come and gone, this quotation from *Hamlet* seems very apt,

> Those friends thou hast, and their adoption tried,
> Grapple them to thy soul with hoops of steel.

Mr. Deming expressed to the author of this biography his regret that so many of his contemporaries, mentioned herein, have passed away. He hopes those who may read these pages will be charitable in their criticism as there have been delays and many difficulties in assembling material, much of it from memory.

Among the young men who came to Cheyenne in the same year Mr. Deming reached Wyoming, was T. Blake Kennedy, now judge of the United States District court.

Of the fifteen original charter members of the Young Men's Literary Club, established forty-two years ago, only four or five survive. Among them is Clyde M.

Watts, able lawyer, and a close friend and neighbor of Mr. Deming. Mr. Watts perhaps has the best record for attendance of any member of the organization.

It is an interesting coincidence that Judge Kennedy, the first secretary and Mr. Deming, the first president, are still in the land of the living.

Judge Kennedy after much success as a lawyer, was elevated to the federal bench where his ability is widely recognized. He takes his judicial duties seriously but he is able to relax and enjoy the lighter side of life when the opportunity presents. That is a happy balance and worthy of emulation.

In one scrapbook is a neat little envelope containing the personal card of William Howard Taft, the only American ever to hold both the office of president of the United States and later chief justice of the supreme court of the United States. The message, in Chief Justice Taft's own handwriting, reads:

"To the Chairman of the Civil Service Commission:

"With the hope that my law clerk may obtain some statistical information concerning the classified service and the regulations and the history of the changes of the law and regulations, for use in consideration of a case pending before our court. Mr. Hayden Smith is my law clerk and he will present this to the Chairman.

January 28, 1926   Wm. H. Taft"

Early in my life in the West, the Union Pacific railroad, cooperating with other lines, invited a large number of newspaper and magazine writers, together with men prominent in official and business life, to be the railroad's guests for about two weeks on a trip through the Rocky mountain states. The company desired to show what it had accomplished in improving the system, under the original Harriman regime, and also give the tenderfeet guests an opportunity to study, at first hand, reclamation problems and public land questions then attracting wide attention in congress and elsewhere.

"Toward the close of our itinerary we reached the little railroad station of the Crow Indian agency or reserve in Montana shortly afternoon on sunday. The stop was made there as we were to be shown over the Custer battlefield. It was before the days of any general use of automobiles, although a few were in operation in the cities. The local committee had assembled two or three hundred Crow Indians, as well as a large number of farmers, ranchmen, cowboys and others. When the train stopped, the Indians gave us a typical western welcome, or at least as much so, as the more or less dignified Crows would be likely to extend.

"Throughout the trip, there had been occasional opportunities to ride horseback. There were about half a dozen in the party who enjoyed that recreation, and I had been constituted a committee of one to contact members of local 'glad-handers' and see that good saddle horses were available. While waiting for the trek of several miles to the battlefield, I inquired if there were any saddle horses not in use, and was advised that there were quite a number tethered behind the railroad station. Gathering up the riding contingent, I stood back while the others made their selections. The result was, that the only mount left for me was an Indian pony about half the size of an average range horse. It was a beautiful afternoon in september and the cavalcade strung out for a long distance over the dusty dirt road, under conditions quite different from those in 1876 when General Custer and his entire command were wiped out by the Sioux. Whites and Indians on horseback were leading the procession, followed by

THE CHEYENNE FRONTIER DAYS CELEBRATION

the original committee, 1897, as follows: Warren Richardson, John A. Martin, John L. Murray, Granville Palmer, Edward A. Slack, Edward W. Stone, Clarence B. Richardson, D. H. Holliday

every conceivable kind of vehicular contraption. There were young and old, men and women, and scores of Indian boys from the reservation school who spoke good English.

"We were riding four abreast, whites and Indians mixing up indiscriminately. On my left was a tall, dignified member of the tribe, a man about forty years of age and he was mounted upon a very fine big bay horse. In order to get a good view of his immobile face I had to look up at him because of my diminutive mount.

"From time to time the dirt road was badly worn with deep ruts because of the heavy travel year after year. A consequence was the Indian's legs and those of the rider on the other side were rubbing and crowding me uncomfortably. With some motion of the hand, I presume, I said to the Indian, 'Too crowded here. You and I can move forward.' Apparently, he did not hear or understand. At least he did not deign to look at me. A bit later when the same situation occurred I repeated my suggestion. Then he seemed to take notice, looked at me passively, but did not change his expression or make any move to relieve me.

"A third time I tried to make myself understood. Then looking down at me disdainfully, as if questioning my sanity or intelligence, he reached over and with his quirt or whip struck my pony upon its haunches a terrific blow. The pony shot out from between the other two mounts as if it had been fired from a cannon. When the Crow caught up with me, he gave my pony another lick and then struck his own horse with the result that we began to attract the attention of those who were near by. Fortunately for me the wind blew my hat away and gave me a good excuse to rein in and stop, while an accommodating Indian boy went back for my headgear.

"The point is, of course, that the Indian thought I was challenging him for a race, and being forced into it, he showed that he not only had a sense of humor but was also a good sport. He was willing to give me the benefit of his quirt and whatever handicap I needed by reason of the fact that he was mounted on a big horse.

"Arthur Capper, a young newspaper publisher of Topeka, Kansas, was in the party. He subsequently became governor of Kansas and has been United States senator for many years. When I was president of the United States Civil Service commission and lived at the Mayflower hotel in Washington, Senator Capper and I frequently breakfasted together and recalled interesting incidents of the trip through the Rockies.

"In my various automobile trips to the east and south I have traveled over a variety of routes, largely in order to see more of the country. This has been true, especially when motoring to Florida. I have enjoyed the various roads through the Atlantic coast states, to and from Washington, and in going from Cheyenne to Florida have traveled through Texas, Louisiana, Alabama, Mississippi, and Georgia.

"A few years ago, I wished to see the development in Oklahoma, since it was known as Indian territory in my geography when I was a boy. I even recalled the mad rush of settlers in 1889 when the lands were thrown open to the whites. Tulsa and Oklahoma City have grown from the grass roots like magic and will continue to expand as the decades pass.

"I was even more curious about the people in Arkansas and particularly the Ozark mountain district.

"In company with a college boy named Bob White, I took that route to the Louisiana line in order to cross the Mississippi river at Vicksburg en route south. It has never been my custom to pick up hitchhikers for several reasons. I felt no obligation to do so. There is always some risk and as a rule my car was pretty well filled with baggage.

"Down in southern Arkansas, as we approached the Louisiana boundary, we were in a swamp country, as poverty stricken, sparsely settled and unattractive as anything I have ever seen. The old highways were being elevated or rebuilt upon drier ground. From time to time we were permitted to use parts of the new road but most of the time were following the old.

"We had just observed a detour sign and pulled up a slight incline to the new grade and headed southeast, when a member of the road building crew raised his hand and we stopped. He came alongside and advised us that a short distance ahead was a one way stretch and we would have to wait for the traffic going the opposite direction. While we visited with him and asked many questions, I observed a big colored man standing a few feet away, probably near enough to hear what we were saying. When there was an interval in the conversation, he walked up to our car and said, 'Boss, could you-all give a fellow a lift down the road a piece?' While he spoke pleasantly and politely enough, I felt no inclination to modify my rule against hitchhikers and replied, 'My friend, on this trip we have had scores of opportunities and requests to take in old and young, men and women, white and colored, but have not done so, because it is against my rule and furthermore you see there is not much room left in the back seat as it is well filled with baggage.' He was a six-footer, about thirty-five years of age, with a fairly prepossessing face.

"Although disappointed, he replied, 'All right Boss, you has the say so, but I shore is disappointed. I'se got a job waiting for me just across the Louisiana line and if I doesn't get there soon I'se afraid I'll lose it.' He was so pleasant about it and looked at me so appealingly that I wavered for an instant, and asked him how far it was to the town at which he wished to stop. He responded, 'About fifty miles.' That meant that he would be with us an hour or more through a country that was strange to us and thinly populated. As we had not yet been given the signal to move forward, the colored man, the road superintendent and I continued to talk, but I did not assent to the negro's request. He was persistent, however, though exceedingly polite, and I finally turned to the road man and asked, 'Do you know this man?' He replied, 'No, sir, I never saw him until a few minutes ago when he appeared here with a bundle under his arm.' At that, the African straightened himself up and seemed to take on about four or five inches of height. His face brightened because he instinctively felt there was a ray of hope in my question. Then he intervened, 'I kin identify myself,' and without another word, he reached in his pocket and pulled out a roll of papers or documents tied up with a red ribbon. Bob White was driving and I was on the front seat with him. The colored man passed the papers to me with the suggestion that I read them. When I opened the package I found that it was an official parole from the warden of the Arkansas state prison, in which the name of the colored man appeared together with the fact that he had been convicted of grand larceny and sentenced for five years. After three years he had been paroled in recognition of his industry and his good behavior.

"The big negro, watching intently, tried to read my mind, I assumed, and when I still hesitated he said, 'And Boss, that ain't all.' I didn't know whether he meant he had a recommendation from another state penitentiary or just what. At any rate, he handed me a letter. It proved to be a To Whom it may Concern document, signed by the warden of the Arkansas prison commending the bearer to the consideration of anyone who might be able to give him a job. I then decided to take a chance, to the alarm, I think, of Bob White, who quietly suggested, 'Don't you think you would better move to the back seat.' I acted upon his suggestion and told the hitchhiker to climb in.

"Then I discovered, I thought, one reason for his weakness of character. His big head and neck were in a straight line. There was not the natural curve of a normal rear view, in striking contrast to his pleasant face.

"We drove along comfortably and I engaged him in conversation and kept him talking, especially about prison life and the people and their habits in Arkansas, particularly the share croppers. He was intelligent and responsive and really entertaining. I felt as long as I could keep him talking that there would be no danger, although it would have been easy for him to control the situation in that God-forsaken country.

"At luncheon time, we stopped, I gave him enough money to buy himself something to eat, although I presume he had received the usual allowance when he left the penitentiary. After lunch, he appeared promptly at the time set and when he left us in Louisiana he was profuse in his thanks and appreciation. My mistake in this little circumstance or experience was that I didn't record his name and address and keep in touch with him in order to see whether he honored his furlough or parole."

During the World war, General John J. Pershing and his staff paid a formal visit to the tomb of Lafayette, who, as a young man of noble birth, joined Washington's army and helped the colonies win their struggle for liberty against George the Third of Great Britain.

The cables, which carried the news, credited General Pershing with the epic statement, "Lafayette, we are here."

These words attracted much attention at home and abroad. It occurred to Mr. Deming that the lines might be made the theme of a bit of verse or some other appropriate expression.

He says: "Wrestling with the subject and, finally, by paraphrasing to 'Lafayette, we are come (a bit of poetic license) I evolved a few stanzas. They bore the title 'A Tribute to France.'"

When General Pershing at the tomb,
    With trembling voice, declared
'Lafayette, we are come, are come,'
    Breathing the spirit of Washington,
Of Valley Forge and Old Yorktown;
    Proud to wear the fleur de lis,
Speaking the hope of democracy,
    Fighting the fight of liberty
Which liveth yet and will not die,
    He spanned a century of brotherhood
Which holds us yet in common good
    And told the story simple and true,
Of the age-long debt we owe to you.

Oh beautiful, beautiful France,
    France of the fleur de lis;
Brother in our distress,
    A sister in liberty.

We are come, yes, with all that we have —
    There's a bond in our kinship with you,
In the Stars and the Stripes when we give
    Three cheers for the Red, White, and Blue
We are come, France, with uncovered head,
    In the name of the now and ago,
In our tribute to de Lafayette,
    And our homage to Rochambeau,

Oh, beautiful, beautiful France,
    Our France of the fleur de lis,
The France that can never die
    In a cause that makes men free!

"Both my enthusiasm for the effort and sentiment for the subject were dimmed somewhat, a bit later when I received the following letter.

City and County of San Francisco
Department of Public Works, December 11, 1922

HONORABLE WM. C. DEMING, Cheyenne, Wyoming

DEAR SIR: There has come to my attention a copy of the *Wyoming State Tribune* under date of november 27th, which contains your poem entitled "A Tribute to France." The article preceding the poem states that the expression, "Lafayette, we are here!" was uttered by General Pershing at the tomb of Lafayette in France.

As this statement is not one of fact, I desire to say that it was I who made use of this expression on july 4, 1917, at Pic Pus cemetery, Paris, France. I accompanied General Pershing abroad as chief disbursing officer of the A.E.F., and held this position until june of 1919, when I returned for station in San Francisco.

About june 25th, we having reached Paris june 13, 1917, General Pershing sent for me and said, in brief, that ceremonies were to be held at the burial place of Lafayette on july 4th under the auspices of the society of the Sons of the American Revolution, and that a representative of the American Expeditionary forces would be expected to make an address.

I was deputed for this duty, prepared my oration, submitted it to General Pershing in person about july 1st, and he marked upon my original manscript "O.K. — J. J. P." I delivered the address and made use of the expression quoted, as can be testified to by many officers of the A.E.F., including Major-general Harbord, Major-general Hines, Marshall Joffre, secretary of war for France, Panlevy, and many others.

General Pershing has never claimed he gave utterance to this expression, and would be glad to say so if you were to question him in the matter.

I only write this letter to you in the interest of historical accuracy, as I do not believe your statement should go uncontradicted. Expressing admiration for the beauty of your poem, and with every kind wish to you in person, I am   Very truly yours,

C. E. STANTON, Col. U.S. Army Retired

Colonel Stanton's statement was subsequently confirmed by the following letter:

Washington, July 30, 1937

MR. WILLIAM C. DEMING, Cheyenne, Wyoming

MY DEAR MR. DEMING: In the absence of General Pershing, who is abroad, I am replying to your letter of july 25th, relative to the authorship of the expression, "Lafayette, we are here."

The following is quoted from General Pershing's book, *My Experiences in the World War* (page 93, vol. 1):

"It was on this occasion and upon this spot that utterance was given to an expression that could have been born only of inspiration, one that will live long in history — 'Lafayette, we are here!'

"Many have attributed this striking utterance to me, and I have often wished that it could have been mine. But, I have no recollection of saying anything so splendid. I am sure that those words were spoken by Colonel Stanton and to him must go the credit for coining so happy and felicitous a phrase."   Yours sincerely,

G. E. ADAMSON, Captain, U.S.D., secretary

"Yet the error continues to travel by radio and printed page and probably always will.

"The General Hines referred to by Colonel Stanton is General Frank T. Hines, who became director of the Veterans' Administration in Washington. General Hines cooperated with the Civil Service commission and was an industrious administrator. I became very fond of him."

Growing out of a simple incident of travel, supplemented by considerable imagination, about fifteen years ago Mr. Deming penned a bit of romance, called *Bluegray Yarn or The Woman at the Rail*. The effort was neatly bound and mailed to a few friends at Easter time.

So many of the acknowledgments expressed a hope or a desire that he would write a sequel that later two chapters were added: the first called "At the Cross Roads" and the concluding one, "When Dreams Come True." The original chapter is printed herewith.

THE WOMAN AT THE RAIL

"What silences we keep year after year,
With those who are most near to us and dear;
We live beside each other day by day,
We speak of myriad things, but seldom say
The full sweet word that lies within our reach
Beneath the commonplace of common speech.
Then out of sound and out of reach they go —
These close, familiar friends who love us so;
And sitting in the shadow they have left,
Alone with loneliness and sore bereft,
We think with vain regret of some kind word
That once we might have said and they have heard."

"The 'Empress' was steaming majestically through placid waters at the close of an autumn day. The ship's heavy whistle sounded curt acknowledgment of a blast from a passing boat. This exchange of signals aroused me from meditation of the calm sea. Looking up, I observed the slender form of a well-dressed woman. No detail of her attire was striking, but she presented an ensemble of harmonious units from her soft hat to her shapely shoes. A pretty scarf of dark red and black was draped becomingly about her neck. Her face was scarcely discernible from the angle of her position at the rail. I felt, however, that it conformed in attractiveness to her taste in dress.

"Rather wistfully, I thought, she gazed at the passing ship, and resumed her knitting. Even the blue-gray yarn she so deftly handled blended with her personality, as I observed it in a somewhat lingering glance that late afternoon. Presently, I approached her with a commonplace remark, and she responded with that free-masonry of the sea which forms a transient brotherhood.

"Her manner was neither inviting nor repelling – merely the naturalness which good breeding commands and which guarantees in return courtesy and good will. To each succeeding remark of mine she was agreeably and intelligently responsive. The ease and simplicity of her manner were delightful in the extreme. Conversation flowed freely and frankly on, touching the war and women's part in it, her knitting, national and world politics, books and people of note. Apparently there was no subject she could not discuss, and everything seemed to interest her.

"When she courteously inquired the time I was surprised to find we had been chatting for more than an hour. I experienced the guilt of presumption, yet there was nothing in her manner indicating that I had intruded upon her reveries. I told her frankly how much I had enjoyed her company. She smiled warmly and I withdrew.

"This casual meeting did not pass quickly from my mind. Throughout the evening, I thought of the unaffected good-fellowship of the slender woman, who did not take her attention from her knitting, yet followed or led the conversation at will.

"As I sought to visualize her features, my memory was hazy. I could not recall the exact color of her eyes, nor did I know the shade of her hair, covered so completely by a soft gray hat. In-so-far as I know, she had not looked directly at me and, if indeed, she gave our meeting another thought, she must have carried away as vague an impression of me as I did of her. I remembered chiefly a pretty and rather unusual movement of her lips, which characterized her speaking – and the soft tones of her voice which carried one along like music at eventide. Then it came to me by a process of recollection and elimination that she had not changed her position at the rail. Her diverted gaze and concentration were natural, apparently, as her eyes seemed to be upon her knitting all the time.

"There was nothing in the situation that impelled her to simulate interest in me or in what I was saying. It was as if I had been talking with someone I had known all my life.

"My dinner was spoiled by my preoccupation, and later I found that I could not keep my mind on my book. There had not been an abrupt or awkward pause during the entire hour. But what she really said – her words, I mean – was lost to me in the clinging memory of the woman herself. I endeavored to recall detail and realized only her spirit which left me in a bewildered state of mind.

"There could not have been any personalities or conventional small talk, because only a fleeting remark about her knitting and how the world had helped idle women to find themselves suggested a clue to her identity. I did recall that she said that many women, like Doggie Trever in the *Rough Road* and Jean Valjean in *Les Miserables* after meeting the old bishop, had found their souls.

"She did not appear again.

"Apparently, I had passed out of her radius of thought and existence as suddenly as I had discovered her at my side. The next, and the succeeding day, however, she filled my memory and my vision as I sought to rebuild the hour's enchantment. Nothing tangible came – all was merged in her subtle simplicity. Try as I might to deduce some expression of interest or tone of sympathy for my lonely meditation, I could recall no word or act that she might not have granted to anyone.

"All my hopes and dreams for another meeting were in vain. As well might she have been swallowed up by the sea, which houses so many mysteries.

"Glad as I was to see my native land, I did not hasten to leave the good ship which had brought me safely home. As I strolled aimlessly about, the woman emerged from her cabin, the personification of grace and good taste. She was following a luggage-laden porter and now wearing a smart, well-tailored blue suit. I looked straight into her eyes, and behold, they were a wonderful brown! For an instant I was not sure it was really she, when – Blessed Damozel – she gave me a smile of recognition – and farewell.

"I walked to the ship's side, and with a deep sense of personal loss watched her disappear in the crowd at the dock. There was a modicum of comfort in the impression that she went away alone and that only the Goddess of Liberty was waiting to bid her welcome home.

"Emerson says, 'A new person is to me always an event, and hinders me from sleep.' I appreciated all that he meant and sometimes must have felt. Long she lingered in my memory – soft hat, blue-gray yarn, gentle voice, alert mind, pervading personality – tantalizing mystery! We were indeed as ships that pass in the night and speak each other in passing.

L'Envoi

"Some man or woman stands on everybody's road to God.'

"After I have climbed up the mountain side of life and am passing down to the valley where the evening shadows fall, the sea, the sunset, and blue-gray yarn will remind me of the slender, nameless woman at the rail."

Recollections and Historic Notes

PINCHOTISM AND FOREST RESERVES, BY W. C. DEMING. When one considers the well-ordered and carefully managed national forests in Wyoming today, it is almost inconceivable that less than forty years ago they were wide open to any and all livestock men. Then, too, fire ravages were common and destructive. Today there are twelve national forests in Wyoming containing 8,500,000 acres of land.

In 1940 the forestry superintendent and his rangers, the fire patrol, the hundreds of miles of excellent oiled roads in the reserves and the protection given to young and growing timber, are the result of a policy and plan inaugurated by President Theodore Roosevelt and administered for many years by Gifford Pinchot of Pennsylvania, later a governor of the Keystone state.

I said, in those days the use of the forest reserves for grazing and timber cutting was a sort of a free-for-all, which meant of course a clashing of interests and a terrific waste of resources. Yet, the bitter feeling engendered by the then new restrictions and regulations became a political issue and almost split the republican party in Wyoming. Only the popularity of Senator Warren and Roosevelt saved the situation.

Today, some of the most pronounced leaders of the opposition frankly acknowledge that Theodore Roosevelt and Gifford Pinchot were right.

This scrap of history would not be complete without a more or less adequate description of the activities and personality of Colonel A. A. Anderson, artist, author, aristocrat, world traveler, stockman, traffic cop, friend of royalty, campfire host and Wyoming forest superintendent, about whose head a regular tornado of criticism circulated and revolved for several years.

Fortunately in his retirement, only a few years ago, the Macmillan company of New York published Colonel Anderson's *Experiences and Impressions*.

In reviewing his autobiography for the *Wyoming Tribune* I said:

"Thirty odd years ago there were at least three acute and bitter issues in Wyoming, to-wit, A. A. Anderson, Gifford Pinchot or pinchotism, and the establishment, maintenance and regulation of federal forest reserves.

"Strange as it may seem, prior to the administration of President Theodore Roosevelt what are now set apart as national forests were largely unsurveyed portions of the public domain, and were used by the cattlemen and sheepmen of the West without charge, let or hindrance.

"Of course the cattlemen and the sheepmen did not agree among themselves as to the division of that particular 'spoils system' and sometimes unpleasant results followed.

"Early in the century Anderson, then a well known portrait painter from New York, who also maintained a studio in Paris, decided to spend a summer vacation in the Rocky mountains of Wyoming. He left the railroad at Billings with a well equipped camping and hunting outfit and proceeded overland to the foot of the Greybull mountains in what was then known as the Meeteetse Rim country.

"Anderson was a contemporary and friend of Whistler, the great English artist and numbered among his loyal Wyoming friends Colonel William F. Cody, or Buffalo Bill, who as early as march, 1903, wrote Anderson from London expressing his pleasure upon the appointment of Anderson as superintendent of the Yellowstone forest reserve.

"Those were the days when Bill Barrow, of Douglas, Atwood Thomas, of Meeteetse, and other opponents of the new regime, set up by Theodore Roosevelt and made effective by Gifford Pinchot, chief of the forest service in Washington, almost split the republican party in Wyoming, because there were few stockmen of importance who believed and frankly admitted that the old order could not go on forever.

"A reviewer in the *Casper Times* finds that Anderson had taken first prizes in the International Art Exhibits in Paris, London and New York. The same writer says the colonel took part in range wars of early Wyoming; that he was a cattleman and a principal actor in the famous incident in which four Utah sheepmen were driven out of the Jackson Hole country.

"Yet, this man of the East and the West, this tenderfoot and hard-boiled superintendent of a forest reserve, this artist, whose name has been written large upon the canvases of two continents, also found time during the last quarter century to occupy an official position in New York City's traffic department, and help work out details of New York's modern traffic system as made necessary by the million automobiles in the city.

"Anderson not only served as superintendent of the Yellowstone forest reserve, which included nearly ten thousand square miles in Wyoming, Montana and Idaho, but he acted as an assistant game warden of Wyoming and was an important factor in preventing the wholesale destruction of big game in this state.

"Through his friendship with Colonel William F. Cody and Honorable George T. Beck he was able to render valuable assistance in having the Shoshone dam above Cody included in one of the earliest appropriations under the Federal Reclamation act.

"It seems that it was through his acquaintance with Anderson that William R. Coe of New York first visited Wyoming, and later became a large property holder and citizen of Wyoming.

"Forgetting the old adage that it is well to catch or secure your rabbit before you skin it, a Wyoming governor and legislature exercised undue haste in placing upon the statute books of the state an inheritance tax which Mr. Coe felt was directed at him.

"He subsequently withdrew his citizenship, although he still has large ranch and livestock holdings in northwestern Wyoming.

"Colonel Anderson went to Lexington, Kentucky, and purchased, in addition to high grade cattle, some well-bred horses which formed the nucleus of some of the best racing stock in the West. Perhaps that is why, in after years, he was made a colonel upon the staff of a Wyoming governor.

"Anderson not only was impressed with the misuse and abuse of the forests in Wyoming, but he observed they were being wantonly destroyed by fire. Sometimes by campers and sometimes, he alleged, by stockmen who blazed their own trails with little or no care as to the result.

"Hence it was a proud moment when he donned the uniform of superintendent of the Yellowstone forest reserve july 1, 1902.

"In his book he says, 'When the reserve was first organized every paper in Wyoming except one – and that one I owned – attacked me most severely. To read their articles one would think that I had horns and hoofs. For instance, the *Meeteetse News* said, "Mr. Anderson can by a single stroke of his diamond-bedecked hand put out of existence that noble animal (the sheep) that clothes his unclean body." ' (Colonel Anderson overlooks the fact that the Cheyenne *Tribune* took a rather broad view of the question and gave Pinchot every opportunity to be heard, much to the disappointment of some sheepmen.)

"Colonel Anderson moved up the Greybull river ten miles above the Pickett ranch where amidst a dense growth of cottonwood and luxuriant buffalo grass, he filed upon a homestead of one hundred sixty acres. This was the beginning of the Palette ranch, more than a generation ago, and there Colonel Anderson's first book was born.

"I doubt whether there were fifty people in Wyoming who knew that A. A. Anderson, of Meeteetse, the fighting champion of the United States forest reserve system, was an aristocrat of the first water and an artist who had painted pictures of notables, including royalty, and had exhibited at the Universal Exposition in Paris in 1889,– and they didn't care.

"Senators Warren and Clark and Representative Mondell were between two fires, but were in a position to see the federal government's side as well as the position of the local sheepmen and cattlemen, most of whom felt their sacred rights were being abused. Our Washington delegation handled a delicate situation well. They needed Teddy. Roosevelt had a tender spot in his heart for Wyoming, as evidenced by his assistance and subsequent visits to the state. Pinchot took most of the punishment and seemed to thrive on it.

"More than ten years ago in a meeting of the Wyoming Woolgrowers association in southwestern Wyoming, I heard one of the biggest sheepmen in the state declare upon the floor of the convention that no one wished to return to the old order of things. The cattlemen have also from time to time given the forest reserve, as a system, 'a few kind words.'

"Carlyle, the great English writer, expressed in a paragraph the entire mission of good books. He said: 'In books lies the soul of Time: the articulate audible voice of the Past, when the body and the material substance of it has vanished like a dream.'

"Colonel Anderson, in his autograph, has made a fine contribution to Wyoming history. He need apologize only for waiting until he was four score and then some.

"Perhaps he thought that one way of beating his critics and reviewers. I might remind him that the good die young, and that there are worse places than Wyoming.

"Perhaps, the greatest compliment Anderson has paid Wyoming was in spending so much time here after having hobnobbed with the crowned heads of Europe, including Queen Victoria, King Edward, the Czar of Russia, former Emperor William of Germany and the Shah of Persia, whose country offers some attractions which interest men, especially artists. He left his hall-mark upon this state."

"While I did not reach Cheyenne until march 1901, I have been surprised, in looking back over books, records, histories, and official rosters, to see how many of the pioneers who figured politically or otherwise in the state's development I have known.

"For instance, the officers of Wyoming's two houses

of the legislature from 1890 to 1939 were as follows, practically all of whom I have known, more or less intimately.

1890 – W. R. Schnitger, Laramie county, president of the senate.
Oliver P. Kellogg, Crook county, speaker of the house.

1893 – Frank W. Mondell, Weston county, president of the senate.
L. C. Tidball, Sheridan county, speaker of the house.

1895 – George W. Hoyt, Laramie county, president of the senate.
Jay L. Torrey, Fremont county, speaker of the house.

1897 – George E. Abbott, Laramie county, president of the senate.
A. D. Kelley, Laramie county, speaker of the house.

1899 – John McGill, Albany county, president of the senate.
Levi R. Davis, Weston county, speaker of the house.

1901 – Edward W. Stone, Laramie county, president of the senate.
Jerome S. Atherly, Albany county, speaker of the house.

1903 – Charles A. Guernsey, Laramie county, president of the senate.
Jerome S. Atherly, Albany county, speaker of the house.

1905 – E. E. Levers, Uinta county, president of the senate.
Lyman B. Cooper, Converse county, speaker of the house.

1907 – O. H. Brown, Uinta county, president of the senate.
Scott K. Snively, Sheridan county, speaker of the house.

1909 – Edward T. Clark, Laramie County, president of the senate.
C. H. Hayden, Big Horn county, speaker of the house.

1911 – J. M. Schwoob, Big Horn county, president of the senate.
L. R. Davis, Crook county, speaker of the house.

1913 – Birney H. Sage, Laramie county, president of the senate.
Martin L. Pratt, Park county, speaker of the house.

1915 – Edward W. Stone, Laramie county, president of the senate.
James M. Graham, Fremont county, speaker of the house.

1917 – Joseph W. Todd, Johnson county, president of the senate.
W. K. Jones, Laramie county, speaker of the house.

1919 – Thomas G. Powers, Goshen county, president of the senate.
E. J. Sullivan, Natrona county, speaker of the house.

1921 – W. W. Daley, Carbon county, president of the senate.
L. R. Ewart, Park county, speaker of the house.

1923 – Simon Skovgard, Big Horn county, president of the senate.
J. D. Noblitt, Lincoln county, speaker of the house.

1925 – Lewis H. Brown, Sweetwater county, president of the senate.
J. C. Underwood, Laramie county, speaker of the house.

1927 – Perry W. Jenkins, Sublette county, president of the senate.
A. W. McCullough, Albany county, speaker of the house.
1929 – Frank O. Horton, Johnson county, president of the senate.
M. L. Bishop, Jr., Natrona county, speaker of the house.
1931 – Clarence Gardner, Lincoln county, president of the senate.
Charles B. Mann, Big Horn county, speaker of the house.
1933 – Roy H. Cameron, Crook county, president of the senate.
Wm. M. Jack, Natrona county, speaker of the house.
1935 – N. A. Pearson, Sheridan county, president of the senate.
Henry D. Watenpaugh, Sheridan county, speaker of the house.
1937 – W. B. Saunders, Campbell county, president of the senate.
Herman F. Krueger, Park county, speaker of the house.
1939 – H. H. Horton, Albany county, president of the senate.
Herbert B. Fowler, Weston county, speaker of the senate.
1941 – Earl Wright, Sweetwater county, president of the senate.
Carl Robinson, Lincoln county, speaker of the house.
1943 – Russell H. Nichols, Natrona county, president of the senate.
Richard J. Luman, Sublette county, speaker of the house.

"I was elected a member of the lower house of the legislature in 1902. Governor Richards, Colonel E. A. Slack and the chairman of the Republican State Central committee requested me to father a bill for an appropriation for the Louisiana Purchase Exposition, which I took pleasure in doing. I had no trouble in securing ample sentiment for the measure, but one unpleasant situation arose. It seemed that in connection with some past litigation Colonel Slack's *Leader* had bitterly criticized a certain young lawyer, then a member of the house. He and his friends on the committee attached an amendment, providing that no one holding a federal office would be eligible for a place upon the commission. This would eliminate Colonel Slack, who was receiver of public moneys in the United States land office.

"I never made a harder fight in my life than in an effort to eliminate this personal thrust from the bill.

However, the majority voted for the amendment, either on personal grounds or because they felt that Colonel Slack, holding a remunerative public position, should be satisfied.

"After the legislature had adjourned, to my surprise, Governor Richards, upon a suggestion from Colonel Slack and his friends, appointed me as a member of the commission along with Clarence B. Richardson, who was commissioner-in-chief."

Miscellaneous Matters and Reminiscences

Among the interesting documents found in the files of Judge O. S. Deming was a two thousand dollar Confederate state's bond presented to him as a souvenir by one of his law partners, a native of Virginia, who had served in the Confederate army. Judge Deming was on the Union side. He was the father of William C. Deming.

"Woman suffrage throughout the United States is so well established in 1940 that it is difficult to realize it was almost a joke and a by-word in 1900, except in Wyoming and a few other commonwealths.

"However, the National Woman Suffrage association had been working for years and was beginning to see some hope for The Cause as they called it.

"Mrs. Harriet Taylor Upton, daughter of Judge and Mrs. Ezra B. Taylor, of Warren, Ohio, was treasurer of the association. Judge Taylor, a fine lawyer, had succeeded James A. Garfield in the house of representatives in congress when Garfield was made senator, and later president. When I arrived in Warren, Ohio Judge Taylor was in practical retirement and his hospitable home, on Mahoning avenue, with its majestic elms and maples, was a meeting place for many friends.

"Mr. and Mrs. George W. Upton conducted the home of Judge Taylor and both were always hospitable and entertaining. Mrs. Upton is now a resident of Pasadena, California.

"Among the visitors from time to time at the Taylor-

Upton home were Miss Susan B. Anthony, president of the National Woman Suffrage association, Mrs. Carrie Chapman Catt, organizer, Mrs. Maud Wood Park, the Reverend Anna Howard Shaw and Alice Stone Blackwell.

"I have heard them discuss woman suffrage and allied questions many times. They were all brilliant women, especially Mrs. Catt, who, upon the lecture platform was the equal of anyone I ever heard.

"Miss Anthony was prim, Puritan and severe. She looked the part of a crusader and expressed herself at all times with much frankness. I recall her saying, 'All great reforms move slowly, especially if they run counter to deep-seated prejudices and the views and opinions of the male sex. The men of America so long have been accustomed to considering women or wives largely as cooks or seamstresses or mothers of their children, that they cannot conceive of them having any ideas upon social, political or economic questions.'

"Mrs. Catt interpolated, 'It is still more difficult for men to understand that women have any rights, when it comes to money and property and those things ordinarily managed by the head of the family.' Just what Mrs. Upton said at the time I do not recall, but she had a great sense of humor and never hesitated to vent it at the expense of the opposition.

"However, I do remember that a modern young woman, who had been converted to the cause, upon hearing Miss Anthony's remark about the wife being largely a cook or seamstress or housekeeper, added with a twinkle in her eye, 'Or merely a lawful mistress.'

"Of course, that brought down the house.

"Most of them lived to see the realization of their dream and long-fought battle for the adoption of the

Nineteenth amendment to the constitution of the United States.

"I would enjoy hearing Mrs. Catt's reaction to the following from Buffalo, New York, november 8, 1939, by Dr. Will Durant, philosopher and author: 'A wife is no longer a useful partner in an ecomonic unit – she is almost a luxury.

" 'With industrialization of society, it (marriage) is no longer a unit of economic production' he told a civic group. 'A wife today is almost a luxury – a thing of beauty and probably a joy forever.' "

Discussing characteristics of many business men and others in relation to new enterprises and investments or needed changes in one's own line, Mr. Deming said: "Many business men seem to look for reasons for not doing a thing rather than reasons for doing something. Often there appears to be a natural tendency to hesitate or delay until all the circumstances are more favorable. That rarely occurs. If one expects to progress, he must be willing to take a chance."

John Charles Thompson, now editor of the *Tribune,* in his reminiscences discusses a visit of President Horace G. Burt of the Union Pacific railroad to Cheyenne during the shopmen's strike in 1902. When the brakeman attempted to throw the switch in order that Burt's private car could take the side track east of the depot, he found a spike had been driven in to prevent the switch from being opened. Burt took matters in his own hands, summarily discharged a division superintendent and forcibly opened the switch himself. The incident was recounted to Mr. Thompson by William H. Redd of Cheyenne, a porter on Burt's car, and for many years a faithful employee of the Union Pacific railroad. Redd served as custodian of the Majestic building, and is a good citizen and a leader among the colored people of Wyoming's capital city.

Mr. Deming adds the following:

"Horace Burt was a very able railroad man and a positive character. He was president of the Union Pacific system during the very serious strike in Cheyenne mentioned above.

"The situation became so alarming, as a result of some disorder, that a rumor spread through Cheyenne, as rapidly as a prairie fire travels, that the Union Pacific railroad shops in Cheyenne would be closed indefinitely. In fact, that statement was published in one of the newspapers.

"The business men and citizens generally were so frightened by the possibility of losing the shops that I, as publisher of the *Tribune,* went to Omaha and asked for an interview with President Burt. President Burt sat quietly in his office and talked very frankly, saying: 'The outcome of the strike, so far as it affects Cheyenne, depends as much upon the citizens of Cheyenne and the railroad men there as with the company. We have done much for our employes there and hope to do more, but, as William of Orange said: 'No nation can always be the assenting nation. The railroad has done practically all the assenting.'

"Mr. Burt also discussed the question of living conditions in Cheyenne. He said: 'If rents are higher than they should be the landlords know it and should settle that matter themselves. If living expenses are too high your business men know it and should find ways and means of improving that situation.' He urged patience in connection with the labor troubles and wound up with a reassuring statement, 'The Union Pacific railroad desires to do no injustice to the citizens of Cheyenne or its employees living there. The company will continue to operate its road and will not abandon its shops in Cheyenne.' That good news, telegraphed to the *Wyoming Tribune,* had a very excellent effect upon all concerned.

William C. Deming has known the various presidents of the Union Pacific Railroad since 1901, and has been a witness to the great improvements made in that system during that time. Grenville Dodge, the original chief engineer, of the Union Pacific Railroad, is credited with finding the pass over Sherman hill between Cheyenne and Laramie.

He wrote an interesting volume under the title *How we built the Union Pacific Railroad.* A few years ago Mr. Deming condensed that bit of history, along with other facts concerning the railroad, into a booklet which was widely distributed.

The life story of William Martin Jeffers is very closely bound up with the Union Pacific Railroad.

Jeffers, often referred to as the modern Horatio Alger, progressed from office boy in 1890 to president of the railroad system in 1937. The Union Pacific is Wyoming's most important transportation industry and William Jeffers is a living symbol of the company.

He is a native of North Platte, Nebraska, born january 2, 1876, one of nine children of Mr. and Mrs. William J. Jeffers. His father was an employe of the Union Pacific shops.

When "Bill" Jeffers was only 14 years old, he left school in order to contribute to the support of the family.

On june 1, 1890, Jeffers, as call boy, began his career with the railroad. During his first four years of railroad, he was successively promoted to clerk in the maintenance of way department, time-keeper and then as extra foreman of the steel gang.

He studied telegraphy during his free time. In 1894 he became telegrapher and after serving in this capacity for two years he was promoted to train dispatcher and in 1900 to chief dispatcher.

In june of that year he married Lena A. Schatz of North Platte, daughter of a Union Pacific employe. November, 1905 he acted as trainmaster at Green River, Wyoming and the following year went to Denver, Colorado in the same capacity.

He returned to Green River in 1907 as assistant superintendent, and in 1909 he became superintendent of the Wyoming division. When the territory, extending from Cheyenne, Wyoming to Ogden, Utah was consolidated into a single division in 1911, he became its superintendent.

Jeffers was only 39 years old when he was named superintendent of the Nebraska division. The same year he was promoted to general superintendent. A year later, june 3, 1916, he became general manager and on july 1, 1917 he served as both general manager and vice-president.

October 1, 1928 he was elected vice-president in charge of operations of the entire Union Pacific system, with approximately ten thousand miles of track extending from Omaha and Kansas City on the east, to Los Angeles and Portland on the Pacific coast.

In february, 1940 the Union Pacific published nationally an advertisement featuring the fact that the Union Pacific was originally planned by Abraham Lincoln for national defense, and stating that the railroad was then and is today the strategic central route connecting the East and the West coast.

The hundreds of trains daily over the Union Pacific, carrying men and material incident to the second world war emphasize the vision of President Lincoln.

Through the years of promotion to the presidency, Jeffers has never lost contact with the men in the ranks. The employees who "knew Jeff when" always feel free to walk into his office and discuss a railroad problem. He still carries a card in the telegrapher's union. He organized and is an active member of the Union Pacific Old Timers clubs, an organization restricted to employees who have served the railroad 20 years and in which no official can hold office. He also organized the Junior Old Timers clubs, whose members have served from 5 to 20 years.

In 1939, he brought to Omaha the world premiere of the motion picture epic, "Union Pacific," and took a prominent part in the organization of the Golden Spike Days celebration held in Omaha in connection with the exhibition, which directed national recognition to the city and to the railroad.

Concerned exclusively with railroad interests for 52 years, Jeffers was appointed national rubber administrator by President Franklin D. Roosevelt on september 15, 1942. Totally unfamiliar with the problems, he stepped into his new work with the same "Let's get it done" vigor he always has shown in his railroad career, and at the end of one year was able to report to the President the completion of the job, after which he returned to the Union Pacific Railroad.

Jeffers has been recognized for his contribution to American life by eminent educational institutions. He received the degree of Doctor of Laws from Franklin and Marshall college at Lancaster, Pa., in october, 1937; from Creighton university at Omaha in june,

1938; from the University of Wyoming at Laramie in june, 1939; from the College of Idaho at Caldwell in june, 1941; and from Notre Dame university in december, 1942.

In the old days as now there were slums and restricted districts and police court dockets and saturday night disturbances, among both the white and the colored. In that respect, human nature and conditions have not changed very much.

The Warren Tribune attempted to publish, as the *Denver Post* formerly said, "All the news that is fit to print," and probably some that was not very important.

"Throughout my professional life I made it a point to see all callers, if practicable, and never to keep them waiting unnecessarily," said Mr. Deming.

"Upon one occasion, Mandy Brown, a buxom colored woman, who was about half white, called to see me. She was exceedingly well dressed and in the vernacular of the day, 'looked like a million dollars.'

"With a subdued and hurt expression, after being seated, and wiping a timely tear from her eye, she handed me a copy of the *Tribune,* with a scarehead and detailed story of her fight with another colored woman, and the penalty imposed by the local police judge.

"She commented, 'Mr. Demmons, I can't tell you how bad I feels over this piece in the paper. It has hurt my reputation most powerful and it is not the first time I'se been written up. I'se been sick in bed ever since this was in the *Tribune* and wonders what I'se done to deserve such treatment.'

"Not thinking of anything better in response to her plea for sympathy, I replied, 'Mandy, you certainly don't look ill, in fact you look fine,' to which she

WILLIAM MARTIN JEFFERS
starting as call boy, became president of the Union Pacific Railroad Company

rejoined, 'That's just the trouble, Mr. Demmons, I always look so well that I never gits no sympathy.'

"I have used Mandy's epigram a great many times since when I felt that I was not getting proper consideration."

"Perhaps not many of the present generation in Wyoming know that the Thermopolis Hot springs are said to be the largest in the world, in flow of water. Neither is it well known that, in a treaty of april 21, 1896, grand old Chief Washakie, always a friend of the whites, transferred to the government of the United States the Big Horn Hot springs, now known as the Thermopolis Hot springs. About sixty-four thousand acres were involved, this being only a part of the Shoshone reservation at that time.

"Later the federal government conveyed or donated to the state of Wyoming the mile square containing the present Hot Springs state reserve. Subsequently the Wyoming legislature carried out Chief Washakie's wish that provisions should be made for free baths to the public, including the Indians.

"There have been very few more beautiful tributes written than Grace Raymond Hebard's life and work of Washakie. The story of his closing hours, on the evening of february 21, 1900, surrounded by his wife, sons and daughters, will appeal to the emotions of the stoutest heart. His last words were an admonition to his family and people to remain at peace with their white brethren and to conduct themselves as good citizens of the United States government which, he reminded them, had been paying him a pension each month for loyalty and service rendered.

"His people, as he called them, supplied fourteen soldiers for the great World war in 1917 and 1918,

five of whom saw over-seas service and others served
in Siberia and the Philippines. His handsome, young
grandson, John Washakie, who enlisted at Camp Lewis,
Washington, died there while in training on may 13,
1918.

"On october 1, 1941, the Devil's Tower in Crook
county, Wyoming attained nation-wide publicity as a
result of a rather simple incident.

"George Hopkins, claiming to be a parachute instructor in the army air corps, wagered fifty dollars
that he could make a descent and land squarely on the
top of Devil's Tower.

"It was much easier to win this bet than it was to
find a way down after the descent and collect the fifty
dollars. Wind, rain, and snow made his situation rather
uncomfortable, although relief in the way of blankets
and food was dropped from airplanes. It is claimed
that seven or eight thousand people were attracted to
the spot during the six days Hopkins was marooned.
In due time skilled mountain climbers from New
Hampshire, Massachusetts, Wyoming and Colorado
pooled their resources and rescued him.

"The Devil's Tower, a picture of which is published
herewith, is about twelve hundred feet higher than the
level of the Belle Fourche river and about eight hundred sixty-five feet from the base to the summit. It is
a very unusual formation of basalt, said to be of volcanic
origin.

"Apparently, ten or fifteen million years ago, there
was an uplift and in the ages that have passed, the less
substantial material and lava, which accompanied the
upward thrust eroded or have blown away. The diam-
eter at the base is about one thousand feet. And the
area of the summit is more than one acre.

Closing Thoughts: or Fifty Years After
by MR. DEMING

If one could look forward as he is able to look backward, the story of each human life might be vastly different.

Some few visit fortune-tellers, others invest in a horoscope reading, while the majority of matter-of-fact, unsuperstitious individuals or Doubting Thomases just plod on, taking things pretty much as they come.

If misfortune threatens, they say it is fate or perhaps blame the signs of the zodiac, forgetting, as Marc Antony said: "The fault, dear Brutus, is not in our stars; but in ourselves that we are underlings."

I hesitate to classify myself except to say my life-season's harvest might have been worse and the returns much less.

On the asset side, there have been, for the most part, good health, many loyal friends, a fine father and mother, two brothers and a sister.

My brother David S., a most interesting and lovable character, died july 19, 1940, at his home in Kentucky on the eve of his departure for a visit in Wyoming. David Deming was a conservative businessman, owned considerable property, and had served for many years as director of the local bank at Mt. Olivet, of which his father had once been president. His widow, Sarah Reveal Deming, survives.

David's two sons, Osmer S. and William, also are citizens of the Blue Grass state.

Osmer S. Deming, commonly called "O.S.", has displayed unusual business ability. He began operating gasoline filling stations in southern Florida, chiefly in Miami, after the first World war, and owned or controlled about forty when the second World war began.

Not satisfied with building up one substantial industry under the name of the Superior Oil company of Florida, working in close association with the Cities Service company, he initiated a large enterprise in his home state of Kentucky.

About five or six years ago he quietly obtained options upon a large tract of land in the heart of the tobacco commission house district of Lexington, Kentucky, and proceeded to the financing of a new building which would cover several acres.

He was fully cognizant of the fact that Lexington was the center of a very large tobacco marketing commission business that had been rather closely controlled by old families and long established companies in the Blue Grass district.

His thought was to make his new warehouse the most modern in Lexington and one that would assure competition with old firms. His plans were carried out to the letter, and the war prices of tobacco have made the enterprise a success from the beginning.

Osmer and his wife, Lorena, are the parents of a beautiful ten year old girl, Joe Ann, who much resembles Shirley Temple at that age.

David's second son, William Thomas, and his wife, Katherine, have two bright boys, William T. jr. (Billy), eighteen years old and Jimmy, fifteen, the latter promising to be something of a naturalist. He expects to join the navy in june, 1944.

Billy began investigating and assembling radios

Mr. and Mrs. David S. Deming

brother of William C. Deming and father of O. S. Deming, Jr. and William T. Deming of Kentucky

Mr. and Mrs. Deming W. Morrison of Los Angeles, California

STAFF-SERGEANT WILLIAM T. DEMING

Instructor in Radar, Terminal Island, California   when in the U.S. Marines

JAMES DEMING
son of Mr. and Mrs. William T. Deming,
joins U.S. Navy 1944

HARRY, JOAN, AND ALLEN MORRISON
children of Major and Mrs. Deming W. Morrison

when he was in the grade schools, and according to a recent issue of the *Leatherneck,* a publication of the marines in Washington, D.C., he is the youngest radar technician in the United States. After training as a marine at Treasure Island, San Francisco, he may enter Massachusetts Institute of Technology in Boston. Radar is the new invention for radio detection, and is a highly secret method, controlled by the United States army and navy.

My brother, Thomas H. Deming, remained a bachelor, why I do not know, as he always has been fond of womankind and is a favorite with the fair sex. He adheres closely to newspaper work, plays golf and bridge as a diversion, and keeps in close touch with his young nephews and nieces, encouraging them in many substantial ways to prepare for the battle of life. He is still editor of the Warren, Ohio, *Tribune,* takes life philosophically, has accumulated a reasonable competence, and is liberal with his benevolences. He never held political office and never wanted to. He cares little for society, and has no illusions about life. He is blessed with good friends. His ability has gained for him recognition in "Who's Who in America."

My sister, Adah Deming Morrison, after many years of happy married life with her husband, William H. Morrison, a native of Kentucky, is now a widow. She is active in the Christian church, the P.E.O., Daughters of the American Revolution, Woman's club, and other local organizations. She has shown remarkable capacity in looking after her own business affairs. She has a beautiful home in Wheatland, Wyoming, and spends part of the winter in California. She is all that a loving sister could be.

Adah was the youngest, and by far the best in every

way of the four children. Her son, Deming W. Morrison, is a graduate of Leland Stanford University and is an authority on many forms of civil engineering. As chief of the division of dams on the ten-year, seventy-million-dollar flood control project in Los Angeles county and vicinity he carried heavy responsibility. He is now a major in the United States army, as chief engineer of construction, and has been transferred from his headquarters at San Bernardino, California to Salt Lake City, Utah. He has a fine wife, Agnes, and two alert young boys, Allen, sixteen years of age, and Harry, fourteen, and a clever little girl, Joan, ten years old. She is also very attractive.

When I was a boy in Kentucky, the most affluent man in the community was said to be worth fifty thousand dollars, equal in purchasing power to one hundred thousand dollars today. Lawyers and newspaper men rarely got a very high rating in Dun & Bradstreet, and I did not expect to do any better than the "run-of-the-mine" professional men.

However, I did discover that I had some talent for organization and certain business instincts that might be developed under favorable circumstances, but that was the rub – the field or the opportunity seemed remote.

As I survey my youth and early manhood, it appears I had but two ambitions, if such they may be called. One was to give vent to my aptitude, I thought, for public speaking, which began, no doubt, with "Twinkle, Twinkle, Little Star," "The Boy Stood on the Burning Deck," "The Village Blacksmith," or "The Seminole's Reply."

I was thrilled and fascinated by the platform or political orator, of which there were many, especially

MAJOR DEMING W. MORRISON
son of Mrs. Adah Deming Morrison

at campaign time. That naturally suggested some form of public life, perhaps congress in the days to come.

It was merely a fleeting fancy, no doubt.

The other conviction, hope, or belief, was that I would marry young and become the father of children, without which, it seemed to me, life would be as Dead Sea fruit.

Now I find myself called upon to strike a balance. The verbal or rhetorical outlet has been intermittent. Effective, popular discourse or public reasoning requires constant practice and application.

As to married life and family, that phase appears in earlier pages of this book.

I do not pretend to say the whole could or could not have been better or worse. I must, of necessity, leave it as Byron said in *Childe Harold's Pilgrimage*, "And what is writ is writ – would it were worthier."

Without any special desire or effort to possess money or property other than enough for comfort and some luxuries, including travel, I find that I have exceeded such limitations measurably. I trust my stewardship has not been wholly selfish.

I am willing to close this anthology – collection of "flowers" from my friends with these lines:

> "How great would we be, have I often conceived,
> Had we really achieved what we nearly achieved.
> We but grasp at the skirts of the thing we would be
> And fall back in the lap of a false destiny.
> Thus it is, thus it has been since this world began,
> The truest, the noblest, the best part of man
> Is that part which he hath ne'er fully played out;
> The first and last word in life's volume is doubt."

One of my Wyoming critics, who has looked over this manuscript, objects to my closing words as set forth in the quotation above. Perhaps the tenor was influenced somewhat by the fact that almost every writer from Bible days to Pythagoras, Shakespeare, Burns, Pope and modern authors seems to emphasize the frailties, the disappointments, the weariness, the pains, the struggles, the hardships, the emptiness, the solemnity and the vanities of human life rather than its achievements, its pleasures, its satisfactions, and its compensations.

In deference, therefore, to my friend's opinion, it may be worth while to add these lines:

> "Our lives are albums, written through
> With good or ill, with false or true;
> And as the blessed angels turn
> The pages of our years,
> God grant they read the good with smiles
> And blot the ill with tears."–*Whittier*.

WILLIAM THOMAS DEMING
son of David S. Deming

OSMER S. DEMING
son of David S. Deming;
in World War I cadet uniform

DEMING W. MORRISON
son of Adah Deming Morrison;
as a high school graduate

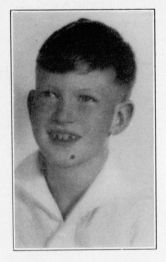 

ALLEN MORRISON   HARRY MORRISON
and Joan (below) Children of Major and Mrs. Deming W. Morrison of Calif.

JOAN MORRISON   JOE ANN DEMING
                            daughter of Osmer S. and Lorena
                                    Deming of Ky.

MR. AND MRS. OSMER S. DEMING OF CYTHIANA, KENTUCKY

MRS. WILLIAM T. DEMING
of Mt. Olivet, Kentucky

WILLIAM T. DEMING
son of above

JAMES DEMING
son of above

Appendix

Generations in the Deming Family

David W. Deming   Pennsylvania
Almira Sage Deming   Pennsylvania

. . .

Osmer S. Deming   Kentucky
Leona Rigg Deming   Kentucky

. . .

William C. Deming   Wyoming
David S. Deming   Kentucky
Thomas H. Deming   Ohio
Adah D. Morrison   Wyoming

. . .

Osmer S. Deming   Kentucky
William T. Deming   Kentucky
Deming W. Morrison   California

. . .

William T. Deming   Kentucky
James Deming   Kentucky
Joe Ann Deming   Kentucky
Allen D. Morrison   California
William Harry Morrison   California
Joan Morrison   California

Positions Held by William C. Deming

President, Philomathean Literary Society, Mt. Olivet, Kentucky.

President, Allegheny Literary Society, Meadville, Pennsylvania.

President, Alpha Chapter, Delta Tau Delta Fraternity, Allegheny College, Meadville, Pennsylvania.

President, Class of Ninety, Allegheny College, Meadville, Pennsylvania.

President, Joshua R. Giddings Club, Warren, Ohio.

President, Tribune Company, Warren, Ohio.

President, Young Men's Christian Association, Warren, Ohio.

President, Tribune Publishing Company, Cheyenne, Wyoming.

President, Stockman-Farmer Company, Cheyenne, Wyoming.

President, Deming Realty Company, Cheyenne, Wyoming.

President, Original Cheyenne Radio Corporation.

President, Young Men's Literary Club, Cheyenne, Wyoming.

President, Wyoming Press Association.

President, Board of Trustees, University of Wyoming.

President, United States Civil Service Commission, Washington, D.C.

The more important Published Writings of William C. Deming

America's Disabled Veterans: in *Current History,* april 1931, vol. XXXIV, no. 1.

Application of the Merit System in the United States Civil Service. Articles and addresses of William C. Deming, president of the U.S. Civil Service commission, Washington, G.P.O., 1927) 76 pp.

Balaam and his literary mule. 6 pp.

Blue-gray yarn or the woman at the rail (fiction) 26 pp., 1927.

Buying a newspaper by Burn Brunk: in *The Independent Magazine,* vol. 75, no. 3380, september 11, 1913.

Directions to Wyoming Tribune Correspondents. 1 p.

Don'ts for Editors and Reporters. 1 p.

Give us more "Muracals." Hundreds of children sit reverently through the Passion Play. Folder, 6 pp., october, 1943.

He was a "Forty-niner." William Packard, grandfather of the inventor of the Packard Automobile lost in California for many years. 8 pp. 1943.

Helen Hamilton Gardener (Alice Chenoweth Day). 1853-1929. 31 pp.

Inception and building of the Union Pacific-Central Pacific Railways. History of early proposals for transcontinental lines and legislation authorizing construction of Union Pacific and Central Pacific prove conclusively that congress contemplated one continuous railroad from Missouri river to the Bay of San Francisco. 19 pp.

The Miracle of Helen Keller.

My Interview in 1897 at Ellsworth, Ohio, with James R. Greene who saw the Battle of Waterloo. 8 pp.

Old Stage-Coach Days: being a more or less True Story of Two Tenderfeet and a Lone Woman. 4 pp. april 1943.

Presidents and the Senate: in *Washington Star.* 9 pp.

Roosevelt in the Bunk House and other sketches: Visits of the Great Rough Rider to Wyoming in 1900, 1903, and 1019 (c 1927). 80 pp.

Seeing Europe with the editor of the Wyoming Tribune. Cheyenne,
    1913. 43 pp.

Theodore Roosevelt, as he appeared in 1910. (1919) 8 pp.

Sixty-five Years of the Tribune-Leader.

The Tamiami Trail.

Thomas Jefferson, statesman and inventor.

The Valley of the Shadow (1942). 4 pp.

What the Old Preacher Said (october 1, 1942). 4 pp.

Who Was Cain's Wife?

Magazine and Newspaper Articles
by William C. Deming*

After graduation, what?

Asia may be Kaiser's undoing.

Bridge work—past and present, by the dentist.

Business methods that encourage crime.

Chicago brownstone house yields rare art treasures.

Cops are not ducks.

The double-deck bus, by the rubberneck.

Dry farming receipt from state commission of dry farming experiments.

Dying at 57.

The ecstatic venture of life, by a wayfarer.

Examination of a master, by Masters.

First classified civil service employee still going strong, Doctor Doyle.

General U. S. Grant.

The girl and her dad, by one of the boys.

God moves in mysterious ways.

Have pigeons a sense of humor?

Horace Greeley, Nathan C. Meeker and the Union colony in Colorado.

How do they do it? by the traffic cop.

How to succeed though rich.

"I could love your baby, too." Lyrics by W. C. Deming, music by Jimmy Maxwell and J. Paul Monson.

Is apple pie extinct?

Is the bath brush passé?

It is not sufficient that a city should be prosperous – it should be beautiful also. Miami, Florida. april 1937.

June weather in San Diego, 1915.

Key West, like Job, has had many trials and tribulations.

---

*Miscellaneous writings of W. C. Deming are being prepared for publication, to be included in a collection of his addresses, editorials, essays and other papers.

Lafayette, we are here! (A poem.)

"Lafayette, we are here!" Spoken by Colonel C. E. Stanton not General Pershing, the commander-in-chief said.

Link in "Linkum" Highway, by the tourist.

Lo, the poor Indian, still a mere ward of Uncle Sam.

A Mexican bull fight.

Miracles, ancient and modern – people always wanting a sign.

The night air mail, by the star gazer.

Notes here and there.

Our most privileged character.

Pennsylvania Avenue street cars should go – also Treasury building.

Pension hysteria subsiding in California.

The pound sterling recognized in Virginia.

President of Civil Service commission thinks passage of Brookhart bill to bring present prohibition employees into classified service without examination would be a breach of faith with thousands of applicants.

President Theodore Roosevelt's letter written in 1903.

Question for "Information Please."

Radio, spirit and immortality, by a layman.

The Reclamation act and farming by irrigation.

The Red devils, by the semaphore.

Safety of bank deposits the desideratum.

Some suggestions relating to dry land farming.

Something about dry farming, 1912.

Suggestions for resolutions at Salt Lake republican meeting, october 18 and 19, 1935.

Thomas Jefferson while president was hard pushed for funds.

The *Tribune Chronicle* – past and present (Warren, Ohio).

Washington needs a matrimonial agency, by the accelerator.

What do you know about rainbows?

What is the answer?

What's in a name? by the referee.

Why the fair lady screamed.

White lines and a dark cop, by the bumper.

Women and oriental mysticism.

Yes, girls, it's coming! by the moss back.

Yes, it all depends – no formula for success.†

---

†There were hundreds more on a great variety of subjects.

Addresses of William C. Deming*

Abraham Lincoln.

Address at Allegheny college, Meadville, Pa., october 7, 1924.

Address before the alumni and active members of the Delta Tau Delta at Philadelphia, Pa., march 29, 1924.

Address before Illinois federation of women's clubs, at Chicago, Ill., may 19, 1926.

Application of the merit system in the United States civil service: articles and addresses of William C. Deming, president, U.S. civil service commission. (Washington, G.P.O., 1927) 76 pp. *(printed)*.

Bank advertising: address before Wyoming Bankers' association.

Benjamin Franklin. 21 pp. *(printed)*.

California and the Japanese: address before Young Men's literary club, 1921.

Cheyenne, past, present and to come: a prophecy and a retrospect. 1922.

Classified civil service of United States: address before Virginia federation of women's clubs, Richmond, Va., may 21, 1925.

Constitution of the United States: address before the Laramie county bar association on the anniversary year of the birth of the United States's constitution.

Decoration day address.

The drama as an educational and moral factor: address before Woman's club, Cheyenne, Wyo., 1912. 8 pp. *(printed)*.

Essentials of success: address before the Rawlins high school graduating class.

The evolution of popular government. Patriotic address, wednesday evening, december 6, 1916, at the close of the Knight Kadosh Degree, thirty-first reunion, Wyoming consistory. (Quality Print Shop, Cheyenne, Wyo.). 8 pp. *(printed)*.

The Federal civil service. Address before the Public Service institute, at Hotel Somerset, Boston, Mass., march 16, 1927.

Flag Day address at Elks home, Cheyenne, june 14, 1938.

George Washington, the Mason.

How a letter of a country lawyer became international law. (Wyo. Labor Journal, Cheyenne). 11 pp. illus. *(printed)*.

Isms and schisms, scrip and scripture in California. An address before the Cheyenne Rotary club, july 12, 1939.

Life of George Washington. (Pioneer Pr. Co., Cheyenne). 28 pp.

Life of Robert Burns. Address before the Burns club at Cheyenne, january 27, 1913 (published by request in Wyoming-Tribune).

Mary, Queen of Scots.

The opportunity and duty of the press in relation to world peace. Address at Lake Mohonk Conference on International Arbitration, on may 17, 1912. (Washington, G.P.O., 1912). Senate document no. 764, 62d congress 2d session. 8 pp. *(printed)*.

Major opportunities for the local Chamber of Commerce and the city of Cheyenne during 1935.

The making of a nation. Address before the Pennsylvania State society, Sons of the American Revolution, Pittsburgh, Pa., february 22, 1926. 14 pp. (printed).

Napoleon.

Our good neighbor Nebraska.

Presents strong case against Roosevelt administration and its policies and programs. Address before Lincoln club, Cheyenne, Wyoming. may 8, 1939.

Presidents I have known. (Douglas Enterprise, Douglas, 1942). 23 pp. (printed).

Remarks of William C. Deming, president of the Tribune publishing company and president of the United States Civil Service commission at the dedication of the new Tribune-Leader building in Cheyenne, saturday, july 20, 1929, by the National Editorial association.

Remarks before Kiwanis club, Washington, D.C., may 24, 1923.

Remarks before national spelling bee contest, New National Museum, Washington, D.C., june 17, 1925.

Remarks at railroad day banquet, Cheyenne, june 13, 1935.

Richard Mansfield. Address given before Young Men's Literary club.

The twelfth legislature (1913) and its opportunities. Address before the Young Men's Literary club.

A tribute to John B. Kendrick, the man and statesman. Address at First Methodist church, Cheyenne, november 12, 1933.

What do you know about Texas? Address before the Cheyenne Rotary club, september 1941.

Young Men's Literary club still going strong – is now 40 years old.

*The Addresses in the above list which have not heretofore been printed are being prepared for publication. They will be included in a collection of Mr. Deming's Addresses and Writings.

The Young Men's Literary Club

MEMBERSHIP 1942-1943

BENNETT, REV. C. A. – Rector, St. Mark's church (Episcopal); former Rotary club president.

BLACKMAN, REV. J. C. – Pastor, Congregational church.

BLUME, JUDGE F. H. – Justice, Wyoming supreme court; former attorney, Sheridan, Wyo.; state senator; authority on Roman law.

BREWSTER, WILLETS

CLARK, DR. JOHN D. – Attorney; vice-president, Standard of Indiana; nationally known economist and college lecturer.

CLARK, ROBERT G. – Attorney (resigned). In U.S. Army.

DINNEEN, W. J. – Automobile dealer; president, Cheyenne chamber of commerce.

GRIER, R. S. – Young business man; assoc. mgr. Grier Lumber company; former member, Wyoming legislature; colonel U.S.A.

HENDERSON, H. B., SR. – Retired former state bank examiner; former banker.

HENDERSON, H. B., JR. – Captain of artillery in World War I; lawyer, Cheyenne city attorney; former Nat. vice-commander American legion; chairman republican state committee.

HEWLETT, GEORGE W. – Retired lieut.-commander U.S. navy; former republican state chairman; ranchman and business man; former member Wyoming legislature.

HOFMANN, R. J. – Owner and manager Cheyenne Elevator company; county commissioner; member, Cheyenne frontier committee; business leader.

HUNT, DR. L. C. – Dentist; former state senator; twice secretary of state, Wyoming; governor of Wyoming.

JOHNSTON, DR. GEO. P. – Physician and surgeon; former city councilman.

KENNEDY, JUDGE T. BLAKE – Judge of U.S. district court for district of Wyoming; former attorney; prominent mason; elk; church, and club matters.

KIMBALL, JUDGE RALPH – Justice of Wyoming supreme court; former prominent attorney, Lander, Wyo.; state senator.

KLINE, M. A. – Practicing attorney.

LAUGHLIN, R. B. – Attorney; member, Wyoming legislature. In U.S. Army.

LAZEAR, E. T. – Local Union Pacific attorney; former president, chamber of commerce; state senator.

LOOMIS, JOHN U. – Union Pacific attorney; former president, chamber of commerce; former president, Cheyenne Rotary club.

MARBLE, FRED W. – Vice-president, Stock Growers National bank.

MILLER, L. A. – Twice governor of Wyoming; former state land commissioner and state senator; former U.S. internal revenue collector for Wyoming; regional director of W.P.B.

MULLEN, W. E. – Attorney; formerly attorney-general of Wyoming.

NORRIS, W. A. (PAT) – Proprietor, Wortham Machinery company; state senator.

RINER, JUDGE W. A. – Justice, Wyoming supreme court; former attorney of Cheyenne.

ROEDEL, A. E., JR. – Proprietor, Roedel's drug store.

SAMPSON, L. C. – Attorney; formerly asst.-attorney-general, Wyo.

SWAINSON, C. A. – Attorney and U.S. referee in bankruptcy.

THOMPSON, J. C. – Secretary to acting-governor Houx; editor, *Wyoming State Tribune;* authority on Wyoming history and pioneer characters.

THOMPSON, JUDGE S. M. – Judge, district court, first judicial district, Wyoming; formerly, Laramie county attorney.

WALTON, A. D. – Attorney; formerly U.S. district attorney for Wyoming; active in masonic circles and politics.

WALTON, J. H. – For several years business manager of the *Wyoming Tribune;* now president, Walton Motor company; former cashier, Stock Growers National bank.

WALTON, ROBT. B. – Secretary, Walton Motor company; active in Wyoming national guard; lieutenant-colonel, U.S.A.

WATSON, H. G. – City engineer; formerly asst. state engineer; active in state masonic work; formerly on state land board.

WATTS, C. M. – Attorney; former district judge; asst.-U.S.-district attorney; member, Wyoming legislature.

Early Members of the Club

ARGESHEIMER, J. C. – Chief clerk of house and senate and city auditor and assessor; former newspaper editior.

BAKER, A. – Chief of Cheyenne field division of U.S. general land office; state land commissioner; district governor of Lions international.

BARTLETT, S. B. – Civil engineer.

BEELER, H. C. – Former state geologist.

BENNETT, H. M. – Prominent physician and surgeon.

BRECKONS, J. A. – Secretary and right-hand man of U.S. Senator F. E. Warren.

BREWSTER, PAUL – Aristocratic citizen and gentleman of leisure.

BRISTOL, E. L. – Head of S. A. Bristol Printing company.

BURGESS, DR. W. A. – Physician and surgeon; county health officer.

CALDWELL, THE REVEREND R. G. – Pastor First Presbyterian church.

CAREY, ROBERT D. – Cattle ranchman; president Wyoming Stock Growers' association; governor of Wyoming; chairman of state highway commission; U.S. senator.

CARLISLE, C. C. – City engineer; assistant state engineer and other responsible technical positions.

CHAPLIN, W. E. – Editor *Laramie Republican;* member of first state constitutional convention; register of U.S. land office; secretary of state.

CLARK, E. T. – Asst. United States attorney; member of legislature.

COCHRAN, GRIFFIN – Former newspaper man; died in France during World war.

CONWAY, J. H. DR. – Financier and physician.

DEBELLE, K. W. – Former newspaper man.

DEMING, W. C. – Member of Wyoming legislature; receiver of public moneys, in U.S. land office; president, board of trustees, University of Wyoming; president, U.S. Civil Service Commission nearly eight years; former owner, Wyoming *Tribune-Leader;* and president Deming Realty company.

DUBOIS, WILLIAM – Architect (leading Wyoming); member of legislature; director, Stock Growers National bank.

DUNTON, W. H. – Former Cheyenne attorney and sheep rancher.

EVANS, GEORGE H. – Former Cheyenne newspaper man.

FEE, I. B. – Former superintendent of Cheyenne schools.

FISHER, REV. C. F. – Minister.

FULLER, R. P. – State land commissioner; assistant secretary of state.

GOODRICH, R. D. – City engineer; assistant state engineer; dean, engineering department of University of Wyoming.

HAAS, WILLIAM G. – Postmaster, chairman of Frontier Days committee.

HAGGARD, AVERY – Cheyenne attorney; president, Cheyenne Lions club and director of Lions international.

HANNUM, J. E. – Former manager, Continental Oil company, Cheyenne.

HARRIS, REV. R. L. – Rector, St. Marks church, later a Bishop.

HARTUNG, M. H. – Member of state senate.

HAY, HARRY G. – Former Cheyenne banker.

HILLS, REV. L. C. – Pastor, First Presbyterian church.

HOWELL, D. J. – Assistant, United States attorney; attorney-general for Wyoming.

HUNTER, THOMAS – Attorney and rancher; member of legislature; president of Lions club; president, Cheyenne Chamber of Commerce.

HUSTON, REV. S. A. – Rector, St. Mark's church; later became a bishop in Episcopal church.

JOHNSTON, A. D. – Former prominent Cheyenne banker.

JOHNSTON, CLARENCE T. – State engineer; professor of engineering, University of Michigan.

KELLEY, A. D. – Several times member of house of representatives and state senate; speaker of house; former sheriff, Laramie county.

KELLEY, E. J. – Former Cheyenne business man; prominent elk.

KENDRICK, JOHN B. – State senator; former governor of Wyoming; United States senator; prominent in ranching, banking and business, Sheridan, Wyo.

KINGDON, J. E. – Former asst. state engineer.

KIRK, LOUIS – Clerk, United States court; secretary, J. M. Carey and Bro.

LARSH, W. L. – Postmaster; former state agent New York Life Insurance company.

LeCRON, JAMES D. – Secretary to Governor J. M. Carey; later prominent newspaperman of Des Moines, Iowa; private secretary to Secretary of Agriculture Henry A. Wallace.

LEE, A. K. – State senator and banker.

LEE, RAY E. – State land commissioner; attorney-general; prominent Cheyenne attorney.

LIKERT, GEORGE – Union Pacific railway coal expert.

MALLIN, CHARLES F. – Attorney.

MATSON, R. N. – Member Wyoming legislature; Judge of first judicial district; president, Wyoming Bar association; member, board of trustees, University of Wyoming; commissioner of United States to International Exposition at Seville, Spain, in 1928; Doctor of Laws, Syracuse University, 1929; appointed minister to Greece in 1933 by President Hoover.

MATHEWS, J. Q. – Former superintendent of Colorado and Southern railroad.

McFETRIDGE, REV. R. J. – Rector, St. Mark's church.

MENTZER, WILLIAM C. – Judge of first judicial district.

MERRILL, GEORGE E. – Former prominent lumber dealer.

MOORE, REV. F. L. – Pastor, First Congregational church.

OHNHAUS, C. J. – Clerk, U.S. court; vice-president, AmericanNatl. bank.

O'LEARY, WILFRID – Successful corporation attorney; deputy attorney-general.

PALMER, W. S. – Former meteorologist of Cheyenne weather bureau.

PHELAN, W. Q. – Attorney; chairman, democratic state central committee; commander, Knights of Columbus for southern Wyoming.

RENO, MAJOR W. W. – United States army.

RICHARDSON, C. B. – Commissioner in both St. Louis and Portland Expositions; American consul, Chihuahua, Mexico; large oil operator.

RIGDON, C. L. – U.S. attorney; county attorney.

RINER, C. W. – Member of Wyoming house and senate; councilman and mayor of Cheyenne.

ROSS, WILLIAM B. – County attorney; president, Kiwanis club; governor of Wyoming.

ROYER, D. C. – President, Cheyenne Business college.

SCHROEDER, J. H. – Former Cheyenne business man; member legislature.

SCHWEIRING, O. C. – Principal, Cheyenne High school; dean, college of education, University of Wyoming.

SEVISON, Z. E. – State highway engineer.

SHELDON, F. B. – Deputy state treasurer.

SINCLAIR, BURKE H. – Private secretary to Governor Kendrick; Colonel of 148th field artillery, World war; major, Wyoming national guard.

SKINNER, MAJOR G. A. – United States army.

STEEVER, E. Z. – Colonel in American expeditionary forces and originator of present system of high school military training.

STONE, E. W. – Member of state senate; president, state senate; mayor of Cheyenne; high ranking Mason.

STRADER, DR. GEORGE L. – Eye, ear, nose and throat specialist; member of Wyoming house of representatives; member, Cheyenne school board.

TYSON, L. R. – Railway mail clerk.

VANCE, A. J. – Manager, Mountain States Telephone company.

VREELAND, J. E. – Grocer.

WALKER, G. S. – Former Cheyenne newspaper and business man.

WARREN, FRED E. – President, Warren Livestock company; Cheyenne business man and banker.

WETLAUFER, N.R. – Former physician.

WHITING, J. A. – State engineer; city engineer; member, Cheyenne city council.

WILCOX, T. PAUL – Official reporter of first judicial district; assistant attorney-general; city attorney, Cheyenne; president, Rotary club, Cheyenne.

WYMAN, DR. W. A. – Secretary, state board of health; county physician and city physician.

Members of the State Highway Commission

Name	Qualified	Term of Office	Address
Francis C. Williams	Mar. 21, 1917	For 4 yrs. from feb. 24, 1917	Sheridan
Joe Kinney	March 20, 1917	For 2 yrs. from feb. 24, 1917	Cokeville
Gus Holm's	Feb. 28, 1917	For 4 yrs. from feb. 24, 1917	Cody
Robert D. Carey	March 1, 1917	For 6 yrs. from feb. 24, 1917	Careyhurst
M. R. Johnston	Feb. 27, 1917	For 2 yrs. from feb. 24, 1917	Wheatland
William R. Weeks	Feb. 20, 1919	For 6 yrs. from feb. 24, 1917	Lander
Joseph C. Kinney	April 8, 1919	For 4 yrs. from feb. 28, 1919	Cokeville
LeRoy Laird	March 5, 1919	For 2 yrs. from feb. 28, 1919	Worland
L. R. A. Condit	Feb. 28, 1919	For 6 yrs. from feb. 28, 1919	Barnum
W. R. Weeks	Feb. 28, 1919	For 2 yrs. from feb. 28, 1919	Riverton
M. R. Johnston	Feb. 28, 1919	For 4 yrs. from feb. 28, 1919	Wheatland
LeRoy Laird	Feb. 26, 1921	For 6 yrs. from feb. 28, 1921	Worland
S. W. Conwell	Feb. 25, 1921	For 6 yrs. from feb. 28, 1921	Casper
John M. Snyder	June 1, 1921	June 1, 1921 - feb. 28, 1927	Lovell
(Vice L. E. Laird, resigned)			
Hiram D. Lingle	April 24, 1923	4 years from april 24, 1923	Lingle
Thomas O'Neill	Feb. 3, 1924	6 years from feb. 28, 1923	Big Piney
Roy Seney	Feb. 25, 1925	6 years from feb. 1925	Sheridan
Francis Johnstone	Sept. 28, 1925	Sept. 15, 1925 - feb. 28, 1931	Carlile
(Vice Roy Seney, resigned)			
John M. Snyder	March 4, 1927	6 years from march 1, 1927	Lovell
S. W. Conwell	March 4, 1927	6 years from march 1, 1927	Casper
Fred G. S. Hesse	April 1, 1927	March 1, 1927 - feb. 28, 1931	Buffalo
(Vice F. Johnstone, resigned)			
Fred M. Mills	Feb. 28, 1929	6 years from feb. 28, 1929	Rock Springs
Nels H. Smith	April 4, 1929	March 25, 1929-feb. 28, 1931	Horton
(Unexpired term of Fred G. S. Hesse, deceased)			
Royce F. Tebbet	May 3, 1929	6 years from april 24, 1929	Torrington
Nels H. Smith	March 17, 1931	6 yrs. from feb. 28, 1931	Horton
Ralph E. Foe	Feb. 24, 1933	6 yrs. from march 1, 1933	Greybull
Wilson S. Kimball	Feb. 28, 1933	6 yrs. from march 1, 1933	Casper
Louis J. O'Marr	Feb. 23, 1933	Feb. 18, 1933 - -mar. 1, 1937	Sheridan
(To succeed Nels H. Smith)			
W. J. Witherspoon	Feb. 7, 1935	6 yrs. from feb. 28, 1935	Kemmerer
(To succeed Fred M. Mills)			
Royce F. Tebbet	Feb. 7, 1935	6 yrs. from apr. 24, 1935	Torrington
(To succeed W. S. Kimball)			
Dist. No. 3			
Gwynne Schoonmaker	Feb. 18, 1939	6 yrs. from march 1, 1939	Lander
(To succeed Ralph E. Foe)			

Dist. No. 4
THOMAS O. COWGILL   Feb. 18, 1939   6 yrs. from march 1, 1939   Cody
Dist. No. 5
WILLIAM E. TAYLOR   Feb. 28, 1939   4 yrs. from march 1, 1939   Gillette
(To succeed Louis J. O'Marr whose term expired March 1, 1937)
E. D. CRIPPA   March 1, 1941   6 yrs. from feb. 28, 1941   Rock Springs
(Succeeding W. J. Witherspoon)
G. M. WORTH   March 8, 1941   6 yrs. from April 24, 1941   Wheatland
(Succeeding Royce Tebbet)
J. M. KEAHEY   March 1943   6 yrs. from march 1, 1943   Buffalo
(Succeeding W. E. Taylor)

STATE HIGHWAY SUPERINTENDENTS
AND ENGINEERS

Title	Name	Length of Service
State highway engineer	Z. E. Sevison	April 1, 1917 - march 1927
State highway superintendent	D. S. McCalman	Feb. 28, 1919 - feb. 1922
State highway superintendent	LeRoy Laird	Feb. 1922 - 1927
State highway supt.-engineer	Z. E. Sevison	March 1927 - june 1933
State highway supt.-engineer	C. H. Bowman	June 1933 - sept. 1933
State highway supt.-engineer	James B. True	Sept. 1933 - sept. 1937
State highway supt.-engineer	C. F. Seifried	Sept. 1937 - march 1939
State highway superintendent	Frank Kelso	March 1939 - jan. 1943
State highway engineer	C. F. Seifried	March 1939 - jan. 1943
State highway superintendent	C. F. Seifried	January 1943 - july 1943
State highway superintendent	J. G. Smith	July 1943 -
State highway superintendent	J. R. Bromley	1944 -

STATE HIGHWAY DEPARTMENT
Receipts and Disbursements
April 1, 1917 - Sept. 30, 1942

RECEIPTS

CASH:

Motor Vehicle License Tax	$ 7,430,943.54
Gasoline License Tax	23,064,001.85
Commercial Vehicle Compensatory Fees	1,872,757.40
Gasoline Dealers License Fees	18,007.00
Oil Royalties	10,053,585.24
Federal Aid	42,447,293.89
City, County, and Other Aid	1,915,261.56
Public Service Commission Permit Fees	105,785.22
Bonds	7,400,000.00
Bond Premium	19,573.00
State Appropriations	1,200,000.00
Miscellaneous Cash	861,386.52

OTHER THAN CASH:

Trade-in allowances, offsets, and deductions	602,234.19
TOTAL RECEIPTS	96,990,829.41

DISBURSEMENTS

OPERATING EXPENSE:

Administration	2,749,681.26
GASOLINE TAX DIVISION (including refunds)	351,317.43
Commercial vehicle division	76,792.07
State highway patrol	579,904.64
Maintenance	16,593,093.49

CAPITAL INVESTMENT:

Construction	72,734,917.93
Property and Equipment (less depreciation)	2,128,098.24

OTHER:

Special services	157,248.81
Profit and loss or adjustment account	194,567.35
Suspense accounts	140.48
Miscellaneous: refunds, interest, etc.	68,366.23
TOTAL DISBURSEMENT	95,634,127.93

CASH ON HAND: Sept. 30, 1942	.$1,357,901.48	
Accounts payable	1,200.00	
		$96,990,829.41

Index